The Story of Irish Rugby

THE
STORY OF IRISH
RUGBY

Edmund Van Esbeck

Stanley Paul

London   Melbourne   Auckland   Johannesburg

Stanley Paul & Co. Ltd

An imprint of Century Hutchinson Ltd

62–65 Chandos Place, London WC2N 4NW

Century Hutchinson Australia (Pty) Ltd
PO Box 496, 16–22 Church Street, Hawthorn, Melbourne, Victoria 3122

Century Hutchinson New Zealand Limited
PO Box 40-086, Glenfield, Auckland 10

Century Hutchinson South Africa (Pty) Ltd
PO Box 337, Bergvlei 2012, South Africa

First published 1986
© Edmund Van Esbeck

Set in Sabon
by Avocet Marketing Services
Bicester, Oxon

Printed in Great Britain by
Butler & Tanner Ltd, Frome and London

British Library Cataloguing in Publication Data

Van Esbeck, Edmund
The story of Irish rugby.
1. Rugby football — Ireland — History
I. Title
796.33'3'09415   GV945.9.I73

ISBN 0 09 166270 2

Contents

Appendices

Foreword

By Sir Ewart Bell K.C.B., President IRFU 1986–87

Followers of rugby will welcome another book on Irish rugby from the pen of Edmund Van Esbeck, who, for many years, has been the rugby correspondent of the *Irish Times*.

His dedication to rugby football is unflagging, his knowledge of the game and its participants is unsurpassed and he espouses and articulates its best traditions with unbounded enthusiasm. As always, his views are expressed with consistency and conviction.

In 1974, he wrote the centenary history of the Irish Rugby Football Union, *One Hundred Years of Irish Rugby*. That book traced the history of the game in Ireland from humble beginnings and gave credit to the great players, the great games and the personalities that did so much to develop the game in the country.

History gives value to the present and, with this in mind, much of the text of that book is included in this publication with special emphasis on the major developments that have taken place in Irish rugby since 1974. In that period, two Triple Crowns and two international championships were won. Ireland went on no fewer than four overseas tours. There have been major innovations at game development level and, of course, a major rebuilding programme at Lansdowne Road.

In addition, Ireland entered the realm of schools and 'B' internationals. All these happenings are dealt with in great detail in this book, which also includes most comprehensive appendices relating to the records of the game at every level in the country. It is, in fact, a history of Irish rugby right to the present day.

There are many fascinating aspects of the way in which the game of rugby football has developed in Ireland since the mid-nineteenth century. Its federal structure, based on the ancient provinces of Connacht, Leinster, Munster and Ulster, is somewhat different to what obtains in other countries and has shown itself to be remarkably durable against a recurring background of civil commotion and political controversy.

Foreword

Not only do the four branches cherish their independence, but in turn the Irish Rugby Football Union remains sensitive to the wishes of its constituent parts and seeks assiduously to lead and not to dictate.

There is, no doubt, something special in the Irish temperament which emphasises the comradeship inherent in the game. It can, therefore, be anticipated that, in reacting to the pressures for change in the ethos and management of the game, the Irish aim to be a moderating and beneficial influence. I think this publication illustrates those points and it is a worthy record of Irish rugby.

Preface

When, to mark the centenary year of the establishment of the first administrative body for organised rugby football in Ireland, the Irish Rugby Football Union asked me to write a history of the game in Ireland, they presented me with a task that was both a labour of love and an onerous responsibility. With the generous help of many, the book *One Hundred Years of Irish Rugby* was published in the autumn of 1974.

It was the story of a great organisation born from humble beginnings. It was also a tale of what can be achieved by single-minded dedication and honesty of purpose, the story of a game and an organisation that has triumphed over political, social and religious divides.

When it was suggested to me that the time had come to chronicle yet again the story of rugby in Ireland, its rapid growth and development in recent years and to update the record of the game in Ireland, it was a task I undertook with some measure of trepidation, but no little enthusiasm. There have been many major developments since the official history of the IRFU was published 13 years ago. Yet in order to give substance to the present, I felt it imperative that the story of the past should be left substantially intact.

I have made amendments in some instances to the original text, much of which still forms the basis for this book. I have laid emphasis on what has happened in the last 13 years and I hope rectified some omissions. There is a chapter on the history of Lansdowne Road, one devoted to the administrators, one to the schools, one to game development and, of course, more than one to what has happened on the field of play since 1974. Since that date the Triple Crown and the international championship has been won twice by Ireland. There have been no fewer than four overseas tours by Ireland and major developments in many aspects of the game in the country.

Preface

Many new photographs appear and some of the old remain. The appendices have been completely updated and many additional facts included such as the schools internationals and the lists of the cup winners at school level as well as the senior cup and league winners in all four provinces.

Following the publication of *One Hundred Years of Irish Rugby*, quite a lot of new information came to light and amendments are made where necessary. For instance the list of Ireland captains is now much more substantial.

I have set out to give, in so far as has been possible, a comprehensive record of Irish rugby, to pay tribute to those who fashioned the tradition and to those who have maintained it.

Edmund Van Esbeck, 1986

Acknowledgements

In offering thanks to the many who helped me in the compilation of this book, I wish initially to express my deep appreciation to the Irish Rugby Football Union, who so generously and graciously allowed me to use much of the text of the official history of the Union, which I wrote in 1974. Their co-operation was essential for this book to fulfil its central purpose.

I wish to thank in particular, Sir Ewart Bell, president of the IRFU for 1986–87. He went to considerable trouble on my behalf and also kindly wrote the foreword for this publication.

Bob Fitzgerald, the secretary-treasurer of the IRFU, who retired after long and distinguished service in that onerous dual role at the end of June 1986, was ever-willing to answer my queries and to help when I sought assistance. I want to couple with his name those of George Spotswood, Technical Director of the IRFU and John Murphy, Technical Officer of the Union. They were both most helpful.

Mr Bobby Deacy, of the IRFU committee and President of the Connacht branch in 1985–86, was generous with time and effort and particularly so with regard to the records of the Connacht Schools Senior and Junior Cups, as was Mr Roy Loughead, of the Ulster branch, in unearthing the schools records in that province.

There is no greater authority on Irish rugby than Mr G.P.S. 'Sarsfield' Hogan, eminent legislator and former player, and he gave me invaluable assistance and well considered encouragement.

When I wrote the official history, I was grateful for the help of many and, consequently, I would like to reiterate my gratitude to such as Mr Stan Polden (Old Wesley), Mr Eric Pembrey (Blackrock College) and the late Ross McWhirter for the use of books that proved so valuable when I was writing the IRFU history. To those names I would add that of the late Mr Padraig Purcell, one time eminent Gaelic Games Correspondent of *The Irish Press*.

Acknowledgements

I want to thank the secretarial staff at the IRFU Offices and, in particular, the late Miss Sheila MacSweeney, who sadly did not live to see this book published as she died in March 1986.

I am especially indebted to Mr Peter Thursfield, of the photographic staff of the *Irish Times,* who prepared the photographs for this book and, in fact, took many of them himself. I would add my gratitude to the Sports Editor of the *Irish Times* for freedom to use so many photographs and also the library staff of that paper for their help.

Mr Willow Murray, rugby man extraordinary, gave me help of the most valuable nature in compiling the list of those men who captained Ireland and eminent journalist and author David Guiney, who delved into the great store of his knowledge to assist in the early history of Lansdowne Road, notably that concerning the first Athletics International at the venue.

The support and encouragement of my family were essential and I am deeply grateful to my wife Mary, my son and two daughters for their patience and their help in a household disrupted for quite a while. To those I would add my brother Frank, without whom this or any other book I have written would not have appeared.

I want in conclusion to acknowledge the assistance derived from consulting the following publications. *Playfair Rugby Annual, Rothman's Rugby Yearbook*, the club histories of Wanderers, Lansdowne, Bangor, Dublin University, University College Cork, NIFC, Old Wesley and Blackrock College. May I also thank Mr Roddy Bloomfield, of the publishers Stanley Paul, for his patience, support and encouragement and, perhaps, above all for his faith.

Edmund Van Esbeck
May 1986

1

Ellis's indiscretion and the Irish connection

Dawn broke sombre and murky over the city of London on 15 February 1875. A clinging grey mist pervaded the suburbs and thickened to the consistency of a dirty fog within the heart of the great city. No one unused to the urban gloom of the English Industrial Revolution could have viewed such a dawn without feelings of dismay; and to a little group of Irishmen who surveyed the cheerless scene from the windows of the Golden Cross Hotel, that morning must have seemed singularly grim and forbidding. But their minds were occupied with more important matters than the unpromising prospects of the weather.

A match had been arranged for two o'clock that afternoon between the rugby players of England and Ireland. And if that was a matter of some indifference to the great majority of London's teeming millions, it was, nonetheless, an historic occasion, for it marked Ireland's first venture into international competition on the rugby field.

Ireland's sporting prowess was already very well known in an England then in the middle of the Victorian era. The Irish were regular and by no means unsuccessful competitors at Wimbledon; in the field of athletics they had long since revealed an ability to compete on level terms with the best that Britain had to offer, while, as *Saunders' News Letter* put it, 'there is no crew more feared at Henley as the Dublin Four, who have thrice had their names inscribed on the Visitors Cup.' Whatever the result of their match against England, the Irish rugby team of 1875 had the heavy responsibility of maintaining their country's established reputation as a sporting nation.

In 1871, rugby football had entered the arena of international competition when England met Scotland at Raeburn Place, Edinburgh. From the moment that this game took place, the thought was exercising the minds of rugby fraternity in Ireland generally and the students of Trinity College, Dublin, in particular, that Ireland too, should take her place among the rugby-playing nations of the earth.

Ireland's appearance at the Oval, Kennington was, then, the culmination of a dream nurtured in Trinity where, at the annual general meeting of the football club on 24 October 1874, it had been decided to set up an executive committee with the short-term objective of drawing up a team to meet England that season and with the long-term aim of establishing the game on a properly organised basis throughout the country. Both objectives were attained. The first was accomplished, without undue difficulty, in collaboration with a union that had been formed in Belfast immediately after Trinity's initiative had established the Irish Football Union in Dublin. The Irish team that played at Kennington was therefore the product of a co-operative venture between the north and south of Ireland. This set a pattern which has endured for a century: by crossing great political, religious and social divides it has been possible to recruit successive rugby teams on an all-Ireland basis.

History records that the weather that February day in 1875 cleared up dramatically. The state of the ground at the Oval still bore testimony to the drenching rain that the people of London had endured during the preceding week and it may have proved a deterrent to the players, but it did not prevent the game from taking place. History also records that England won by two goals and a try to nothing and that 3000 people came to see how proficient the Irish were in this new art of football called rugby.

The roots of football in its various and assorted forms ran deep in the heritage of those who represented both Ireland and England that day at the Oval, but the distinctive features of this version of the game as it was then practised have been attributed to an indiscretion by a boy at Rugby School in 1823.

Whether legend or fact, it is generally accepted that it all started when the sixteen-year-old William Webb Ellis, while playing in a Bigside game on the Close at Rugby School, caught the ball, and, instead of claiming a mark, ran forward with the ball in his hands. His action, if not strictly illegal, breached the accepted conventions of the game at that time and the other players may well have given him abuse rather than applause. However, as a result of that act Ellis has been given the credit for creating the distinctive features from which rugby football was later to evolve.

Many eminent and learned historians of rugby have closely examined the suggestion that Ellis was responsible for initiating the game. The claim made on his behalf has survived all their curiosity and ingenuity, as it has survived that of the present writer. So before we turn to the development and growth of the rugby game in Ireland, it may be of interest to consider Ellis and his background in some detail and to investigate, in particular, his alleged connection with Ireland.

One theory popularly held in Ireland is that Ellis was born in the county of Tipperary. A different theory favours Manchester. However, no firm documentary evidence has yet been uncovered to bear out either theory. Rugby School cannot confirm his place of birth; nor can Oxford University, within whose walls he was to continue his studies; nor can the Church of England, which he was later to serve as an ordained minister.

The entry under his name in the *Alumni Oxonienses*, 1715-1886 refers to his father as being 'of Manchester, gent.', and on the return which Ellis made for the 1851 census he gave his place of birth as Manchester. This is strong evidence, but it may not be conclusive. Although we cannot be sure where Ellis was born, we do know for certain the month and year of his birth–November 1807.

Thanks to Irish researchers, we know that Ellis's father, James, married Ann Webb, of Bristol, at St Peter's Church, Exeter, in 1804 and that at that time James Ellis was in the British Army. He served in the 18th Royal Irish Regiment and, at a later date, in the First Dragoon Guards. It was while he was with the latter regiment that he served in Dundalk, Clonmel, and Dublin in the year in which William was born, 1807. In 1808 he was posted to the regimental depot in Manchester, before going to the Peninsular War in the following year.

Thus at the time of William's birth there was a definite connection with Ireland, as indeed there was with Manchester. His subsequent statement that Manchester was his birthplace was conceivably born of expediency or perhaps even simple ignorance. Irregular and inaccurate census returns in the middle of the nineteenth century were by no means a rarity, especially by some Irishmen who found fame and fortune in England and chose, for their own personal reasons, to conceal their origins.

James Ellis died while his son was still a small boy. After buying a commission in the 3rd Dragoon Guards for the sum of £735 on 14 September 1809, he was killed in the battle of Albuera on 16 May 1812, receiving a posthumous commendation for his gallantry. After the death of her husband, his widow Ann was left with two young sons, William, aged five, and Thomas, aged eight. She was granted a pension of £10 per annum for each of her sons and subsequently moved to live in Rugby, presumably so that the boys could qualify for education at Rugby School on the grounds of local residence. William eventually entered Rugby School in 1816 and remained there until 1825 when he was admitted to Brasenose College, Oxford. After enrolling at Oxford, his sporting interests no longer included football, but he clearly had a talent for cricket. He represented Oxford University against Cambridge in 1827 and scored twelve runs in the match at Lord's.

Ellis took his BA degree in 1829 and two years later his MA. He was later ordained a minister of the Church of England, serving in Albemarle Street, London and St Clement Dane's, where there is a plaque erected to his memory. The *Church of England Directory* establishes that he was later Rector of Chipping Ongar in Essex and at the same time priest-in-charge of the parish of Laver Magdalen in the same county. The *Church of England Directory* also clearly discounts another belief that he served as Rector of St George's, Hanover Square, London. Further research at the Public Record Office in London has failed to produce a census return for him in 1861 or 1871 from any of the areas in which he ministered at those times.

Not a great deal is known of Ellis's life, and indeed the circumstances of his death and place of burial had an air of mystery about them until 1959, when Ross McWhirter traced his grave to caveau no. 957 in the Cimetière des Vieux, Château Menton, in the south-east corner of France. McWhirter suggests that Ellis was probably spending part of the winter on the Riviera, as did many Englishmen of means at that time. It is a suggestion that warrants the greatest respect, for if it was his custom to winter in France, it would account for the absence of census returns in 1861 and 1871.

Certainly the discovery of his grave aroused tremendous enthusiasm in France, and the man who is credited with starting the rugby game was, and still is, duly honoured by the French Rugby Federation, who tend his grave. Ellis died a bachelor and left the sum of £9000, a substantial fortune in those days, when as Disraeli said, the world was for the few and the very few.

While some information is available about his career in the Church of England, there is no evidence that once he left Rugby School, he took any interest whatsoever in the development of football in any of its various forms. Nor does he seem even to have been aware that shortly before his death the game's first administrative body, the Rugby Football Union, was formed in London. Those who were in Rugby School at or around the same time as Ellis have said that he was not especially adept at or keen on football. If this is true, his indiscretion may well have sprung from sheer boredom, and it would therefore not be surprising if the subsequent developments of the game failed to interest him.

Ellis was the author of a number of works on religion, and one sermon he preached was of sufficient moment to warrant a mention in the *Illustrated London News*.

It is perhaps more interesting to record that he also wrote a poem on beer. The partiality of rugby men towards this particular drink has been proverbial for generations, and Ellis's work was undoubtedly inspired by the virtues of ale as a palatable beverage. Many will agree that he had his priorities right.

There is no doubt that the years between Ellis's celebrated 'indiscretion' in 1823 and his death in 1872 were crucial to the development of rugby football. Indeed, there was a tremendous upsurge of interest in sport generally throughout Britain and Ireland during this period, a factor due in no small measure to the immense amount of social reform that was then taking place. Sport began to take on distinctive and organised forms; and before Ellis died administrative bodies were in existence to legislate on rugby football and association football. And in 1884 the Gaelic Athletic Association was formed in Ireland to propagate the gaelic form of football and the ancient and noble art of hurling. The fraternity that existed between the various 'gaelic' and 'non-gaelic' groups can be gauged from the sporting backgrounds of two of the founders of the Gaelic Athletic Association, Michael Cusack and George St J. McCarthy. McCarthy had played rugby for Ireland and Trinity, while Cusack was a player of no mean skill and apparently a coach of some ability while teaching at Blackrock College and at his own school, Cusack's Academy.

A number of publications, including *A History of Football* (1954) by Morris Marples, make it quite clear that different types of football were beginning to develop during the middle of the nineteenth century, and some interesting information about rugby as a distinctive form is to be found in an article by Matthew Bloxham (1805–88) which appeared in *The Meteor* (the Rugby School magazine) in the issue of 10 October 1876. Bloxham was a contemporary of Ellis at Rugby, but left the school before the celebrated 'indiscretion'.

Thomas Hughes, author of the classic *Tom Brown's Schooldays* which immortalised Rugby School, also provided valuable evidence on the evolution of rugby. Hughes's first year at Rugby was 1834 and, according to him, running with the ball was not then forbidden but it was 'not prudent'. The practice grew, however, and by 1840 it was an accepted part of the game. Hughes was captain of Bigside in 1841–42, by which time the debatable question of running with the ball had been finally settled.

In 1846 the first laws of rugby football were drawn up at Rugby School. Similar forms of football were certainly being played in other English public schools at this time, but the laws as practised by each school were very far from being uniform for a long time after 1846. Sir Montague Sherman in *Football, its History for Five Centuries* arrived at the very plausible conclusion that each particular school had its own rules, which were often modified to meet the size of the playground available.

An exhaustive enquiry into the early history of the game was carried out by the Old Rugbeian Society in 1895. The report issued by the society produced, among other things, signed statements and letters, a number of drawings and maps of Rugby Close, the 1846 laws and the revised laws of one year later. Regarding the all-important question of the game's true origin, the society found that:

In 1820 the form of football in vogue at Rugby was something approximating more closely to Association than what is known as rugby football today. And that at some date between 1820 and 1830 the innovation was introduced of running with the ball; that this was in all probability done in the latter half of 1823 by Mr W. Webb Ellis.

That is probably as near the truth as anyone will ever come. Whether England or Ireland can rightly claim his birthplace, to William Webb Ellis belongs the credit for having 'in all probability' invented the game of rugby football.

2

Early days in Ireland

Mr Morris Marples, who has carried out detailed research into the origins of football in all its forms, confesses that he is unable to trace the game back beyond the seventh and eighth centuries in England. However, in his *History of Football* he suggests that the modern football games may have had their beginnings among the Celtic peoples.

Football was definitely popular in Britain during the fourteenth century and was considered a sufficient threat to the status quo to warrant a ban by a royal proclamation proscribing certain sports in 1365. Ireland followed where England led, and within twelve months the Irish authorities issued a similar edict as part of the Statutes of Kilkenny. What effect these bans had on the populace is difficult to assess; their regular reiteration suggests that they were fairly ineffective. It is, however, significant, that the proclamation of Kilkenny differed in one important aspect from the 1365 decree of Henry III in that it substituted hurling for football. Unless we are to assume that football was unknown in Ireland at this time, it is clear that it was not considered by the rulers of the day as a threat to the status quo of Irish society.

By the sixteenth century football was still considered to be of too little consequence to have an adverse effect on the compulsory military training of the population. In a decree by the mayor and aldermen of Galway in 1527 it was specifically exempted from a general ban when the people were ordered not to play with the stone or the shot, but urged to practise with the longbow and to hurl the dart or spear. It was further ordered that 'at no tyme to use ne occupye the hurlinge of the litill balle with the hookie stickies or staves, nor use no hande balle to play without the walls, but only the great foote balle'.

It seems that the 'great foote balle' continued to enjoy popularity in England during the next century, despite the vigorous efforts of authority to discourage it, but if it was equally popular in Ireland, those who ruled continued to tolerate it, either because they did not know how wide the practice was, or because they saw fit to ignore it.

By the middle of the seventeenth century, there is evidence that a football match was played in the Slane area of County Meath. In a poem written by Séamus Dall Mac Cuarta (1647–1732) he described a match played on the south bank of the Boyne in the townland of Fennor. The poem, entitled *Imirt na Boinne*, suggests that the author was present when his side from the Boyne valley defeated a team from the area south of the town of Drogheda. It is of more than passing interest to note that carrying the ball was one feature of the play.

John Dunton, an Englishman who found Ireland a good source of material for his literary works, described football in the later years of the seventeenth century in Ireland as being played only in the small territory called Fingal, near Dublin. Dunton came to Ireland in 1698 and apparently travelled quite extensively. Dunton's *Conversation in Ireland*, in which his account of football appears, was published in 1699. Dunton recorded that the players of Fingal 'tripped and shouldered very handsomely'. But he also drew the conclusion that even the best of the participants would not come off well if pitted against the exponents who operated in Moorfields, London, a sporting arena of no small consequence. Later references confirm that football was indeed played in the area of Fingal, but, unlike the present day when sporting events are fully chronicled by the press, not many writers saw sufficient romance in sport to deem it worthy of their attention either in prose or verse.

There is evidence that football was played on quite a large scale in Ireland throughout the eighteenth century. One intriguing example of this is a poem, written in 1780 by Edward Lysaght (1763–1810) in which he describes football as he saw it played in College Park. The pitch was presumably situated on the strip of ground that lies adjacent to Nassau Street. Lysaght's treatment of his theme is very revealing. He suggests that the wealthy refrained from indulging in such pursuits as football, a comment that supports the contention of a succession of historians that football was frowned upon by the aristocracy in Ireland as well as across the channel.

Lysaght was an interesting character. Born at Bird-Mill, County Clare, he was the son of John Lysaght, who was related to the noble family of Lisle. His mother was a cousin of Lord Eyre of Eyrecourt, County Galway. By his genealogy he would certainly be regarded as one of the gentry. His father died when Edward was young and the family fell into straitened circumstances. Lysaght entered Trinity in 1779. In 1784 he enrolled at the Inner Temple as a law student. He was also a student at St Edmund's Hall, Oxford, where he took his MA. He was called to the English Bar in 1784 before returning to Ireland. In Ireland, Lysaght was also called to the Bar and went on the Munster Circuit. He was very active in the Volunteer organisation, and used his considerable talents as orator and writer to assist the movement. He wrote a large number of poems and songs, his best known work being 'The Man who led the Volunteers'. He is also credited with the authorship of 'The Rakes of Mallow' and 'Kitty of Coleraine'. The circumstances which led to the poem about football throw an interesting sidelight on the general attitude towards the game in 1780.

In Trinity in Lysaght's student days fellow-commoners thought that they were superior beings to pensioners. Every evening the pensioners played football in College Park. The fellow-commoners were above taking part in such vulgar pursuits. A pensioner, whose name, according to the conventions of eighteenth-century satirical verse, appears semi-disguised as 'C-lf-rd', was vain enough to associate entirely with fellow-commoners and never played football until one evening he accidentally deigned to do so. Scarcely had he made his attempt on the field when some of his fellow-students, indignant at his past folly, tripped up his heels, to the no small gratification of the assemblage present and much to the mortification of the unfortunate C-lf-rd. That night Lysaght wrote a short poem called 'Impromptu', a copy of which appeared in every student's letterbox next morning. The poem read:

> Dear C-lf-rd play football no more I entreat;
> The amusement's too vulgar, fatiguing and rough;
> Pursue the conduct you followed of late;
> And I warrant, ere long, you'll get kicking enough.

References to sport in Ireland became much more frequent in the press of the nineteenth century, and although the amount of space and detail devoted to the football was very small, it is enough to show that it was played in various forms throughout the country, though we cannot be absolutely specific about any of these forms. The inter-parish game played across fields and in the open country was in all probability the most common form. Here we are reminded of Ellis and the question of whether he was influenced by what he might just possibly have seen in the Tipperary area.

One of the games most popular in south Munster and especially in the Kerry area was *cad*. Thanks to the work of the Rev. Liam Ferris, Parish Priest of Ballylongford, County Kerry until his death in 1972, we can be fairly specific about its rules, the type of ball used, and other details.

Fr Ferris wrote a treatise on the game and carried out wide research into its origins. A letter written by him on the subject which appeared in the *Irish Times* on 23 January 1968 is worth reproducing in full.

The Game of Cad

Sir,

The carrying ball game called Cad was played by all branches of the Celtic race; Gaelic, British, Welsh, Cornish and Gallic. Cad was thus far more extensive and by millenia more ancient than hurling, which was confined to the Gaels of Ireland and Scotland.

There are two varieties of Cad; Cross-country Cad (Inter-parish) and Field Cad (definite space and number of players).

Dinneen's dictionary quotes Ballyferriter as retaining the expression '*ag imirt Caid*' for 'playing football'.

In Britain during the eighteenth century the carrying game of Cad was dropped through the influence of half a dozen great public schools, including Rugby. It was replaced by the kicking game, later called soccer, whose rules were definitely formulated by the Football Association in 1867.

In Ireland, however, up to 1885, there was not even a whisper against the carrying game of Cad. Not only so, but Cad was re-introduced into Britain through Irish influence. An English boy, William Webb Ellis, learned the game from his cousins in Tipperary and by running with the ball restarted it at Rugby School in 1823.

His action was later called 'inspired insubordination' and the old game of Cad was once more re-established within the decade, though the Rugby Union was founded only in 1871. The word Cad means the scrotum of the bull, the bag containing its testicles. With extraordinary tenacity, the Rugby Union has retained the shape.

The GAA was established in 1884, but it was only in the following year that the Clareman, Cusack, introduced the kicking game which he called 'Gaelic'. It merely modified the soccer rules of 1867 slightly by allowing the use of the hands.

With the powerful new organisation at his back, Cusack, by the stroke of a pen, killed the thousand-year-old game of Cad. It was not quite dead, however, but it gave what was probably its last gasp in Castleisland three years later in 1888 in a match between the two out-parishes of Cordal and Scartaglen.

Cusack's kicking game may be the wonderful thing which through powerful propaganda it is alleged to be. But to call the kicking game 'Gaelic' pretending thereby that it is traditional football, is nothing but the veriest impudence, paralleled only by Whateley's calling his primary school national.

Irish traditional football is Cad, now improperly called 'Rugby'. It would be a gracious act for the GAA to admit an error which has lasted only a lifetime and to restore the national game of Cad once more to its position of honour.

After writing the letter Fr Ferris said that he, like many others, was relying on hearsay when he pointed out that Ellis had learned the game of cad from his cousins in Tipperary.

Yet it is worth taking a more detailed look at the game of cad, for certainly there were marked similarities between it and rugby football. The outer case of the ball was inflated by a natural bladder so that its shape was not round, but elongated in the manner of the later rugby ball. The cross-country version of the game was usually played between parishes, with the issue often apparently being disputed in a day-long duel, the object of the exercise apparently being to take the ball home. The field version was much more akin to rugby, and in this, trees bent in the shape of an arch were used as goals. Fr Ferris even discovered a very old man from the South Kerry area who clearly remembered having seen the game played and who actually claimed to have taken part in the game himself when a youth.

It is by no means impossible that Irish boys attending English public schools brought back to Ireland something of what they had seen and learned on the sports fields of their academies, and that the games they introduced in vestigal form evolved into what we know today as rugby football. Time has, however, kept most of its secrets about the absolute origins of football in Ireland and elsewhere. But we do know that football had been played in Ireland for many hundreds of years before the beginning of the nineteenth century. We also know that it incorporated carrying and running with the ball. Could those Irish boys have brought with them to their English schools something of what they had seen and played while at home?

3
Trinity leads the way
1854–74

Dublin in the 1850s presented a face very different to that of the thriving, bustling city we know today. It is possible, with the aid of old drawings, photographs and maps, to re-create an impression of the city as it appeared in the early days of what has sometimes been called the Grand Victorian era. But there are still tangible reminders of the past, and a careful inspection of the vicinity of Trinity College reveals the sharp contrast of the multi-storey office blocks side by side with houses that still display all the elegance of Georgian architecture at its most perfect. Trinity College itself is a place of contrasts, the intermingling of the old and the new, in its buildings and in its character. It was here, in the year 1854, that the earliest recorded Irish rugby club was founded.

The Trinity club's foundation date of 1854 makes it the second oldest rugby club in the world; only Guy's Hospital can claim seniority. For reasons that are difficult to explain, one seldom finds acknowledgement in rugby reference books to Trinity's true year of origin.

Football traditions in Trinity, of course, go back far beyond 1854, a point made clear by Edward Lysaght's poem. As in Lysaght's time, the sporting scene in Trinity in the middle of the nineteenth century was largely influenced by Irish boys returning from the English public schools. As is pointed out in the centennial history of the club published in 1954–an event incidentally in which the centrepiece of the celebrations was appropriately a match against Blackheath, a founder member of the Rugby Union in 1871 and a leading influence–several of the early members of the Trinity club had been entered at the college some years before the club was officially formed. The earliest known members of the club included many from Cheltenham and Rugby schools and the first three listed all entered Trinity in 1848–six years before the club was formed. W. Stackpool and E. Lloyd were both

Cheltenham boys, while E.S. Forester was educated at Mr Ryder's School.

The first public reference to the existence of a club in Trinity is, according to the records, a notice which appeared in the Dublin *Daily Express* on Saturday, 1 December 1855, to the effect that a game would take place that day at two o'clock between original and new members of the club. It was signed by Robert Henry Scott, the new club's first officer. Scott, born in Dublin in 1833, was, significantly, an Old Rugbeian. He entered Trinity in 1851, became a classical scholar in 1853 and First Moderator in Experimental Physics in 1855. He held the joint offices of honorary secretary and treasurer until 1856.

As is perhaps indicated by the teams selected to play in the match of December 1855, one of the club's main initial difficulties was in finding opponents, and for several years the members had to be content to play games organised within the college with Freshmen taking on the Rest; those with initials A to M facing those that remained; the Football Club *v.* the Boat Club (a fixture which survived until 1874); Rugby and Cheltenham boys *v.* The Rest; and English-educated boys *v.* Irish-educated boys.

The first record of a match against outside opposition if outside it can be called, is of a match against the 'Wanderers' in 1860. Those Wanderers were not the club that bears that name today, though they, like Trinity, can proclaim a record that goes back over a hundred years, having been founded in 1869. The Wanderers of 1860 were apparently a collection of former students of Trinity. It is worth noting, too, that the Wanderers formed in 1869–70 had a decidedly Trinity influence as well. The connection between the two Wanderers must however be left in the realms of speculation and imagination.

The match was, at any rate, deemed worthy of an advertisement in the press of the day. The *Dublin Evening Packet* of 27 November 1860 carried a notice signed by Anthony Traill, honorary secretary of the Trinity club, and the *Irish Times* of 6 December 1860 carried a report of the match, stating that darkness called a halt to the proceedings and that the game would be resumed on the following day.

The honorary secretary must have been a powerful figure in those distant days for it was not until 1863–64 that Trinity elected a captain; to Richard Traill goes the distinction of being the first holder of that office. He led the club until 1864–65 and was succeeded by A.M. Dobbs, who also held the office for two seasons, and then A.F. Graves, who was captain in 1866–67.

The next man to lead Trinity was Charles Barrington, who was in control in 1867–68. His influence was to stretch far beyond the confines of the close circle around which the club's affairs revolved. Barrington was a member of a distinguished Irish family, whose old residence, Glenstal Abbey, just outside Limerick City, is now a rugby academy of some standing. Barrington, later Sir Charles, died on 12 August 1943 in Botley, near Southampton, at the age of 95. His maternal uncle, Charlie West, is believed to have been the person on whom Thomas Hughes based the character 'East' in *Tom Brown's Schooldays*, and Barrington had himself also been a pupil at Rugby School.

Barrington was captain of Trinity for three years, with Richard M. Wall, honorary secretary since 1865–66, continuing in that post when Barrington took over the leadership on the field. Barrington was obviously a man of administrative as well as playing ability; together with Wall, he drew up a set of laws that bore many similarities to those Blackheath–one of the founding clubs of the Rugby Union–had drafted in 1863. In a letter written in 1931 to Dr Edward Watson, a Trinity stalwart to the day he died in 1947, Barrington vividly recalled working on the laws with Wall in 1867, though they were not, of course, presented until the annual general meeting of the club in October 1868. Needless to say they were passed.

Barrington's arrival at Trinity coincided with a general expansion and reorganisation of the club. There was a big increase in membership and a second XV was formed. With the arrogance that comes from a superiority that is total, Trinity decided that any team that wished to play their First XV, must first prove their worth by defeating their second string. In 1867 the seconds played St Columba's College, which still maintains a thriving rugby tradition, with enthusiastic participation in the Leinster Schools Cups to this day. Hume Street School and Dungannon School also played Trinity Seconds in this period, so rugby had spread its net to Ulster and within a short period to points south and west as well.

The reorganisation of the Trinity club in 1867–68 ensured that proper records were kept from the year 1867. It was in 1868 that the club colours of red and black were officially adopted and they still survive. Honours caps were first awarded in 1868, an innovation that was, apparently, also decided at that momentous meeting at which the rules were passed. The caps were red and black, quartered, with a gold shamrock embroidered on the front. Opponents for these stylishly equipped players were, unfortunately, still hard to find.

Rugby football was beginning to spread in Ireland and the laws passed at that meeting in 1868 had important repercussions on the expansion of the game within the next six years. Clubs began to emerge that were to contribute handsomely to Irish rugby; indeed, many of them are still contributing over a century later.

Wanderers (1869) had their motivating force in Richard Milliken Peter, later to play an important role in the setting up of the first administrative body in Ireland. Other clubs formed at about this time include Lansdowne (1872), variously known as the Irish Champion Athletic Club and Lansdowne Road, Dungannon (1873), and Queen's College, Cork (1874). But it is possible that UCC may be denying themselves seniority, for in 1972 a printed copy of the Rugby Football Laws as played in Queen's College, Cork, in 1872, came to light. Carlow (1873) and Ballinasloe (1875) are still prospering, and Cork FC and Cork Bankers made a significant contribution before time took its toll of them, as it did of several others such as Arlington, Phoenix, Engineers, Monaghan, Scott's Military Academy, Merrion, Kingstown, Kingstown School and Bray.

The Jesuit colleges of Belvedere and Clongowes Wood had their own set of laws in those early days; latterly they follow those laid down by the ruling body. Tullabeg College, near Tullamore, the sister college of Clongowes, with which it was amalgamated in 1886, also played football. Football was the winter game in Tullamore until the canal froze, whereupon skating took over. The type of football played in Tullabeg and Clongowes until 1890 was neither rugby nor soccer; it was a game which resembled the field cad referred to by Fr Ferris in his letter to the *Irish Times*. The game was played under what are variously called the 'Jesuit Rules' or the 'Catholic College Rules'. Another early starter was Portora Royal School, near Enniskillen, County Fermanagh, and this school sent out and is still sending out some of Ireland's finest rugby players.

At the time the Barrington laws were introduced, rugby in the Belfast area was non-existent, but cricket was a thriving sport, and nowhere more so than in the North of Ireland Cricket Club, which had been formed in 1859. At this period Mr John Lawrence operated as a well-known supplier of sports equipment in Grafton Street, Dublin. He was also a keen sports enthusiast and annually produced a handbook on cricket. Lawrence quickly recognised how rugby football was spreading and reproduced 'The Laws of Foot Ball as played at Trinity College, Dublin' in his handbook, which was avidly read and disgested by members of the North of Ireland Cricket Club.

That handbook and the boys coming home to Belfast from the English public schools were profound influences in the Belfast area and, in particular, rugby in and around the North of Ireland Cricket Club's ground at Ormeau. To those influences could be added yet another, E.H. Moeran, a cricketer of repute, but also a rugby enthusiast who was willing and able to inspire his love of the game into others. The fact that a rugby section of the North of Ireland Cricket Club was formed in the autumn of 1868 is not without significance. At the time, several of the cricketers objected strongly to this invasion, but their objections were brushed aside as this extract from the *Belfast News-Letter* of 27 November 1868 reveals.

The North of Ireland Football Club

The idea of establishing this club originated a short time ago with some members of the North of Ireland Cricket Club, who had been at English schools and who knew and appreciated the game. Great difficulties lay in their way. Few in this part of the world had ever seen the rugby game played, still fewer had ever played it. After some hesitation the consent of the North of Ireland Cricket Club was gained to permit the erection of goals on the lower part of their ground and about a month and a half ago the North of Ireland Foot Ball Club played its first practice match. Since that time many new members have been enrolled.

Saturday is the club match day and the following have been elected to form a committee: P.M. Dudgeon, R.H. Orr, J.T. Reade, J.M. Sinclair, and E.H. Moeran, honorary secretary and treasurer.

Moeran was to North, the name by which the club is known throughout the rugby world, what Barrington was to Trinity, and the fact that he was a leading bowler with the cricket club no doubt gave him the influence and the standing needed to propagate the rugby cause.

Like Trinity, North found it difficult to find opposition, but, unlike Trinity, did not impose such qualifications as beating the Second XV before getting a match against the First XV. The formation of a rugby club in Queen's University in the autumn of 1869 gave North their first outside opposition and on 16 January of the following year the clubs met for the first time at Ormeau. The match apparently went on for three days, Queen's fielding eighteen players to North's thirteen, which probably accounted for the fact that Queen's got the first score, McIlreavy getting a try and J.M. Sinclair converting. That try, however, took a long time to come, for it was not obtained until the second day of the match, which was not until 23 January. Queen's finished that afternoon leading by a goal to nil. Hostilities were resumed a week later and the account in the *Belfast News-Letter* of 1 February does not tell all but it reveals much.

> The match was finished on Saturday last, the third day of play. The club [North] won the toss and selected the upper goal, the wind being in their favour. At the end of the first half hour the club had obtained two points and the sides changed goals. The College then pressed their opponents more vigorously making five points in succession. Shortly before four o'clock, Mr W. Bottomley succeeded in obtaining a touch down for College and Mr Sinclair secured a goal by a well directed kick. The College had made a goal on the previous Saturday, and as their opponents had made none, victory was theirs.

The indications are that the laws as practised in Belfast were not exactly orthodox even for those times, but it was a good start.

In the next few years the shortage of opponents was acute, but interest was maintained and more players were learning the game. Eventually North looked outside the Belfast area for opposition and readily found it in Dublin and Scotland in the 1871–72 season. In the interim North fulfilled fixtures with Queen's University and the Royal Schools at Dungannon and Armagh.

On 16 December 1871 North and Trinity met for the first time. The match was fifteen-a-side and was played at Ormeau. Trinity won by one goal and one touch down to nil. A week later the first match between Scottish and Irish clubs took place when North entertained West of Scotland and lost by a goal to nil. By 1873–74 North had embarked on a Scottish tour, during which they lost to Glasgow Academicals. By this time the game had spread to the RA Institution and Methodist College in Belfast, where masters were included in the school team. Meanwhile Trinity had opened their fixture list to more than North, for in 1873–74 they travelled to the Dingle Club, Liverpool, where they drew the game. All these connections with England and Scotland which were being established by Trinity and North were to have beneficial results in the near future.

The game was spreading in Dublin and Belfast and to points south and west, but it was not until 1875–76 that Wanderers had earned the right to meet Trinity's First XV. In the north the establishment of clubs such as Windsor, Ulster, Belmont, Lisburn and Albion, all now defunct, helped in no small way to establish the rugby traditions of the province of Ulster, where, undoubtedly, North made the biggest contribution of all.

4

Two unions
1874–75

Our story has brought us once again to that fateful day, 15 February 1875, when Ireland for the first time put an international rugby team in the field. The season of 1874–75 was the most significant in the history of the game in Ireland, for it saw the formation of the Irish Football Union, the game's first administrative body in this country. It is interesting to note that this momentous development was brought about as a direct result of pressure from England.

England and Scotland had been engaged in the field of international combat since 1871. It was therefore only natural that with two clubs of the calibre of Trinity and North, both of whom had sampled the delights of cross-channel football, the thought should cross the minds of their officials that Ireland too should be represented in the international arena. In 1873–74 Trinity made valiant attempts to arrange a match against England, but the principal stumbling block was England's objection to the fact that there was no national administrative body in Ireland.

Following the annual general meeting of the Trinity club in October 1874, it was decided to call a meeting of the 'principal clubs' with a view to forming an executive. It was even announced after the Trinity annual general meeting that an international between England and Ireland would 'very probably be played' in London in the not too distant future. With the Trinity influence so strong among such 'principal clubs' as Wanderers and Lansdowne, there was no difficulty in making the arrangements for the gathering and it took place, according to the *Irish Sportsman and Farmer* of 12 December 1874, at 1.30 pm on the afternoon of 7 December in the rooms of George Stack at No. 27 Trinity College.

There have been many inaccurate reports written about that meeting. The lack of any surviving minutes probably accounts for the accretions of myth and legend that have been perpetuated about it—an unfortunate characteristic of much of the early history of Irish rugby.

The assembly that gathered in Stack's rooms consisted of Messrs Barlow (in the chair), Stack, Peter, Casement, Walsh, Neill, Malet, Ogilby and Robinson. Many of these men played a major part in subsequent developments. Richard Milliken Peter probably emerges as the key figure in the early days of Irish rugby administration, though he was later to sever his connections with the game and to depart under a cloud. He was a clerk in the offices of the Commissioners of Church Temporalities in Ireland, and in addition to being a skilful and enthusiastic rugby-player, he was also a leading figure on the rowing, yachting and swimming scenes in Ireland.

The match against England was discussed and the dates of Saturday, 6 February and Monday, 8 February were suggested as possible dates for the game, but significantly, it was decreed that 'no firm decision could be taken until an executive was formed'. It was, however, decided that this task would take place one week later at John Lawrence's rooms at 39 Grafton Street.

Wanderers certainly took due note and they called a meeting for Thursday, 10 December and appointed Messrs Peter and Barlow as their representatives. They duly took their places in Lawrence's rooms at 3.30 pm, on the afternoon of Monday, 14 December, 1874. So too did others. George Hall Stack represented Trinity, and he was joined by Richard Galbraith. Engineers were represented by H.D. Walsh and D. Neill, and they were joined by J.D. Ogilby and G. Burke (Lansdowne), H. Adams and W.H. Wilson (Bray), C. Murphy and E. Galbraith (Portora), W. Smyth and W. Beatty (Dungannon), A.P. Cronyn and J. Cronyn (Monaghan).

As befitted the status of the captain of Trinity, Stack was in the chair. Peter was elected honorary treasurer, and Walsh took over the onerous duties of honorary secretary. A working committee of five members was elected to carry out the day-to-day chores connected with arranging the match against England, which had been the specific purpose in calling the meeting. Messrs Stack, Barlow, E. Galbraith, R. Galbraith and A.P. Cronyn were elected to this committee.

It was decided that the administrative body should be called the Irish Football Union and that all clubs adhering to the rugby code should be invited to join. An immediate recruit was the Kingstown club, though they were not represented at the inaugural meeting. It must be added, too, that Trinity had a more than adequate representation, for several of those who were there in the interests of other clubs and paid their £1 entrance fee could be said to have had a dual commitment. Notable among these were Edgar Galbraith, Arthur Cronyn, who spread his talents around liberally, and Walsh. All three were included in the first Irish team as representatives of Trinity.

Shortly after the establishment of the IFU, a circular was issued stating the aims of the new body and announcing, in a clever example of persuasive democracy: 'The meetings of the IFU are at present held in the metropolis, but this arrangement, it is hoped, will in future years be exchanged if provincial clubs so desire, for some other plan which will enable them to make their wishes better understood and more effectively carried out.'

The formation of the IFU was not exactly greeted with euphoria in the corridors at Ormeau, or so we are told by the leading rugby journalist of the day, one Jacques McCarthy. McCarthy was a man of wit and wisdom; he was also, alas, too often indebted to his memory for his 'facts' and to his prejudices for his jests. Certainly his assertions about the game in the early days do not stand up to historical investigation, not least with regard to the administrative set-up.

In 1892 a Church of England clergyman, the Rev. Frank Marshall produced a monumental work on rugby entitled *Football, the Rugby Union Game*. Marshall's book was for long accepted as the authoritative source on the early years of the game. It must be pointed out, however, that the chapter on Ireland, written by McCarthy, is largely responsible for the many inaccuracies about the early history of Irish rugby. It is surprising, too, that many who have down the years poured scorn on McCarthy's accuracy, or rather lack of it, have, nonetheless, slavishly followed his opinions and accepted them as fact wherever it has been convenient to do so.

McCarthy's conclusion that rugby administration in Ireland began with a split is probably the most widely repeated of all the myths about Irish rugby. Two unions there certainly were in the early days, but a split there was not.

It is not the intention to take McCarthy's assertions here and attempt to disprove them one by one, but we must briefly examine McCarthy's version of the story of how the Northern Football Union of Ireland came into being on 13 January 1875.

In his account in Marshall's book McCarthy suggests that after Wanderers and North had met in a match at Ormeau on 28 November 1874, 'a dreadful row arose when North won the game and questioned the right of those in Dublin to form an "Irish Football Union" without first consulting Belfast. They had shown that day they were the better footballers and furthermore had more money and more enthusiasm.'

If that row arose, then North were a little ahead of their time, for the actual foundation of the IFU was still a fortnight away. Furthermore, an account of the match appearing in the *Irish Sportsman and Farmer* on 5 December states that Wanderers were 'most hospitably received'. In retrospect that phrase has a lot of significance.

So much for McCarthy's story and for the one subsequently written by J.W. Whitehead in the 1925 edition of Marshall, which basically follows the McCarthy line, even asserting that the North members 'there and then formed their own union'.

That they did not do. Certainly the rugby fraternity in Belfast, and the North club in particular, did not take kindly to Dublin running the show, but the notice convening the inaugural meeting of the Northern Football Union of Ireland was more placatory than recriminatory. It read:

> The lovers of football in Belfast and neighbourhood have under consideration what steps should be taken with regard to the success of the Irish Football Union and the establishment of annual international matches between three kingdoms. It has been decided to call a meeting for 13 January to see what course should be adopted.

The *Belfast News-Letter* of 14 January 1875 records what steps were decided upon; in that edition the following report appeared.

NORTHERN FOOTBALL UNION OF IRELAND

> At a meeting largely attended by representatives of the various clubs in this district in the Linen Hall Hotel last evening, Mr Combe, captain of North of Ireland Football Club in the chair, it was resolved, on the motion of Mr Heron, seconded by Mr McDonald that, in order to secure a proper representation of Northern clubs, and in general to support and encourage the game, a union for this district be formed, to be named the 'Northern Football Union of Ireland'. It was also decided on the proposal of Mr Shaw, seconded by Mr Cochrane, that the question of Northern clubs competing in the coming international match to be played in London early in the year, be left to the working committee of the Northern Union to confer with the Irish Union in Dublin and to report to a further meeting.

That notice does not tell all about the circumstances and events surrounding the formation of the union in Belfast, but it effectively kills many legends. The most notorious of these is the suggestion that Ulster saw itself as a rival body to the Dublin administrators. Nor does the report bear out the ridiculous contention that anything other than full support would be given to the Dublin initiative for the match against England. Such 'facts' belong more to the faulty memory and fertile imagination of Jacques McCarthy than to the annals of rugby history.

There may indeed have been a row after Wanderers visited North in November. Perhaps in the heat of the moment the North players decided to form their own union. But they obviously had second thoughts on the whole matter, not least because, out of consideration for the other clubs in the Belfast area, they were scarcely justified in going it alone; and furthermore, an Irish team was going into the field and North wanted to be represented on it.

On 12 January 1875, the eve of the big Belfast meeting, a working committee of the IFU convened at No. 8 Trinity College. The earliest extant minutes of the union date from this meeting. It is recorded that Edgar Galbraith laid before the committee a letter to the effect that the Lord Lieutenant of Ireland, the Duke of Abercorn, had agreed to become president of the union. Such matters as the jerseys to be worn by the Irish team and the printing of a circular were also discussed.

Meanwhile Peter, at the instigation of the committee, had already sent out another circular appealing for funds, and the *Freeman's Journal* of 30 December 1874 took up the cry from the heart. In a leading article it commended the proposed international match to its readers. 'We anticipate with pleasure the future encounters of our Irish youths with their compeers of the sister countries,' continued the article, which ended by appealing to 'the practical sympathy of their fellow countrymen of all shades and degrees'. The combined efforts of Peter and the *Freeman's Journal* no doubt had a big bearing on the fact that £30 was raised by public subscription. This money went a long way towards sending the first Irish twenty to London.

Jacques McCarthy in his account of how the first Irish team was picked claims that it was agreed that each union would nominate ten men, thus ensuring an even balance. That, in fact, was not at all how the Irish team was selected.

On 22 January a meeting of the IFU was held at which was read a letter from A.G. Guillemard, honorary secretary of the Rugby Union, confirming that the match against England would be played at Kennington Oval on Monday, 15 February 1875. George Stack then proposed that:

In order to guarantee that the Northern clubs' interests would be duly
regarded in the selection of the interntional twenty, that the Irish Union
shall nominate seven men to play on the twenty, and the Northern Union
a like number and that each Union would then submit the names of ten
further players each from which the remaining six players would be
chosen.

The Northern Union accepted the proposal with a slight amendment:
for some obscure reason they proposed that each union would submit
the names of eleven players from which the remaining six players would
be chosen to complete the team. The Northern Union enclosed the
names of their selected seven, but Stack, obviously a man of character as
well as scholarship, would not allow the names of the seven northern
players to be read at a meeting of the IFU on 3 February until after the
IFU had chosen their seven.

Stack himself was one of the seven selected by the IFU: joining him
were W. Smyth, M. Barlow, E. Galbraith, A.P. Cronyn, F. Hewson and
R. Galbraith. It is interesting to record that all but Smyth did in fact
line-out at the Oval. By a strange coincidence six of the North's original
selections also played: R. Walkington, R. Bell, W. Ash, A. Combe, J.
McDonald and W. Gaffikin. The odd man out was G. Shaw. After the
seven southern players had been chosen, B. Casement, H. Robinson,
H.W. Walsh, J. Magennis, J. Shannon, H. Adams, R. Greer, J. Myles,
J. Allen and A.W. Cuscadden were nominated for further consideration, the IFU here waiving its right to submit a total of eleven names.
The remaining six places on the team would be picked by a sub-
committee of six, three from each union, and Stack, Peter and R.
Galbraith were chosen to represent Dublin interests when the team was
finalised in London.

Myles, Allen, Casement, Magennis and Walsh eventually made the
team, as did H. Cox of Trinity, which meant that the IFU eventually
had twelve men on the field at the Oval, of whom no fewer than nine
were from Trinity College. Wanderers had three representatives, in M.
Barlow and J. Allen and H. Hewson; NIFC had six representatives;
Windsor one; and Methodist College one. It is not recorded how this
balance eventually materialised.

To Stack went the honour of being Ireland's first captain–and a
richly deserved distinction for the man who had been one of the leading
figures in setting up the match and who was not averse to putting his
hand into his pocket to support the cause in practical terms. Stack, as

well as being a man of means and a footballer of considerable skill, was also well endowed intellectually. He took his MA in 1875, having entered Trinity in 1870 after being educated in Raphoe, County Donegal. He was, sadly, not destined to live long enough to see more organised Irish teams in the fields for he died unexpectedly and apparently under tragic circumstances in November 1876.

Whatever fate was to befall him two years later, he was in vigorous good health when he led his side out at the Oval. The Irishmen were attired that day in green- and white-hooped jerseys, white knicker-bockers, and green- and white-hooped stockings. Jacques McCarthy, however, was not impressed by the display of his fellow-countrymen. 'What an enterprise and what a twenty,' he wrote. 'They had never previously seen each other. H.L. Robinson and the celebrated "Darky" Smyth, the two best backs in Dublin University, were absentees, although their names were on the cards sold about the Oval.' One must wonder about McCarthy's assertion once more, for while Smyth was an original selection for the game, Robinson was not deemed worthy of being named among the seven first choices by the IFU. But dignity in defeat was not one of McCarthy's characteristics, a fact made very clear in many of his subsequent offerings on Ireland's early efforts in the field of international competition.

England won the game by two goals and a try to nil, and contemporary reports suggest that the defeat could in large part be attributed to a complete inability to match the England teamwork, an understandable situation when one considers that England had the benefit of three games against Scotland. The Irish kicking was, apparently, very bad as well. McCarthy's sweeping condemnation was not, however, re-echoed in other publications such as *Bell's Life*, the *News-Letter*, the *Irish Times* and the *Freeman's Journal*.

A certain A.T. Mitchell was, apparently, the scourge of the Irish. It was he who scored the first try, an effort that was not converted, for, as the *Freeman's Journal* reported, the try was 'almost on the touchline and the place by Fraser failed'.

England led by that try at half-time and immediately after the interval laid seige to the Irish line, forcing the Irish to touch down four times in succession, before A. Cronyn, who was, apparently, one of the Irish heroes of the day, made a dashing run towards the England line. But Nash then dropped a goal for England, and that was followed by a try from Cheston to which Pearson added the goal points.

That evening the Irish players were entertained to dinner by the

Rugby Union at St James Hall. The *News-Letter* records that though Ireland lost, they 'won the respect of the conquerors'.

The assessment of the game as given in *Bell's Life* was that Bell, Cronyn and Galbraith (though it did not specify which of the Galbraiths) had all tackled well, but, added the commentator, 'Ireland has much to learn in the matter of tactics and play. However, we have no doubt that when an English twenty first plays in the Emerald Isle, a wonderful improvement in the form shown on Monday will be evident to all.'

So at last Ireland was in the international rugby field and the twenty players who had the distinction of being the first representatives were:

Backs:
   E. Galbraith (Dublin University)
   R.B. Walkington (NIFC)
Threequarter backs:
   E. McIlwaine (NIFC)
   R. Galbraith (Dublin University)
Half-backs:
   A.P. Cronyn (Dublin University)
   G.H. Stack (Dublin University), capt.
   R. Bell (NIFC)
Forwards:
   J. Allen (Wanderers)
   G. Andrews (NIFC)
   W. Ash (NIFC)
   M. Barlow (Wanderers)
   B. Casement (Dublin University)
   A. Combe (NIFC)
   W. Gaffikin (Windsor)
   J. Myles (Dublin University)
   H.L. Cox (Dublin University)
   F.T. Hewson (Wanderers)
   J. MacDonald (Methodist College)
   J. Magennis (Dublin University)
   H.D. Walsh (Dublin University)

Many of these men were playing out of position, but in those days this was not a rare occurrence.

The first international out of the way, the IFU and the Northern

Football Union turned their attentions to other things. The IFU began thinking about arranging a return match in Dublin, while the Northern Union tried to organise a match against a team from Dublin. Their invitation was rejected at a meeting of the IFU on 3 March, a meeting incidentally at which the first Munster club became affiliated to the Dublin body, the honour of this seniority going to the Rathkeale club.

Within a short time two other teams came into the union: Arlington and Scott's Military Academy. In the interest of accuracy it must be pointed out that the inclusion of Rathkeale, Scott's Academy and Arlington in the list of founder-members in the 1892 edition of Marshall is erroneous. The minutes of the general meeting of the IFU held on 19 March 1875 clearly state that as 'Rathkeale, Arlington and Scott's Academy had all joined the union so late in the year, their subscriptions be considered their subscriptions for the following season'.

The minutes of that meeting also record that when everything was paid the union showed a credit balance for the year of £2 1s. 3d., not a bad performance when one considered that it had necessitated public subscription to send the Irish twenty to the Oval.

The working committee for the 1875–76 season was also elected; Walsh was again honorary secretary and Peter honorary treasurer, with Stack and Richard Galbraith completing the line-up. It was decided, however, that this committee would resign and a new one be elected at the beginning of the season 'should any important clubs join the union in the interim'. The necessity did not arise, but other happenings of some moment were at hand.

5
A Dublin initiative
1875-79

The officials of the IFU did not sit back and enjoy the sun during the summer months of 1875. The IFU wanted a single controlling body for the whole country, and with that aim in view they sent the following proposals to the Northern Football Union.

(1) That the annual meeting take place in rotation in the north (Belfast), in Dublin and in the south (suppose Limerick). The business of the meeting would be the election of officers and a working committee for the year. (2) That trial matches take place in each of the above named places, and (3) That as a full attendance of the working committee on the occasion of the selection of the Irish team was desirable, that expenses of the various members be paid by the union.

The proposals did not meet with a ready response from Belfast, and Dick Bell, the honorary secretary of the Northern Football Union, informed Dublin that amalgamation for this season was not considered possible.

Meanwhile, England suggested 13 December as a likely date for the first international in Dublin, and at a meeting of the working committee of the IFU that proposal was accepted. The date of 13 December had also been suggested by Bell as the most suitable occasion for the first interprovincial match between Leinster and Ulster. Bell also suggested that a sub-committee consisting of five members from each union would pick the team to meet England following the interprovincial. This was accepted by Dublin with the proviso that the claims of Munster and Connacht players must also be considered. This is, incidentally, the first reference to Connacht in the official records, though there is no record of any Connacht clubs being affiliated to the IFU at this time.

The interprovincial was fixed for 27 November at the Ormeau grounds. Now all that remained was to find a suitable venue in Dublin for the match against England. The IFU had originally turned to Trinity, but College Park was not deemed suitable so the net had to be cast wider. The 'Nine Acres' at Phoenix Park was then proposed and for a time came under active consideration. Then Henry Wallace Doveton Dunlop, honorary secretary of the Irish Champion Athletic Club, who was also a Trinity graduate and an athlete of repute, offered the Lansdowne Road ground, on which he had a lease from the Earl of Pembroke, but his letter of proposal was rejected out of hand on 5 November, in spite of Dunlop's persistent efforts to induce the committee to reconsider their decision. Lansdowne Road, it was claimed, was 'quite inadequate for an international rugby match'. Subsequent events were to give that decision a hollow ring.

The choice of venue for this historic occasion eventually fell on the Leinster Cricket Grounds at Rathmines, and after negotiations the ground was secured at a rent of £10. Although Trinity had been unable to provide a ground, they came to the assistance with ropes, posts and a flag-pole. So now all was ready for the big day, even down to the booking of the Ancient Concert Rooms for the after-match dinner at a cost of £5. There remained, however, the matter of the interprovincial and, even more important, the selection of the Irish team. Both events took place on the weekend of November 27–29.

Leinster and Ulster faced each other at Ormeau on Saturday 27 November, and the fiercely held belief in Belfast that they were the superior football beings was borne out by the result: Ulster one goal, Leinster nil. Trinity supplied eleven of the Leinster twenty, Wanderers six, Lansdowne, Bray and Kingstown one each. The familiar names of Galbraith, Walsh, Cox, Casement and Barlow appeared in the Leinster team. A notable absentee was Stack, but the *News-Letter* recorded that Leinster also missed the services of Mr Cronyn ('one of Ireland's finest men behind the scrummage'), Mr Higginson, Mr O'Connor and Mr Wilson. Thus a built-in excuse was readily available to explain away defeat. For Ulster, the NIFC were represented by twelve players, Windsor seven and Methodist College one—a suitable commentary on where exactly the strength of Ulster rugby was vested. Ulster had seven of the players who had represented Ireland at the Oval in their team: Walkington, Bell, Ash, Andrews, McIlwaine, Gaffikin, and Mac-Donald. A contemporary report rhapsodises: 'The morning broke beautifully and the day was one of the finest that could possibly be expected. It was just cold enough to make sealskin jackets and ulster coats comfortable.'

A crowd of a thousand turned up at Ormeau, a record number for a match in Belfast according to the *News-Letter*, whose representative was much taken by the appearance of the Leinster players in their 'Shetland coloured jerseys and harp, white knickerbockers and club stockings'. Ulster wore white jerseys with the red hand as a crest, white knickerbockers, and red stockings. Only the knickerbockers have changed to this day.

Ulster scored early through Heron and the try was converted by Walkington. Heron was president of the Northern Football Union, and he must have been in a tranquil mood when he presided at the after-match dinner in the Linen Hall Hotel, Belfast.

The vigorous efforts of the players and the after-match celebrations obviously took their toll, for it was not until Monday that the five representatives from the IFU joined their five comrades from the Northern Union to select the Irish team to play England. Seventeen of those selected in Belfast eventually took the field at Rathmines, when Ireland, needless to say with the full blessing of the IFU, was led for the first time by an Ulsterman, Dick Bell. Twelve of those who had played at the Oval were again in the Irish side; while Ulster had the captaincy, Leinster still had the majority representation, eleven to nine, when Ireland lined-out at Rathmines.

When the Irish team, led by Bell, ran on to the Rathmines ground, their uniform was very different to that which they had worn at the Oval. This time Ireland wore navy blue knickerbockers, blue stockings and white jerseys and for the first time had the shamrock as a crest. The fact that England, too, wore white jerseys, did not apparently lead to any confusion, and it certainly did not detract from the merit of England's performance.

Ireland, apparently, showed much improvement in their play from the initial engagement, but England were too strong and too clever for the home representatives and won convincingly by one goal and one try to nothing. Thousands had turned up to witness the spectacle, though their presence is not borne out by the gate receipts, which totalled only £22.9s. As the admission fee had been set at a shilling (ladies, admittedly, being granted free access), large numbers must have gatecrashed the proceedings.

Some consideration had also been given to organising a match against Scotland, and the arrangements were left in the hands of the Northern Union. However, after Dublin had agreed to the game taking place in February, Bell wrote saying that the game would not take place, but failed to give a reason.

Once again the IFU managed to show a profit on the year's workings, and Peter reported a credit balance at the end of the season of £4 17s. 2d. The accounts also reveal that he had managed to get the Leinster Cricket Club to reduce the rent from the original £10 to £7 10s.

The match against England was now firmly established on an annual basis, but when in November 1876 the Rugby Union informed the IFU that the forthcoming game at the Oval would be fifteen-a-side, the suggestion was greeted with something approaching outrage and was summarily rejected. The reduction in the number of players had complications for the two Irish unions other than the fact that any deficiency in playing skill could be more easily disguised when there were forty players on the field.

Negotiations were completed on a more satisfactory basis for the second interprovincial between Leinster and Ulster, and Henry Wallace Dunlop's persistence that Lansdowne Road was a suitable venue for representative rugby was rewarded when the match was fixed for the ICAC ground. The terms of the agreement between Dunlop and the IFU are interesting. Dunlop agreed either to let the ground for £5 or to charge no ground rent but share the expenses of the game and the gate receipts. The IFU chose to accept the latter proposition.

The weather was not very kind for the first interprovincial match to be played in Dublin; the afternoon of 16 December 1876 saw no let-up in the torrential rain that had fallen throughout the morning, but, as the *Irish Times* reported, 'the Interprovincial match–Leinster versus Ulster–did actually come off despite the inclemency of the weather, and the general impression in the city that the game could not possibly take place.' The *Irish Times* also records that Leinster deservedly won by a goal and a try to two tries. After the game the representatives of the two unions met in the Arcade Hotel, Suffolk Street, Dublin, for the purpose of selecting the Irish team to meet England at the Oval on 5 February 1877. The Rugby Union had by this time secured the grudging approval of the Irish to their stipulation concerning the numerical strength of the two teams. Fifteen-a-side they wanted and fifteen-a-side they would get.

Ulster's suggestion that the interprovincial, too, be played fifteen-a-side had been adopted, and the northern committee's initiative in arranging a game against Scotland to be played at Ormeau on 19 February 1877 was also readily endorsed by the IFU. Ireland set off for the Oval once more, and yet again defeat was their portion, this time by two goals and two tries to nil. The score margins in these international defeats were widening and the worst fears about the reduction in playing strength were proved to have solid foundation. Ireland had only three survivors from their first international match: Richard Galbraith, Walkington and Cox.

After seeing the debacle at the Oval, the joint sub-committee of selection retired to the Charing Cross Hotel to pick the team to meet Scotland. Surprisingly only four of those who played against England were dropped, but when the team lined out against Scotland at Ormeau, it in fact showed seven changes from the side that lost at the Oval. The changes were not, however, for the better as Ireland was overwhelmed by six goals and two tries to nil, scarcely an auspicious start to the series.

On the home front, however, many important developments were under way. Munster were about to enter the field of competition. A challenge was issued by the Limerick club and accepted by the IFU at a meeting on 2 March 1877, and the date for the first Leinster *v.* Munster game was fixed for 24 March, with College Park as the venue. This time, however, the weather intervened in full force, and so bad was the day that the game had to be postponed to Monday, 26 March. Munster put up a brave fight, but Leinster prevailed by one goal to nil.

Munster was represented for the first time at a meeting of the IFU when C.B. Croker of Limerick attended the annual general meeting of the union on 15 October 1877, a meeting at which Harry Walsh resigned as the honorary secretary and the post was taken over by Dr William Neville.

Less than a fortnight later an even more important event occurred when the first specific moves were made towards an amalgamation with the Northern Football Union. At a special meeting of the IFU on 29 October 1877 it was decided to call a committee meeting for the following Thursday, 1 November, to draw up a scheme for amalgamation. It was also agreed to call an extraordinary meeting of the union with a view to getting the scheme adopted.

The committee met, in fact, on 2 November and drew up the following scheme for amalgamation with the Northern Union.

(1) That the union be called the Football Union of Ireland.

(2) That branches in connection with the union be established in Leinster, Ulster and Munster to manage the affairs of the clubs in these provinces.

(3) That the committee of the union consist of nine members, three to be elected from each branch annually on or before 20 October each year and that within a fortnight after their election, they elect a secretary and treasurer.

(4) That when possible this committee shall meet in Dublin.

(5) That each club pay an annual subscription of half a guinea to defray the expenses of the union.

The scheme was adopted with slight amendment at the extraordinary meeting held at 63 Grafton Street on 7 November, and things looked set fair for the big union between north and south. But Belfast hedged on the issue and a dispute arose between the two unions about the date for the match against Scotland that season. There was further insistence by the IFU that it was now time that Munster got a say in the running of the national side, and Munster having agreed to meet Leinster at College Park in Dublin on 26 January, the IFU suggested that the north send representatives to attend the game. Leinster once again beat Munster, this time by one goal and a try to nil. But the NFU was not represented at the game.

The cool atmosphere between north and south was eased somewhat when the Northern Union requested a date for the Leinster-Ulster game and also informed Dublin that arrangements for the match against Scotland had fallen through. It was news greeted with some dismay by the IFU committee. However, they suggested 2 March as a likely date for the interprovincial and also took the opportunity to remind the Ulstermen that they had not yet received a reply to their suggestion that Munster be represented at future meetings to select an Irish side. Ulster agreed to 2 March as the date for the interprovincial with Belfast as the venue. Ulster won the match by two goals to nil.

The IFU had several weeks earlier quietly arranged for a visit from England for 11 March. A meeting was held in Belfast to discuss this forthcoming fixture and to select the Irish team. The IFU minutes record that H.L. Robinson, H.Murray, W. Neville, R.M. Peter and F. Kidd represented Leinster and Munster at this meeting.

The presence of the Munster delegates may have irritated the Ulstermen, for the proceedings became heated. Dick Bell, who was in the chair, at one stage threatened to leave the meeting, but his better judgement prevailed in the end, no doubt on the grounds that anything might have happened had he left the room. After a lengthy discussion, the team was finalised. Significantly enough, it contained no fewer than three Munster players: E.Croker, W. Griffiths and J.J. Keon, all of Limerick. Griffiths and Croker were in the side that eventually lined out.

Dunlop, seeing that all was now ready for the fray, again offered

Lansdowne Road for the game against England, but this time at slightly elevated terms. (It was, after all, an international!) The union agreed to Dunlop's terms that he be paid £5 and half of any profit over £50 after deduction of expenses.

Only one player now survived from the 1875 game against England at the Oval. This was R.B. Walkington, who played at full-back and captained the Irish side that day at Lansdowne Road. The story of the game was the old familiar one–another defeat, this time by two goals and a try, and once again Ireland failed to score. Five matches in international competition had failed to yield even one score, but reports of the after-match dinner, which was held at the Shelbourne Hotel, do not suggest that the Irishmen allowed any cloud of depression to settle over them because of this latest reverse.

In October 1878 the IFU again opened negotiations with the Northern Football Union for an amalgamation. This time the south decided to use Munster as their lever, suggesting that if Ulster persisted in standing in the way of the establishment of a single legislative body, then Munster could feel entitled to form a Munster Branch and claim equal representation at all future meetings of selection sub-committees. With Cork and Limerick football clubs both affiliated to the IFU, the suggestion carried some weight. Cork had three representatives at the annual general meeting of the IFU, held on 4 November 1878, and one of their representatives, William Goulding, was elected on what was termed 'a new executive committee' which replaced the old working committee. A nice balance was preserved when J.G. Cronyn of Limerick also found a place.

Dublin kept a firm hold on the Cork connection, and Wanderers and Trinity arranged to visit Cork for matches early in December. It was decided that this would be an opportune time to play the first interprovincial in Cork. The southern public were therefore now to have their full-scale rugby festival, with Wanderers taking on Cork FC on Saturday, 30 November, Trinity facing Cork on Monday, 2 December, while Leinster would meet Munster on Tuesday, 3 December. Cork managed to draw with Trinity, but lost to Wanderers, and Munster lost to Leinster by one goal and three tries to nil.

The proceedings of that programme in Cork did not go unnoticed in the northern metropolis, and a meeting of the executive committee of the IFU held in Neville's rooms at No. 9 Trinity College on 25 November 1878 was attended by none other than Dick Bell. His errand was, according to the minutes, 'to learn the views of the IFU with respect to amalgamation and to assist in drawing up a general scheme'. After lengthy discussion, the following rules emerged.

(1) That the union be called the Irish Football Union.

(2) That its objects shall be to promote and foster the game of rugby football in Ireland and to arrange international and interprovincial matches.

(3) That branches in connection with this union be formed in Leinster, Ulster and Munster respectively, to manage the affairs of the clubs in these provinces belonging to the union.

(4) That the committee of the union shall consist of eighteen members, six from each province to be elected annually, on or before 1 November, and that within a fortnight of their election they shall proceed to elect a president, two vice-presidents, an honorary secretary and honorary treasurer out of their own body.

(5) That in case of any member of the committee retiring during the term of office, that branch of the union which he represented shall fill the vacancy so caused.

(6) That the annual subscription of each club belonging to the union shall be £1 and that there shall be an entrance fee of one guinea.

It was further agreed by the committee that Munster, until they had either drawn or won a match against Ulster or Leinster, should only have four representatives on the committee, the two places to be left vacant in the meanwhile.

These proposals were accepted by the north with one amendment to rule six, which was that clubs at present belonging to either union would not have to pay the entrance fee. At a meeting of the IFU on 11 January 1879 it was agreed to accept the Ulster amendment. The same meeting also finalised arrangements for a double-bill interprovincial programme at Lansdowne Road on Friday, 16 Janaury, when Ulster would meet Munster for the first time, and Saturday, 17 January, when Ulster and Leinster would renew their rivalry.

A dinner was planned for the Saturday night in the Royal Arcade Hotel and it was also decided that members of the Munster team could attend 'provided that they paid their own share'.

The outcome of the games was a double victory for Ulster, Leinster this time losing by one goal to nil. The papers of the day heralded the new set-up as the formation of the Irish Rugby Football Union. Alas, they were ahead of their time, for the amalgamation was still twelve months away. In the intervening period there were occasions when the prospect of the great union looked to be in great jeopardy. Indeed, the first signs of Ulster dissent came the day before Ulster met Munster, when at a meeting of the IFU a letter from the honorary secretary of the Northern Union was read informing the meeting that the NFU did not intend that the rules for amalgamation should come into force that season (1878–9), particularly with regard to the selection of the Irish team. The minutes record that

> After much discussion, it was unanimously agreed to remonstrate with the Northern Union upon this apparent breach of faith and to point out to them the injustice done to Munster in refusing its players a place on the committee of selection, while playing them on terms of equality. In case the NFU persisted in their refusal, it was agreed that the IFU should agree to the old method of selection for the Irish XV to play against England that season, but should refuse to play the Scotch match in conjunction with the Northern Union unless the XV for it was chosen by a committee arranged on the new system.
>
> H.L. Robinson, G. Nugent, R.M. Peter, F. Schute and W. Neville were then selected to act as the members of the committee of selection on behalf of the IFU. In case no Munster representative was allowed on the committee, it was agreed that the two last named representatives would retire from the meeting in favour of W.J. Goulding and J.C. Cronyn, of Munster.

It was in this slightly sensitive atmosphere, then, that Munster met Ulster for the first time the following day.

After the Leinster *v.* Ulster game, the committee of selection met in the Royal Arcade Hotel to select the Irish team to meet England at the Oval on 3 February 1879. R.B. Walkington, J.A. MacDonald, E. Hughes, J.R. Bristow and W. Finlay represented the NFU and, just as they had threatened, they refused to admit any representative from Munster to the meeting. True to their word, Messrs Neville and Schute retired from the proceedings, their places being taken, as planned, by Goulding and Cronyn. Notice was formally given to the representatives of the NFU that the IFU would not consent to play Scotland unless the team was picked by a committee representing all three provinces as agreed under the scheme of amalgamation.

The team to meet England was chosen without the assistance of the Ulstermen, but fate was to deal Ulster a kind hand when the match against England had to be postponed because of frost and the NFU suggested that the team originally selected to play against England now line-out against Scotland in Belfast on 7 February 1879. The Northern Union also proposed that after the match in Belfast an amalgamated committee of the three provinces, six representatives from Ulster and Leinster and four from Munster, should meet to draw up rules for the guidance of the IRFU, which should come into force at the commencement of the following season.

With the long-cherished union now in peril, the IFU agreed to these proposals at a meeting in Dublin on 12 February. The date of the match against England was also fixed at this meeting for 24 March.

The withdrawal of J.Heron and J. Cuppaidge from the team that met Scotland made way for the advent of Goulding and A. Archer of Trinity to the Irish team, which once again maintained its undesired tradition by losing and failing to score. After the match a meeting was held in the Linen Hall Hotel in which all three provinces participated and, according to plan, drew up the rules for the guidance of the IRFU. Suffice it to say that they made only very minor amendments to the regulations originally accepted by both major bodies.

Ireland made their now customary unsuccessful excursion to London, where, even though they played ten forwards and five backs, they failed to contain the opposition, who won easily by three goals and two tries to nil.

6
A new beginning: the 1880s

The last meeting of the IFU took place on 28 October 1879 at 63 Grafton Street, premises owned by John Lawrence, who had also been the host five years earlier when the inaugural meeting had been held, on that occasion at 39 Grafton Street.

The new union was finally a fact of life. The inaugural general meeting of the IRFU was held at 63 Grafton Street at noon on 5 February 1880. William Neville was elected president, with Richard Bell and William Goulding as vice-presidents, thus creating a nice balance of three provinces. Peter was elected the first honorary secretary, while Edwin Hughes, from Ulster, was entrusted with the office of honorary treasurer. The Leinster representatives were Neville, Peter, F. Kennedy, G.P. Nugent, G. Scriven and F. Schute. Ulster's six were Bell, J. MacDonald, Hughes, W.T. Heron, H.C. Kelly, G.M. Shaw, while William Goulding, William Kelly, T. Harrison and J.J. Keon were looking after Munster's interests.

At the time of the IRFU's foundation Ireland had played seven matches, lost them all and had failed to register even one score. Now with one controlling body and the game expanding at club level, surely the first score, if not the first victory, would not be too long delayed.

By a happy coincidence the first try for Ireland came in the inaugural year of the first union, and to a Trinity student, John Loftus Cuppaidge, went the distinction of scoring it. Cuppaidge was a medical student who subsequently set up practice in Queensland and lived to recall his singular feat until 1934. His effort did not, however, preface a long career in the Irish jersey, for he was capped but once subsequently, in a match against Scotland that same year.

That Ireland's first try should have been scored by a Trinity player and at Lansdowne Road was of course fitting and contemporary reports reveal that Cuppaidge grounded the ball right between the England posts. Those reports also inform us that R.B. Walkington, despite his international experience at the time, 'was shaking like a leaf' while he was taking the kick. Not surprisingly, he missed, an omission of some consequence at a time when a goal was considered superior to any number of tries. England went on to win the match by a goal and a try to a try. On 14 February that year Scotland were hosts to Ireland for the first time and the match followed a familiar pattern when in Glasgow, Scotland won by three goals and two tries to nil.

Munster had the honour of providing the IRFU with the president in 1880-81 when William Goulding defeated Richard Bell in a ballot for the office. Goulding was to have the distinction of presiding over the first Irish victory dinner for the big breakthrough was at hand. It came on 19 February 1881 when Ireland defeated Scotland by a dropped goal to a try at Ormeau.

Jacques McCarthy, who had been singularly unimpressed after another defeat by England, displayed an appreciative pen when he recorded that famous victory.

> Although Scotland were warm favourites, the odds against Ireland had been reduced in rather odd fashion, however, for several of the original Scottish XV had to be replaced at the last moment owing to the secession of a section of Edinburgh players who felt aggrieved at the committee's choice of captain.

After revealing, and not for the first time, his dislike of Belfast, graphically illustrated by his remark that 'by as yet some unexplained miracle the amphibious inhabitants of the Northern Athens were favoured by a fine day', McCarthy went on to state that Ireland should have won, but did not turn first-half superiority into tangible benefit on the scoreboard so that at half-time there was no score, a situation that continued until five minutes from the end when disaster struck in the shape of a Scottish try. McCarthy described the effort as follows:

> McMullan, of Cork, making a mis-catch at a long kick, placed the whole of the Scottish team on-side and Graham, who was leaning against the Irish goalpost, rubbing his shin, after a recent hack, leisurely limped over the line and touched the ball down.
>
> Nothing could be more galling or tantalising than this; but some slight relief was forthcoming when Begbie missed the kick which was as easy as possible.
>
> Only five minutes remained, could we now win? Surely we deserved it as we had been up on the Scottish line all day and thrice compelled them

to touch down in defence with very narrow escapes. The spectators became simply hysterical and never ceased shouting from this to the very end.

Their exhortations were rewarded, however. McCarthy graphically described the winning score in the last minute.

> J.W. Taylor got possession immediately after the drop out and with all his team attending him, ran up to the Scottish 'twenty-five', where he passed to 'Merry' Johnston, who returned him the leather on the very verge of the Scottish line.
>
> Here it was heeled out from the scrummage to Johnston, who, amidst vociferous profanity, missed his pick-up, and Campbell, darting in, shot the ball into touch ten yards down.
>
> Barney Hughes, however, rapidly realised the situation and threw it out to Taylor before the Scots could line-up, and Taylor transferred to Johnston, who quicker than you could think or write, tossed to Bagot, who dropped the ball over the Caledonian bar.
>
> Such frantic excitement as these lighteningly executed triumphant movements evoked was never previously seen, and men and women and children embraced each other indiscriminately.
>
> The spell of sorrow was broken and we returned to Dublin by the five o'clock train supremely happy.

So Ireland had won a match at last and the fifteen noble players who achieved that first victory were:

R.E. McLean (Dublin University)
J.C. Bagot (Dublin University)
W.W. Pike (Kingstown)
M. Johnston (Dublin University)
H.F. Spunner (Wanderers)
A.J. Forrest (Wanderers) capt.
D. Browning (Wanderers)
J.W. Taylor (Queen's College, Belfast)
J.A. MacDonald (Queen's College, Belfast)
R.W. Hughes (NIFC)
J. Johnstone (Ulster)
W. Finlay (NIFC)
H. Purdon (NIFC)
A.R. McMullan (Cork)
H.B. Morell (Dublin University)

The team was led by A.J. Forrest of Wanderers, and while McCarthy made reference to the fact that Scotland were not at full strength, it is worthy of note that of the Irish team elected for that season by open ballot among the members of the union, no fewer than five of the Irish side that beat Scotland were originally only named as substitutes: McLean, McMullan, J. Johnstone, Purdon and Morell.

That victory was to have a sequel at the annual general meeting of the union in Dublin on 17 December 1881. When the accounts were presented it was discovered that there was only £23 4s. 7d. in the kitty and that the sum of £24 5s. was still due to the Imperial Hotel, Belfast, for the dinner to the Scottish team. Worse still, a balance of £8 5s. 6d. was also due to the Shelbourne Hotel, Dublin, for an international dinner given to the England team that had conceded that try to Cuppaidge in February 1880. The IRFU now faced something of a financial crisis; indeed, money troubles were to beset the union for the next decade. The only reward received by the fifteen heroes who had beaten Scotland was a bill from the union for one guinea each. There is no record that any of them ever paid it.

That meeting in December 1881 also saw Dick Bell sever his connection with the IRFU. No reason was given for his resignation; possibly he may have been discouraged by his defeat in the 1880 election for the presidency. So Bell, who had done so much for the organisation of the Northern Union and the IRFU, was destined never to be honoured with the supreme office.

A similar fate was to befall R.M. Peter, whom Jacques McCarthy had described as 'the father of Irish rugby', a title that was perhaps rather exaggerated. Peter severed his connection with his club, Wanderers, and the IRFU in 1882 after a dispute about a match report he wrote in the *Irish Times*. Shortly before he departed from the rugby scene, he attempted unsuccessfully to organise a national cup competition and even went as far as drawing up the rules for what he termed 'The Irish Rugby Football Union Challenge Cup'. His project was not, however, greeted with any great enthusiasm and it fell through. Peter was, however, more successful in Leinster, where he had been very active as a club representative for both Wanderers and Dundalk.

The Leinster branch realised the potential of such a competition within its own province and established the Leinster Senior Cup in 1882. Not unexpectedly, Trinity won the inaugural tournament and retained the cup for the following two seasons before Wanderers broke their monopoly in 1885.

It was to Ulster, however, that the credit for initiating cup football in Ireland belongs, for as early as 1875–76 the Ulster Schools Cup was established. Armagh Royal School were the first winners, beating the Royal Academical Institute by a dropped goal to nil in the second replay, after the teams had played two scoreless draws.

Leinster followed the Ulster lead in 1887 when they, too, started a senior schools cup, with Blackrock College the first winners. The eighties may not have been a particularly auspicious decade for Ireland's performances on the playing-field, but it was nonetheless a period of tremendous development on the home front. The Ulster Senior Cup was started in 1884–85, and, as might be expected, NIFC were the first winners, while Munster and Connacht soon followed suit, Bandon winning the first Munster Senior Cup in 1886, and Galway Town taking the inaugural Connacht title in 1896. Cup football has never since been an integral part of the game in Ireland, and the last two months of each season are always a period of frenzied activity in the field of competitive rugby.

In 1882 Ireland met Wales for the first time, the game taking place at Lansdowne Road on 28 January. In the light of subsequent events in the field of international competition, it seems strange in retrospect that it was with something approaching condescension that Ireland granted Wales a fixture. Wales had made the initial approach in 1880, but after first accepting the fixture for the following year on condition that the game took place in Dublin, the IRFU decided against playing the game.

Munster did, however, undertake a Welsh tour in 1881, led by William Goulding. They played three matches, one against Newport, which they lost, one against a South Wales XV, which they also lost, and then ended their campaign on a successful note by defeating Neath. It was an effort that earned a severe reprimand from the ruling body, for Munster had not sought permission from the IRFU, and Wales had taken the opportunity to count the victory by their South Wales XV over Munster as a win for Wales over Ireland.

Perhaps Ireland's attitude to the first match against the principality can best be put into perspective by the fact that only four of the selected team turned out at Lansdowne Road on 28 January 1882. Ireland duly paid the penalty, losing by two goals and two tries to nil.

A week later, also at Lansdowne Road, Ireland achieved her best result yet against England, a draw, two tries each. It was a game that aroused more than a little controversy, to say nothing of the ire of that trenchant critic, Jacques McCarthy.

Without any possibility of contradiction [wrote McCarthy], Ireland won by a goal and a try to two tries, but the official result was a draw. This was the famous Pike cum Nugent match, Pike the player winning it, while Nugent, the umpire lost it. McLean kicked a goal for Ireland off a try by Taylor, but Dr Nugent decided that it was no goal. Stokes scored for Ireland immediately after the kick-off, but Walkington missed the kick, then Hunt got in for England, Rowley missing. W.N. Bolton (an Irishman by the way), then scored for England and finally M. Johnson got a try which was virtually scored by Taylor. Off this McLean kicked the goal above referred to and which was disallowed by Nugent amidst universal dismay.

So a draw it was, despite McCarthy's claims. Even so, the result was encouraging for Ireland, though it was to prove no deterrent to Scotland, who exacted due retribution for their defeat the previous season by gaining a victory of two tries to nil in Glasgow.

The annual general meeting for 1882–83, held on 20 January 1883, was not without its dramatic moments. At the outset of the meeting, the statement of accounts was rejected on the grounds that 'they were quite unintelligible', and J. Atkinson, the honorary secretary for the previous season who had resigned the post prior to the 1883 meeting, was requested in his absence to furnish a detailed account of his stewardship. A special committee was set up to investigate the accounts and instructed to take 'whatever steps they deemed necessary for the recovery of any balance they found due'.

History does not record what they found nor what steps they took. Meanwhile the Imperial Hotel in Belfast was still seeking the money due for the dinner to Scotland in 1881 and the union was still seeking one guinea from each of the players who had taken part in the game.

Munster, who in 1880 had beaten Leinster and had thus enjoyed equal representation on the committee, provided the treasurer when William Goulding was appointed in succession to Atkinson, while the new president was George Scriven, by now qualified as a doctor from Trinity. Still at the height of his playing career he was not only elected president of the union, but was also appointed captain of the Irish team for the season. As the union committee still picked the team on a system of ballot, Scriven had the unique distinction of being president of the union, captain of the Irish team and chairman of selectors in the same season. H.C. Cook took over as honorary secretary. Showing a fine appreciation of the possibilities contained in the decision to set up an investigating committee on the financial position, Cook promptly informed all and sundry that he was accepting the honorary secretary's position on the strict understanding that he would not be held in any way responsible for outstanding debts.

That the union's difficulties, financial and otherwise, got a thorough airing in the press of the day was evident when at the general meeting the following season, A.R. McMullan proposed that in future, the press be barred from reporting the proceedings of the union's meetings. Despite strong support from Cook for this motion, the committee, showing a fine regard for the democratic process, rejected it, so McCarthy and his ilk were not to be denied free access to any contentious material. Rather less democratic, perhaps, was the reduction of the representation of each province from six to five during the season.

Scriven had led Ireland against England and Scotland in the previous season, but the match arranged against Wales had been dropped. The failure to honour the fixture against Wales was the subject of a lively debate. Cook informed the meeting that the Irish players were just not interested in travelling to play Wales and that he found it quite impossible to raise a team to make the journey to Cardiff. At this juncture it was proposed and carried that any man who played in the Welsh match only would not be awarded an international cap. Then making an impassioned plea that a truly representative side should be sent to Cardiff in March 1884, the president said that every effort must be made to select a team, worthy to meet Wales. However, those sentiments did not deter the union from deciding unanimously that while Ireland would fulfil its commitment in 1884, Wales would thereafter be dropped from the international schedule.

The 1883–84 season was the first year in which a complete international programme took place, with the four home countries meeting each other. England won in Dublin and Scotland won in Edinburgh in 1884, but once again the union had extreme difficulty in getting a really representative team to travel to Cardiff–so much difficulty, in fact, that Cook, who travelled in his capacity as honorary secretary, was forced to play for Ireland. And even then, in order to field fifteen players Ireland had to borrow two from Wales. To this day there seems some doubt as to who the two players were, but most authorities name them as H.M. Jordan and H. McDaniel both from Newport. Jordan subsequently played for Wales against England and Scotland the following year and against Scotland in 1889, but McDaniel never achieved the distinction for his own country that was conferred on him by Ireland that day in Cardiff, albeit by default. That Irish team was led by D. Moore as J. MacDonald, captain that season, was one of those who failed to make the trip to Cardiff, where Ireland's rather mixed XV were beaten by a goal and two tries to nil.

MacDonald's game for Ireland against Scotland in 1884 was his last and severed the final connection with the first twenty, which had included the Ulsterman. It was in view of his sterling service to Ireland that he was given the captaincy in 1884, having stated that this would be his last year in international football.

Ireland's difficulties in Cardiff were not the only problems that beset the rugby world that season. When England met Scotland at Blackheath, a dispute arose in the course of the game that had major repercussions. While Ireland was not directly involved, the referee at Blackheath was George Scriven, who had added the distinction of being an international referee to his other achievements. Sir Rowland Hill, one of the leading legislators of the era, and a legendary figure in the Rugby Union, summed up the incident thus: 'In the course of play, the ball was knocked back by a Scotsman (ruled so by the referee G. Scriven, a well known Irish player), one of the English team secured it and a try was scored. The Scotsmen claimed that the knocking back was illegal.'

The English and the Scots were unable to reach an agreement on the matter and so in 1884–85 Scotland did not meet England. There the matter rested until Ireland considered the matter at the general meeting of the IRFU held on 11 December 1885.

W.J. Moore proposed and R.G. Warren seconded a successful motion 'That the honorary secretary be directed to write to the honorary secretaries of the English and Scotch Unions stating that an International Board would be very useful for the settlement of international disputes.' England and Scotland consented and a conference was held in Dublin on 6 February 1886. As a result of its deliberations, Scotland awarded the 1884 match to England on the understanding that England would join an international board composed of an equal number of representatives of each of the four unions. Thus was born a body that has since been the ruling authority of the game. And while, like many other great institutions, it had its teething troubles, it was founded on an Irish initiative, a fact which is scarcely ever mentioned in rugby reference books.

But the 1884–85 season was in many other ways a momentous one for Ireland. At the annual meeting of 1885 the honorary treasurer, William Goulding, was able to report that at long last the financial position was improving, the union now having a credit balance of £20 8s. 4d.

It was at this meeting, too, that the clubs attached to the Irish

Provincial Towns Rugby Union, which had been formed some years earlier by a few provincial clubs, were finally brought in under the senior body. They had applied to the IRFU the previous season for amalgamation and were informed that they should affiliate to the respective branches in their area. With the exception of Dundalk, all the clubs concerned were in Ulster.

It was in 1885 also that the province of Connacht made an attempt to form its own branch, although there were only four clubs in the province. The meeting decided that if a fifth club should be formed in Connacht, the province would have the right to form their own branch and be given representation on the union committee and admitted to the interprovincial programme. In the meantime a Monkstown FC proposal that Galway Grammar School, Ballinasloe, Connacht Exiles and Queen's College, Galway, be elected to membership of the IRFU was accepted. It was the start of what proved to be a long, hard road for administrators in the west and it was another fifty years until the objectives envisaged that December day in 1885 were brought to full fruition.

Finally, at the same meeting the design for the crest on the Irish team jerseys was changed to the shamrock pattern that Irish teams have worn ever since and Scriven was elected once again as president of the union, the only man in history to have been appointed to that office twice with a break between the two terms of service.

During this season the team actually played Scotland twice, which in some ways made up for the fact that the Scots did not meet England at all. Ireland was led for the first time by a Munsterman, W.G. Rutherford, and lost to England by two tries to a try in Manchester on 7 February. For some undefined reason, five of the Irish players refused to play: L. Kidd, H.M. Brabazon, R. Nelson, J. Forrester and J.J. Johnston. The match against Scotland at Ormeau on 21 February lasted exactly fifteen minutes and was called off because of bad weather. Scotland insisted on a return match to be played in Edinburgh; it took place in March, and Ireland, badly depleted, lost the game by two tries and one goal to nil.

The season of 1885–6 saw things return to normality. England had a full programme of games, but rumblings of discontentment were still evident as the International Board was still not framed to England's liking. At a meeting in October 1886 England decided to change the scoring system, allowing three points for a penalty goal, where previously a penalty did not count. But the other countries could not go along with England's wishes and for a time it looked as if England would be without a fixture in 1887. Indeed, the IRFU called a special meeting on 29 November 1886, when it was proposed by J.F. Blood (Leinster) and seconded by S. Harris (Leinster) that 'It would not be advisable to play England in Dublin in 1887.' The proposal was defeated by thirteen votes to three. The meeting also decided that the old system of scoring would operate and England subsequently agreed to that principle. This was, incidentally, the first meeting of the IRFU at which Connacht was officially represented, and one of their three delegates was none other than Jacques McCarthy.

The subject of Sunday rugby was also raised at that special meeting when Kincora FC, a recently-formed Munster club, wrote to request a union ruling on the subject and were informed that there was nothing in the laws of the IRFU which prohibited Sunday play. The matter was accordingly referred back to the Munster Branch.

England came to Lansdowne Road on 5 February 1887, which turned out to be a memorable day for Ireland. On twelve previous occasions Ireland had faced England, and with the exception of the draw in 1882 it had been one defeat after another for Ireland. Ireland put a young side into the field, a team that in fact contained ten new caps, and at long last England was humbled. Ireland not only won, scoring two goals, but for the first time did not concede a score. Jacques McCarthy was ecstatic. He opened his article in *Sport* of the following week thus:

> Ladies and gentlemen–with your kind permission and attention I shall now sing you a few verses of a little parody on Joe Coburn's original favourite 'Two Lovely Black Eyes' ahem, Mr Conductor, will you oblige please?
>
> Two goals off two tries,
> Oh, what a surprise;
> Were ever Englishmen leathered like this?
> Two goals off two tries.

McCarthy's great rival 'Green and Gold' who operated for the *Irish Sportsman* was, however, even more jubilant for he had greeted the announcement of the team with far greater confidence than had McCarthy. 'Green and Gold', looking ahead to the game against Scotland, had this to say:

> Gentlemen of the Irish fifteen, thus far by means of play that was grand,

you have marched on despite impediment. England, the erstwhile successful boar, whose ravenous appetite had swallowed up our teams, gave our poor country a taste that rudely cropped its ripened hopes of fair prosperity, is now even chockful of bile.

St Patrick, who after all was a gentleman, has caught St George between wind and water and the latter eminent personage is now weeping by the waters of Babylon with a leg on each side of his tail. You have licked the Saxon and you have done it nobly. Now you face the representatives of brown heath and shaggy wool, oaten cakes and Islay whisky. Having settled St George and Merrie England, are you going to play second fiddle to Bonnie Scotland? Gentlemen, you have begun well and your country looks to you to go on and finish the work. I say then in the familiar but immortal words of the 'Iron Duke', 'Up guards and at them', break the thistle as you have plucked the rose and plant on the heights of victory the great immortal shamrock.

One suspects that 'Green and Gold' saw infinitely more in Ireland's win than a victory on the rugby field over England. Not even McCarthy could equal the invective of his tirade, though he did have a good try. Their exhortations were, however, all in vain, for Scotland put a stop to Ireland's Triple Crown ambitions, and Wales, with whom Ireland had resumed negotiations, followed by winning as well that season. Yet victory over England was something to shout about, especially when little confidence had been expressed in the young side that had been elected by the IRFU committee.

McCarthy had been at his vitriolic best when describing the team selection for *Sport*. He declared that four of the selected side were unfit through injury and that the selection meeting 'all wound up with a hot battle for the last place, which finally went to the Munsterman John Macaulay after his portrait, war paint and all, had been handed around the room'. But McCarthy had a vivid imagination and did not hesitate to bend the facts in the interest of a good story and readable copy. He concluded his assessment of the team selection by remarking: 'All the mischief was now done, the Irish XV for 1887 had been elected. And directly after the team had been made known, R.M. Bradshaw offered to put down £50 as a guarantee and pick an outside fifteen which would play as well as the chosen one.' McCarthy asserts that Bradshaw formally challenged the Irish XV but that E. McAlister, who that day was elected honorary secretary of the union and was later to emerge as a distinguished legislator, was unable to get the latter together, so that the bet fell through. Suffice it to say that the IRFU minutes of the proceedings do not bear out McCarthy's statements; indeed, if Bradshaw was even present at the meeting, it was not in an official capacity.

It is instructive to look a little more closely at the achievements of that little-fancied Irish team which by its victory wrote a glorious chapter in the history of rugby in Ireland. Robert G. Warren was captain that day. As a youngster of twenty-one, he had come into the Irish side in 1884 against Wales and in all won fifteen caps. His service on the field was invaluable and he could be said to have been the first really accomplished back that Ireland produced. He was destined to have an even more distinguished career as a legislator.

Legend has it that another player, John Macaulay (who figured in McCarthy's alleged 'portrait' incident), had arranged to get married that weekend. Having taken all his annual leave, it was the only way he could think of to get time off from an employer not apparently well disposed towards sport. Macaulay was to play in only one more international, but, like Warren, he later became a distinguished legislator.

Ireland, apparently, beat England 'fore and aft' and Warren, who was playing at half-back, must have given his threequarters a good service, for two of them, C.R. Tillie (Dublin University) and R. Montgomery (Queen's College, Belfast), scored the tries, both of which were converted by Dave Rambaut (Dublin University).

'Green and Gold's' address to the troops did not have the desired effect when Scotland a week later won convincingly by two goals and two tries to nil in Belfast.

The restoration of the game against Wales that season, did not result in any further glory for the Irish, but it was, nonetheless, an historic occasion, for the game, played at Birkenhead, is the only international on record to have been contested at a neutral venue. Birkenhead was chosen to save Ireland expense, being an infinitely more convenient location than Cardiff or Swansea. Wales won the game by a dropped goal to three tries, all of them scored by Montgomery.

None of the other home countries played England in 1888. At a meeting of the English Union in March 1887, invitations were sent to Ireland, Scotland and Wales to attend a meeting at which the laws of the game would be discussed. When no replies were received from the other unions by September 1887, England decided that the interests of international rugby would be best served if they played their future internationals according to the laws of the country in which the matches took place. The IRFU at a special general meeting on 20 September 1887 showed independent spirit and its contempt for the whole affair by deciding that they would not send any delegates to a meeting of the Rugby Union 'having no wish to interfere with the laws of the game in England and that we should retain our right of legislating on the rules to govern the game in this country.'

A meeting of the International Board in Crewe on 5 December 1887 decided that 'All international matches must be played under rules approved of by the International Board, in terms of which no international match with England can take place until the English Rugby Union agrees to join the International Board.' England recognised that decision for what it was and finally accepted the principle that the International Board would become the lawmakers for the game generally.

The vexed question of scoring continued to cause dissension, and again in 1889 England did not meet any of the home countries. The method of scoring that obtained since 1875 was still good enough for the IRFU, but at a general meeting in January 1888, the Irish Union ruled that a match should be decided on a majority of points. A try would count as two points; a goal from a try (the try not to count) as four points; a dropped goal or a goal from a free as three points. In 1892 these values were altered by reducing a goal from a free to one point. By 1894 the IRFU had agreed to assimilate the scoring in international matches to that adopted by the other unions. A try was now to count as three points; a goal from a try (the try not to count) as five points; a dropped goal as four points; a penalty goal or a goal from a mark as three points. And that was how the scoring stood until 1948 when the dropped goal was reduced in value to three points. In 1972 the try was raised to four points.

The period of the late eighties and early nineties could be said to have been the second great period of development within the game. In addition to scoring values, many other practices were under constant consideration. These included alterations in the line-up of the backs, originally introduced by the Welsh when they experimented with four threequarters. Another highly contentious question, which still arouses a fair share of controversy, was the role of the wing forward.

When the Irish team was being elected for the 1888 matches, the question of wing forward play was raised by E. McAlister and W. Stokes. There was also a request that the press should not report any details about the picking of the team, a request that the irrepressible

McCarthy did not comply with, as the following passage from *Sport* illustrates.

> Messrs Stokes and McAlister spoke strongly against the pest of the wing forward, but Mr Warren (note R.G.), was just as fervent in favour of it. He was mainly the man to be considered, or at least one of them, and gave personal reasons for his opinions. In the end it was as much as could be done to prevent two wing men from being decided on.

Nothing daunted, Ireland picked the team to meet Scotland and Wales. The match against Wales on 3 March at Lansdowne Road was, in fact, the first that took place as the game against Scotland was postponed until 10 March because of frost.

There was not much confidence in the Irish side as Wales had already beaten Scotland and were regarded as 'a tricky lot'; their tactics had certainly incurred the wrath of the termagent critic McCarthy, who wrote:

> Scotland was simply swindled out of the match. There is not the least use in using nice words when dealing with such shabby subterfuges as those which were adopted by the Welsh.
>
> To put the case in a nutshell, they got a surprise try early in the first half and then killed the remainder of the time by lying down on the ball, kicking out of play and every other trick and dodge that the rules have not provided against, as prostitution of a noble, fair and chivalrous game. . . . Since Ireland was swindled out of her first game with Wales, I have fought tooth and nail in these columns to have the Ireland and Wales fixture abandoned and I think I have a few converts to my view now.

But the match and its result had a truly remarkable effect on McCarthy's previously held views. Ireland won by two goals and a try to nil, and he decided that these Welsh were not so bad after all. 'If we are always to meet Welshmen like these,' he conceded, 'even though they may be better players, and beat us, they will be welcome for I never saw a more gentlemanly lot on a field'.

R.G. Warren again led the side and proved to be one of the heroes of the day, together with the Monkstown back M. Carpendale, who apparently had a hand in every score. Warren had obviously got his way with regard to the wing forward, for T. Shanahan (Waterford) apparently played in the role of a rover. Carpendale, Warren and

Shanahan shared the scoring between them. The Irish side also included D.B. Walkington at full-back. He regularly wore a monocle when playing. It was his habit to take off the monocle when making a tackle and then replace it.

The team that defeated Wales for the first time included six of those who had shared in the win over England in the previous season. Walkington was one of the six. The full team was:

D.B. Walkington (Dublin University)
C.R. Tillie (Dublin University)
D.F. Rambaut (Dublin University)
M.J. Carpendale (Monkstown)
R.G. Warren (Lansdowne) capt.
J.H. McLaughlin (Derry)
H.J. Neill (NIFC)
E. Stoker (Wanderers)
F.O. Stoker (Wanderers)
W.G. Rutherford (Lansdowne and Clanwilliam)
T. Shanahan (Lansdowne and Waterford)
C.M. Moore (Dublin University)
J. Moffatt (Albion)
R. Mayne (Albion)
E. Ekin (Queen's College, Belfast)

The victory over Wales did not inspire a performance of similar moment against Scotland at Raeburn Place a week later, when Ireland lost by a goal to nil.

The annual general meeting of the IRFU in 1888 was an eventful occasion. Proposals that Munster's representation be reduced to three and Connacht's to two were successfully resisted, as was a motion from Ulster that the Irish XV in future be picked by sub-committee. Connacht were struggling on with the aid of annual subsidies out of union funds; nevertheless, this meeting saw the election for the first time of a Connachtman, Richard Biggs, to the presidency.

The season of 1888–89 was notable for the visit of the first team from overseas, when a side from New Zealand, led by Joe Warbrick and named the Maoris, came to these shores. An Irish team was selected to meet them, although its members were not awarded international caps. Playing Ireland on 1 December 1888, the Maoris won by four goals and a try to a goal and a try, but lost to both Wales and England (the latter's only international engagement of the season). Ireland also lost to Scotland in Belfast but beat Wales in Swansea, so the eighties which had opened with Ireland seeking her first international win, closed on a note of victory. The win against Wales in Swansea, Ireland's first victory on foreign soil, was a good omen for the nineties.

7

The gay nineties and glory

The gate receipts of £210 that had been taken at Lansdowne Road for the match against England in 1887 did much to put the union's finances on a sound footing. Meanwhile the workings of the union were beginning to take on a much more efficient aspect. The new president for 1890 was Frederick Moore, a leading figure in Wanderers and one of three brothers who had played for Ireland. Frederick was in four Irish teams between 1884 and 1886; he was capped for the first time at the age of twenty-seven, and while his international career was now over, he continued to assist his old club until 1901 when he was forty-one. He was, too, the first member of Wanderers to be elected to the presidency of the union. Frederick's younger brother Frank had also been capped four times, while a third brother, Malcom, who assisted Trinity, won three caps and was in the first Irish team to beat Wales in 1888. Frederick Moore, who was knighted in 1911, proved to be an able president and under his guidance the union flourished.

When the nineties dawned, Ireland had played thirty-two matches, won four, drawn one and lost twenty-seven, and one game against Scotland had been abandoned. Not a very auspicious record, but the performances on the playing field did not really reflect the progress the game was making internally.

The four seasons between 1890 and 1893 were not exactly vintage years for Ireland in the field of international competition. In twelve matches, Ireland only managed to get one win (against Wales) and two draws (one each against Wales and Scotland). In 1893 England won readily enough by two tries to nil at Lansdowne Road; Ireland played a scoreless draw with Scotland in Belfast, and lost rather unluckily by a try to nil against Wales in Llanelli. There were, however, definite signs by this time that things were improving.

A revisionary committee had already been set up under Moore's presidency in order to facilitate changes in teams selected by the whole union committee, but the idea of forming an autonomous body to pick the Irish team had also been exercising the minds of the union, particularly the Ulster Branch, for some time, and an experiment with a rather unwieldly committee of nine in addition to the president of the union was subsequently approved. It was not until October 1892, however, that the specific words 'selection committee' were mentioned. Bob Warren proposed that a committee, 'called a selection committee' and consisting of six members, two each from Munster, Leinster and Ulster, be established. The first record of a 'selection committee' operating appears in the minutes for the annual meeting in January 1894, a meeting at which J. Redmond Blood, the president for the previous year, presided. Blood, Bob Warren (Leinster), R. Garrett and R. Stevenson (Ulster) and J. Hook and H. McOstrich (Munster) were appointed selectors. Their appointment coincided with Ireland's first Triple Crown triumph.

Scotland had won the Triple Crown in 1890–91, England in 1891–92 and Wales in 1892–93; in the case of both Wales and Scotland it was their first time to capture the coveted trophy. Ireland was very much the poor relation then, which probably accounts for the fact that they were quoted at odds of five to one, or so a contemporary informs us, when they faced England at Blackheath.

Wales had been experimenting with four threequarters for the previous ten years and had used them with profit in 1893. It was probably in the natural order of things that Ireland should follow suit.

The Irish selectors, like many of their successors, decided to put their faith in experience when they named the side to meet England. The team contained three new caps, all in the pack. They were Tom Crean of Wanderers, George Walmsley of Bective Rangers, and the NIFC man Jim Lytle, whose brother John was one of the veterans of the Irish side, having been capped first in 1889. But John Lytle was not the only experienced campaigner in the Irish eight that day. The captain, E. Forrest of Wanderers, had also been in the team on various occasions since 1889. The pack was completed by John O'Conor of Bective Rangers, Charles Rooke of Trinity and Harry Lindsay, another Trinity man. O'Conor and Rooke in particular had built up tremendous reputations since their appearances on the international scene in 1890 and 1891 respectively. Both were to play their full part in Ireland's triumph.

But the class and experience were not confined to those up front. Ireland had a threequarter line of Willie Gardiner, Sam Lee, Lucius

Gwynn and H.G. Wells. Lee had come into the side in 1891 and had
been a tower of strength ever since. He was highly regarded by the
leading critics of the day, notably by that prolific rugby writer E.H.D.
Sewell, for many years rugby correspondent of the *Evening Standard*
and the author of numerous books, who declared him to have been
among the greatest threequarters he saw before or since, an opinion
shared by another respected critic of the era, W.J. Townsend Collins,
who wrote under the pen name of Dromio. At half-back Ireland had the
combination of Ben Tuke (Bective Rangers) and Trinity's W.S. Browne,
two players who apparently had the ability and intellect to use
threequarters when it was prudent and ignore them when it was not.

Writing about the 1894 series, many years later, John O'Conor
recalled the Triple Crown triumph.

Although it was a famous victory when we beat Wales in Belfast, I must
admit it was not a great match.

In those days handling was not developed to the extent that came
later. The game was left almost entirely to the forwards and the scrums
were grim affairs, with all their forwards giving the full weight to the
shove. There were no specialised positions such as hooker or wing
forward, and every forward was expected to be an accomplished hooker.
First up, first down was the rule. The backs were used mainly in defence.

We got off to a good start when beating England by a dropped goal
and a try to a try at Blackheath and thus had the satisfaction of scoring
the first Irish victory over England on English soil.

Generally we were pleased with the performance of the side which was
not a particularly hefty one–I was the heaviest at 13½ stone–but all the
players were tall and speedy. That English game was also notable for the
fact that it was the first time Ireland used four threequarters. Until then
we had played nine forwards.

We had a full-back problem that year and after the English match
Sparrow (Trinity) was replaced by Grant (Bective) who had started the
season in his club's second XV.

He played very soundly against both Scotland and Wales. Walmsley
broke a leg before the Scottish match and Bond of Derry replaced him in
the pack, but we got through against Scotland by a goal to nil, Wells
getting the all-important try. But Wells was injured for the big day
against Wales in Belfast and Dunlop of Trinity replaced him on the
wing.

The Lagan had overflowed on to the Ormeau ground shortly before
the Triple Crown match and the pitch was in a frightful condition for
the match. The mud was over our ankles and it was almost impossible to

keep a foothold. But we were less affected by the conditions than Wales. We relied on fast foot rushes to keep their defence in trouble and prevented their backs from developing attacks.

The conditions and the ability of our forwards to maintain a non-stop onslaught won us the day. John Lytle got the only score of the game in the early stages, when he kicked a penalty goal from in front of the posts. That kick won us the Triple Crown.

In all Ireland used eighteen players in the three matches; the heroes who carved out that first crown and championship triumph were:

P.J. Grant (Bective Rangers)
R. Dunlop (Dublin University)
L.H. Gwynn (Dublin University)
S. Lee (NIFC)
W. Gardiner (NIFC)
B. Tuke (Bective Rangers)
W.S. Browne (Dublin University)
E.G. Forrest (Wanderers) capt.
T. Crean (Wanderers)
C.V. Rooke (Dublin University)
H. Lindsay (Dublin University)
James Lytle (NIFC)
J.H. O'Conor (Bective Rangers)
A.T. Bond (Derry)
W. Sparrow (Dublin University)
H.G. Wells (Bective Rangers)
G. Walmsley (Bective Rangers)
John Lytle (NIFC)

Bond and Grant replaced Walmsley and Sparrow after the English match. Dunlop came in for Wells for the match in Belfast, so twelve of the players were engaged in all three matches.

O'Conor's reference to wing forwards is especially relevant, for Rooke apparently brought a new dimension to the game in this respect during his career, which saw him help Ireland to another championship success in 1896 before he retired from the game the following season. He subsequently became a minister in the Anglican Church and died in Wellington, New Zealand, in 1936. Charles Vaughan Rooke did not exploit the possibilities of the wing forward position quite as far as an illustrious player who was to follow shortly after he left the playing field, the legendary New Zealander, Dave Gallagher, but he impressed Dromio more. It is interesting to note that neither of these players impressed that great judge of rugby, E.H.D. Sewell.

The first Triple Crown success and the outright win in the championship that went with it were greeted with tremendous enthusiasm in Ireland and nowhere more so than within the IRFU itself. It was decided that the players who had participated in the three games would be given special presentations to mark their achievement, but someone had second thoughts on the issue and at a meeting of the committee held in December 1894 it was decided not to proceed with the matter, no doubt on the grounds that amateur status might be violated, a consideration that will have a familiar ring for many present-day rugby players.

The season 1894-95 was notable for much, not least the fact that, despite having nine of the Triple Crown heroes in the side for the three internationals, Ireland lost every game, thus going from zenith to nadir in record time. Munster lost their second selector that season on the grounds that their club strength was inferior to that of Leinster and Ulster; indeed, at one stage in the early season the Munster Branch stood suspended by the union for non-payment of club affiliation fees. Either by accident or design they did manage to pay the sum of £6, which ensured that all was forgiven in time for the championship.

Three notable additions to the Irish strength that season were the Magee brothers, Louis and Joe, and Andrew Clinch. Both Clinch and Louis Magee were to play significant parts in subsequent triumphs, even if their initial appearances against England at Lansdowne Road were not marked by any signs of impending greatness.

The following season, Ireland used only sixteen players. Gardiner, Lee, Crean, O'Conor, Jim Lytle, Lindsay and Charles Rooke of the Triple Crown-winning combination were still on active service. Louis Magee was now firmly established at half-back. James Sealy, later to have a distinguished career as an administrator, came into the pack against England, who were warm favourites, having destroyed Wales by 25 points to nil at Blackheath.

But England could perform no similar demolition job on Ireland, who took control of the proceedings from an early stage and, with tries by Sealy and T.H. Stevenson, won by 10 points to nil.

There was one change made for the match against Scotland, G. McAllen of Dungannon RS was brought in for Fulton at full-back.

McAllen's selection made him the first schoolboy to play for Ireland. He was aged eighteen years and two months when he made his first appearance against Scotland at Lansdowne Road. Regrettably, his debut was not marked by an Irish success, and against the predictions of most and the desires of all in Ireland, Scotland managed to get away with an honourable 0–0 draw. However, that result enabled Ireland to go on to achieve their second triumph within two years for, fielding an unchanged side, they secured the championship by defeating Wales by 8 points to 4 in Dublin, Jim Lytle and Tom Crean getting tries.

The strength of the Irish side was subsequently reflected in the fact that no fewer than six of the sixteen who had shared in it, were selected for the British and Irish team to tour South Africa in the summer of 1896. In all there were nine Irishmen on that tour: the six who had shared in the championship triumph were Louis Magee, Larry Bulger, Jim Sealy, Andrew Clinch, Tom Crean and Andrew Meares; they were joined by Louis Magee's brother Jim, who was never capped for Ireland at rugby but who was an international cricketer, Robert Johnston (Wanderers), who had played twice for Ireland in 1893, and the as yet uncapped Trinity man C.V. Boyd. Availability rather than ability was often the yardstick for the early touring teams, but nine representatives was, nonetheless, a singular tribute. These were the first Irish rugby players to tour abroad for the 1888 team that toured Australia and New Zealand did not contain any Irish representatives.

The 1896 team to South Africa was led by the Cambridge Blue, J. Hammond, and played four Test matches, winning three and losing one. Bulger, Crean, Louis Magee, Clinch and Sealy played in all four Tests; Meares played in three, while Jim Magee and Johnston in two and Boyd in one. This was no mean contribution.

Both Crean and Johnston were to go back to South Africa within a short time, but on a very different mission. Both fought in the same regiment in the Boer War three years later, and both were also awarded the highest military decoration, the Victoria Cross, for valour.

That match against Wales in 1896 was the last Crean played for Ireland, but the nucleus of the previous season's championship side was still at hand, and they opened next season's campaign by defeating England by 13 points to 9 at Lansdowne Road. With this match, two brothers, Mick and Jack Ryan from Cashel, County Tipperary, came into the Irish pack for the first time. The Ryans were members of the Rockwell College club, where a famous contemporary of theirs who also wore the college's blue and white jersey with distinction was

Eamon de Valera, a full-back and centre of some calibre.

An 8–3 defeat by Scotland in Edinburgh terminated Ireland's championship aspirations and also their international programme for that season, as neither Ireland nor Scotland met Wales.

The question of payment for 'broken time' had been creating difficulties in the north of England since 1886. Differences of opinion reached a critical point at a general meeting of the English Union in September 1893, when it was proposed that players be allowed compensation for *bona fide* loss of time. The proposal was not carried, and the issue continued to cause trouble, with the result that in 1895 twenty-one clubs broke away and formed what subsequently became the Rugby League.

It was against that background then that what has become known as the 'Gould dispute' occurred. It caused a major problem for the International Board that culminated in Scotland and Ireland refusing to play Wales in 1897 and Scotland again refusing to meet Wales in the following year.

Arthur Gould, a magnificent Welsh centre who had just retired from international football, was to be the recipient of a house from his admirers, but the board stepped in to bar the presentation. The Welsh RU did not accept that the board had jurisdiction in the matter. However, Gould himself declined the offer and eventually Wales, after resigning from the board, was permitted to rejoin in February 1898 on the specific condition that they recognised its bye-laws.

In 1897 Ireland lost an outstanding administrator, Eddie McAlister, honorary secretary of the union from 1886, and also honorary secretary of the International Board from 1887 to his untimely death in 1897. He was succeeded as honorary secretary of the union by Charles Ruxton, who occupied the position until 1925, and as honorary secretary of the board by another Irishman, Robert Warren, who held that position until 1933. McAlister was only the first in a long line of Irishmen to act in that capacity for the board,* for when Warren resigned in 1933 he was followed by Harry Thrift (1933–56), who in turn was succeeded by Eddie Kirwan (1956–71).

Ireland's campaign in 1898 opened against England at Richmond, and after a 9–6 defeat, Sam Lee retired from the international scene. Scotland then won by 8 points to nil in Belfast. With cordial relations now resumed with the Welsh, the match was arranged for Limerick on

*For a full list of Irish representatives on the International Board, see Appendix 1.

19 March. It is the only international that has been played in that great rugby city, and it ended in a Welsh victory by 11 points to 3.

Thus the omens did not look good for the closing season of the nineteenth century, and when Ireland faced England at Lansdowne Road in the opening match of the 1899 campaign not one of the 1894 Triple Crown team remained. Andrew Clinch of the 1896 championship-winning side had also departed, so that when Ireland lined up against England the most experienced members of the pack were the Ryan brothers, James Sealy and W.G. Byron. Fulton was still at full-back and, of course, the incomparable Louis Magee was at half-back to lend his talents and experience. One of the newcomers for that England game was a schoolboy at Campbell College, J.B. Allison. The combination of the old and the new proved potent enough to resist the demands England put on it at Lansdowne Road, where Ireland won by a try, scored by Magee's half-back partner G.G. Allen, and a penalty goal.

While injuries had severely restricted the selectors' scope for the match against England, they did not account entirely for the fact that only two of the seven backs who faced England were in the side against Scotland at Inverleith. The pack showed three changes, including the recall of Jim Lytle, thus re-establishing a connection with the 1894 Triple Crown team. A.D. Meares of Trinity was given his first cap and Tom Little of Bective Rangers, who had played against Wales the previous season, was also brought back. Ireland won by three tries to nil, with E.F. Campbell of Monkstown, C. Reid of NIFC and James Sealy making the scores.

So Ireland went on to tackle Wales, this time at Cardiff, where they had never won. For this match, which was fixed for 18 March, Ireland made two changes in the pack. McIlwaine and C.H. Moriarty coming in for McGown and Lytle; it was to be Moriarty's only Irish cap. Behind the scrum, George Harman, who had played against England but was injured at the time of the Scottish match, was recalled in the centre, and G.G. Allen resumed his half-back partnership with Magee, Barr of Methodist College being omitted. Many years later the game and its background was described by Mick Ryan in the *Rockwell College Annual*.

> You know the feeling a player has when his team has reached a cup final–a feeling of satisfaction for having done so well, and a feeling that if this game is lost, all that was hitherto gained is quite undone; that the

hard training, the gallant deeds and the plucky defence have gone for nothing.

Such a feeling intensified is what a player has when it comes to a chance of winning the Triple Crown. Would all our previous efforts be for nothing or would we emerge victorious?

Wales had studied the Irish methods and at 'a council of war' had selected and constructed their team and prescribed their tactics with a view to frustrating the Irish forwards.

The fact that the game was played in Cardiff proved to be no small matter. The rails of the enclosure gave way and an unruly crowd took up whatever positions they chose. They crowded on the touch and goal lines and at times it seemed an impossibility for Ireland to score; as one reporter said afterwards, 'Wales had a thousand full-backs, some of whom came up even to the "twenty-five".'

Play had to be stopped time and again to clear the field. The Cardiff police had apparently just received new uniforms which they were not going to trust to the mercy of the mob. They simply kept out of the way and even the horse police declined to go on the ground.

Our team had been changed out of recognition and only five of us played in both the English and Scottish games: Louis Magee, James Sealy, Billy Byron, Jack and myself. Influenza had done a lot of the damage with regard to the many changes made during the season.

We were accorded a hearty welcome when we came on to the field, then Wales, led by Bancroft, came to the strains of 'Men of Harlech'. By that time the spectators had practically taken possession of the field and it was obvious that a start could not be made until they were cleared.

That took a considerable time and both teams withdrew while it was being done. Nearly half an hour was lost before the ground was playable.

At last we were off. It was desperate stuff. We got away from the first scrum on a good rush and 'Blucher' Doran kicked ahead, but Skrimshire fielded and brought play back to midfield.

The Welsh threequarters tried some flashy movements, but Butler and Campbell tackled splendidly. Frees were numerous to both sides and we had a few chances of penalty goals, but luck was decidedly against us.

After play was held up, when the spectators invaded the pitch, Wales were very dangerous on the resumption. We were beaten back to our own line, but Butler saved the situation with a beautiful punt to touch at halfway.

Then it was our turn to attack. Sealy made a splendid opening and passed to me. I saw the line within easy distance, but alas heard the referee whistle for an infringement. Wales cleared, but only for a while until Sealy tackled Nicholls in possession inside the Welsh 'twenty-five'. Scrum; we will have this ball back or die. Ah! we've done it.

Allen picked up and set the whole back line in motion. Doran took his pass in masterly fashion and romped past the opposition.

During the interval, the mob again invaded the pitch and more time was lost before the game could resume. Louis Magee had to go around with Mr Turnbull, the referee, and beg the over-enthusiastic ones to move back.

The second half was thrilling. Wales, not beaten by Doran's try, opened up some brilliant movements, Nicholls and Llewellyn made great efforts to score, and twice we were forced to touch down. Skrimshire broke through to be taken down by Butler, while Magee eased the pressure twice in succession by good runs.

Still Wales pinned us inside our own 'twenty-five' and it seemed as if nothing could prevent a score. And then came the most exciting incident of the game.

Lloyd whisked the ball out to Nicholls. Straight through all opposition he went, swerved and transferred to Skrimshire, who seemed to have a perfectly clear field. He had lightning speed and there appeared to be nothing to prevent him scoring between the posts. Suddenly Magee flashed up and dived for his heels. Amidst frantic cheers from the Irish supporters, Skrimshire came down and lost the ball.

After that, the game was ours. We stormed the Welsh defence, but it was remarkably sound. We were still on the Welsh line when the final whistle sounded. The Triple Crown was ours.

Twenty-four players helped to achieve that second Triple Crown success for Ireland and, as Mick Ryan pointed out, only five players participated in all three matches. The players (with the Triple Crown appearances shown in brackets) were:

T. Ahearn
   (Queen's College, Cork) (E)
G.G. Allen
   (Derry and Liverpool) (E W)
J.B. Allison
   (Campbell College) (E S)
A. Barr
   (Collegians) (S)
W.H.Brown
   (Dublin University) (E)
W.G. Byron
   (NIFC) (E S W)

E.F. Campbell
   (Monkstown) (S W)
I.G. Davidson
   (NIFC) (E)
G.P. Doran
   (Lansdowne) (S W)
J. Fulton
   (NIFC) (E)
G. Harman
   (Dublin University) (E W)
T.J. Little
   (Bective Rangers) (S W)

J.H. Lytle
(NIFC) (S)
L.M. Magee
(Bective Rangers) capt.
(E S W)
A.D. Meares
(Dublin University) (S W)
C.H. Moriarty
(Monkstown) (W)
H.C. McCoull
(Albion) (E)
T. McGown
(NIFC) (E S)

J.E. McIlwaine
(NIFC) (E W)
P. O'Brien-Butler
(Monkstown) (S W)
J.C. Reid
(NIFC) (S W)
J. Ryan
(Rockwell College) (E S W)
M. Ryan
(Rockwell College) (E S W)
J. Sealy
(Dublin University) (E S W)

A happy footnote to that victory is that it could still be recalled by one of the Irish players, George Harman, in the summer of 1974 when he celebrated his hundredth birthday at his home near Looe in Cornwall.

So despite the gloomy forecasts by the journalists of the day that Ireland would be struggling that season, the second Triple Crown and third championship were brought back in triumph. The words of the *Freeman's Journal* of 2 January 1899 have a hollow ring in retrospect: 'The trials in Dublin and Belfast must be regarded as unsatisfactory and where an Irish XV is going to come from is purely a matter of enterprising conjecture.'

The year 1899 saw the outbreak of the Boer War and much other conflict in the world, but in Ireland at least it was made memorable by twenty-four men in green. The president of the union in that triumphant season was John Moore, a man who gave almost forty years' service on the union committee and who was an International Board representative from 1892 to 1927. Lucius Gywnn, Sam Lee and John Macaulay were on the selection committee, and Macaulay was still there thirty-one years later. He first served in 1895–96 and sat on the selection committee for no fewer than twenty-six seasons.

A combined British and Irish team set off in the summer of 1899 for Australia. It contained three Irishmen, two of whom, 'Blucher' Doran, and Tom McGown, had helped to win the Triple Crown. The third member of the Irish contingent was the Trinity player E. Martinelli, a rather mysterious figure, who is not recorded as having played for Trinity at first-team level.

But an event of even greater significance took place in September 1899 when an Irish team set sail for Canada. It was led by J.G. Franks (Dublin University), who had won three caps as a forward in 1898, but the only Triple Crown hero in the side was Ian Davidson of NIFC, who had played against England. 'Blucher' Doran's brother Bertie, one of three brothers to play for Ireland (a third brother, Eddie, having won two caps in 1890), was also in the party. Irish rugby has long been noted for its strong tradition of fraternity (in the original meaning of the word as well as in the commonly accepted sense), as is demonstrated by the fact that two other sets of brothers, the Boyds and the Rowans actually took part in the Canadian tour. The full party of seventeen players was:

J.C. Lepper (NIFC)
P.C. Nicholson (Dublin University)
T.A. Harvey (Dublin University)
R.R. Boyd (Lansdowne)
J. Byers (NIFC)
H.A. Boyd (Dublin University)
R. Stevenson (Dungannon)
B.W. Rowan (Lansdowne)
F. Dinsmore (NIFC)
I. Grove-White (Dublin University)
J.S. Myles (Derry City)
I.G. Davidson (NIFC)
H.A. Macready (Dublin University)
J. Stokes (Lansdowne)
B.W. Doran (Lansdowne)
J.G. Franks (Dublin University)
A.C. Rowan (Lansdowne)

The tour was sponsored by 'Duke' Collins, a native of Dublin living in Toronto, and apparently no voice was raised in objection to an act of sponsorship. Whatever the cost or the profits (if any), there is no record in the IRFU accounts of the tour for the 1899–1900 season or for the following term.

The team sailed to Halifax, and arrived a couple of days before the outbreak of the South African war. The Irishmen played eleven games, winning ten and losing one. The games took place in Halifax, Montreal, Ottawa, Brockville, Peterborough, Quebec, Toronto and Hamilton. The sole Irish defeat was suffered in Halifax at the hands of a combined side picked from seven cruisers of the Atlantic Fleet and the province of Nova Scotia. The Irish played a man short in the game, as J. Sproule Myles, later to serve as a member of Dáil Éireann for East Donegal, broke a leg in the early stages of an earlier match in Toronto. This accident, combined with other injuries, left the Irish with only fourteen fit players. Myles's injury necessitated a protracted stay in Canada and he did not arrive home until late in December, the remainder of the party having returned over a month earlier.

The Canadian tour was the closing chapter in the story of Irish rugby in the nineteenth century. Ellis had started something more than a scientific exercise that day at Rugby School in 1823. There had been many faltering steps en route to two Triple Crowns and three championship triumphs for Ireland, but surely the gayest day of the gay nineties had been 18 March 1899 in Cardiff.

8
A new century
1900–14

Comparisons between the great sides of different eras is always difficult, not only because of the lapse in time, but even more because of the game's constant evolution. The great success enjoyed by Ireland in the nineties, made it difficult for those who followed and wore the green jersey in the early 1900s, and if the period between 1900 and the Great War did not herald achievement of similar moment, there were occasional displays of brilliance and some Homeric battles were won and lost. The championships of 1906 and 1912 were the high points in the story of Irish rugby in this period.

It was, too, a period of advancement at home, with the Triple Crown triumph in 1899 giving the spur for many new clubs to emerge. The First All-Blacks came and went, leaving a trail of destruction behind them. The First Springboks came too and if not quite as successful as the New Zealanders, they added a further dimension to the rugby game in these islands.

Ireland opened the challenge for the Triple Crown against England at Richmond in 1900 with a team which had been built around the nucleus of the previous season's championship side. Louis Magee was still at half-back; Doran, Allison, Reid and Campbell, the threequarters, had all worn the Irish jersey previously, as had full-back O'Brien-Butler. The Ryans, James Sealy, and Meares were in the pack, and to their strength were added the newcomers Jack Coffey, Fred Gardiner, Sam Irwin and P. Nicholson, the last of whom had toured in Canada.

Sam Lee, who had played with many of them, was president of the union. His term of office did not get off to a very auspicious start when England won by 15 points to 4, with Allison getting Ireland's solitary score, a dropped goal. A draw with Scotland at Lansdowne Road and defeat by Wales in Belfast left Ireland at the bottom of the championship table. The wheel of fortune seemed to have turned full circle back to the gloomy days of 1895.

It was a bad start to the new century. The year 1900 saw Wales take over as Triple Crown and championship winners, their Crown victory being only the first of five which they were to achieve within the space of eleven seasons. Ireland alone of the four nations failed to win a Triple Crown between 1900 and 1914; Scotland won it three times in this period and England twice, statistics that seem to point to the fact that Ireland was very much the sick man of the rugby scene. Yet statistics can be misleading, for of the fifty-four matches Ireland played in the fifteen seasons preceding the Great War, twenty-one were won, including six against England, six against Scotland, three against Wales and six against France. Two games were drawn, against Scotland in 1900 and against England in 1910, while New Zealand and South Africa (twice) proved beyond the range of Ireland's capabilities.

In those fifteen seasons there flourished some of the most distinguished players ever to wear the Irish jersey. Magnificent forwards such as Fred Gardiner, Jack Coffey, Alf Tedford, C.E. ('Ellie') Allen and George Hamlet are all unforgettably associated with that era. Tedford, who arrived on the scene in 1902, was to make a tremendous impact on forward play, while Hamlet, who made his debut in the same season, wore the green jersey with honour on no fewer than thirty occasions. Nor was all the talent contained in the heart of the scrum, for there flourished backs of equally high quality in E.D. Caddell, James Cecil Parke, an international lawn tennis player of world renown, Harry Thrift, the flamboyant Basil Maclear, Alex Foster, Harry Read and the incomparable Dickie Lloyd, described by E.H.D. Sewell in *Rugger: the Man's Game* as 'an ace at all three aspects of kicking, punt, drop and place. For sustained accuracy', continued Sewell, 'I never saw anything like the kicking achievements of this boy from Portora School. His accuracy was phenomenal.'

That victory by Wales in the 1900 Triple Crown series was the preface to a run of four successive victories over Ireland, the gloom being broken by wins over England at Lansdowne Road in 1901 and 1903 and a 5–0 success against Scotland in 1902. By the time of the England-Ireland match of 1904 the Ryan brothers, 'Blucher' Doran and J. Fulton were all that remained from the glorious nineties. Louis Magee was also still on active service, but was recovering from injury at the time of the encounter at Blackheath. England won that day by 19 points to nil, and the match signalled the end of international rugby for Jack Ryan. Mick played in the 19–3 defeat by Scotland at Lansdowne Road, as did another pair of brothers, James and Joe Wallace, who had gained their first caps in the game against England. The game against Scotland proved to be the last international for both Mick Ryan and James Wallace, but Joe was there when Ireland faced Wales in Belfast in 1904 and played his full part in a great Irish success.

Louis Magee came back for the game against Wales, and at full-back Ireland had a newcomer, Mossy Landers from the recently formed Cork Constitution club, and there was another new cap on the wing, Harry Thrift.

This has been described as Tedford's match, and quite apart from his contribution of two tries, he proved the scourge of a remarkably talented Welsh team that included Teddy Morgan, Willie Llewellyn and Dickie Owen. A notable absentee was Gwyn Nicholls, but Wales did not attribute their 14–12 defeat so much to Nicholl's absence as to the 'blindness' of the referee, Mr Crawford Findlay from Scotland.

The scene for a thrilling climax was set in the first half, at the end of which Ireland led by 6–3, Tedford and Joe Wallace getting tries and Teddy Morgan replying with one for Wales. After Wales equalised in the second half with a try by Gabe, Ireland lost their left wing, C.G. Robb, and Joe Wallace went on to the wing. Robb returned to the fray but was barely able to walk, and Wales took advantage of the situation to score two tries, after which Robb left the field for good. With a 12–6 lead and Ireland reduced to fourteen men, nothing other than a Welsh win could be envisaged. But the Welshmen had reckoned without Tedford and his colleagues in the forward line and a magnificent seven they proved.

Thrift signalled his entry into international football by getting a try. Its circumstances were somewhat controversial but it could hardly be allowed to hold up the game at such a crucial and thrilling moment. Now within striking distance and playing like men possessed, the Irish forwards, brilliantly nursed by Magee, were subduing the Welsh eight. A great passing movement initiated by Magee, reached Wallace, who was hemmed in; but he cross-kicked, the Welsh full-back Winfield misfielded it, and Tedford grabbed the ball and went in under the posts. The winning conversion was a formality for Landers.

With Limerick having seen one international and with Dublin and Belfast on the regular schedule, the clubs in Cork decided that it was time that an international match took place in the southern capital, and the win over Wales in Belfast gave added impetus to the demand. The Cork Constitution and Cork County clubs put a request to the union that the match against England in February 1905 should be played in

Cork, but the proposition was rejected out of hand at a meeting of the union committee on 29 March 1904, and the match against England was fixed for Lansdowne Road on 11 February. It was also pointed out at the meeting that no request had been made from the Munster Branch. That omission was quickly rectified, however, and when the committee met again on 11 May, they had before them a letter from the Munster Branch asking that the previous decision be reconsidered. Once again the appeal fell on deaf ears. No doubt the fact that the number of clubs in Munster had decreased from thirteen to six was a weighty part of the argument for refusing to play another international in the province. But other Munster demands met with a more positive response, for at that meeting Garryowen, now becoming a power in the world of Munster rugby, were granted a sum of £250 towards obtaining a lease on a ground in Limerick. At that meeting, too, Connacht, after yet another period in the wilderness, were granted official branch status once again, as there were now five clubs in the west: Galway Town, Old Galwegians, Queen's College, Galway Grammar School and St Ignatius' College.

The Munster clubs were by no means prepared to abandon so readily their case for providing an international venue. If their numerical strength had dwindled, their resolution was not impaired, and they knew their union laws. A requisition summoning a special meeting of the union committee to consider yet again the playing of the match against England in Cork was immediately prepared by the Munster Branch and signed in accordance with union laws by the honorary secretaries of five clubs. On 24 August 1904 the IRFU honorary secretary, Charles Ruxton, sent the following circular to all members.

I beg to inform you a special meeting of the Council will be held on Saturday the 10th day of September 1904, at the Hibernian Hotel at 8 p.m., for the consideration of the following requisition from the Munster Branch of the IRFU.

'We the undersigned honorary secretaries of Munster clubs affiliated to the IR Union hereby request you to convene a special meeting of the Council of the Union for Thursday, August 25th in accordance with rule 9, for the purpose of considering the application of the Cork County and Cork Constitution clubs to have the international match, England *v.* Ireland, of 1904–05 played on the new grounds of these clubs, situate at the Wellington Bridge, Mardyke Walk, Cork.'

The necessary £5 was enclosed in accordance with rule 9 and the requisition was signed by George Hutchinson, honorary secretary of Constitution, A.E. Bennet (Limerick County), J.M. O'Sullivan (Garryowen), E. Mason (GPO) and George J. Daly (Cork County).

Suddenly the vociferous opposition to Cork as a venue for an international was stilled, with scarcely a dissenting voice. Munster had won the day and the match was fixed for Cork. There was one stipulation, however: Munster had to guarantee the union the sum of £200. The accounts for the season reveal that they met their obligations; and so the Mardyke, a ground that enshrines so much that is best in Munster rugby, became the scene of a famous Irish victory over England. Strangely enough, it was to be an Englishman who proved the main instrument for the Saxon debacle.

If ever there was a case of revenge being sweet, it was Maclear's international debut that February day in Cork. An English officer in the Royal Dublin Fusiliers, Maclear was stationed in Fermoy, County Cork, a circumstance that did not prevent his occasional appearance for Blackheath. With the international season approaching, the eyes of the English and Irish selectors were turned towards him, and it was his rejection by one of England's most famous legislators that gave him to Ireland. In January 1905 Maclear played for Old Bedfordians against Old Paulines at the Richmond Athletic ground. An interested spectator at the match was Sir Rowland Hill, who, having seen Maclear convert eleven tries and score two, then pronounced the verdict 'Not good enough, no opposition to test his true ability.'

So the way was clear for Ireland and when the team to meet England was announced Maclear was named in the centre. It was the first of eleven appearances for Ireland; and in each of his three games against England he was on the winning side.

At full-back for Ireland that day in Cork was Mossy Landers, later to become an Irish selector and respected rugby correspondent of the *Cork Examiner*. Landers himself played a noble part in Ireland's great victory–the biggest over England up to that time and a record that was to stand for another forty-two years. Many years later he recalled that famous match in the following account.

The Mardyke ground was part of the site of the Cork Exhibition at the turn of the century. When the Exhibition closed in 1903, negotiations between the Exhibition committee and those three great sportsmen, Frank Morrogh, John Reese and Alderman P.H. Reade, resulted in the Mardyke grounds being handed over to Cork County and Cork Constitution as joint tenants.

The 'Dyke' was soon in excellent condition and in 1905 came the outstanding event in the history of rugby in Cork–the international between England and Ireland. Ireland won by seventeen points to three, after one of the greatest displays ever put up by the wearers of the green.

I have some outstanding memories of this game, the first being that it was Basil Maclear's initial game in international football. In between my own spells of work at full-back, I watched the Cork County man as he flashed up the field time and again–always dangerous to the English defence–and I came to the conclusion (to which I still hold) that he was the greatest back Ireland ever had...

Incidentally I might mention that the Irish team that year and the side that defeated Wales the previous season, in spite of gloomy critics, included at least three forwards who had played for their provinces as backs.

For instance Alf Tedford and Fred Gardiner played as backs for Ulster and Joe Wallace was an excellent half-back both for Trinity and Leinster.

'Ellie' Allen and Moffatt of Old Wesley got tries just before half-time, both made by Maclear, who got among the tries himself after the interval, adding the goal points to supplement tries by Joe Wallace and Moffatt again. Landers is not alone in his opinion of the Irish performance that day, for E.H.D. Sewell in a description of the game says that Maclear's opponent, S.F. Cooper, later to become secretary of the Rugby Union, spent the day 'stern-chasing'.

It was a record day all round for the attendance was 12,000 and the gate receipts were £900, which left the Munster Branch smiling and some red faces in the corridors of power in Dublin. The match was also notable for the new stand which had been specially erected for the occasion. In his description of this stand Landers wrote:

> The stand was probably the most unique ever used for an international match. It was made possible by the generosity of the local brewers, Beamish and Crawford and J.J. Murphy. They lent the committee hundreds of empty barrels–large and small.
>
> The whole stand was bound very securely with thick strong wire and it was passed perfectly safe by the official engineers the day before the match. Thousands of spectators occupied the stand, as the structure ran along the whole length of each touchline outside the paling.

Ireland went to Inverleith to meet Scotland, fortified by that great victory and, not unnaturally, with an unchanged side. With Coffey,

Tedford and Joe Wallace at their brilliant best in the Irish pack and Maclear again stamping his class on the proceedings, Ireland won easily by a goal and two tries to a goal, with Tedford, Wallace and Moffatt gaining the tries and Maclear adding one conversion. So the Triple Crown beckoned yet again, and the campaign was carried onto Welsh soil.

With Wales having defeated both England and Scotland, this was a Triple Crown match for both contestants. The stakes could not be higher on 11 March in Swansea. Wales were at the height of their power, seeking their fourth Crown in six seasons, with Gwyn Nicholls, Rhys Gabe, Owen Llewellyn and Morgan to give the class behind the scrum and the hardy miners from the valleys up front to slog it out with Tedford and his comrades. The Welsh back division was probably the greatest produced in the world up to that time. Many will argue that it has never been surpassed.

Ireland made one change, James Parke, who had been injured for the earlier matches, coming into the centre in place of A.D. Harvey (Wanderers). But the mighty Welsh combination of class behind and aggression up front proved too much for a gallant Irish side that lost by 10 points to 3.

Ireland had a huge following that day at St Helen's Ground. The contingent from Cork included the Barrack Street Band. A violent storm had given them a rough crossing, but not even the loss of some of their instruments overboard could dim their enthusiasm as they marched proudly through the streets of Swansea.

On six further occasions in a span of just over thirty years Wales were to prove an insurmountable final obstacle for Ireland's Triple Crown hopes. But if Wales claimed world supremacy after that win in 1905, the claim was about to be disputed by a team from New Zealand.

The First All-Blacks, captained by an Irishman, Dave Gallagher, came to Britain in September 1905, an unknown quantity. They played in Ireland, England, Scotland and Wales, participating in thirty-three matches, thirty-two of which they won; they scored 830 points and conceded only thirty-nine; twenty-four of their opponents failed to score against them and the only game they lost, to Wales in the twenty-eighth game of the tour, provoked a controversy that still goes on. They brought a new concept to the game and gave birth to a legend that grew rather than diminished with the passing of the years.

The New Zealand team opened their tour in a sensational fashion that gathered momentum as the tour progressed. They beat Devon by 55 points to nil at Exeter, a result that was greeted by such scepticism by the news agencies that the result was reversed in the belief that it was wrong. But it was all too true, and Cornwall were the next to fall victims to the awesome brilliance of the invaders.

As the tour progressed, the full realisation of the true powers of the tourists shook the complacent rugby world in Britain and Ireland, and the IRFU decided that, in view of the results achieved by the invaders, it would be prudent to play a special trial match before Ireland met them on 25 November. Munster were also on the tour schedule, and a request from New Zealand that the game fixed for Limerick on 28 November might be cancelled as they wanted a week's rest before they met England four days later was rejected out of hand by the IRFU.

When the New Zealanders arrived in Dublin for the game against Ireland their record stood: played 21, won 21; points for 646, points against 22. Their tactical appreciation, superb physical fitness and astonishing team work had destroyed all opposition, including Scotland, who had the unenviable privilege of meeting them in the first international.

New Zealand raised again the question of the function of the wing forward a thorny subject which had exercised the minds of rugby pundits and legislators for a decade, but this time the All-Blacks raised the controversy to a new pitch when Gallagher, who filled the role, also put the ball into the scrum. Accusations that he was putting 'bias' on the ball, and committing sundry other acts, such as obstruction, were levelled, and not all the accusations were coming from the conservative elements in the game. They scarcely troubled Gallagher and his men, who drew record crowds at every match they played, a circumstance that influenced the IRFU to make the international in Dublin an all-ticket game, the first in international rugby history.

Ireland called on all the tried and true warriors for the match against the All-Blacks, and H.G. Millar (Monkstown) and Moffatt were the only players missing from the side that had lost in Swansea. Moffatt was replaced by C.G. Robb, who had played in all four games in 1904, while H.S. Sugars of Trinity came in for Millar. It was Sugars's first cap, and a tough baptism it proved for him.

The Irish put up a tremendous display in the first half, but eight minutes before the interval R. Deans, a threequarter who was setting the rugby scene alight by his prowess, got in for a try, which full-back Wallace converted. Wallace achieved similar feats in the second half when Deans and A. McDonald ran in further tries to give New Zealand a 15–0 win in a performance that embellished still further their legendary prowess. No wonder Wallace said after the tour: 'The best time I had personally on the whole tour was in Ireland. The Dublin people gave us a grand reception.' Similar sentiments were to be voiced sixty-eight years later by a New Zealand side, but under less happy circumstances.

An injury sustained while playing against Scotland had prevented Gallagher from participating in the match against Ireland, but his absence made little difference on that occasion or against Munster three days later in Limerick.

Basil Maclear was the only one of the Munster team who had played in the international, and in fact that match in Limerick was Maclear's fourth appearance against the tourists as both Blackheath and Bedford had summoned his services earlier in the tour–not with any great profit, for Blackheath lost 32–0 and Bedford went down by 41–0. Maclear was to suffer a similar fate in the Munster colours, for the All-Blacks scored 33 points that day in Limerick when Munster got the now customary total against them of nil.

The extent of the touring side's impact on the Irish population was illustrated by a contemporary report of their arrival in Limerick, where 'Loyalists and Nationalists alike turned out to meet the New Zealand team at the railway on their arrival from Dublin.'

Later touring teams were to have a much harder passage when they encountered Munster on their own territory, but if the Munster team of 1905 did nothing else, they created history by being the first interprovincial team in Ireland to play a touring team.

A member of the Munster back line was Dickie Magrath, who later won one cap for Ireland and was president of the IRFU in 1921–22. He lived to the ripe old age of ninety-five, and recalling the First All-Blacks in 1970, two years before his death, he stated that they were 'unquestionably the greatest rugby team of all time.' The full Munster team that lined-out in Limerick was:

A. Quilligan (Garryowen)
A. Newton (Cork County)
B. Maclear (Cork County)
W.O. Stokes (Garryowen)
R. Magrath (Cork Constitution)
J. McQueen (Queen's College, Cork)
J. O'Connor (Garryowen)

J. Reeves (Cork County)
J. Wallace (Garryowen)
S. Hosford (Cork Constitution)
J. Lane (Lansdowne and Limerick)
M. White (Queen's College, Cork)
A. Acheson (Garryowen)
W. Churchwards (Cork County)
R. Welphy (Queen's College, Cork)

It fell to Wales to lower the All-Blacks' colours, but the match at Cardiff is still a matter of dispute for New Zealanders still contend, nearly seventy years later, that Deans scored a legitimate try, which was disallowed by the referee, J.D. Dallas of Scotland. Dickie Magrath, who was present at the match, concurred with the New Zealanders' opinion.

The New Zealanders returned home, leaving behind them a new appreciation of the art of rugby football, but those who sought to emulate their tactics did not always do so with beneficial effects. The mixed blessings of the All-Black's influence were particularly apparent in Ireland.

The wiles and strategy employed by Gallagher became something of an obsession with some members of the Irish rugby fraternity, and when Ireland faced England in Leicester in February 1906 it was decided to play only seven forwards, with Maclear being given a roving commission. Ireland got away with it against a weak English side, winning by 16 points to 6. Tedford, once again in magnificent form, scored two tries and Bill Brooke Purdon signalled his advent to international football at half-back getting a further try. Maclear's contribution was seven points—a try and two conversions.

The quality of opposition encountered against Scotland at Lansdowne Road was of an altogether different calibre. The Scottish pack, which included such notables as Pat Munro and 'Kimo' Simpson, capitalised to the full on Ireland's new methods and won by 13 points to 6.

Wales, meanwhile, had beaten England and Scotland, and so came to Belfast with the Triple Crown in their sights yet again. Describing the Belfast match in *Rugger: the Man's Game*, E.H.D. Sewell wrote:

About the only certain thing concerning Irish rugby is its uncertainty. As an example, was there an Irishman anywhere, on that March morning in

1906, which heralded the greatest victory recorded in rugby's stirring history, who would have risked a ha'penny that the Irish team, if playing one short throughout the second half and two short for the last ten minutes of it, would beat that Welsh side?

The Irish team that walked on to the field at Belfast in 1906 was:

C. Henebry (Garryowen)
B. Maclear (Cork County)
F. Casement (Dublin University)
J.C. Parke (Dublin University)
H. Thrift (Dublin University)
E.D. Caddell (Wanderers)
W.B. Purdon (NIFC)
C.E. Allen (Derry and Liverpool) capt.
A. Tedford (Malone)
H.G. Wilson (Malone)
H.J. Knox (Dublin University)
J. Coffey (Lansdowne)
F. Gardiner (NIFC)
Joe Wallace (Wanderers)
M. White (Queen's College, Cork)

The half-back Purdon was carried off just before half-time with a broken leg, at a time when Ireland led by 8 points to 3, Harry Thrift scored a try which Fred Gardiner converted, with Joe Wallace adding another try and Teddy Morgan getting one for Wales. Joe Wallace took over at half-back, and the ever-eager Tedford, Jack Coffey and their colleagues on the Irish forward line pressed on, magnificent in face of adversity.

With about ten minutes to go, further disaster came Ireland's way when Tommy Caddell had to retire with a broken ankle, and Fred Gardiner joined Wallace at half-back. Nothing daunted Ireland added a further try through Maclear, who that day wore his customary white kid gloves, though he had also added a khaki puttee for good measure as if in anticipation of a great occasion. All Wales could muster in a last assault was a solitary try, and so once again Belfast and the Irish had proved the stumbling block to the principality, reawakening vivid memories of a similar result two seasons previously.

That was Gwyn Nicholls's last game for Wales. In his pre-match address to the Irish team, the captain, 'Ellie' Allen, had told his men to pay Nicholls the compliment of tackling him on every conceivable occasion. Allen had also apparently informed the Irish selectors that he did not want to lead the side if Ireland persisted with the ploy of playing only seven forwards. He got his wish and Ireland accomplished what Sewell described as 'the greatest of all wins in international or any rugby. None can snatch that laurel from the Shamrocks, though botanists may cavil.'

By an extraordinary coincidence, the total number of caps won by each of the two teams came to 202.

Belfast was to be the scene of Ireland's next appearance in the international arena, and when the First Springboks came to Britain and Ireland in the early season of 1906–07 the Ulster crowd was once again treated to a magnificent match. However, this time the ending was not so happy, for South Africa won by 15 points to 12, with the winning try coming two minutes from the end when A.C. Stegmann pierced the Irish cover. That match was notable for one of the greatest tries ever scored, with Maclear running from his own 'twenty-five' after an Irish back movement had broken down. He gathered the ball, and jumped a Springbok tackle. Then swinging for the open country, he was engaged by S. Joubert, the South African full-back, but Maclear disposed of the challenge with a superb hand-off and completed his assignment with a try half-way between the posts and corner flag. Douglas Morkel, one of the famous South African rugby family, was in the South African side that day and kicked a penalty goal; indeed, he was to kick himself to rugby immortality on that tour.

A 17–4 win over England at Lansdowne Road in February 1907 augured well for Ireland's Triple Crown hopes, but the team's progress in that direction came to a summary halt when Scotland won by 15 points to 3 at Inverleith. Worse was to follow, however, for Wales extracted full retribution for recent indignities by defeating Ireland by 29 points to nil in Cardiff. It was Maclear's last match and an inglorious exit for one of the great threequarters of an era when there were many talented backs in international football. Maclear was killed in the 1914–18 war.

But the year 1907 was a significant one in Irish rugby for developments other than Maclear's departure from the Irish team. In December 1906 the honorary treasurer of the IRFU, Harry Shepperd, died unexpectedly and his death brought a complication for the union that was later turned into a shrewd stroke of business from which Irish rugby followers have derived the utmost benefit. Shepperd's death set in action a chain of events which eventually led to the establishment of the Lansdowne Road ground as the mecca of Irish rugby (see chapter 27).

Despite the glory of the win over Scotland in 1908, the acquisition of the ground by the union did not herald a period of particular distinction for Ireland on the international front, and apart from a draw with England in 1910, Ireland lost every game against the other home countries up to 1911.

There was, however, some consolation to be found when France were entertained for the first time in 1909. England had been playing France since 1906 and recording big scores against these newcomers to international rugby. Wales brought France on to their fixture list in 1908 and Ireland then decided to follow suit. The first match took place at Lansdowne Road on 20 March 1909. Most of those who had played such a noble part in the great victories over Wales in the middle of the decade had gone, but two notables who remained behind the scrum were Harry Thrift and James Parke. Fred Gardiner, too, was in the pack, together with George Hamlet. Whatever the deficiencies of the Irish team at this time (and contemporary reports leave no doubt at all that there were many), Ireland coasted home against France by 19 points to 8. This was Fred Gardiner's last international, and having before the game announced his decision to retire, he and his colleagues were most anxious that the occasion be marked by a score from the old warrior. He duly got a try–and converted it for good measure. Thrift and Parke, too, made their last appearances in the Irish jersey that day and Thrift later described his grand finale as a 'light-hearted affair'. Unlike Fred Gardiner, Thrift did not celebrate with scores, but there is no evidence that he was aware of his impending retirement. Parke, however, collected five points with a penalty goal and conversion.

International rugby, like all other sporting events, was having to compete in this era with the new wonder of the age, the cinema, though the attraction in the Round Room of the Rotunda of 'Perfection New Living Pictures' hardly accounts for the meagre attendance that turned up to see the French, who drew a gate of only £399 13s. 6d., as opposed to the England match, which enriched the union funds to the extent of £1,201.

The win over the French was repeated in Paris the following season at the Parc des Princes, while a draw with England was a reasonable reward for Ireland's first visit to Twickenham, which was opened for the first time that season. Two youngsters came into the Irish team for the first time that day at Twickenham, and while they performed with a reasonable degree of distinction, few recognised in the play of the Irish half-backs Dickie Lloyd and Harry Read, both of Trinity, that this combination would later make such a profound impact. Lloyd was the dominant figure, not only of this powerful new partnership but of the whole Irish team; he may not have been a great contributor to the fluid movement of his threequarters but he was a master-kicker and his skill as a strategist and tactician was unparalleled. He was a product of Portora Royal School which only twelve months earlier had sent out what is still believed by many to be the best school team ever seen in Irish rugby. They not alone destroyed all opposition at their own level but took on and defeated senior club sides. A measure of their true brilliance can be gleaned from the fact that in Lloyd's time they had supplied the whole Ulster schools back line in a team that had defeated Leinster by the record score of 72 points to nil.

The advent of Lloyd and Read, later to become president of the IRFU, gave an entirely new shape to the Irish team. Previously the half-backs had a fluid role, each operating at scrum-half and out-half. This all now changed, with each man specialising in his own fixed position, Read at the base of scrum and Lloyd at out-half. With George Hamlet an inspiring forward and captain, the Irish pack, which also included Tom Smyth of Malone, who had led the British and Irish side to South Africa in 1910, laid on the kind of possession on which Lloyd and Read thrived.

The 1911 campaign opened well for Ireland, who defeated England in Dublin by a try to nil, Tom Smyth getting the all-important score. Lloyd demonstrated all his considerable talents against Scotland at Inverleith on 25 February, converting two of the four tries Ireland scored in a great 16–10 victory. With Wales having beaten both England and Scotland, Ireland's game in Cardiff on 11 March was the Triple Crown final of that season.

It was, however, Wales who won the day, proving themselves far too accomplished for their Irish opposition. It was their sixth Triple Crown victory in the space of eleven seasons. The 16–0 result tells its own tale. There was, however, consolation for Ireland when once again they defeated France by 25 points to 5 a fortnight later in Cork. That game was the last of thirty appearances George Hamlet made for Ireland, a world record for a forward at that time.

Lloyd took over the leadership of the side in the following year and the initial match against England did not give birth to great hopes for the immediate future, ending as it did in a 15–0 defeat. However, against Scotland, Lloyd dropped a goal and kicked a penalty and Alex Foster, a forceful threequarter who had come on the scene two years earlier, also got a try in a 10–8 win. Welsh power had been curbed that season by England and it was further diminished when Ireland won by 12 points to 5 in Belfast; that victory, combined with an 11–6 win over France in Paris, enabled Ireland to share the championship with England.

A more doubtful distinction was not far away, however, for the visit of the South Africans, the Second Springboks, brought a defeat of record proportions at Lansdowne Road on 30 November 1912. Ireland lost that day by 38 points to nil. This was not alone the biggest defeat ever inflicted upon Ireland, but also upon any country in the realms of international competition up to that time. Not even France in their faltering advent to the top echelons had suffered a similar indignity.

The match against South Africa was due to be refereed by Mr Potter Irwin, a noted official of the day, but when he was unable to make the journey, the whistle was taken over by Mr J. Tulloch, a past president of the Scottish Union and an official well known to the Lansdowne Road clientèle. However, Mr Tulloch had to retire midway through the proceedings and Fred Gardiner took over as referee while the Springboks wove their by now familiar patterns of destruction. Ireland's net return in two seasons consisted of two wins over France and one over Scotland.

9

War calls a halt
1914–23

So shall you, when morning comes
Rise to conquer or to fall.

(Sir Henry Newbolt)

At midnight on 4–5 August 1914 Britain declared war on Germany and
for the next four years the talk was not of Lloyd or Poulton Palmer. The
battles on the international front were fought not with an oval ball but
by mechanised armies that wrought the greatest devastation ever known
to mankind. Among the hundreds of thousands who fell were many
rugby men. Nine Irish internationals lost their lives: J.T. Brett, R.B.
Burgess, E.C. Deane, W.V. Edwards, B. Maclear, V. McNamara, R.S.
Smyth, A.L. Stewart, and A.S. Taylor. These were only a few among
the numerous Irish players who were killed or permanently disabled in
that great conflict. Many who survived brought back with them
decorations and honours earned on the battlefields of France, Gallipoli
and elsewhere.

The disruption of rugby football caused by the Great War was
accentuated when the uneasy peace in Ireland was shattered by the
Easter Rising in 1916, which also brought much death and destruction.
The storm-clouds that gathered over the country did not clear until
1923, when the Irish Free State was set on a firm footing.

Just as so many rugby men had, in response to their sense of duty and
the call of their leaders, fought and died in the war against German
aggression, so also there were others, fewer in number, who took up
arms in the cause of Irish independence. Some, notably Kevin Barry of
UCD Rugby Club, died for the cause. Fortunately the friendships and
good fellowship of Irish rugby men were not affected by differing
loyalties and political sympathies, and this great sporting bond
continues to be a bright feature in the most gloomy times.

One sad casualty was the president of the IRFU, Frederick Browning,
who had presided over the union meeting in September 1914 which
decided that all club games and representative matches should be

suspended for the duration of the war. Consequently, only school competitions and interprovincial school matches kept public interest in the game alive. Browning was tragically killed when his unit of the Veterans' Corps, returning to Beggar's Bush Barracks after a route march on Easter Monday 1916, was fired upon by outposts from Commandant Eamon de Valera's garrison in Boland's Mills, under the mistaken impression that the advancing men were combat troops. It was a sorrowful incident, and a grim quirk of history that the president of the union should have lost his life in a confrontation, however remote and undesigned, with another man who played and loved rugby football.

The Great War ended in 1918 but turbulent clouds hung over Ireland for four years as the 'Troubles' continued, to be succeeded by a civil war. Yet despite the great difficulties, the game went on in Ireland, although it was virtually confined to the schools in the season of 1918–19. There were only five schools playing the game in Munster that season, and only two or three in Connacht. The position in Leinster and Ulster, however, was much healthier and immense interest was taken in the schools cup competitions in those provinces. There was also considerable activity in the University Colleges. In Dublin an unofficial league competition included teams from UCD, College of Science, Blackrock College, St Mary's, Merrion and Trinity South Africans. The competition was unfinished after UCD and Trinity had played two exciting drawn finals in College Park.

The Trinity South Africans included many fine players, including Jan Van Druten, subsequently to become one of the greatest of Springboks forwards. He continued to play for Trinity until 1923. There was strong public opinion in favour of his being selected for Ireland, as would have happened in England and Scotland, but the Irish Union adhered to what may be termed its strictly 'racialist' policy in such matters. Irish blood, however diluted, is considered a necessity.

In the season of 1919–20, club competitions and a full international programme were once again restored. A notable addition to the senior club scene in Leinster was that of University College, Dublin. This outstanding club was later to give many great players to the Irish side and was destined to make a signal contribution to the game generally.

When Ireland faced England at Lansdowne Road on 14 February 1920, football in Ireland was still in a parlous state, and the Irish selectors had some difficulty finding fifteen players of international calibre. Some of the selections in that season have with at least an element of truth been described as 'truly Gilbertian' choices. Yet despite all the obstacles and restriction of choice, the first game in the international sphere bade fair to produce a surprise of the first magnitude.

Weak in playing strength, but not apparently in will, Ireland could still call on the genius of Lloyd. His brilliance and a personal contribution of eight points left Ireland ahead by 11 points to nil with just thirty minutes to go, even though faced by an England team led by one of her most distinguished rugby sons, W.J.A. Davies. But at this critical juncture and, alas, not for the first time, the Irish forwards cracked, and England were the masters in the final reckoning, winning by 14 points to 11.

The season had not begun well, but Irish optimism was still high. However, the downward trend continued in the later games of the season, when Ireland were thrashed 19–0 by Scotland and 28–4 by Wales in Cardiff. The final indignity came in Dublin on 3 April, when France beat Ireland for the first time and did so in comprehensive fashion with a result of 15 points to 7. That was Lloyd's last match for Ireland and he was partnered at half-back by another great veteran Stan Polden, who had played three times before the war and whose career had extended over a period of twenty years. He was later to play a very active part on the administrative side of the game, being an Irish selector for eleven years and president of the union in 1933–34.

The inglorious beginning of the post-war campaign on the international front prefaced some further dismal days ahead, but all was not on the debit side during that 1919–20 season for the internationals of that season brought forth two players who were later to stamp their vigorous presence on the international scene.

Whether in desperation or by conviction that he was the best man for the job of full-back, the selectors had finally picked Ernie Crawford, at that time a veteran of twenty-eight years, for the game against England. His debut was characterised by a splendid display in the art and craft of full-back play. A Belfastman resident in Dublin and a member of the Lansdowne club, Crawford went on to win thirty caps for Ireland and shared in many of the considerable triumphs that his club were to enjoy during a magnificent spell in the twenties.

In the game against France, George Stephenson, a youth who had started the season in the Queen's University third XV, won his first cap in the centre. From that April day in 1920 until he received an injury in February 1929 Stephenson played in every game, a truly remarkable sequence. Stephenson's reputation in an international career that saw him win forty-two caps, a world record that stood for a quarter of a century, was built mainly on his defensive powers and his ability as a place kicker.

With the advent of Crawford and Stephenson and despite the departure of Lloyd, the nucleus of a formidable back line was formed but the strength in depth was not at hand, and the next few years were ones of trial and error. A 9–8 win over Scotland was the only reward during the 1920–21 season, which saw the arrival on the international scene of yet another Irish back of quality, Denis Cussen, but the shortage of youthful talent was emphasised by the fact that two other pre-war stalwarts, Alex Foster and Harry Jack, played in the championship series.

There was one other pre-war stalwart, however, still chasing the ball with vigorous pursuit and renewed enthusiasm. This was Billy Collopy of Bective Rangers, who had played against England in 1914 and in the three subsequent matches that season. He was to remain on the scene for some time yet.

Billy Collopy's father had played for Ireland in 1891, and this is only one example of those strong family traditions that were such a notable characteristic of top-class Irish rugby in the 1920s. A sizeable list of illustrious fathers, sons and brothers could be compiled for this period. George Stephenson was joined by his brother Harry during that 1921–22 season, and Billy Collopy was soon to be accompanied by his brother Dick. 'Jammie' Clinch, a forward of some substance who, like his famous father, Andrew ('Six Hundred') Clinch, was never referred to by his baptismal appellation, was about to emerge on the international scene and leave his stamp as a wing forward of quality and determination (not to mention wit). From the north would come the Hewitts, Frank and Tom, and up from Tipperary the Pikes, Ted and Victor, two of the eleven children of a Tipperary clergyman, who saw five of his sons play for Leinster and two for Ireland, with a couple of near misses in Andrew and Robert. The name McVicker was to appear in an Irish team for the first time in 1922 when Sam from the Queen's University played in all four matches. His career was eclipsed, however, by two more of the clan, Jim and Hugh, who came into the side in 1924 and 1927 respectively.*

Dick Collopy had joined his brother Billy in the Irish pack in the

---

*For a full list of fathers, sons and brothers who have played for Ireland, see Appendix 5.

1922–23 season, and after Ireland had lost to England and Scotland 'Jammie' Clinch made his debut against Wales at Lansdowne Road and shared in a 5–4 win which was only Ireland's third success in the post-war era. But a new dawn was breaking: many of the boys who had played with distinction in the schools cups in the years immediately after the war were now emerging as players of international quality, and the difficulties that had beset the game in Connacht and Munster in particular were receding. In 1923–24 Ireland won two of the four matches played and from this point on, great things began to happen.

Club football had received a major stimulus in the organisation of a national competition in 1922. A cup presented by a rugby enthusiast, Mr Robert Bateman, was contested at the end of the season between the winners of the respective cup campaigns in the provinces. Not surprisingly, Lansdowne were the first winners in 1922.

On the international front, Ireland, having lost to both England and Scotland, faced Wales in Cardiff with the knowledge that they were long outsiders. Desperate situations often preface what could be called a gamble rather than a calculated risk and the Irish selectors' choice for the game in Cardiff could certainly be put into the category of a gamble of major dimensions. In desperation the selectors picked a nineteen-year-old schoolboy from Belfast, Frank Hewitt, to play at out-half. The name Hewitt came into the international sphere in the grand manner, for Frank's elder brother Tom was also chosen for his first cap in the same game, being named on the left wing. The paternal instincts of a bygone age were reflected in the choice of another new cap in the forward Bob Collis, whose father had played for Ireland in 1884. And Ernie Crawford, who had been dropped for the match against Scotland, was recalled to the position of full-back.

Within fifteen minutes Tom Hewitt celebrated his elevation to international status by scoring a great try and Crawford signalled his return by kicking the goal points to put Ireland five points up. This was a good start, but better was to follow. Less than five minutes later Harry Stephenson ran diagonally across the field for his own line and when faced by two Welsh defenders passed to Tom Hewitt. He held the ball for only a fraction of a second before giving a return pass to Stephenson, who got in at the right corner, and even when Crawford hit an upright with the conversion attempt, Irish joy was not dimmed.

With Frank Hewitt giving a masterly display at out-half and the Irish forwards playing with spirit and skill, opportunity was strictly limited for the Welsh, who, however, shortly before the interval laid siege to the

Irish line. They were helped by a superiority in the tight scrums, and intense pressure culminated in Cliff Richards getting an unconverted try for Wales. The interval score of 8 points to 3 in Ireland's favour suggested the Welsh were in for a struggle and the spectators for a memorable spectacle when hostilities were resumed.

A few near misses were all Ireland had as a reward for a lot of pressure early in the second half, and it was Wales who scored first with a dropped goal, so the whole issue hung on a single point. Forty thousand Welsh voices rose in chorus to urge on their countrymen. But a cruel surprise was in store for them. About twenty minutes before the final whistle Frank Hewitt received a perfect pass from his scrum-half Joe Clarke and proceeded to make a tremendous run. He beat Griffiths, one of the Welsh half-backs, and then sold two glorious dummies before crossing for a gem of a try beside the posts. The conversion was a formality, but the thrills were not over yet.

Wales rallied, and one of the Welsh pack, Pugh, got in for a try. The score now stood at 13 points to 10 in Ireland's favour; time was running out and the Irish pack was tiring rapidly. The crisis point was at hand and it came in the form of a splendid run by Welsh winger Rowe Harding, who seemed certain to score. Harry Stephenson raced across from the other wing to head Harding off. In an amazing burst of speed, the Irishman shortened the gap with every stride and then, staking all on a last despairing leap, took Harding down a yard short of the Irish line.

It was a glorious tackle, the closing thrill of a memorable struggle. The victory was the first that Ireland had won on Welsh soil since Louis Magee's team had travelled to that same Cardiff pitch exactly a quarter of a century before to take the Triple Crown. Their successors could now feel that they had earned the right to regard themselves as the equals of their legendary forbears. Their day of glory was a milestone in the history of Irish rugby, for it marked a turning point in Ireland's international fortunes.

10
The dawn of a new era
1924–29

Now free from political strife, the people of Ireland had more time to devote to sport. Rugby in particular enjoyed greater popularity than ever before. In 1923 the IRFU purchased a new ground in the Ravenhill district of Belfast for the sum of £2300. The ground was enclosed and a stand built at a cost of £15,500, an adequate commentary on how the union finances had improved. A paid administrative assistant, Rupert W. Jeffares, had already been appointed by the union, and in 1924 he was carrying out secretarial duties under the direction of the honorary secretary, C. Ruxton. In the following year the office of honorary secretary was discontinued and Rupert Jeffares was appointed secretary of the union. With the game spreading and administration imposing increasing demands on honorary officers, Jeffares's appointment was a logical development. He was to occupy the position for twenty-six years and to see many changes take place in the committee-room and on the field of play. In this latter respect the opening years of Jeffares's reign coincided with a period of brilliance for Ireland unmatched since the glorious days of the gay nineties.

The 1924–25 season opened with a visit to the home countries by the Second All-Blacks. Ireland was the first country to feel the weight of their talents when, on 1 November 1924, New Zealand, later to reach a peak of perfection that earned them the title of the 'Invincibles', was hard put to it to defeat a gallant Irish side that lost by 6 points to nil, a penalty goal and a try. That Irish performance took on added significance when New Zealand subsequently beat Wales by 19–0, England by 17–9 and France by 30 points to 6 and ended with a tour record of played 30, won 30. The fact that Scotland did not play the All-Blacks hardly seemed to matter.

Time had at last caught up with Billy Collopy and he was gone when Ireland faced the challenge of the championship in 1925. There was, however, a notable new recruit in the Irish team that defeated France by

9 points to 3 in Paris. He was yet another product of Trinity College, and of Anglo-Irish stock. His name was Mark Sugden.

Sugden's career had been one of some success when he played for Trinity and Leinster as a threequarter. His advent to the scrum-half position came out of need rather than of conviction when Trinity found themselves short one afternoon of a scrum-half and Sugden was drafted to fill the gap because of the reluctance of others to take over the duties. Never was opportunity taken to such devastating effect. Sugden went from strength to strength and even on that day in Paris had not yet revealed the whole range of his talents, though he certainly demonstrated sufficient ability to be retained for an important assignment against England at Twickenham.

One of the two new caps in the forward line for that game was George Beamish, later to earn distinction as an air ace and no little reputation on the golf links. (His brother Charles was later capped too.) The second newcomer to the pack was a former captain of Campbell College, William Fraser Browne, better known by the soubriquet of 'Horsey', a name spoken with reverence in every rugby-playing nation. Once a threequarter of indifferent skill, he found his true vocation in the pack, and prior to his departure to the British Army training camp at Sandhurst, he was already a player of personality, courage and skill. Ruthless tackling was his *métier*. His advent to the Irish side was a protracted business on the grounds that some of the selectors thought him too small and light for the demands of international competition.

Browne helped Ireland to a 6–6 draw with England at Twickenham, the first time since 1911 that England had failed to win against the Irishmen. H. Wakelam in his book *The Game Goes On* probably summed up this encounter correctly when he wrote: 'The game was marked by the happy and strange phenomenon of an Irish pack of forwards sticking it out to the last and finishing with something in reserve.' Certainly Wakelam is correct when he says that with this pack modern Irish forward play came into being; Browne, as much as any and more than most, deserves the credit for its creation. His subsequent matches were characterised by his courage, and while lack of weight and height took toll of his stamina throughout a career that was all too short, he was to share in some great matches and moments in his international appearances that spanned three years and gained him twelve caps.

In 1926 Ireland beat England, Scotland and France before Swansea proved the graveyard of Triple Crown hopes yet again. This was the third time since 1905 that Wales had foiled the Irish Triple Crown effort.

That draw against England in 1925 did not presage any deeds of moment against Scotland, who won readily enough by 14 points to 8 at Lansdowne Road, but a 19–3 win over Wales at Ravenhill was the prelude to greatness which was to be tangibly rewarded in the following year. On that day in Belfast Sugden had a new partner at half-back, his Leinster colleague Eugene Davy, then a student at University College, Dublin. Sugden and Davy made their contribution to that historic win over Wales, and they were to be the lynch-pin of a great Irish back line in 1926.

The back line of that season was arguably the greatest ever fielded by an Irish side. Sugden, the master of the dummy, was the scrum-half supreme; Davy, the complete footballer, took over at the half-back position; Ernie Crawford, who mixed subtlety of movement with sarcasm of tongue and was never afraid to use both attributes, was at full-back; Denis Cussen, first capped in 1921, still retained the pace that made him a sprint champion; George Stephenson and Frank Hewitt, now moved into the centre, had Tom Hewitt outside them on the left; while J.H. Gage of Queen's University, who had the distinction of also being capped for South Africa, was included in the side against Scotland when Frank Hewitt was unable to play.

In the pack, Bradley was the experienced man of the front row, and the campaign also saw A.M. Buchanan, Charlie Hanrahan and C. Payne gain their first caps. James McVicker, who had spent much of his career as a threequarter with a junior club in Belfast, had developed into a second row of substance after joining Collegians in 1924 and beside him was another newcomer in J.L. Farrell of Bective Rangers. S.J. Cagney played in all four games, but C.F. Hallaran, now a well-tried veteran, was dropped after the English match. 'Horsey' Browne was unable to play against France or England, but appeared against Scotland and Wales, while Clinch was still very much in the picture mapping out territory of forward play never previously traversed. Great in defence, Clinch had the distinction, if that it may be called, of playing in thirty matches for his country without scoring a single try and without impairing his unimpeachable reputation—a salutary lesson for some present-day players.

A notable absentee from the Irish pack in 1926 was George Beamish, who was out of action with a serious leg injury. His absence, combined with the unavailability of Browne, probably accounted in part for a sluggish display by the Irish forwards against France, who were, nonetheless, defeated by 11 points to nil in Belfast. There was little evidence in this game of the brilliance that lay ahead.

Still without the formidable pair, Ireland nevertheless reached the pinnacle against England in 1926, a performance and a match that many assert were the greatest they have yet seen. The events are worthy of at least a brief description. England took an early lead when their out-half Kittermaster cut through and laid on a try for his half-back partner Arthur Young. T.E. Francis converted: –0–5 to England. The England full-back Catcheside was caught in possession by Cussen, dropped the ball, and George Stephenson was presented with a try: –3–5. A splendid English movement culminated in H.G. Periton getting a try, and Francis was again on target with the conversion: –3–10. Obstruction against England and a long-distance penalty goal by Stephenson, who was given the kick by the captain, Crawford, against the advice from the crowd. At half-time the score was 6–10 to England, and then, after the interval, Sugden began to weave his pattern of magic.

Twice within the space of five minutes Sugden outwitted the English defence with swerve and dummy and twice Stephenson kicked the goals from the same mark, a yard from the touchline, after Cussen had capitalised on Sugden's ploys: –16–10 to Ireland. Then, near the end of the game, Haslett, a new cap in the English side, broke through from a line-out to get a try for England and Francis added the goal points, so it was 16–15 and all to play for. An English attack was foiled and Cussen, instead of finding a safe touch, kicked across the field. An English defender was deceived by the flight of the ball and failed to field it, but Frank Hewitt, following up quickly, did get it and ran in for a try that assured a win for Ireland by 19 points to 15.

Now, having beaten England in a victory that was acclaimed by an Irish invasion of the Lansdowne Road ground, it was on to Scotland and Murrayfield, the new home of the Scottish Rugby Union. Ireland brought more than a victory over England to Murrayfield; they also brought with them the innovation that had marked out that game against England on 13 February as historic for a reason which had nothing to do with its being the occasion of the first Irish defeat of the Saxons for fourteen years. On that day in Dublin Ireland had worn numbered jerseys for the first time, and they were similarly clad for their initial visit to Murrayfield. The game was played under appalling conditions which were a test of endurance rather than skill. Ireland won on both counts, with a movement between Stephenson, Clinch, Davy and Gage producing the only score of the game, a try in the last minute.

Davy's defensive qualities were seen at their best that day, while Crawford played with the utmost steadiness in conditions calculated to test the mettle of a full-back. Now the last hurdle was to come at Swansea yet again; the result was an 11–8 win for Wales, a bitter disappointment to the Irish team but a just tribute to the strength of the Welsh pack. Yet it was a close-run game which nearly turned into a win for Ireland, as Tom Hewitt was only inches from his objective with a last-minute drop at goal which, had it gone over, would have given Ireland a one-point victory. (At that time the drop had the inflated value of four points.)

So Triple Crown honours were missed literally by inches, and a share in the championship with Scotland was the rather poor substitute for what might have been. The game against Wales marked the close of Tom Hewitt's career, and his brother Frank retired in the following season. These were premature retirements that may have cost Ireland the glory that looked imminent but which was not to materialise in the immediate future.

While chance had made Sugden a scrum-half, so also it cost him his place for Ireland's first match the following season. Paul Murray, a young and versatile back, was making an impression in his games for Wanderers, but with Sugden secure on the Leinster team, Murray's chances of representative honours in the scrum-half position seemed limited in the extreme. But an injury to an Ulster player in the match against Leinster in December 1926 gave Murray an unexpected opportunity to display his talents. He was called into the Ulster side during the match and played with sufficient authority to displace Sugden in the selectors' favours when the team to meet France was picked. An 8–3 win in Paris did not help Murray keep Sugden out for long, however, for he was recalled against England at Twickenham, a match in which Hugh McVicker made his international debut alongside his brother Jim. It was not, alas, an auspicious partnership, for Ireland lost by 8 points to 6.

Wins over Scotland and Wales followed that season, which marked the end of Crawford's international career and the advent to the Irish team of two threequarters of great merit, Jack Arigho, one of a splendid Lansdowne back line, and J.B. Ganly of Monkstown. The game against Scotland was played at Lansdowne Road in atrocious conditions; this was the day already referred to, when patrons in the new East Stand received a severe drenching. Subsequent incumbents of the stand have viewed proceedings in greater comfort, well protected from the weather.

In the 1928 series of internationals Sugden and Davy were prominent at half-back and George Stephenson's solid presence still dominated the threequarter line. 'Horsey' Browne, 'Jammie' Clinch, Ted Pike and Charlie Hanrahan were experienced members of the pack, in which George Beamish, who had been out of action for the previous two seasons because of injury, was also a conspicuous and formidable figure. With men such as these in the team, it is small wonder that Ireland won against Wales in Cardiff, against Scotland at Murrayfield, and against France in Belfast. However, they lost to England and to the touring team from New South Wales, and England took the 1928 championship.

The great side assembled in the mid-twenties was, however, breaking up; but while no Triple Crown or outright win in the championship had been gathered as a testimony to their undoubted ability, many of them, including George Stephenson, Beamish, Sugden, Davy, Clinch and C.T. Payne, were still together when Ireland at last laid the Twickenham bogey on 13 February 1929. It was victory achieved against a background of misfortune in the shape of an injury in the early stages to Stephenson, who fractured several ribs. If fate had not always smiled benignly on Ireland at Twickenham and elsewhere, they hung on grimly to win an historic victory over England by 6 points to 5, with Davy and Sugden scoring the tries that saw Ireland home on the strength of a magnificent forward effort.

Paul Murray was back in the Irish side, but in the centre, and his contribution that day, like those of Davy and Sugden, was complementary to the forwards' efforts. And Stephenson, always magnificent in defence, won the game for Ireland with a great saving tackle in the dying minutes despite his broken ribs. The victory, not unnaturally, was greeted with euphoria, and Twickenham, by no means unused to the theatrical, especially when Wales played there, was the scene of overflowing Irish emotions. (The seat cushions proved a handy wherewithal for releasing the pent-up feelings.)

Now a Triple Crown beckoned again, but Scotland called a halt to those aspirations when they won surprisingly a fortnight later at Lansdowne Road, where the crowd actually overflowed onto the pitch throughout the game, a circumstance that deprived Ireland of at least one score when Jack Arigho was unable to ground the ball near the posts after scoring an early try. Stephenson was still an absentee because of his rib injury, the first game he had missed since 1920. But he was back again for the game against Wales in Belfast, when Morgan Crowe also came into the side in place of Paul Murray. Another new arrival in the Irish team which faced Wales that year was Mark Deering, a fine forward from the Bective Rangers club. By a strange coincidence, Crowe's brother Phil and Deering's brother Séamus were later to make their debuts on the same Irish team against England in 1935.

So the twenties, which had opened with the game in such an uncertain state in Ireland, closed on an altogether different note. The achievements at international level were reflected in a growth domestically that bordered on the dramatic. At the close of the 1929 season there were no fewer than 160 clubs and 59 schools affiliated to the IRFU. Nowhere was the strength more pronounced than in Munster, where in 1920 the game was in a perilous condition. Munster could now boast of having 54 clubs and 10 schools. In Connacht, too, where the struggle to survive had gone on for so long, the situation had improved immeasurably: there were now 15 clubs and 5 schools playing rugby in the province. In Leinster and Ulster, where the main strength of the union had always lain, the improvement was steady, if less dramatic. Leinster had 45 clubs and 25 schools, while there were 46 clubs and 19 schools affiliated to the Ulster Branch.

Ireland had, too, made a significant contribution to international rugby in 1923, when Ellis's exploits of a century before were celebrated with a game that saw six players from Ireland join forces with nine from Scotland to meet a combined team from England-Wales. It was an excellent game, worthy in every way of the event it commemorated. England-Wales won by 21 points to 16. A similar game took place at Twickenham in October 1929, when to honour the memory of one of England's most famous sons, Sir Rowland Hill, Scotland-Ireland exacted revenge by winning an exhilarating match by 20 points to 13. Paul Murray, Eugene Davy, Mark Sugden, George Beamish, Michael Dunne (a Lansdowne forward who had made his mark on the international scene the previous season), C.T. Payne and J.L. Farrell all displayed their talent and skills to great effect that day at Twickenham.

A most important feature of the twenties was the emergence of organised associations of referees, which both recruited new aspirants and vastly improved the general standard of refereeing. In earlier days it had often been the case, particularly in junior games, that a referee was conscripted haphazardly from the touchline spectators. It was vitally important as the game spread that referees should be available on an organised basis. Ulster and Leinster took the lead in this vital work, and the names Wallace Harland, Sam Donaldson, Tom Bell, Jim 'Cocky' Rowlands, and Billy Jeffares can be gratefully remembered. Munster soon followed, being inspired by Dickie Magrath, himself an international referee of the pre-war era. Not long afterwards, a Connacht association was formed. The fruits of this pioneering work were clearly seen in the later emergence of Irish referees of world stature, such as Ham Lambert, Michael Dowling, Ray Williams, Kevin Kelleher and Paddy D'Arcy. There followed in the 1970s two others of international repute in John West and David Burnett. Burnett, who has refereed 13 internationals, is still at the height of his powers.

11

Controversy and achievement 1929–39

Wales, who had three times since 1905 foiled Irish Triple Crown aspirations, were unquestionably the bane of the Irish team in the thirties, a decade, nevertheless, of some considerable achievement and no little controversy within the corridors of power of IRFU administration.

Growth and expansion invariably bring with them attendant problems and there were those in Irish rugby who rightly felt that the game's administration needed overhauling. Old traditions die hard in rugby, as elsewhere, and while those charged with the responsibility of guiding the game within the country had contributed handsomely, it was time for changes and not all of them were palatable to those in power.

The growth of the game in Munster and Connacht brought with it major problems, not least in respect of playing accommodation. In an effort to cater for an ever-increasing playing population, Munster and Connacht led a call for Sunday rugby. Although it was a reasonable request, it did not meet with favourable reaction from the more conservative element of the IRFU, and initially the attempt was resisted strongly. But Munster and Connacht were not alone, for there were strong voices in Leinster too who saw that if there was to be healthy development and progress, then the rigid views of those who resisted the call for Sunday rugby would have to be challenged and overcome. The challenge was made, and the contentious issue was eventually resolved.

The first rumblings of discontent, ironically, did not centre round Munster or Connacht, but around a provincial competition in Leinster, the Midland League. The union refused to allow any games under its jurisdiction on Sunday and several times reiterated that stand. The whole issue was therefore ready to be aired openly, and in October 1929 a deputation from Connacht and Munster met the union and explained their difficulties. The union refused to review their attitude and, in so ruling, offered as one of their reasons for forbidding Sunday play the quite extraordinary allegation that, according to reports that had reached them, the behaviour of players and spectators at games that had taken place on Sunday strengthened them in their resolve to oppose such games. But the matter was far from over.

University College, Dublin, asked the union to investigate Sunday play, proposing that a special committee be appointed to look into the structure of the game, particularly in Munster and Connacht. Unfortunately the union saw no reason to do so and the request was turned down. But matches were taking place on Sundays, including the universities tournament, the Dudley Cup. The demands were growing and culminated in a special general meeting of the union being called in January 1930 to investigate the whole question of Sunday play.

Compromise eventually solved the problem at the meeting in January, as it could have done much earlier. The proposal that averted what was certainly building up to crisis-point came from Sam Lee, the man who in the nineties had played so many distinguished games for Ireland. The union decided that 'League and cup matches and all friendly matches shall be played on week-days except by the special permission of the branch or branches to which the competing clubs belong.'

The establishment of the Irish Free State in the early twenties had left the union in the position of governing the game for one island which contained two separate political entities. It is not surprising, therefore, that the next controversy that afflicted the committee centred on what flag should be flown at international matches, as Ireland played both in Belfast, which was politically part of the United Kingdom, and in Dublin, the capital of the Free State. The question was resolved in 1925 by the union designing a special flag of its own. But there were many who felt that when Ireland played at Lansdowne Road, she should do so under the national flag. It was not a request that met with the approval of all the committee, perhaps an understandable position among a body of men who shared a common interest in rugby but whose political outlooks were diverse in the extreme.

Connacht raised the issue again in January 1932 in a letter to the union asking if it was the intention to fly the Irish flag at future international matches at Lansdowne Road. The union, no doubt wishing to maintain a nice balance, replied that the flag which had been designed in 1925 and which incorporated the arms of the four provinces was the only flag flown at Ireland's home international matches, and that it was not intended to depart from this procedure.

But the call for the flying of the national flag was taken up by the press and by many of the clubs. Yet again, University College, Dublin, lent its weight to the argument. More important, the Minister of External Affairs in the Free State government asked to meet the president of the union on the matter. That meeting resulted in the union, without a dissenting voice, deciding on 5 February 1932 that in future the national flag would be flown alongside the union flag at all international matches at Lansdowne Road. So an issue that had initially raised the passions of many inside and outside the game was resolved yet again with the fine balance that has maintained the unity of purpose within the game in Ireland, even if that balance has not been matched in the political arena.

There is no doubt that the union committee of the period comprised people who had done splendid work for the game. They had seen it through a period of crisis in the aftermath of the Great War and had presided over its organisation and development. They were men with distinguished records of service on the field and in the council chamber, men such as R.G. Warren, Stan Polden, Jack Coffey, Harry Thrift, Fred Strain, John Macaulay and Andrew Clinch. Yet it was none the less true that to a large extent the unit had been geared to a common viewpoint and, perhaps, to principles that were too rigid. Nowhere was the common bond of thought more pronounced than in the selection committee. John Macaulay had served no fewer than twenty-six times on it starting in 1895 and was still there in 1930. Stan Polden had been a member of every committee from 1922 to 1931 and was back again in 1932 for a further period of two years. John Warren, like Polden a distinguished legislator, held office for twelve years, from 1922–23 to 1933–34.

Change was needed within the union and the clamour for it came from outside, notably from Leinster, where once again the UCD club were the architects of the dramatic changes that took place within the Leinster executive in the mid-thirties, and subsequently the wind of change blew, with beneficial results, through the IRFU executive committee and selection committees. The new school of thought, which had been frowned upon by the establishment as too radical, nonetheless represented the views of the majority of the players and clubs within the game.

The new set-up in Leinster brought renewed vigour and impetus to the game, both within the province and in a more general aspect. It was reflected in the selection committee for the 1934–35 season, when

Leinster's representatives were Paul Murray and G.P. Sarsfield Hogan.

Murray had just retired as a player, having represented Ireland nineteen times in three different positions, centre, out-half and scrum-half. He had also toured New Zealand with the Lions in 1930. He was to make a contribution of similiar moment on the administrative side, eventually serving as president of the union in 1965–66.

Sarsfield Hogan had been a leading figure in setting the UCD club on the road to success when the college entered senior ranks in 1919, nine years after its foundation. A threequarter of high class, he was on the first UCD team to win the Leinster Senior Cup in 1924 and subsequently a member of the great Lansdowne side of the twenties. His playing career did not follow a similar course to that of Murray, but the ultimate honour, an international cap, only just evaded him, for he played in two final trials, and was several times on the panel of reserves for Ireland. His term of service as an administrator was both long and distinguished.

There were many other able men who came into the administrative sphere at branch and union level during that period of transition in the mid-thirties. One of these was Judge C.F. Davitt, and he too succeeded to the union presidency in 1936–37.

Connacht, too, came into the interprovincial fold in its own right, and for the first time established fixtures with all the other provinces on an annual basis, though it was not until 1947 that Connacht competed officially in the interprovincial championship, thereby giving the annual series the status of an all-Ireland fixture. Connacht had long been blessed with dedicated souls who kept rugby football going within the province despite great difficulties. Foremost among them was Henry Anderson. He was the first Connachtman to be capped for Ireland, receiving that honour four times between 1903 and 1906 while a member of the Old Wesley club. At the annual general meeting of the union in October 1937 Connacht gained direct representation to the union committee for the first time since the old haphazard days of the nineteenth century. Henry Anderson was nominated as Connacht's representative and a worthy one he proved. In 1946 he was elected to the union's highest office.

At that meeting in October 1937 the changing administrative scene was reflected in a lively debate on the constitution of the committee, but a proposal to increase the direct representation of Leinster, Ulster and Munster from one to two members and reduce the elected representatives from eight to four was rejected.

While circumstances and events had brought about the retirement of some of the old established figures of the union in this period, it was time itself that caught up with one of the most remarkable rugby careers of all, that of Robert G. Warren, the former captain of Ireland and a player of considerable ability. Warren had attended his first IRFU meeting in 1885 and had an unbroken spell on the committee until, in 1936, he announced his resignation but agreed to act as one of Ireland's representatives on the International Board. He had acted in that capacity since 1887 and had been honorary secretary of the board from 1897 to 1933, being succeeded in that office by Harry Thrift. R.G. Warren thus served on the union committee for fifty-one years. He had seen many changes, and none of these was more important, dramatic or effective, than those that had taken place during his closing years on the committee. His period on the International Board had spanned forty-nine years, and during that era he had had as his fellow Irish representatives men whose contribution to the game generally and to Irish rugby in particular cannot easily be measured: J.B. Moore (1892–1927), Andrew Clinch (1928–36), Eddie McAlister (1886–97), H.C. Sheppard (1897–1906) and, in the closing years, Fred Strain (1932–46) and Harry Thrift (1931–56).

The thirties, in retrospect, added up to one of the most significant periods in Irish rugby history, but all the drama was not confined to the council chamber. The changes at executive level took place against a playing record for Ireland of near misses, great successes and the winning of the championship for the first time since 1899. The long, barren spell was broken by a fine Irish combination in 1934–35.

By that time France had departed from the championship scene which she had first entered in 1909–10. The break with the four home unions came in March 1931, when, against a background of allegations of rough play and professionalism, it was decided that fixtures against France would be discontinued.

Before that championship triumph for Ireland in 1935, the team had contested two Triple Crown finals, in 1930 and 1931. Ironically, Ireland lost to France in both seasons, but beat England and Scotland before Wales yet again proved the stumbling block.

In 1930 a team that still included George Stephenson, with Eugene Davy in the centre and Paul Murray at out-half, beat England by 4 points to 3 at Lansdowne Road and Scotland by 14 points to 11 at Murrayfield. The match against Scotland on 22 February was notable for a brilliant performance from Davy, who scored three tries in the space of thirty minutes. Stephenson's career ended with the following match against Wales at Swansea, where Wales won by 12 points to 7.

The following season, Ireland, with an all-Lansdowne three-quarter line of Ned Lightfoot, Eugene Davy, Morgan Crowe and Jack Arigho, defeated Scotland by 8 points to 5 in Dublin. They had earlier accounted for England at Twickenham by 6 points to 5, a match that completed a hat-trick of victories over England. The Lansdowne threequarters were still together when Ireland faced Wales in Belfast in March, but the combination was not effective enough to deal with the opposition, and Wales won by 15 points to 3.

Leading figures in the pack now were two notable players from Cork, Noel Murphy from the Constitution club and Jack Russell from University College. 'Jammie' Clinch was still around too, while Jack Siggins from Collegians had come into the side in 1931. The latest of the Pike brothers, Victor, also made his debut that season. And George Beamish was still on hand to lend his experience to that of Clinch and Farrell from Bective.

A great South African team under the leadership of Benny Osler came to Dublin and beat Ireland on 19 December 1931. This was 'Jammie' Clinch's last game for Ireland, by which time Mark Sugden had departed and Paul Murray was now established at scrum-half. Murray's half-back partner was Larry McMahon, who had made his first appearance as a centre against England in the previous season and who subsequently gathered twelve caps in an international career that extended until 1938. There are many who still find it difficult to understand why McMahon's career was frequently interrupted at the whims of the selectors, for he was a centre of the highest class.

Ireland figured in a three-way tie with England and Wales in the 1932 series, when the outstanding feature of the season was a magnificent display against Scotland at Murrayfield. Ireland won by 20 points to 8, Lightfoot and Paul Murray causing the destruction of Scotland. Lightfoot scored two tries that day, and Murray converted all four tries that Ireland got. Michael Dunne, who had missed the 1931 season, was a leading figure in the pack that dismissed the Welsh challenge by 12 points to 10 at Cardiff.

Murray's career ended the following season when in his last match he helped Ireland to defeat Wales by 10 points to 5, an unexpected victory since Ireland had previously lost to both England and Scotland. Ireland had been wonderfully served at scrum-half since Sugden had made his initial appearance in 1925. Sugden and Murray had shared the place between them during eight seasons for all but one match, the game against England in 1932, when the Limerickman, Danaher Sheehan, then playing with London Irish, partnered Eugene Davy.

Murray's retirement brought to the scrum-half position another great player and one who was to remain in the national side until 1939. This was George Morgan, who was initially attached to the Clontarf club and who was later a leading figure in establishing Old Belvedere, a senior-ranking club composed of past pupils of his old school. Morgan's first season in the Irish jersey was something of a traumatic experience, however, for in 1934 Ireland lost all three matches and Davy's international career ended with the game against England.

In 1935 there were four new caps against England: Phil Crowe in the back line and three new forwards, P.J. Lawlor and Séamus Deering (Bective Rangers) and H.J. Sayers (Lansdowne), in the pack. The new formula did not add up to a potent force, and England won by 14 points to 3. Morgan's partner at half-back was Aidan Bailey, who had made his debut in the previous season while still a schoolboy at Presentation College, Bray.

For the match against Scotland, Bailey was restored to his proper position in the centre, and another Hewitt, Victor, a brother of Frank and Tom, came in at out-half for his first cap. Jack Siggins, the Irish captain, led a pack of forwards that included herculean workers in Deering, Bob Graves and Sammy Walker, all recent assets to the front line. Ireland won by four tries to a goal, the tries being scored by Joe O'Connor of UCC, Lawlor, Ernie Ridgeway and George Morgan.

Only one change was made for the match against Wales on 9 March 1935: Jack Doyle of Bective Rangers came in on the wing for Dave Lane of UCC. The Irish pack was again magnificent, but the feature of the match was the manner in which Bailey put the great Welsh centre Wilfred Wooller out of the game. Two penalty goals, one each by Siggins and Bailey, gave Ireland a 6–0 interval lead. Doyle celebrated his first and, as it transpired, his only cap by getting a try and Wales's only achievement that day was a penalty goal.

That victory at Ravenhill was to end a long wait as it gave Ireland the championship for the first time since 1899. But as the programme had not been completed for a fortnight, Ireland had to wait for the result of the last match before knowing that the title was theirs.

The Third All-blacks came on tour the following season and Ireland failed to register their first win over a touring team, losing by 17 points to 9, despite the fact that there were sixteen Irishmen on the field, for the referee that day was an Irishman, Billy Jeffares, son of the IRFU secretary and one of a long line of distinguished Irish referees. One such referee was Kevin Kelleher, who established an all-time record of taking charge of no fewer than twenty-three international matches before his retirement from the international scene in 1972.

Narrow victory, but victory nonetheless, over England (by 6 points to 3 in Dublin) and Scotland, beaten with greater ease by 10 points to 4 at Murrayfield, set the stage for another Triple Crown match against Wales in Cardiff in 1936. Cardiff, where four years earlier Ireland had foiled Welsh Triple Crown hopes, was no happy hunting-ground for Ireland, who travelled as reigning champions. And while Wales could not win the coveted title, having been held to a draw by England, victory in the match would give them the championship.

The Arms Park was packed to capacity for the game, with thousands locked outside the gates. The game was better in the expectation than the realisation however, for it was decided by a penalty goal, kicked by the Welsh full-back Vivian Jenkins after only twelve minutes' play.

The Irish forwards worked tremendously hard to open the way for the backs, but all the endeavours of Deering, Russell, Siggins, Walker and their comrades proved in vain, and the Welsh goal was the only score of a most disappointing encounter.

Wales and Scotland were both defeated in 1937, when George Cromey took over the out-half position, but England took the Triple Crown and the championship. Their 9–8 win over Ireland at Twickenham was surrounded by controversy. England had scored a try in doubtful circumstances, the ball appearing to go out of play, but A. Butler, the England right wing, immediately went in for a try, which gave England the lead. That advantage was short-lived, as Fred Moran, an Irish sprint champion who had come into the team the previous season, gained an equalising score following a great passing movement. Within ten minutes Ireland was in the lead: George Morgan paved the way for Moran to cross for a second try, to which Aidan Bailey added the points from the touchline. With ten minutes' play remaining, Peter Cranmer reduced the lead with a penalty goal for England. And then, five minutes from the end, came the incident that provoked the controversy and gave England the winning try.

H.V. Sever, the England left wing, put in a great dash down the wing. As he grounded the ball, he was bundled into the corner flag by the combined efforts of Vesey Boyle and Fred Moran. The referee, Mr J.W. Faull of Wales, was unable to decide whether or not Sever had been bundled into touch in goal and the Irish linesman, Stan Polden, was asked to adjudicate. He decided that Sever had scored a legitimate try. Recalling the incident many years later, Stan Polden was adamant that Sever had grounded the ball before being knocked into touch in goal. So victory went to England.

In the season of 1937–38 Ireland suffered a humiliating 36–14 defeat by England at Lansdowne Road. This was to be Scotland's season, for both the Triple Crown and championship went to them—they did not win either again until 1984—and Ireland took the wooden spoon after losing to Wales in Swansea. But better days were ahead.

The Lions went to South Africa in the summer of 1938, travelling under the leadership of Sammy Walker. That, however, did not deter the selectors from dropping Walker for the game against England in 1939. It was, nevertheless, a useful-looking side that travelled to Twickenham. Charlie Teehan, a young hooker from UCC, and J. Ryan of UCD were brought into the pack, while at full-back the selectors opted for the diminutive Lansdowne man, Con Murphy. Among the experienced members of the team, Harry McKibbin, who had toured in South Africa, was partnered in the centre by Des Torrens of Bohemians, and Fred Moran and V.J. Lyttle were on the wings. Like the half-backs Cromey and Morgan, all had played in the international arena previously. The pack was fortified by the presence of Blair Mayne, a tremendously strong forward and a boxer of repute, and Dave O'Loughlin, who had made his mark as a forward in the previous season.

H.J. ('Mike') Sayers of Lansdowne and Aldershot Services had been on the scene for some time, while his back-row colleagues, Sinclair Irwin and Robert Alexander, were established internationals, Alexander since 1936 and Irwin since the match against Scotland in the previous season. Sinclair Irwin was following in his father's footsteps, for Sam Irwin had played for Ireland nine times between 1900 and 1903 and was president of the union in 1935–36. In that respect, too, Sinclair was to emulate his father, for he attained the presidency in 1969–70. Harry McKibbin, his colleague that day, had the distinction of being elected president of the IRFU for the centenary season (1974–75) and is one of Ireland's representatives on the International Board.

It was the combined efforts of McKibbin and Irwin that gave Ireland a 5–0 victory over England at Twickenham on 11 February 1939, Irwin scoring the try and McKibbin converting.

While it was a success gained against the expectations of most, it was thoroughly deserved, and the same team was named to meet Scotland at

Lansdowne Road. One change was necessary before the game, as D. Tierney of UCC was forced to withdraw; his departure brought in Tommy Headon of UCD for his first cap. In conditions of rain and mud, Ireland won convincingly by 12 points to 3. McKibbin kicked a penalty goal, Torrens and Moran scored tries, and Mike Sayers marked a Scottish drop-out and then dropped a goal from the mark, a rarity at the best of times but a truly remarkable feat in the prevailing wind and rain. It was the first score of that nature in international football for eight years, and only the eleventh in international rugby. A crowd of 35,000 was present to witness the novelty.

A crowd of 30,000 packed into Ravenhill on 11 March to see an Irish side that showed just one alteration from the team that beat Scotland. Vesey Boyle was recalled on the left wing. The spectators did not, however, see an Irish victory, for the Irish forwards were outplayed and Wales won. However, in spite of the disappointment, the future looked bright and there would be other opportunities in the years that lay ahead. But the opportunity to contest another Triple Crown was not to come for another seven years. Seven times in all had Wales foiled Ireland at the last obstacle, and four of the frustrations had been suffered since 1930.

12
Europe erupts
1939–46

The political situation in Europe had for several years been clouded by a growing menace as Germany made territorial demands on some of her neighbours. What many expected finally occurred on the first Sunday of September 1939, when Britain declared war on Germany. Eire was not involved but a war situation was not one in which international rugby could be played.

The proposed tour of Australia to Britain and Ireland scheduled for the autumn of 1939 was cancelled and, in common with the other unions, Ireland lost £1050, their share of the guarantee towards the Wallabies' tour expenses. The Australians returned home without playing a match. All official internationals were cancelled for the duration of a war that lasted until 1945 and ravaged mankind to a degree never previously known.

The effect of the previous conflict in 1914–18 had been to stifle effectively all rugby other than in the schools. This time the series of cup campaigns in the provinces, with the exception of Ulster, continued throughout the war and brought in some much-needed revenue, but the Bateman Cup, suspended in 1939, was never again contested.

There were also Services internationals in Britain, including a four-countries match at Richmond in December 1939. Such games as an Irish XV *v.* Defence Forces gave opportunity to players who would in ordinary circumstances have worn the Irish jersey in full internationals. In 1942 further spice was added to the representative scene when an Irish XV met the British Army at Ravenhill. It was the first of five such matches that took place and it was not until the last of the games, in December 1945, that the Irish side managed to win, beating the British Army by 19 points to 3. These games gave tremendous experience to Irish players who were later to form the backbone of the national side when full internationals were resumed in 1947, while some of those who had distinguished themselves in the Irish jersey in the period immediately before the war also figured in the series.

Yet many fine players were deprived of the ultimate distinction because of the war, notably Austin Carry, a splendid out-half who played for Trinity and Old Wesley, Des Thorpe of Old Belvedere, a scrum-half who just missed a cap, Hugh Greer, an accomplished back from the NIFC club, Jack Guiney of Bective Rangers, and his namesake, Jack Guiney of Clontarf.

The war in Europe ended in 1945 and international rugby reverted to civilian control in Britain, where the Services had organised what games had been possible during the war period. When international rugby was resumed in 1946 with unofficial internationals there were many missing faces. Two of the Irish side of 1939, Robert Alexander and Mike Savers, were killed in 1943. C.F. Hallaran, a sterling forward of the twenties, was killed in 1941, while P.B. Coote, who had won one cap in 1933, lost his life in the same year. J.B. Minch of Bective Rangers, capped five times in 1913 and 1914, also fell in 1943, and there were many others. On the home front, the union's affairs had been guided by John Warren, elected president in 1938, until he too died in 1945.

In 1946 there was a full programme of matches and, happily, France had now returned to the fold. The 1946 games were not, however, recognised as full internationals, so those that participated in them did not get caps. Ireland's first assignment was against France at Lansdowne Road in January 1946. France's return to the international scene did not bode well for the Irish, who lost by 4 points to 3. The French side that lined out at Lansdowne Road in 1946 showed no signs of being the products of a ravaged and hungry land. It included two giant second-row forwards, A. Soro and R. Moga, both of whom played a major role in Ireland's defeat. That day the Irish crowd got a first glimpse of a back-row forward in the French team, Jean Prat, later to leave his imprint on the rugby scene by his brilliant application and execution of line-out technique and other facets of wing forward play.

Ireland lost to England by 14 points to 6, while Scotland and Wales also applied sufficient pressure on the Irish XV to win. And if Britain had felt the hardships of war and the severity of food rationing, there was as yet enough rugby talent around to ensure that the 1947 championship would not be conceded to a team from across the Irish Sea.

Rugby football in its first season after the war, 1945–46, owed a great debt to a touring party of New Zealand soldiers. They played as the 'Kiwis' but wore the black jerseys for so long associated with the All-Blacks, and they added lustre to the proud traditions of New Zealand football, reviving happy memories of All-Black teams by their standard of play. The Kiwis played two games in Ireland, beating Ulster by 10 points to 9 in a splendid game at Ravenhill on 14 November. Three days later they faced Leinster at Lansdowne Road. The game ended in a 10–10 draw and provided a magnificent match. It was a splendid performance by Leinster against a team that succeeded in beating Wales, England and France twice subsequently.

Meanwhile, the IRFU had elected Henry Anderson as president for 1946 and all was back to normal on the domestic front. The task was now to build up a team for a worthwhile Triple Crown challenge.

13

The golden years 1947-52

One crowded hour of glorious life
Is worth an age without a name.
(*T.O. Mordaunt*)

Almost half a century had passed since Ireland's last success when, once again, an Irish team set out in quest of the Triple Crown. Those forty-nine years of waiting had seen much disappointment and frustration, most of it inflicted by Wales. But the crowded hour of glory was at hand, and it came in Belfast on 13 March 1948, when Wales was defeated by two tries to nil. That win gave Ireland the Triple Crown and, for the only time in history, the grand-slam victory over all the home countries and France. It did not give Ireland the international championship, for when Ireland took the field at Ravenhill the result of the championship contest had already been decided.

Ireland had used twenty-six players during the 1946 campaign of unofficial internationals. Only three of the players, Con Murphy, the full-back, wing Fred Moran, and Dave O'Loughlin of the forwards, had been capped in the pre-war era. But while that 1946 campaign proved one of no joy for Ireland, it did provide valuable experience for the players, two of whom were to make such an impact in the immediate future. By coincidence, they were both medical students, one from Belfast and one from Dublin. Jack Kyle from Queen's University and Karl Mullen from the Old Belvedere club played in the positions of out-half and hooker respectively on the Irish side that by its victory over Wales in 1948 wrote the preface to a tale of glory that has become known as the golden years of Irish rugby. Mullen and Kyle played together on an Irish side for the first time against the British Army in December 1945. Later that season they got a better appreciation of the international atmosphere during the unofficial contest against France, England, Wales and Scotland. Mullen played in all four matches in 1946, while Kyle played in those against France and England.

Mullen was already a top-class international hooker in 1947 and when given the opportunity to lead the side the following season, he proved a splendid captain and a great tactician at a time when the tactics employed by the Irish side were very much a matter for the captain. Mullen's name will always be identified with Ireland's golden years, during which he gave ample proof of his qualities of leadership and of his depth of thought and ability to analyse the potential of his own team and the strength and weakness of the opponents. He brought a new dimension to the Irish captaincy and was a worthy successor to two of the shrewdest Irish captains of an earlier age, Louis Magee at the turn of the century and Ernie Crawford in the 1920s. And any comparison must take account of the fact that the evolution of the game may have made Mullen's task more difficult than those of his two illustrious predecessors.

Kyle, every inch an athlete, stamped his class and authority on the international scene in 1947 when the championship series was resumed and if, as yet, the greatness soon to emerge was not revealed in all its full bloom during the 1947 campaign, the potential was there for all to see.

In January 1947 international rugby was restored to the calendar in its full official form when France met and beat Scotland in Paris. Ireland's first match that year was against France in Dublin on 25 January, and the journey from representative to international rugby was not smoothly made by the Irish, who lost by 12 points to 8. Con Murphy of Lansdowne was the only player who survived from the pre-war era. Although Ireland lost, there were plenty of players in the Irish side that day who would be around in sunnier times. Barney Mullan, on the left wing, had come from the same club, Clontarf, as that flier Fred Moran, whom the war deprived of anything up to twenty more caps. Kyle was at out-half, and the nucleus of a great pack was on view, with Karl Mullen being propped on one side by M.R. Neeley and on the other by a formidable figure in stature and accomplishment, John Christopher Daly, who for much of the war period had been engaged in battles of a very different nature on the high seas. Colm Callan, a tough and uncompromising second-row from Lansdowne, Bob Agar from Malone and Bill McKay, another medical student from Queen's University, all wrote the preface to greater things that day before the enthusiastic gathering that had assembled at Lansdowne Road.

The French did not in those days attract the capacity attendances that gathered at the shrine when England and Wales were the visitors, though later French teams were of sufficient skill to be greeted by the 'house full' sign in Dublin.

The defeat by France induced no feeling of depression among Irish supporters nor panic decisions among the Irish selectors for the next assignment, the match scheduled against England at Lansdowne Road on 8 February. Ireland brought in a newcomer on the right wing, Bertie O'Hanlon of Dolphin, and his was one of many fine contributions to an Irish victory of historic proportions. His play was clearly of sufficient character and skill to suggest that greater things were at hand.

Ireland won by 22 points to nil, and there never had been, nor has there been since, an Irish victory over England by so wide a margin.

The Irish forwards had hustled and harried the French a fortnight earlier before eventually yielding territory and possession to a heavier French eight, who capitalised on an injury to Karl Mullen. But in the match against England there was no injury, and from start to finish the Irish pack gave England a roasting. Kyle, partnered by his university colleague Ernie Strathdee, was magnificent at half-back and the backs responded splendidly to the service laid on for them. Barney Mullan with two tries, two conversions and a penalty goal contributed thirteen points to Ireland's total, O'Hanlon scored two tries and McKay one.

After this great victory Con Murphy's long and successful career as a full-back, small in size but a giant in performance, came to an end. He was replaced by Dudley Higgins and the captaincy passed to J.D. Monteith, one of the Irish centres.

Fortified by that astounding win over England, Ireland faced Scotland at Murrayfield a fortnight later and justified the confidence they carried. In bitter cold and on a snow-bound pitch, Barney Mullan's unconverted try in the closing stages proved decisive.

That victory at Murrayfield set up a Triple Crown opportunity yet again, and Ireland's task against Wales was to be at Swansea, where Ireland had not won since 1889, five years before their first Triple Crown success. Ireland included a new cap for the game, Michael Lane of University College, Cork, who made his debut as a centre, although his experience and talents were more suited to the wing. Once again Swansea proved a place of doom and gloom for Ireland and her supporters. Ireland did reasonably well in the first half, at the end of which there was no score. Then W.E. Tamplin of Cardiff landed a penalty goal for Wales, who held the lead in precarious fashion until the genius of Haydn Tanner, the brilliant Welsh scrum half, was utilised to open the way for a try near the end. So Wales had managed to blight Irish hopes once more for the fifth time since 1930 and for the eighth time in all. But the Welsh sceptre was soon to be removed from over the

Irish head. Ireland would lay the Swansea bogey, and many of the players who walked dejectedly from the St Helen's ground were soon to return to the territory and not have to make the journey to the pavilion by their own resources when the battle was over.

The Australian team which visited Britain, Ireland and France in the 1947–48 season, came as the Third Wallabies but they were, in fact, only the second fully representative side from Australia, for the Second Wallabies came and went in 1939 without playing a match. One of the 1939 team, W.M. McLean, came back in the autumn of 1947 as captain of these first post-war tourists. A broken leg sustained in the sixth match of the tour ended McLean's active participation for the duration, but despite his absence Australia beat England, Scotland and Ireland.

That match against Ireland in Dublin on 6 December, proved a bitter disappointment, for Ireland was comprehensively beaten by 16 points to 3. Not even the stimulus of an early penalty goal, kicked by Kevin Quinn, a player who for some reason could not reveal in international games the full extent of his immense talents, succeeded in lifting the Irish. The Australians also played Ulster and Munster and found that both these teams, especially the latter, provided much stiffer opposition to their ability than had the national side.

Neither O'Hanlon nor Mullan, each of whom had contributed so handsomely the previous season, were in the Irish side. The wings were Des McKee, later in the season to solve a problem in the centre, and Kevin O'Flanagan, an all-round sportsman of truly astonishing versatility if not every man's idea of the complete rugby player. O'Flanagan was also a soccer international and a champion athlete, and he later turned his attention to golf with no little success. His brother Michael later also made one appearance for a later Irish side and he, too, was a soccer international. Thus if the O'Flanagan brothers both had a short tenure in the Irish rugby team, the fact that both were capped at rugby and soccer was a unique double.

Ireland met France at Colombes on New Year's Day 1948 in the first match of the international championship and to general surprise gained a decisive victory by two goals and a try (13 points to 6). Less than a month previously, ten of those who played at Colombes had been in the side against Australia. But the display in Paris was in complete contrast to the performance against Australia. Barney Mullan was back in the threequarter line, as was O'Hanlon, and the centre positions were taken by McKee and the Garryowen man Paddy Reid, who had made his debut against Australia. In the pack Colm Callan was recalled to the second row, and among other changes was the inclusion of a new cap at wing forward, Jim McCarthy of Dolphin. His arrival had an instant impact on the quality of play, and on that day he formed with Bill McKay a useful partnership that was to become devastatingly effective when the back row unit included the Old Belvederian Des O'Brien. McKay was a tackler of the highest quality, McCarthy an opportunist who brought a new concept to wing forward play and who was to prove the principal agent of Kyle's plan for breaching the opposing cover. The team lacked penetration in the centre but played to the strength of a superb pack of forwards.

That win in Paris was the prelude to the finest accomplishments in the whole history of Irish rugby. The teamwork of the Irish side was at almost its greatest pitch of perfection and was ready to be exploited to the full, first by Jack Kyle and later by Karl Mullen. The finishing touches to the team's composition were made when Mullen took over in time for the next game against England, and until then Kyle was able to achieve the desired dominance by his superb improvisation and by skilfully manipulating his forwards' rhythm and control.

The terminology of rugby, like much else, has changed today. In 1948 there was no talk of second-phase attack, nor of good ball. Ireland won two Triple Crowns by what today would be termed second-phase attack but which then was referred to as a magnificent pack of forwards, as well as the ability of others to eliminate error and grab opportunity when it presented itself in the shape of penalty goal chances and try-scoring opportunities—to say nothing of the sheer genius of Jack Kyle, surely among the greatest of all rugby players.

In Jim McCarthy Ireland had the ideal ally to Kyle, once the ball came back on the Irish side. Barney Mullan (like George Norton in the following year) was a place kicker who had full mastery of his craft. Daly, injured early in the season, was recalled for the game against England, and despite the win over France, Strathdee lost the scrum-half berth to Hugh de Lacy and the captaincy to Karl Mullen. Des O'Brien came in at number eight, Daly was restored to the front row in place of Jim Corcoran of UCC, and Jack Mattsson of Wanderers was at full-back.

D.R. Gent, the former English international who was for many years a highly-respected rugby correspondent for *The Times,* was one of many impressed by Ireland's 11–10 win over England at Twickenham on 14 February 1948. 'A great Irish side this and a great victory,' he wrote.

McKee, Kyle and McKay scored tries and Mullan converted one, and that was enough for the needs of the hour.

Scotland at Lansdowne Road was the next assignment, and the visiting side included no fewer than three pre-war internationals, one of whom, W.C. Murdoch, had first been capped in 1935. Ireland restored Dudley Higgins to full-back and had Michael O'Flanagan in the centre for Paddy Reid. Victory for Ireland against Scotland meant that Ireland would win the championship irrespective of how they fared later against Wales. And victory came, following a faltering and nervous first half. Kyle scored a magnificent try which assured success after Barney Mullan had given Ireland the lead with a similar effort after the interval. So Ireland were champions for the first time since 1935 and the championship was won at Lansdowne Road for the first and only time in history.

Ireland faced the supreme test when they lined out at Ravenhill against Wales in front of a capacity crowd of 30,000 on 13 March 1948. Had there been room to accommodate another 100,000, it is safe to assume that the capacity would still have been stretched to the limit, such interest was there in the game. A championship had been won, and Ireland were meeting Wales for the Triple Crown and the grand slam. Karl Mullen, recalling what it was like in the Irish dressing-room that March day, said:

> We were tense and anxious, yet I knew, and the players knew, we could win. The whole team discussed tactics, the Welsh strengths and what we thought were their weaknesses. And that was a procedure that we always went through. Every man had his say, it was an important part of the pre-match preparations in a side whose hall-mark was team spirit. Forward supremacy was all-important and we knew we had to win in the pack if victory was to be ours. The atmosphere was tremendous. The realisation that we could win the Triple Crown came first, I think, after the win over England at Twickenham. The main worry we had before the match in Belfast was that things might go wrong on the day and that old Welsh bogey would assert itself once more.
>
> We decided on a policy of seeking to win through our forwards and the genius of Jack Kyle, undoubtedly one of the great players of any era. A plentiful supply of possession for the Welsh, we felt, would probably mean disaster for they had a splendid back line and we feared three players in particular, Haydn Tanner, Bleddyn Williams and Ken Jones.
>
> A little incident just after the kick-off inspired great confidence in me. Barney Mullan took a penalty that went just over the Welsh full-back

Frank Trott's shoulder and trickled into touch near the Welsh line. For some reason, I felt then that this was going to be our day.

There is a widely held belief that apart from Kyle, our backline was not good. It is an opinion that I do not subscribe to. Kyle was certainly the master outside the scrum, but the defensive qualities of the backs were excellent, and that day in Belfast Paddy Reid and Des McKee were magnificent in defence and did not give Bleddyn Williams an inch. Our defence behind the scrum was invariably good, even if the attacking ability was a little limited.

At half-time the score was 3–3, with Bleddyn Williams having scored a great try to bring Wales level after Barney Mullan had given us the lead with a try when he took a long pass from Kyle in full flight. Rhys Stephens had been giving us a lot of trouble in the line-out and Jimmy Nelson was given the job of subduing him. Nelson well and truly performed his task. The 'council of war' we held at the interval gave us a lift and we were, I believe, the better team in the second half.

When J.C. Daly got the try in the second half that gave us the lead, the whole team played like men possessed. In the closing stages Kyle used the touchline superbly and we felt that we had only to avoid doing something rash. We held out to the final whistle and when that went, there was, initially, only a dim realisation that we had won the Triple Crown.

Dim the realisation may have been, but within seconds Karl Mullen and his fourteen heroes had to bear the full brunt of long-pent-up emotions. Few in the crowd at Ravenhill had seen Ireland's last triumph forty-nine years earlier. Souvenir-hunters of an historic victory made Chris Daly the primary target, and as he left the field shoulder-high the shirt was stripped from his back. Daly, who had started the season with a bad injury that threatened to end his career, was not to play for Ireland again as he turned professional after the Triple Crown triumph. As a league player he revealed the athletic ability that had made him a priceless asset to Ireland.

That match against Wales was not vintage rugby, but it was a champagne occasion, a long-cherished dream realised. It was a just reward for effort and ability, for determination and character.

Nine of the team in Belfast had played in all four matches in the championship: Bertie O'Hanlon, Des McKee, Barney Mullan, Jack Kyle, A.A. McConnell (a strong and durable prop from Collegians), Colm Callan, Karl Mullen, Jim McCarthy and Bill McKay. Three more had played in the three Triple Crown matches: Jimmy Nelson, Des

The Story of Irish Rugby

O'Brien and Chris Daly. Dudley Higgins, injured for the game against England, had played against France, Scotland and Wales; Paddy Reid had played against France, England and Wales; Hugh de Lacy against England and Scotland; and Ernie Strathdee against France, after which game he was surprisingly dropped in favour of de Lacy, though he was recalled for the Welsh match. Jack Mattsson, Mick O'Flanagan, Ernie Keeffe, a fine forward from Sunday's Well, who was yet another player deprived by the war of further honours, Jimmy Corcoran and Bob Agar had all played in one game each, Mattsson against England, and Agar, Corcoran and Keeffe against France.

Thus twenty-four players contributed to Ireland's success and attained a level of achievement without equal either before or since. It was the privilege of a Corkman, the late Teddy McGrath, to be president of the union in that season of triumph, one that gave a tremendous stimulus to the game in Ireland. Meanwhile as Karl Mullen's men carved out their path of glory, time caught up with four stalwarts who had served nobly in an earlier age. In the space of six weeks, and at the height of Ireland's glory, four Irish internationals died: John Fulton, who had played against England in the 1899 Triple Crown-winning year and who had in all played sixteen times for Ireland; Mossie Landers, like Fulton an accomplished full-back in the early 1900s; Bertie Doran, one of the three brothers from the Lansdowne club to play for Ireland; and Eddie McCarthy, who was in the Irish team against Wales in Limerick in 1898. They may not have been in full accord with all the concepts of the game as played in 1948, but they would undoubtedly have appreciated Mullen's men and rejoiced in their deeds.

Ireland opened the 1949 campaign in the role of defending champions, secure in the knowledge that the great majority of the championship-winning team was still at hand. Two exceptions were Chris Daly and Paddy Reid, both of whom joined the Rugby League. Once again they were team-mates, but in the cause of the Huddersfield club.

Ireland included four new caps for the first assignment of the 1949 campaign. One of the newcomers who faced France at Lansdowne Road on 29 January was full-back George Norton. His advent to international status did not have happy consequences on his initial appearance, but the benefits of his presence would be gained in the immediate future. With Daly gone, there was a vacancy at prop forward and the selectors turned to another Munsterman, Tom Clifford from

Sir Ewart Bell (president IRFU 1986-87). He is a former Ireland international and former Ireland selector

The Dublin University team of 1866-67 pictured in College Park. This is the earliest photograph of any Irish rugby team in existence

Second time around. The gay nineties were very productive for Ireland and this side led by Louis Magee won the Triple Crown and Championship by beating Wales in Cardiff in 1899. *Back row, left to right:* W. Byron, M. Ryan, J. Sealy, J. Ryan, C. Moriarty, A. Meares. *Sitting:* J. McIlwaine, E. Campbell, J. M. Lyttle, L. Magee (capt), G. Allen, C. Reid, J. Harman. *Front:* G. P. Doran, P. O'Brien-Butler

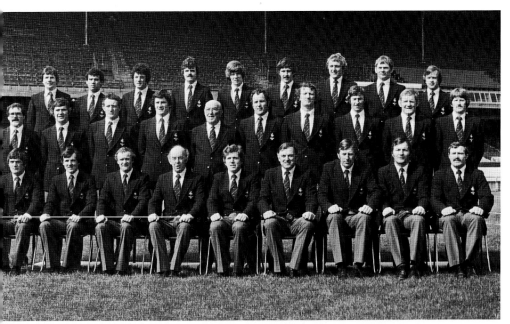

The Ireland party that toured Australia in the summer of 1979 and created history by becoming the first of the countries to win a Test series in the southern hemisphere. They beat Australia 2-0 in the Test series. *Back row, right:* T. Kennedy, T. Ward, R. O'Donnell, A. McLennan, O. Campbell, F. Ennis, A. McLean, C. Fitzgerald, tterson. *Middle row:* P. Andreucetti, C. Cantillon, N. Byrne, J. O'Driscoll, Dr T. O'Connell (medical officer), ley, W. Duggan, D. Irwin, G. McLoughlin, P. McNaughton. *Front row:* P. Whelan, J. Moloney, M. Gibson, ffey (manager), F. Slattery (capt), N. Murphy (coach), M. Keane, H. Steele, P. Orr

ve: The Ireland team that toured Japan in the summer of 1985, winning all five matches played. It was Ireland's our to Japan. *Back row, left to right:* B. Mullin, P. Matthews, P. Collins, P. Kenny, B. Spillane, W. Anderson, cCall, J. McCoy, N. Carr, H. Harbison. *Middle row:* K. Crossan, R. Brady, M. Bradley, P. Kennedy, itzpatrick, P. Rainey, M. Finn, T. McMaster, R. Keyes. *Front row:* P. Orr, T. Ringland, D. Lenihan, J. Gallagher ical officer), D. McKibbin (manager and president of the IRFU 1985-86), C. Fitzgerald (capt), Mick Doyle ch), H. MacNeill, M. Kiernan, P. Dean

The only seven players in history who have played for
Ireland at all four levels, at which the country has
participated: Schools, Under 23, 'B' and full
international. *Above left:* Jimmy Bowen (PBC, Cork and
Constitution), *above right:* Donal Spring (Cistercian
Roscrea, Dublin University and Lansdowne); *right:* Jim
McCoy (Portora Royal School, Dungannon and Bangor);
above: Moss Finn (PBC, Cork, UCC and Constitution)

Left: Harry Harbison (Blackrock College, UCD and Bective Rangers); *above left:* Brian McCall (Armagh Royal School, Queen's University and London Irish); *above:* Donal Lenihan (CBC Cork, UCC and Constitution)

Above: Five great Ireland forwards in action during the season of triumph in 1982. The front row trio are Gerry McLoughlin, Ciaran Fitzgerald and Philip Orr, with behind John O'Driscoll *(left)* and Moss Keane

Right: Pointing the way to victory: Ciaran Fitzgerald, the man who led Ireland out of the wilderness in 1982 when he captained the side that won the Triple Crown and Championship. He led the Lions in New Zealand in 1983 and was at the helm again when Ireland captured the Triple Crown and Championship in 1985

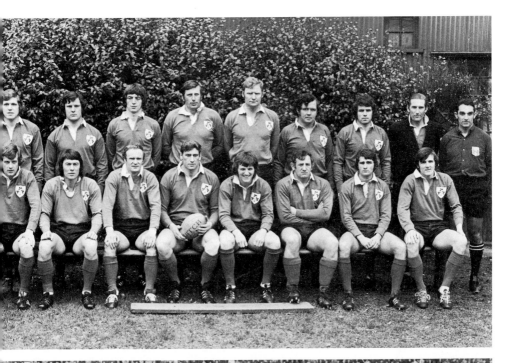

he Ireland team that won the International
pionship in 1974, Ireland's first win in the
ionship since 1951. *Back row, left to right:*
ery, S. McKinney, T. Grace, M. Keane, T. Moore,
ch, D. Milliken, P. Darcy (touch judge), R. Palmade
e). *Front row:* A. Ensor, K. Kennedy, M. Gibson,
IcBride (capt), M. Quinn, R. McLoughlin,
Master, J. Moloney

Above: United We Stand. The Ireland team that won the
Triple Crown and Championship in 1985, seen here
linking arms in Cardiff as a gesture of defiance and
solidarity prior to the match against Wales. *Left to right:*
C. Fitzgerald (capt), J. McCoy, W. Anderson,
P. Matthews, D. Lenihan, M. Kiernan, N. Carr, P. Orr,
K. Crossan, H. MacNeill, B. Mullin, M. Bradley,
T. Ringland, B. Spillane

Top: Two of the greats of Irish rugby and central figures in the Lions triumph in South Africa in 1974. Willie John McBride *(left)* and Syd Millar, outside the room in the Ballymena clubhouse named in honour of the club's most famous sons

Top: Ireland's most successful captain: Karl Mullen, who led Ireland to unprecedented success in 1948 and 1949 when the Triple Crown and Championship were won both years under his leadership, with Ireland's only grand slam being completed in 1948. Mullen also captained the team to win the Championship in 1951 and led the Lions in Australia and New Zealand in 1950

Above: Ray McLoughlin, capped forty times for Ireland, twice a Lions tourist and a man who brought a new concept to captaincy when he led Ireland in the mid 1960s

Above: Tom Kiernan, capped fifty-four times for Ireland at full back and captain of Ireland on twenty-four occasions, a record. He captained the Lions in South Africa in 1968, Ireland in Australia in 1967 and Ireland in Argentina in 1970. He coached the Munster team that beat the All Blacks in Limerick in 1978 and then coached the Ireland side that won the Triple Crown and International Championship in 1982. This was Ireland's first Triple Crown success since 1949. Now a member of the IRFU Executive Committee, he was elected junior vice president of the IRFU in June 1986

the Young Munster club, and a very fortunate choice he turned out to be. The international careers of the other two caps were of shorter duration. Tom Cullen, at scrum-half, made his only international appearance that season against France. Two seasons earlier he had been selected for the international side but was unable to play. The fourth newcomer to the side came into the problem spot on the team, the centre. He appeared to have a most unlikely background, for he was a Roman Catholic priest. Father Tom Gavin of London Irish did not have a lengthy or distinguished international career, but is unique in so far as he is the only Catholic priest ever to have been capped for Ireland.

It was once again a case of the unpredictable Irish when France were entertained in 1949. Ireland had opened the previous season by being well beaten by the Australians, and yet had gone on to take the Triple Crown and championship. This time a French team which had lost earlier to Scotland travelled to Dublin and won by two goals and two dropped goals (16 points) to three penalty goals (9 points), a scoreline that revealed almost the full range of the scoring system, but one that was an anti-climax for the Irish after their previous fine performances. George Norton kicked all three penalties for Ireland. Had the game taken place in the previous season, Ireland's margin of defeat would have been two points wider, but the International Board, in their wisdom, had reduced the value of the dropped goal from four points to three, a happy decision that went some way towards putting that particular facet of scoring into something approaching its proper perspective in relation to the try.

Despite the reverse against France, Ireland once again went on to win the championship and the Triple Crown, with which legendary honour the French were not of course concerned.

From the French match onwards, Ireland had the best pack of forwards, notably in the set scrums, in support of the outstanding hooker of the age, Karl Mullen, and the best out-half, Jack Kyle. The Kyle-Strathdee partnership was restored for the game against England, a match in which the threequarter line was moderate with Gavin unable to provide the thrust the line needed. The wing positions were occupied by O'Hanlon and Mick Lane who, having been capped in 1947 as a centre, now found his natural environment. Clifford, a forward in the typical Munster mould, tough and uncompromising, proved an able ally to Mullen in the front row.

Norton's three penalty goals against France had made no difference to the end product, but such was not the case against England. He kicked two in the first half of that match, when a try by O'Hanlon gave Ireland a 9–5 lead, at the interval. Norton brought his points total to seventeen in two matches when he converted a second-half try by Des McKee, and Ireland won comfortably by 14 points to 5. And if the Irish display was not of a quality that appeared to presage another title, the win over England was important, not least in psychological terms.

Callan and McConnell were both omitted for the game against Scotland at Murrayfield. Ireland also replaced Gavin, bringing in a youngster from Queen's University, Noel Henderson. He had been a brilliant schools player and emerged on the senior representative scene that season in the Ulster team. His first cap against Scotland was the start of a brilliant international career that extended over the next decade, and his presence in the 1949 series turned a moderate threequarter line into what was at least now an ample force. In the pack Bob Agar took over from Callan in the second row and Les Griffin of Wanderers came in at prop for McConnell.

By the time Ireland reached Murrayfield, Scotland had championship aspirations, having beaten both France and Wales. However, they proved no match for the Irish side. George Norton again made a rich contribution, scoring a penalty goal and two conversions. The Kyle-McCarthy combination bedevilled the Scots, McCarthy getting both the Irish tries. Scotland's only reply was a penalty goal.

Ireland took an unchanged side to Swansea on 12 March for a match in which both the Triple Crown and the championship were at stake. The Welsh side had shown erratic form and their selectors had therefore brought back the experienced Billy Cleaver for Glyn Davies at out-half. The crucial score came before half-time. Kyle began a brilliant tactical movement which culminated in a try for Ireland, scored, as so often, by McCarthy. Norton then converted it to register the full five points. It was the only score of the match. The Triple Crown was Ireland's once again.

Ireland owed much to McCarthy that day, for quite apart from his try, he did a most effective spoiling job on the Welsh half-backs. Kyle had made a remarkable blind side break, which he turned to full account by a cleverly lofted kick inwards over the heads of the converging defence. McCarthy's speed of thought and movement did the rest. Jumping high for the ball just short of the Welsh goal-line, he defeated the desperate efforts of several defenders to prevent him from scoring.

The try was the reward for enterprise and thought, qualities that epitomised the play of McCarthy and (even more so) of Kyle. Kyle not only possessed excellent hands and a fine turn of speed, but also had the facility for knowing just the right moment to seek and make the breaks. He was the outstanding back of that entire championship series, in which Ireland used nineteen players. Only three times previously had the Triple Crown been won by the same country in successive seasons: England won it in 1913 and 1914 and achieved the double again in 1923 and 1924, as did Wales in 1908 and 1909.

It was a happy Irish party that returned to their headquarters at Porthcawl to celebrate the victory and to enjoy the festivities arranged by the president of the union, Sarsfield Hogan, who had been a selector when Ireland had won the championship fourteen years earlier. George Norton had more reason than most for celebration, for he could reflect on a contribution of twenty-six out of the forty-one points Ireland had scored in the championship. That total was a record for an Irish player in one season and stood until 1973, when Ireland's out-half Barry McGann contributed twenty-eight points, also in four matches, though one of these was against New Zealand.

The 1950 international season was surrounded by a time-worn argument about the eligibility of players. The controversy basically concerned England, who fielded what amounted to a Dominions team liberally sprinkled with South Africans and including one All-Black. The question of proper qualification had never been solved, or indeed really faced, except by Ireland. Agreement of a kind was reached towards the end of the season, when it was decided that no overseas player could be offered a cap once he had played for his own country, but that hardly settled the matter, especially at a time when the number of outstanding Dominion players resident in Britain was increasing rapidly. Ireland thus remained in almost splendid isolation by the IRFU's long-standing unwritten agreement to select only players of Irish birth (or at least one Irish parent) who had never appeared in a trial for another country.

On the playing field, Wales relieved Ireland of both Triple Crown and championship, and Ireland achieved a win and a draw in the four matches. It was little consolation to Ireland that Wales paid her the compliment of imitation, winning the series by close co-operation among the forwards and halves, supported by the opportunism of those behind. One notable divergence from Irish practice, however, was that Wales possessed adroitness in the centre that had not been at Ireland's disposal. Nowhere was it used more effectively than at Ravenhill on 11 March 1950, when Wales won by 6 points to 3, Ken Jones and Malcolm

Thomas getting tries for Wales, while George Norton kicked a penalty goal for Ireland.

Ireland's first match of this season was played in arctic conditions in Paris. Ireland included two new caps, J.H. Burges, a scrum-half from Rosslyn Park, and the Instonians man Des McKibbin, whose selection to prop forward position strengthened still further the family tradition in Irish rugby, for his brother Harry, the centenary president, had been a centre for Ireland and the Lions before the war.

It was a penalty goal by Burges in the last minute that earned Ireland a draw after France had held on grimly to a three points lead, established by means of a dropped goal by their out-half P. Lauga. Lauga had taken three drop shots at goal during that first half; apart from the one that counted, another also went over the bar, but as the whistle had gone for off-side, the goal was disallowed. Adding some weight to the opinion that Ireland had been extremely lucky were the facts that Jean Prat had missed a penalty from in front of the posts and the full-back R. Arcalis had hit a post with a superb drop kick in the second half. It was an unimpressive start to Ireland's championship defence and Jim McCarthy's absence was sorely felt.

An injury to Des McKee, which forced him to leave the field for good at half-time, was something that Ireland could not afford against England at Twickenham, and Bill McKay's removal from the pack to fill the void at centre was another change that the Irish pack could ill afford. England won the match, yet the margin of their victory was a narrow one, 3 points to nil. Nevertheless, it ended all hopes of the hat-trick of championship and Triple Crown success that so many had expected Ireland to achieve.

Ireland, with three new caps in the side, demolished Scotland by 21 points to nil at Lansdowne Road a fortnight later, an event that did not go unnoticed in Wales, whose team did not face the prospect at Ravenhill with any degree of equanimity. As it transpired, Wales won at Ravenhill, and deservedly so, but had to endure periods of intense danger before getting home by two tries to a penalty goal. Jim McCarthy was back after missing three games through injury, but this time Wales managed to circumvent the Kyle-McCarthy link.

In the summer of 1950 the first British and Irish side to go on an overseas tour since the war left for New Zealand, and Ireland's accomplishments in the recent past were reflected in the choice of Karl Mullen as captain. Eight Irishmen accompanied him. George Norton, Michael Lane, Noel Henderson and Jack Kyle were among the backs, a clear indication of the selectors' awareness that not all the talents of the Triple Crown sides were hidden in the heart of the scrum. Tom Clifford, Jimmy Nelson, Bill McKay and Jim McCarthy were the Irish representation in the forward line-up.

Not for those tourists the quick jet-flight that takes today's teams across the world in little more than a day. They went by boat and had to endure a rough passage on the initial stages of the voyage. On the field the demands were no less severe and New Zealand won the Test series by three games to nil with one drawn. George Norton broke an arm while playing against Southland at Inver-cargill during the sixth match of the tour and took no further part in the proceedings. Karl Mullen was also injured and did not play in the third and fourth Tests.

The 1950–51 season was one in which the form of participants varied to an astonishing degree throughout the series. But for Ireland all ended happily, for the title was regained. Mullen again proved an able captain and his educated foot-work ensured a smooth service for Kyle, who still revealed the form that had captivated the New Zealand public, perhaps the most discerning critics in the rugby world. Kyle was a real match-winner and match-saver.

When Ireland played France at Lansdowne Road on 29 January 1951 fortune was on the side of the home team. The side included four new caps: C.S. Griffin on the right wing, R.R. Chambers in the centre, J.H. Smith of Queen's University at prop, and John O'Meara of UCC at scrum-half. O'Meara was in the side after the original choice, Hubie McCracken, had withdrawn because of an attack of pleurisy. They were surrounded by experience and expertise, and tries by Jimmy Nelson and Tom Clifford and a penalty goal from Noel Henderson saw Ireland safely through by one point (9–8).

Ireland selected the same side for the game against England at Lansdowne Road, but Michael Lane had to withdraw because of a broken rib. His defection brought in a new cap, the Queen's University player Harry Millar. It also brought to a total of five the Queen's University representation on the side. (The other four were Henderson, now firmly established in the centre, Kyle at out-half, and Bill McKay and Smith in the pack). Des McKibbin, operating in the second row, kicked a penalty goal in the second half and that sufficed to decide the issue in a game notable for excitement rather than quality.

An injury to George Norton after fifteen minutes of the match against Scotland at Murrayfield did not augur well for Ireland's Triple Crown chances, but Millar played heroically at full-back and, with

McKay on the wing, the seven Irish forwards performed splendidly. But once again it was primarily Kyle's brilliance that saw Ireland through. He opened the way for the match-winning try ten minutes from the end, and Des O'Brien applied the finishing touch to Kyle's break. McKibbin missed the conversion, but Ireland held on to a 6–5 lead. Noel Henderson had dropped a goal in the first half which had cut Scotland's advantage at the time to 5–3. It was no mean achievement to leave Murrayfield with victory after playing for sixty-five minutes with fourteen players.

That was Norton's last appearance for Ireland. His place for the Triple Crown match against Wales went to Aengus McMorrow of Garryowen; McMorrow, who played for Connacht, was the first man from that province to be capped in the post-war era. Tom Clifford, too, had gone, and McKibbin had moved to the front row for the game against Scotland. J.R. Brady of CIYMS came into the second row to form a new partnership with Paddy Lawler of Clontarf. A 3–3 draw against Wales in Cardiff on 10 March gave Ireland the championship, but not the Triple Crown. Norton's absence was never more sorely felt, for three kickers failed to take opportunity with chances ranging from the reasonable to the simple. The scoring pattern was decided in the first twenty minutes with Ben Edwards kicking a penalty for Wales and Kyle equalising with a great try for Ireland. The second half was a battle between the forwards, with the monotony broken by the attempts of Kyle and his opponent on the Welsh side, Cliff Morgan, to find a way through tight defensive cover. That was the first confrontation between Kyle and Morgan, later to emerge as one of the game's great outside halves.

The golden years were now over, but despite a defeat at the hands of the Fourth Springboks in Dublin on 8 December, Ireland went to Colombes and defeated France by 11 points to 8 early in 1952. Ireland's performance against the Springboks had been of reasonable dimensions, and with Clifford now back in the pack and a most promising second row from Ulster, Robin Thompson, having made an impressive debut against South Africa, Ireland looked capable of taking any opposition up front. And Kyle was still a master of his craft at out-half. Tries by Henderson and McCarthy, a penalty goal from Henderson and a conversion by a new cap, Jack Notley, added up to more than the French could handle. The victory nurtured hopes that were not, however, realised.

The match against England was scheduled to take place at

Twickenham on 9 February but was postponed to 29 March because of the death of King George VI. So Scotland was to provide the next examination for Ireland in Dublin on 23 February and with Notley now in the centre and two new caps, Mick Dargan of Old Belvedere at flank forward and Archie O'Leary of Cork Constitution in the second row, Ireland met the needs of the occasion and won by 12 points to 8.

Lansdowne Road on 8 March provided proof that Ireland had reached the end of a glorious era, for Wales completely outplayed the home side and won even more decisively than the 14 points to 3 on the scoreboard suggested. It was Karl Mullen's last match for Ireland, for he lost his place for the rearranged game against England at Twickenham on 29 March. His replacement, Robin Roe, proved a worthy successor to Mullen as a hooker. Ireland gambled with five new caps at Twickenham for, in addition to Roe, there were two newcomers in the pack, Paddy Kavanagh and Billy O'Neill both from UCD, the club which also provided a new wing, Mick Hillary. The name Bailey figured on an Irish side yet again when Noel Bailey of Northampton was picked for the threequarter line.

Des O'Brien took over the leadership from Mullen, but his tenure of office did not start in the winning vein, as England defeated Ireland by 3 points to nil. The whole did not add up to a memorable season for Ireland, but there had been satisfactory features. The high spot of the season had undoubtedly been the win at Colombes. This took on added significance later, for twenty years were to elapse before an Irish team was able to manage a similar feat at the ground. Munster, too, had put up a tremendous display against the Springboks, maintaining their great tradition of fighting qualities against touring sides.

14
Low intensity operations
1952–59

Only once in history had an Irish team embarked on an overseas tour. Fifty-three years after that initial crusade an Irish side, captained by Des O'Brien and with Sarsfield Hogan as manager, undertook the second mission, this time to Argentina. It was not unexplored rugby territory, for three times previously the English Rugby Union had sponsored tours, while two years before the Irish visit the full strength of France had played Argentina at Buenos Aires. Several landing players, such as Mullen, Kyle and Henderson, were not available for inclusion. If Kyle's absence did nothing else, it gave an opportunity to the man who had stood in his shadow for Ulster and Ireland, the Instonians outhalf John Hewitt. Hewitt was later to gain the elusive Irish cap, but a total of four appearances for Ireland hardly bore testimony to an ability that would have been more widely recognised had he not been unfortunate enough to be of the same era as Kyle. Hewitt later had the task of sorting out similar difficulties himself as chairman of the Irish selection committee in 1973–74.

Those whose task it was to choose the party for the Argentine in 1952 originally settled on a combination that included fourteen internationals, but defections reduced the number of capped players who eventually travelled to thirteen, one of whom, Michael Dargan, was not an original choice. The party also included a referee, Mr O.B. Glasgow and, as secretary to the manager, Billy Jeffares, who was soon to succeed his father R.W. Jeffares as secretary of the IRFU. The team and officials left Dublin on 20 July. The first match was played in Santiago, Chile, and resulted in a 30–0 win for the Irish.

Argentina was in a sombre mood when Ireland's rugby tourists arrived in Buenos Aires, where the people were still mourning the recent death of Eva Péron, the wife of the Argentinian president, an event that had threatened to put the tour in jeopardy.

Ireland, plagued by injuries and with limited scoring power, won six, drew two and lost one of the nine matches played. This was quite a respectable performance against unexpectedly strong opposition. Ireland won one and drew one of the two Test matches and ended the tour with a record of having scored 126 points and conceded 43. John Hewitt was the star performer among the Irish backs in a side that lost some prestige by a defeat early in the tour, but largely regained it before the expedition ended.

For the players and officials the tour was a most enjoyable experience and the 'Shamrocks', as the team was called, served a worthy purpose in supporting the game in South America. The large Irish community in Buenos Aires were pleased to have a chance of seeing and supporting a national team from the homeland.

The South American journey over, the prospects on the home front were not reviewed with a confidence similar to that which had preceded the championship series in recent years. The doubts in the minds of the Irish supporters were confirmed in a series in which Ireland used nineteen players and awarded nine new caps. Ireland beat France and Scotland, but could only draw with England and lost to Wales. Among the newcomers to the side was yet another forward in the true Munster tradition, Tom Reid of Garryowen; a splendid back row from UCD, Ronnie Kavanagh; and a wing from Bective Rangers, Maurice Mortell. Kavanagh's elevation added still further to the growing list of brothers who had been honoured for Ireland. He had laid his claims while in the Argentine, where he was accompanied by his brother Paddy, who had been capped in 1952.

Des O'Brien had gone and Kyle had taken over the leadership. McCarthy was still present and John O'Meara remained a fine link at scrum-half. But together with Mullen, O'Brien, Clifford and McKay, O'Meara played his last game against France in 1952. Now that these fine players were to be seen no more in the green jersey, much of the old zest was gone and as yet had not been recaptured. Nevertheless, a feature of the 1953 campaign was a resounding 26–8 win over Scotland; and Murrayfield, where once Eugene Davy had scored three tries and Paul Murray had kicked four conversions, witnessed another scoring feat by an Irishman when Séamus Byrne, a wing from UCD, signalled his entry to the international sphere by scoring three tries. It was not, however, the prelude to a long and distinguished career for he was capped but twice subsequently.

The Fourth All-Blacks came in the autumn of 1953, and the Irish got a glimpse of a powerful pack of forwards and one of the greatest of all full-backs, Bob Scott. They also got another beating from the New Zealanders. But the distinguished visitors, like so many touring teams before them, had discovered Munster territory to be ground where not an inch was given, and it took a last-minute try to avert the Munster challenge.

An Ireland team now took the field for the first time without the assistance of Kyle, for when England were encountered at Twickenham on 13 February 1953 Kyle had to withdraw because of injury. So at last John Hewitt got his chance. Despite Kyle's continued absence, Hewitt was omitted for the remaining games against Scotland (won 6–0 in Belfast) and Wales (lost 12–9 in Dublin). Ireland therefore ended the season with one win and four defeats, used twenty-seven players and awarded eight new caps, including a full-back later to give distinguished service, Paddy Berkery of Lansdowne and Garryowen.

Ireland achieved less than promised over the next three seasons. Kyle and Henderson were still in the team, but McCarthy had retired in 1954. In 1955 a young centre from Old Belvedere came on the scene in a match against France. Tony O'Reilly's red hair made him easy to identify on the field, while his physique made him a difficult opponent to stop. If he promised more than he attained in the Irish jersey, he emerged as one of the stars of the Lions tour to South Africa in the summer of 1955, when once again the Lions were captained and managed by Irishmen, Robin Thompson and Jack Siggins respectively. The side also included five Irish players, Thompson, Tom Reid and Robin Roe among the forwards, and O'Reilly and Cecil Pedlow, a recent recruit to the Irish side, among the backs.

Thompson and Siggins could reflect on a splendid tour during which their side drew the Test series by two wins to two and ended with a record of eighteen wins and a draw from twenty-four matches. O'Reilly amassed sixteen tries, a record number, and ended the tour as top scorer.

On the provincial front, the 1955–56 season was marked by Connacht's consolidation as a first-class rugby power. The reward for their honest endeavour and dedication was gathered in the form of a share in the interprovincial championship in 1956, when they divided the spoils with Ulster, having beaten Munster by 10 points to 3 in Cork to record their first victory on Munster soil. Connacht lost to Leinster, but ended the season with a splendid 6–3 win over Ulster at Ravenhill, where two years earlier they had scored their first victory away from home.

No really worthwhile challenge was mounted by Ireland for the

Triple Crown and championship during the remainder of Kyle's career, which came to an end in 1958 against Scotland in Dublin. Kyle won his forty-sixth cap that day to establish a world record of international appearances in matches involving the International Board countries and France. And if Kyle did not play at his brilliant best, at least he ended on the winning side. He had a new partner now, Andy Mulligan, who had come on the scene in 1956, thus becoming the eighth man to partner Kyle in international rugby.

A month previously Kyle had been a member of the first Irish team to beat a touring side when Australia was defeated by 9 points to 6 at Lansdowne Road. John O'Meara was recalled for the game after two seasons out of international rugby, and Ireland had six new caps in their side, including four who were later to render sterling service. One was the latest of the Hewitt clan, David. His father Tom had proved his worth in the 1920s and the son further embellished the family tradition. Among the five newcomers to the pack was Noel Murphy, another son of a famous father, also named Noel, who had been a stalwart in the Irish pack of the 1930s. Noel junior would go on to earn forty-one caps and captain his country. Two other new men were also future Irish captains: Bill Mulcahy in the second row and Ronnie Dawson, the hooker, for whom the honour was indeed at hand.

Dawson scored a try for Ireland on his debut against Australia, as did Pedlow. But the match was won for Ireland by the veteran Noel Henderson, who scored the all-important try that decided the issue in the closing minutes. Ireland had at last beaten a touring side and Kyle, who had been the biggest single contributor to the unprecedented run of success between 1948 and 1951, was appropriately in the first Irish side to accomplish such an historic victory. Henderson, his able right-hand man in so many of the glorious battles fought and won during the golden years, was the captain. The Irish team that beat Australia in 1958 was:

P.J. Berkery (London Irish)
A.J.F. O'Reilly (Old Belvedere)
N.J. Henderson (NIFC) capt.
D. Hewitt (Queen's University)
A.C. Pedlow (CIYMS)
J.W. Kyle (NIFC)
J.A. O'Meara (Dolphin)
B.G.M. Wood (Garryowen)

A.R. Dawson (Wanderers)
P.J. O'Donoghue (Bective Rangers)
J.A. Donaldson (Collegians)
W.A. Mulcahy (UCD)
N.A. Murphy (Cork Constitution)
J.R. Kavanagh (Wanderers)
J.B. Stevenson (Instonians)

It was no easy task to follow Kyle. The job fell to a player from Bohemians, Michael English, who was given a veteran partner in John O'Meara. Sadly, O'Meara ended his international career against Wales in 1958 by being carried from the field on a stretcher midway through the second half, after having scored a try, which together with a penalty goal from Henderson gave Ireland a 6–0 interval lead. But weight of numbers up front and the speed and thrust of the Welsh backs proved too much for Ireland, who conceded three tries in the second half. And with Henderson in the full-back position, the season ended with an 11–6 defeat in Paris.

The aura of greatness that surrounded the Irish team at the outset of the 1950s was not attendant upon the side that represented Ireland in the series of 1959. But if the side itself could not be classed as great, it contained great players. The leadership was given to Ronnie Dawson, the first sign of the team selectors' recognition of his depth of thought, tactical appreciation and knowledge of the game. Those attributes would grow with experience and be applied in a different capacity at a later date when international rugby came to take on a new meaning and when the strategy and, indeed, the very idiom of the game underwent a dramatic change.

Dawson was supported by two strong and able performers in Syd Millar and Gordon Wood, and if Ireland did not have the best team in 1959, they had probably the best front row, and arguably the best pack, since the Mullen era. Mulcahy and a new cap, Gerry Culliton, both of whom were to enjoy protracted careers, were in the second row, while Noel Murphy had the experience and craft of Ronnie Kavanagh and the exuberance and courage of a Connachtman, Tony O'Sullivan, as his back row colleagues.

The back line that faced England at Lansdowne Road in 1959 had a less settled look about it. Henderson was still filling in at full-back. O'Reilly was in the centre with another Conacht debutant, John Dooley, while the wings were occupied by the experienced Pedlow and

Niall Brophy, a fast and intelligent player who had enjoyed a brilliant schools career in the colours of Blackrock College and who was now a student at UCD. He had made a quiet entrance to the Irish side the year before, but greater things were in the offing. English and Mulligan were at half-back.

England blunted Triple Crown aspirations with a 3–0 win and David Hewitt was recalled for the game against Scotland at Murrayfield where an Irish victory was now looked upon almost as a divine right. Expectation was realised in the shape of an 8–3 win. John Hewitt, who in 1954 and 1956 had deputised for Kyle, got an unexpected opportunity to add to his caps total when a bout of influenza forced English to withdraw from the team to meet Wales in Cardiff. So Ireland once again took two Hewitts to Cardiff, as they had done in 1924, when a great victory had been gained against all the odds. History did not repeat itself on this occasion, however, as Wales won a narrow 8–6 victory.

But it was not Wales who was the dominant force of the season. That honour belonged to France, who, under the shrewd leadership of Lucien Mias, came to Dublin on 18 April as champions for the first time in history. They had beaten Scotland and Wales and drawn with England, and the five points thus amassed left them in an impregnable position. Victory over Ireland was naturally expected not alone by France but the rugby world at large, who now at last recognised France for what she was, a major rugby power.

Dawson and his forward colleagues kept up a sustained and furious attack that completely disconcerted the French pack and prevented them from weaving the pretty patterns that had destroyed earlier opposition. The backs responded, none more so than the nineteen-year-old new cap in the centre, Kevin Flynn of Wanderers. Flynn it was who made a brilliant break that laid on a try for Brophy during the first half. Then English, now restored to full health and vigour, scored a dropped goal which gave Ireland a 6–0 interval lead.

There was no way back for France when David Hewitt landed a penalty goal and a try from left wing J. Dupuy. A conversion from P. Lacaze was the only French consolation. So the fifties ended on a victorious note for Ireland. Noel Henderson made the last of his thirty-eight appearances in the Irish jersey, and with his retirement the last tangible link with the golden years was gone.

After the close of the European rugby season the Lions went to New Zealand and Australia. They travelled under the leadership of Ronnie

Dawson, just as almost ten years earlier they had been led by another Irish captain and hooker. The strength of the Irish pack was emphasised by the fact that Dawson was one of five Irish forwards selected, the others being prop forwards Gordon Wood and Syd Millar, second row Bill Mulcahy and wing forward Noel Murphy. Tony O'Reilly, David Hewitt, Niall Brophy, and Mick English were also included, while Andy Mulligan was sent out on an errand of mercy after the team had been hit by injuries. There were two serious casualties: English had to retire from the side after three games, and Brophy after only one. Tony O'Reilly, in contrast, played in more matches than any other player, twenty-four in all, and collected the massive haul of twenty-two tries. David Hewitt was top scorer, however, with 106 points, made up of twenty conversions, ten penalty goals and three tries. The Lions lost a wonderful Test series by three games to one, winning the last of the four internationals. They visited Canada on the way home.

So the fifties came to a close. There had been major changes at Lansdowne Road with the West Stand being completely reconstructed and the capacity of the ground increased to just over 50,000. Rupert Jeffares, the first secretary of the union, retired in 1951 and was succeeded by his son Billy, and it was Billy who helped organise the four-countries match that took place on 31 December 1955 to celebrate the opening of the new West Stand. The ceremony was performed by the president of the union, Harry Read, a man who had rendered such distinguished service on the field of play in an earlier and less organised era. England-Wales beat Ireland-Scotland by 18 points to 15. What was more important, the quality of the game was entirely in keeping with the occasion.

The fifties also saw the retirement of Harry Thrift as honorary secretary of the International Board. He announced his official departure from active participation at the board's annual meeting at Edinburgh on 17 March 1956. He was succeeded by yet another Irishman, Eddie Kirwan. Harry Thrift's connection with the game had extended over half a century; he had played a major role in the development of the game and was an international figure as a player and legislator. The IRFU marked his retirement by presenting him with a silver salver and the presidents of the English, Welsh and Scottish unions, together with the vice-president of the French Federation, were present at the ceremony which took place on the morning of the four-countries match in Dublin.

Rowland Hill of England, Aikman Smith of Scotland, Horace Lyne of Wales and R.G. Warren of Ireland had all played major roles in moulding rugby football. Harry Thrift was worthy to be ranked with that distinguished quartet. He died in February 1958. Another great Irish rugby man, John Macaulay, had died a few months earlier at the age of ninety-one.

15

A momentous decade: the 1960s

Prior to 1960 rugby football could be said to have had four great periods of development: the early days of international rugby when faltering yet decisive steps were taken; the closing years of the nineteenth century and the opening years of the twentieth when backs at last became more than agencies of defence and when Welsh influence was brought to bear on three-quarter play and Irish influence on the distinctive role of each half-back; the period between the two world wars when forward play took on a new meaning; and the aftermath of the 1939–45 war when international rugby became a highly organised sector of the game and the first really great ball-carrying forwards emerged. Here the French influence was probably the predominant factor. Yet when the future generations come to study the game and its evolution, the happenings in the sixties will be seen as having been truly momentous.

It was in this period that the short tour by individual countries came into its own as modern travel facilities put practically every part of the world within reach in little more than a day. It was also in this decade that substitutes were first permitted in international and representative football. But above all it was the time when the coach came into his own, when new tactical concepts were born and a new terminology evolved. Time will tell whether all the innovations were for the better, but on balance the evidence thus far is that the majority of the changes made rugby football a better game to play and a better game to watch.

The improvements were manifest in the game in Ireland as elsewhere, and if no Triple Crown or championship was won during the sixties, the players who wore the national jersey did so to a large degree with distinction. Historic victories were recorded, two overseas tours undertaken, and great players emerged on the scene. Two of them stayed in the game long enough to shatter, in turn, the cap record set by Jack Kyle.

Tom Kiernan, a member of a Cork rugby family with a long tradition in the game, came into the Irish team against England at full-back in the match at Twickenham in 1960. He went on to play fifty-four matches for Ireland before his international career ended at Murrayfield in 1973. Yet that record number of appearances lasted no longer than twelve months before it was broken in 1974 by the Ballymena second-row forward Willie John McBride, Kiernan's colleague for so long in the Irish side. Kiernan retired from international rugby as the most capped full-back in history, having also established two other landmarks that are likely to stand for a long time to come: he scored 158 points for Ireland, more than any other player, and he led his country on a record number of twenty-four occasions.

McBride was first capped against England in 1962 and was still present in 1973–74 to lead the national side. The previous year he set a record of forty-three consecutive appearances in international rugby, eclipsing the record held by the great Scottish prop forward Hugh McLeod, who made the last of forty successive appearances in 1962.

To the names of this distinguished pair could be added yet another, that of Michael Gibson, who while a student at Cambridge University came into the Irish team at out-half in 1964 and for a long time bade fair to equal the degree of proficiency attained by Jack Kyle in that onerous position. Gibson was later switched to the centre, a position in which he also achieved world status.

Kiernan, McBride and Gibson formed a mighty triumvirate, dominating the era which had produced them.

Kiernan was the only one of the three who was a member of the Irish party that toured South Africa in the summer of 1961.

In the previous winter the Fifth Springboks had come to Britain and Ireland and had escaped from Lansdowne Road with a victory that came in injury time through the medium of a push-over try. They had also been given very hard games by Munster and Leinster, so there was some reason for optimism when the Irish party set out in May 1961. If the Irish hopes were not fully realised, the tour was, nevertheless, a major success, and there were to be happier consequences four years later when the South Africans returned the compliment with a short tour of Ireland and Scotland in 1965.

The Irish touring team of 1961 was led by Ronnie Dawson, and Noel F. Murphy, once a respected international player, was the manager. One of the players he had under his guidance was his son, Noel A. Murphy. Ireland played four games, won three and lost one, which was, admittedly, the most important engagement, the international. Ireland scored fifty-nine points and conceded thirty-six in the four matches; Kiernan contributed forty-four, including all eight that Ireland scored in a 24–8 international defeat.

All but one of the team that played in the international had been capped previously, the exception being the Queen's University back Ken Houston. But even with such experience in the back line as that embodied in the presence of Tony O'Reilly and Andy Mulligan, and with the solid defensive qualities of a recent recruit to international rugby, Jerry Walsh of UCC in the centre, Ireland could not provide an effective answer to their opposition. The South Africans' tremendously strong and able pack proved altogether too formidable for an Irish eight that included Dawson, Syd Millar, Gordon Wood, Bill Mulcahy and Noel Murphy, all five of whom had toured New Zealand with the Lions in 1959.

Despite the presence of so many fine players, Ireland could not mount a really serious challenge for the honours on the home front, suffering, as they have so often done, from being short of just a few really good players that would complete a competent line-up. Yet they had a good representation on the Lions team that toured South Africa in the summer of 1962: Tom Kiernan, Niall Brophy, and David Hewitt in the back positions and Syd Millar, Bill Mulcahy and Bill McBride among the forwards. It was the first of five Lions tours for McBride, but was not attended by the glory that followed later for the Ballymena man on other foreign soil.

A six strong Irish respresentation for this tour had hardly seemed likely at one stage in 1962, notably after a visit to Twickenham, to which location the Irish selectors decided to take nine new caps. Ireland took a fearful 16–0 hammering and some who shared in the experience were not destined to have the responsibility of wearing the green jersey again. Two of the forwards who had to endure a tough baptism that February day were still considered good enough, however, to be selected for Ireland in 1973; one was McBride and the other a prop forward, Ray McLoughlin.

Time was when a prop was a prop. McLoughlin, however, begat an era when the defined lines of duty were specifically separated into tight and loose head. And it was in the latter role that he established a worldwide reputation, not alone for his physical attributes and his ability to use them in the cause of his side, but as a thinker on the game and a wily strategist. His reputation in that direction reached its zenith when he took over the leadership of the Irish side in 1965, a year that promised at last to see the Triple Crown returned to Irish soil, though Wales not for the first time ended all thoughts in that direction.

McLoughlin's scientific approach had not yet fully asserted itself, however, when Ireland met England at Twickenham in February 1964, Ireland's win that day was their first victory at Twickenham since 1948. The 18–5 win ended the losing sequence in the grand manner, and none contributed more richly to the victory than Michael Gibson, who had experienced a moment of equal brilliance on the same pitch two months earlier when he had inspired the Cambridge victory over Oxford. He performed a feat of similar moment for Ireland on this his first appearance in the national side. Ireland led by 3 points to nil at half-time through a try by Noel Murphy, but when that great forward 'Bydge' Rogers had got a try for England after the interval and John Willcox converted it, the Irish began to think in terms of the Twickenham bogey again. The doubts were reinforced when Kiernan missed an easy kick, but it was to take more than a bogey to keep the Irish from claiming their rights against England this time.

Kevin Flynn, who as a nineteen-year-old youngster had made such an impressive debut against France in 1959 but to whom fate had dealt some unkind hands in the shape of injuries in the intervening period, was Gibson's able ally this time. He started the Irish blitz that came in the final fifteen minutes by getting a try which Kiernan goaled. Now all was forgiven the Corkman. Then Gibson stamped his genius on the hour. He pierced the English defence with a break from near his own 'twenty-five'. The ball was transferred inside to centre Jerry Walsh after a diagonal run. Walsh changed the direction of the attack from left to right and the movement ended with the Irish right wing Pat Casey scoring a try almost under the posts after the English defence had been disconcerted yet again by a change in direction. It was a score to rank with Basil Maclear's effort against South Africa more than half a century earlier. Flynn completed a day of glory by scoring for the second time near the end, and Kiernan once again landed the conversion. This time the cushions did not fly to herald the Irish triumph when no-side was called, but thoughts of a Triple Crown were uppermost in the minds of the huge Irish following, who saw at last the man they believed to be the logical successor to Kyle.

That win, following a fine effort against the Fifth All-Blacks in Dublin the previous December, did not condition the Irish mind to accept easily the anticlimax that ensued. Ireland was beaten by Scotland in Dublin for the third successive time, and this was followed by further defeats by Wales and France. Ireland had again exercised her almost unique facility for going from the sublime to the ridiculous in the shortest possible time, and ended the season at the bottom of the championship table.

When Ireland opened their 1965 championship programme against France in Dublin on 23 January, they did so under a new captain, Ray McLoughlin, whose prowess as a prop forward was quite exceptional. Ronnie Dawson had gone, having made his last appearance against France in Paris the previous April. Dawson had surprisingly been dropped for the match against Wales, being one of four players who had to pay the penalty for the defeat by Scotland. Two other distinguished heads rolled too, those of Kiernan and Syd Millar. Kiernan's absence was not prolonged, however, for his successor, Fergus Keogh, failed, as so many others before had subsequently failed, to match the Corkman's all-round accomplishments. Kiernan was back for the game against France in 1965, when the hooking duties were entrusted to a young medical student from Queen's University, Belfast, Ken Kennedy. This was the start of another long career. Length of service was indeed a characteristic of many of the players who made their mark in the sixties.

It has been said of McLoughlin that he brought a new dimension to the captaincy of Ireland and killed once and for all any remnants of the old 'laissez-faire' attitude to preparation and tactics. His contribution and tactical appreciation were certainly of major proportions, but it would appear wrong to claim that his was the initial breakthrough in this direction. While McLoughlin's approach to this task was certainly thorough and scientific, it has been argued by his critics that some of his methods were too rigid in concept and not workable by the players at his disposal. Karl Mullen had proved fifteen years earlier that he too was an accomplished strategist as well as a great hooker and he made his point tell with two Triple Crowns and three championships. Ronnie Dawson was not as well endowed as Mullen with regard to his team's strength in depth, yet he was another before the McLoughlin era who had been fastidious in his approach to the job as Ireland's captain – to such outstanding effect when he had led the Lions in New Zealand. Kiernan, also, in his long reign had made a valuable contribution.

McLoughlin did not enjoy a long term of office as captain of Ireland, perhaps because he tried to do too much too soon, perhaps because he was unable to command the ultimate success for which he so zealously strove. What is not in doubt is that McLoughlin's approach would be totally in accord with the game as it is played today and perhaps his greatest accomplishment is that he helped to prepare the way for many of the traumatic changes that followed in the wake of his leadership.

Ray McLoughlin's captaincy was not rewarded in the shape of a Triple Crown. As it transpired, Ireland, after beating England and Scotland in 1965, failed yet again to Wales at the final hurdle, losing in Cardiff by 14 points to 8. For both teams it was a Triple Crown occasion, for Wales had previously beaten England and Scotland.

The atmosphere at the Arms Park is at any time demanding on the visitor, but on 13 March 1965 it was positively electric, a circumstance that probably was a contributory factor in Kiernan's missing an early penalty from in front of the posts. The kick was taken against a background of booing, not the customary silence afforded a penalty-taker. It was a disappointing match, not least in terms of the result. Ireland was in with a chance until five minutes from time, at which stage Wales led by 11 points to 8, but Terry Price, the Welsh full-back, landed the penalty goal that finished the contest and gave Wales the Triple Crown. Not everyone was satisfied with the tactics of either team.

Less than a month later, Ireland, with McLoughlin as captain, had a much more rewarding experience when the first international victory over South Africa was achieved at Lansdowne Road on 10 April. South Africa had come on a five-match tour of Ireland and Scotland. They opened their itinerary in Belfast on 3 April and managed to get away with a draw against a Combined Provinces side. But they were to learn a lesson that others who engaged on similar short tours had endured before them, that the time for preparation for the international games during the long official tour is an invaluable asset in ironing out deficiency and building up team-spirit. No such opportunities are available to quick-striking raiders.

Three days after the Belfast match South Africa met the Combined Universities, some of whose best players, such as Tom Kiernan, Roger Young, Pat McGrath, Ken Kennedy, Ray McLoughlin and Bill Mulcahy, were not available by the wish of the Irish selectors. It was thus all the more remarkable that this depleted team, captained by Jerry Walsh of UCC, earned the distinction of being the first Irish XV to beat the South Africans. In view of the number of times that Munster had unluckily failed to beat touring teams, it was appropriate that the win should have come on Munster soil. It was a most exciting match, during which every university player performed with distinction, South Africa met unexpected resistance from their smaller and lighter opponents, who, incidentally, wore red jerseys in order to avoid confusion with the Springbok's green.

The Universities led 6–0, 6–5, 12–5 and 12–10 and managed to hold out desperately in the closing minutes. The South Africans got enough possession of the ball to win a dozen matches, but the Universities deserved victory for their sheer courage and opportunism. Tony Hickie (penalty goal), Eamonn McGuire (try), John Murray (dropped goal) and Mike Grimshaw (try) scored for the Universities, while Tommy Bedford got both tries for the Tourists, one in each half, and both were converted.

At the subsequent dinner the chairman of the Irish Universities Rugby Union, Sarsfield Hogan, praised South Africa for their most sporting acceptance of their unexpected defeat. Avril Malan, the captain, replied: 'We are glad to hear Mr Hogan's words because we Springboks have very little practice in how to behave as losers.' It was a reasonable enough comment at the time.

The Universities team that recorded that historic win at Thomond Park Limerick was:

A. Hickie (UCD)
M. Lucey (UCC)
J.C. Walsh (UCC) capt.
M. Grimshaw (Queen's University)
W. Glynn (UCD)
J.B. Murray (UCD)
M. Whiteside (Queen's University)
M. Carey (UCD)
M. Argyle (Dublin University)
A. Moroney (UCD)
M. Leahy (UCC)
O. Waldron (UCC)
J. Davidson (Queen's University)
H. Wall (UCD)
E. McGuire (UCG)

Ireland could scarcely have asked for a better stimulant than that given in Limerick and McLoughlin and his colleagues responded by defeating the Springboks by 9–6 at Lansdowne Road on 10 April. Jerry Walsh was the only player who shared in both triumphs; the Universities selection had been restricted to players who were not engaged in the international, but the Irish selectors had conceded that the Universities should not be deprived of their captain.

Conditions were not ideal for the game, even though it took place in the middle of April. An appreciable wind blew and the odd shower of rain made control and ball handling difficult. South Africa had the benefit of the wind in the first half, but it was Ireland who opened the scoring. Scrum-half Roger Young, who had come into the side that season, kicked the ball over the South African line and Pat McGrath, one of the Irish wings, got his hand to it before any of the Springboks could touch down to safety. South Africa then drew level with a penalty goal, but despite sustained pressure, the Irish defence was not breached during the opening period, at the end of which the sides were level at 3–3.

With the wind behind them in the second half, Ireland looked set to strike gold, but it was South Africa who scored again, centre W.J. Mans getting an unconverted try. Tom Kiernan soon brought the sides level, however, with a penalty kick, and when Mike Gibson went over for a try the acclamation that greeted the effort turned to despair when play was recalled for an apparent infringement.

But Irish supporters were not denied a grand finale. It came through the agency of a wonderful penalty kick by Tom Kiernan. There was a breathless moment of suspense while the ball was in flight, and an explosion of thunderous acclamation when it reached its objective. It was enough: South Africa had been beaten twice within the space of five days, and by Irish opposition. And if that was an unlikely happening in the days of Danie Craven and Benny Osler, it hardly mattered to the 45,000 Irish supporters who were in Lansdowne Road in April 1965. Some of them had probably seen Osler and Craven weave their own particular brand of magic in the distant past; this time the spell was not strong enough for the needs of the occasion.

Ireland made the now accustomed unrewarding journey to France for the first match in 1966, a game in which Willie John McBride got a new partner in the strong and durable Connachtman, Mick Molloy. Molloy proved a worthy successor to Bill Mulcahy, whose international career had ended the previous season. A draw with England at Twickenham was a reasonable if not a fair return from a game that Ireland had dominated territorially. Similar dominance had been exerted previously to no effect whatsoever.

Ireland was then defeated by Scotland for the fourth successive time at the Lansdowne Road ground. There were several alterations in the team selected to meet Wales, including a change in the captaincy, Tom Kiernan taking over the job from Ray McLoughlin – a selectorial decision that may have cost McLoughlin the leadership of the Lions side that went to New Zealand that summer. The Welsh match also saw the return on the right wing of the Lansdowne player Alan Duggan, who had been capped twice in 1964 but overlooked subsequently. He did not score that day in Ireland's surprising but welcome 9–6 win, but his try-scoring feats in later matches enabled him to establish an Irish record.

The Fifth Wallabies came to Britain and Ireland in the autumn of 1966, and though they proved good enough to beat Wales and England, Ireland once more registered a win over a touring team by beating Australia by 15 points to 8 on 21 January 1967 at Lansdowne Road. Mike Gibson dropped two goals, Duggan got the first of the eleven tries he scored for Ireland, and Tom Kiernan, making his twenty-eighth appearance at full-back for Ireland, kicked a penalty goal.

Four days later at Musgrave Park, Munster at last got the long-sought and well-deserved win over a touring team when they beat the Australians by 11 points to 8, thereby becoming the first Irish province to win against a side from overseas. Kiernan kicked eight of the eleven points Munster scored, and John Moroney of London Irish and Garryowen and subsequently an international, scored a try. The Irish side that day was led by Noel Murphy, who also had the distinction of captaining the Munster team that had defeated the Wallabies.

Murphy remained in charge throughout the 1967 championship series. After losing to England at Lansdowne Road, Ireland won against Scotland at Murrayfield, where Murphy scored the decisive try and Kiernan landed the conversion for a 5–0 win. Ireland then went to the Cardiff Arms Park and won by 3 points to nil, Alan Duggan getting the only score the match produced.

Meanwhile, the results of the other international matches had ensured that the Ireland-France match at Lansdowne Road on 15 April would decide the championship. As a result of the win in Cardiff, there was considerable confidence backing Ireland's chances of taking the title for the first time since 1951.

As it transpired, the celebrated kicking ability of the Camberabero brothers, Guy and Lilian, effectively countered the Irish challenge, and France deservedly won by 11 points to 6. Noel Murphy was named as captain of the Irish team to tour Australia, and an official party of twenty-four members, with two officials, Eugene Davy as manager and Des McKibbin as assistant manager, left Dublin Airport on 22 April.

Murphy, however, was not able to accompany them, and so Kiernan took over the leadership.

Ireland accomplished the main business of the six-match itinerary in magnificent fashion when on 13 May she beat Australia by 11 points to 5 in Sydney. That was the first, and to date the only, win achieved by Ireland in a full-scale international overseas. After losing heavily by 21 points to 9 to New South Wales on the same Sydney ground a week previously, thought and application for the international were needed. The position was slightly complicated because of a thigh injury to one of the centres, Barry Bresnihan, who had come into the Irish team in 1966. Pat McGrath, normally a wing, was placed at centre and the veteran Niall Brophy went on the left wing. There was one new cap in the pack, Terry Moore of Highfield, and his performance that day suggested that many more caps would follow in the immediate future, but it was not until 1973 that he was again included in an Irish team. Kiernan, meanwhile, was making his thirty-third appearance in the full-back position for Ireland, and by so doing equalled the world record held by the great Welshman, W.J. Bancroft.

Brendan Sherry, the Irish scrum-half, got Ireland off to a good start by creating the opening from which Jerry Walsh scored a try and Kiernan added the goal points. Just after the interval Kiernan dropped a goal. Australia reduced the deficit to 8–5 with a try by their clever scrum-half, Ken Catchpole, and the veteran J.K. Lenehan converted. But the suspense lasted for only four minutes as McGrath quickly capitalised on good work by Duggan to stretch Ireland's lead to 11–5; and that was the final score. Ireland ended the tour with a record of four wins from six matches and a points total of 119, with 80 being registered against.

An outbreak of foot and mouth disease in Britain caused the cancellation of the international between Ireland and the Sixth All-Blacks, which was due to take place in December 1967. It was unfortunate in every way, not least in that Irish followers were deprived of seeing one of the greatest rugby combinations ever to visit Britain and France. The All-Blacks played fifteen matches, won fourteen and drew one; and they beat England, Wales, France and Scotland in the international engagements.

So when the championship campaign started, Ireland did not have the advantage of a match as was the case with the other participants. Ireland lost to France in Paris (as usual) and were deprived of a win against England when Bob Hiller, the English full-back, kicked a last-minute penalty goal from the right touchline to earn his side a 9–9 draw. Hiller that day struck the first of many blows he later inflicted on the Irish. A win over Scotland at Lansdowne Road was not entirely unexpected, but the 9–6 victory over Wales in Dublin provided both excitement and controversy.

Ireland, with a penalty goal from Kiernan and a dropped goal from Gibson, led 6–3 well into the second half. Then Gareth Edwards, the Welsh scrum-half, took a drop at goal that apparently went wide of the left-hand upright. To the astonishment of the capacity crowd, the referee, Mr M.H. Titcomb of England, deemed Edwards' kick good, and it was a decision that for a few moments threatened to have dire consequences in the form of an invasion of the pitch by a section of the crowd. But the incident ceased as quickly as it had started and the game was restarted without undue delay. The Irish players showed no outward signs of dissatisfaction with the decision, but it was a bitter blow.

But Ireland won in the end, when Mick Doyle, a flank forward who had seen service with UCD and Cambridge University and had first been capped in 1965, got a try just before the end of the match. Justice was done.

Doyle had been joined for the game against England by his brother Tommy, from the Wanderers club; they are the most recent of the many sets of brothers to play for Ireland.

Kiernan was subsequently chosen to captain the Lions team in South Africa, and Ronnie Dawson was appointed coach and assistant manager. That appointment epitomised the new approach to the game that had been adopted by the home countries, where coaching at national level had now become looked upon as a necessity. Wales had shown the way with the appointment of David Nash as coach to their national side in 1967, and the other countries were soon to follow the lead. Such happenings as squad training-sessions, unknown in earlier times, soon became commonplace, with national selectors summoning groups of players to assemble at weekends so that tactics and stratagems could be perfected. Despite the appointment of an Irishman as coach to the 1968 Lions in South Africa, the idea had not as yet fully caught on in Ireland, nor was it altogether acceptable to many of those who ran the game, mainly because of fears that the status and authority of the captain would be diminished or, at least, misunderstood.

Kiernan and Dawson were accompanied by seven Irish players: Barry Bresnihan; Mike Gibson; Roger Young; Syd Millar, who that season had again found favour with the Irish selectors after four years in the wilderness; Bill McBride; Mick Doyle; and Ken Goodall, a number eight forward of top quality. Goodall had come into the Irish side that season and had made an immediate impact. He joined the Lions as a replacement during the tour, but was injured in the first game he played and took no further part in the proceedings.

One significant example of the changes that were being implemented in the game was the International Board's decision in March 1968 that in future replacements would be allowed for seriously injured players during the course of official trial games and international representative matches involving touring teams. The Lions South African tour saw the first such replacement, and to Barry Bresnihan went the distinction of being the first substitute in representative football when he came on for Mike Gibson fifteen minutes from the end of the opening game of the tour against Western Transvaal.

The Lions did not win the Test series, but they did win fifteen of the twenty matches they played and drew one, the second Test. Kiernan scored eighty-four points in thirteen matches to set another record for a Lions player in South Africa, and his contribution of thirty-five points in the Test series accounted for all but three of the points the Lions amassed in the internationals.

In October 1968 Australia came on a five-match tour of Ireland and Scotland, and once again Ireland won the international by 10 points to 3. This game gave Irish followers a first glimpse of top-class rugby under an experimental law that restricted kicking the ball directly to touch outside the 'twenty-five' yard lines. The game was not a good advertisement for the experiment. That match apart, the new law speeded up the game appreciably on a general level and was subsequently incorporated into the laws on a permanent basis. Substitutes, kicking laws and coaches truly had the wind of change blown through the game.

Ireland had not as yet appointed a coach to the national side when the 1968–69 season opened, but coaching was gradually becoming an accepted principle within the country, and nowhere more than in Leinster, where since 1964 an annual course had been run at the Butlin's Holiday Camp at Mosney, County Meath. Ronnie Dawson was one of the prime movers in the project and he had a willing and able accomplice in Judge Charles Conroy, the then honorary secretary of the Leinster Branch and president of the union in 1972–73. Desmond Scaife, who succeeded Judge Conroy as Leinster honorary secretary in May 1972, was another leading advocate and did an immense amount of work in the organisation of the course, which is still run annually and is attended by many of the game's leading authorities from other lands, notably Wales and France.

Wales also had a coach in 1969, the job having passed from David Nash to a former Welsh captain and scrum-half, Clive Rowlands, and he mobilised them for their Triple Crown and championship victories, two distinctions earned over Ireland's head as the result of the decisive game in the series between Wales and Ireland at Cardiff Arms Park on 8 March 1969.

Ireland had failed to beat France for the quite astonishing period of eleven years, but the trend was finally arrested at Lansdowne Road on 25 January 1969. Ireland was without Mike Gibson, who had fractured his jaw in the final trial, and the out-half position was taken over by Barry McGann, who had been a brilliant schools player at Presentation College, Cork, Kiernan's old academy, and who was now attached to Lansdowne. McGann made a great debut and Ireland won by 17 points to 9, a victory that equalled one record and established another.

Only once before, in 1948, had Ireland won four matches in succession, and now the win over France had brought a similar run of success, following wins over Scotland and Wales in the 1968 championship and the victory over Australia in October 1968. The second record was an individual one, created by a wing threequarter. John Moroney, who had played at out-half for his club, London Irish, had been selected on the left wing for the game against France and scored fourteen points, made up of three penalty goals, a try and a conversion. McGann, with a dropped goal, completed the seventeen points. Moroney's scoring spree broke the previous individual record set in 1948 by Barney Mullan with thirteen points. The same game was also the first match in which Ireland made a substitution, Mick Hipwell of Terenure College coming on during the second half for Noel Murphy, who had retired injured.

England, with Hiller in his usual kicking form, gave Ireland a hard time of it in Dublin before a 17–15 win for Ireland stretched the winning sequence to five games, and once again Ireland had to take advantage of the substitution law, Colin Grimshaw of Queen's University coming on during the second half for Roger Young at scrum-half.

Things were distinctly promising now. The five successive wins became a record sixth when Scotland proved no match for Ireland at Murrayfield. Tries by Alan Duggan, his third in two matches against the Scots, Mike Gibson, Barry McGann and Barry Bresnihan and two conversions by John Moroney gave Ireland a 16–0 win.

Ireland did pay a price for that win, however, for Ken Goodall was injured and replaced by Mick Hipwell, who thus picked up two caps as a replacement to add to the four he had collected between 1962 and 1968. He was named in an otherwise unchanged team to travel to Wales for the game at Cardiff Arms Park on 8 March.

The Welsh programme of matches had been disrupted that season, so that when they faced Ireland it was only the second match of their championship programme. It was, however, the one they knew they had to win. The build-up to the game was tremendous, nowhere more so than in Wales, where Ireland's progress had been watched with respect and, one expects, some trepidation. Despite the tremendous popular interest in the game, it was played before a crowd of only 25,000, as major reconstruction work in the Arms Park had severely limited its accommodation capacity. Proposals that the game be taken to some other venue (Twickenham and Lansdowne Road were widely canvassed) had met with no response from the Welsh Rugby Union.

Suggestions had gone around that the Irish forwards were living dangerously throughout the championship, and imagination became intermingled with fact, which was that Ireland had incurred several penalties throughout the series. The great majority of them had been for line-out infringements, basically of a technical nature, and some for retreating at the back of the line, a law that was subsequently amended.

To what extent reputation preceded Ireland to Wales one can only guess, but within ten minutes of the start there occurred an incident that ruined the game and left Noel Murphy lying stunned after being the recipient of a punch from a Welsh forward, who broke from a ruck to dispatch his message. Assertions that the blow was the result of provocation were simply post-mortem efforts to whitewash a blatant foul and do not merit serious consideration. The referee, Mr McMahon of Scotland, warned and penalised the offender, but he did not send him off, presumably on a merciful application of the 'first offence' rule. Many thought it would have been better for the image and reputation of international rugby if the referee had been more severe.

Ireland did not win, nor on the balance of play did they deserve to do so, and a highly-talented Welsh side took the honours by the convincing margin of 24 points to 11.

It was Noel Murphy's last match and it was regrettable that a magnificent international career, in which he won forty-one caps and went on two Lions tours, should have ended in such an unsatisfactory manner.

Wales went on to beat England and take the Triple Crown, and a draw in France gave them the championship as well, with one point to spare over Ireland. Wales had clearly demonstrated the value of coaching, and the other home countries were not long in following the lead at national level.

16
Tours and torments 1970–71

In the autumn of 1969 the IRFU decided that the national team would be the better for the appointment of a coach and, not surprisingly, one of those who had preached the coaching gospel louder than most, Ronnie Dawson, was given the task of moulding the Irish side to meet the demands of the modern concept of rugby football. His first assignment was to prepare the Irish side for the international against the Sixth Springboks in Dublin on 10 January 1970.

The Sixth Springboks, under the captaincy of the great scrum-half D.J. de Villiers, faced problems that none of their predecessors had been forced to face. They were most unlucky in the matter of injuries, and wherever they went they were greeted by crowds demonstrating against the policy of apartheid. But these were only two of the factors that made their task difficult. The third, despite all that has been written about demonstrations against South African government policy, was probably far more important. Rugby in Britain and Ireland, through the 'coaching revolution', meant that the Springboks met sides that were better prepared than at any time in the game's history. The home countries had at last discovered that the elimination of error and the ability to capitalise on opponent's mistakes had been the stock in trade of the overseas tourists, especially those that came from South Africa and New Zealand. And now they were able to reply to the challenge of these sophisticated foreign teams in a like manner.

The first really fruitful application of this newly-acquired knowledge came in the third match at Newport, which the Welsh club side won by 11 points to 6. By the time the South Africans reached Ireland they had lost four games, including the international against England.

It was a strange-looking Lansdowne Road that greeted the visitors. The terraces behind the goals were empty and the pitch was well protected by barbed wire to keep out unwelcome invaders. The result of the game was a closely fought draw. South Africa, strong in the forward line, but, with the exception of de Villiers, not very potent behind the scrum, almost won and almost lost.

Ireland was 5–3 up at half-time, Duggan scoring a try and Kiernan converting, with H.O. de Villiers gaining a penalty goal for South Africa. In the second half P.J. Greyling scored a try for South Africa and H.O. de Villiers again found the range to put the visitors 8–5 ahead. The advantage was maintained until the eighth minute of injury time, when Alan Duggan kicked deep into the South African 'twenty-five'. With the Irish in full pursuit, the South African full-back had no option but to lie on the ball in front of his posts. He saved a try which would almost certainly have been converted, but he gave Kiernan the opportunity to level with a simple kick from the ensuing penalty. Five years earlier a kick by Kiernan had had more serious consequences for the South Africans.

One of three new caps in the Irish side for the game was a wing forward from UCD, Fergus Slattery, and he has lived up to the promise he revealed on his initial outing in the Irish jersey.

With Dawson at the helm, there was hope of a new dawn, bringing with it a change of fortune, but there was no evidence forthcoming that it was in the immediate offing when Ireland lost by 8 points to nil in Paris. At Twickenham Bob Hiller once again broke the heart of the Irish challenge with two superb drop goals that gave England a 9–3 win. But better times were round the corner.

A 16–11 win over Scotland brought a welcome change in the pattern the season appeared to be taking, but hardly prefaced great things when Wales came to Lansdowne Road in search of the Triple Crown. Nevertheless, Ireland destroyed the Welsh team of all the talents and amazed the rugby world, not because they won, but by the margin by which they won – 14 points to nil.

The Welsh forwards were completely overwhelmed, and the great half-back partnership of Gareth Edwards and Barry John was played out of the game. All the scoring came in the second half, during which Wales collapsed before the Irish onslaught. Barry McGann started the Welsh decline with a well-taken drop goal, and then Alan Duggan scored a wonderful try to which Tom Kiernan added the conversion. Before the end Ken Goodall, one of the stars in a great Irish pack, added a second try, and again Kiernan converted. There were doubtless a few inquests in the valleys that night, and no little celebration in Dublin. Retribution for the previous season's defeat at Cardiff Arms Park had been exacted. Goodall's talents were not to be at Ireland's disposal again, for he turned to Rugby League before the start of the following season.

Ireland went back to the Argentine in August 1970; the party consisted of twenty-three players, with Kiernan as captain, Dawson as coach, and the IRFU president, Pete Patterson, as manager. The experiences of Wales and Scotland, who had recently met defeat in the Argentine, testified to the strength of the game in Buenos Aires and its neighbouring towns, so the fact that Mike Gibson, Roger Young, Fergus Slattery and Ken Kennedy were unable to go on the tour weakened the strength considerably.

Ireland played seven matches and won four, but two of the three defeats came in the two Test matches, the first of which proved to be a torrid affair during which two players, one from each team, were sent off the field. The Argentine won the match by 8 points to 3, and in the last game of the tour, the second Test, they won by 6 points to 3. Ireland also lost to an Argentine 'C' selection by 17 points to nil.

There were many difficulties, not least a spate of injuries, the most serious of which was incurred by wing Bill Brown, who had made his international debut against South Africa in January. Brown broke a leg in the sixth match. Earlier in the tour back row forward Ronnie Lamont, another international, had been forced to spend four days in hospital recovering from severe concussion. Other casualties were Barry McGann, Tom Grace, the UCD wing, at that time uncapped, Syd Millar, the most experienced of the forwards, Barry McGann and Paddy Madigan, a hooker from the Old Belvedere club who had been Ken Kennedy's understudy in the Irish squad for the past two seasons.

All the games were played in Buenos Aires, with the exception of one game in Rosario, and the Irish found the conditions trying and some of the refereeing decisions strange. It added to the difficulties that the tour took place in August, three months after the close of the previous season, so that Ireland had to face players who were match-hardened since April.

Yet the greatest subject of controversy connected with this most unsatisfactory tour was not the events on the field, but an incident which occurred on the journey home. On the pretext of misconduct, but apparently in an effort to cover up some other airline difficulty, the Irish party were ordered off the plane at Rio de Janeiro and compelled to wait some days in the city until alternative flights could be arranged. The IRFU, having fully investigated the matter, issued a strong statement repudiating the suggestion that there had been misconduct or any other reason justifying the arbitrary and inexplicable action taken by the airline or the Brazilian authorities.

Having eclipsed Jack Kyle's record of forty-six caps in the memorable triumph over Wales in 1970, Kiernan was again the choice as Ireland's captain and full-back for the match against France in 1971. He did not see the season out. A broken bone in his right leg caused him to retire in the second half of the match, which Ireland drew, and he was replaced by Barry O'Driscoll, a Manchester-based doctor who played for Connacht. It seemed the end of Kiernan's international career.

England came to Lansdowne Road and once again Bob Hiller brought about the destruction of the Irish by kicking three penalty goals to give England a 9–6 win. Not since Oliver Cromwell had Ireland been harried to a similar degree by an Englishman. Ireland failed to stop Wales winning the Triple Crown, going down by 22 points to 9 in Cardiff after scoring a meritorious 17–5 win at Murrayfield.

England celebrated her centenary season, the highlight of which was a wonderful four-countries match at Twickenham. Things had come a long way since England had met Scotland at Raeburn Place a hundred years before.

The build-up to the Lions tour of New Zealand in the summer was in direct contrast to the preparation for the first rugby international of all. But those who invented the rugby game reasserted their superiority through the medium of their successors, who, for the first time, won the Test series. Wales supplied the coach and captain in Carwyn James and John Dawes respectively, and Ireland supplied six players. Mike Gibson was the only Irish back in the party, but there were five forwards: Séan Lynch, Ray McLoughlin, who had made a return to the Irish side after five years' absence in 1971; Willie John McBride, making a record fourth tour; Fergus Slattery; and Mick Hipwell.

McLoughlin and Hipwell had to leave the tour half-way through the campaign because of injuries and for that reason did not play in any of the Tests. Slattery was chosen for one Test but could not play, also because of injury, but Gibson, McBride and Lynch (who had come into the Irish team in 1971) all played in the four Tests.

17

A sad affair and a happy sequel 1972–74

Ireland's facility for recalling seasoned campaigners has largely been a profitable exercise through the years. When the Irish team travelled to Paris in 1972 there were two in the side whose international careers had at one time appeared to be over. Kiernan had returned to his old position at full-back, having shaken off the effects of the leg injury that might have caused a lesser man to opt out for good. Kevin Flynn, who had last played in 1966 and first played for Ireland in 1959, had shown enough of his former skill while helping Leinster to win the interprovincial championship to earn the favours of the selection committee.

The Irish team that faced France in Colombes was an odd mixture of the old and the new. On the one hand there were Kiernan, Flynn, Gibson, McLoughlin, Kennedy and McBride, whose combined total of caps amounted to over two hundred, while on the other, there were no fewer than five new caps. They were Tom Grace on the right wing, Wallace McMaster on the left, John Moloney at scrum-half, Con Feighery in the second row and Stewart McKinney at wing forward. The blend proved a potent mixture, however, and for the first time in twenty years Ireland won at Colombes and did so convincingly by 14 points to 9.

Yet again the call for change in the laws of the game had been answered by the International Board, who had elevated the value of a try to four points at their meeting in Edinburgh the previous March. The decision made no difference to the match result in Paris, but the wisdom of it was soon evident.

Having laid the bogey at Colombes, Ireland took an unchanged side to Twickenham. This time not even the presence of Bob Hiller could deprive the Irish, who, however, left their winning effort until almost too late. With just five minutes to go, Ireland was trailing by 12 points to 7 and, needless to say, Hiller had made his personal contribution in the form of eight points. Ireland's last hope appeared to be gone when

Mike Gibson missed a penalty goal, but an England player knocked the ball on behind his own line, and from the ensuing scrum McGann dropped a neat goal. Then Flynn made his presence felt when everyone except the most important person, the referee, thought that time was up. A scrum near the English 'twenty-five', a deft pass from Moloney to McGann, who transferred to Flynn, and the veteran cut his way through the English midfield defence for a classic centre try. It mattered not whether Kiernan could add the goal points, but he did and Ireland thus won by 16 points to 12. Now England knew how Ireland had felt on innumerable occasions.

It transpired that Ireland had disposed of England and rid themselves forever of the menace of Bob Hiller at the same time. Hiller was dropped for England's next match against France and subsequently announced his retirement from international football. He had kicked forty-one points in five appearances against Ireland, and the Irish were therefore not exactly sorry to see him go.

Shortly before the game against England there had been rumours and rumblings that Scotland and Wales were not prepared to travel to Dublin to fulfil their engagements. The reason was given as political instability in Dublin. For those in Ireland, who were totally familiar with the true position, the suggestions were nothing short of baffling. Parts of Ulster, notably Derry and Belfast, had certainly borne the brunt of political and civil unrest since 1969. Many soldiers, policemen and civilians had been killed, the most recent tragic incident having been the deaths of thirteen people in Derry when British Army units opened fire. One of the consequences of that tragedy was that some members of a protest march in Dublin succeeded in burning down the British Embassy. Although Dublin and the Republic of Ireland remained otherwise peaceful, the attack on the embassy naturally angered and alarmed some people in Britain.

Two days before Ireland met England the four home unions met in London and decided that there was no reason why the game between Scotland and Ireland, scheduled for Lansdowne Road on 26 February 1972 should not take place. That appeared to end the doubts. But two days after the Irish victory at Twickenham the Scottish Rugby Union informed the IRFU that they did not intend to travel to Dublin. If the Irish could not understand the Scottish fears, they nevertheless made a determined attempt to allay them. Six members of the IRFU, led by the president of the union, Dom Dineen, travelled to Edinburgh on 16 February in an effort to get the Scottish Union to change its previous decision. The Irish delegation included Judge Charles Conroy, vice-president of the IRFU; Tommy O'Reilly, the union's honorary treasurer; Harry McKibbin and Sinclair Irwin, Ireland's two representatives on the International Board; Ronnie Dawson; and Bob FitzGerald, the union secretary, who had taken over the duties of secretary-treasurer of the union in 1964 after the death of Billy Jeffares.

The persuasive powers of this formidable team, which included men eminent in public life as well as in the rugby world, succeeded in getting the SRU to reconsider their earlier decision, but after a further meeting of the Scottish Union on 17 February, Mr John Law, the SRU secretary, read a prepared statement to the effect that Scotland would not travel to Dublin out of consideration for the safety of their players and supporters. It was a bitter disappointment to Ireland, who having won their first two games away from home for the first time since 1948, appeared at last to have a wonderful chance of bringing off the Triple Crown-championship double with their two home games.

Fears that Wales would follow the Scottish lead were realised ten days later, and once again the same delegation travelled to Cardiff and met the Welsh committee. This time it was the turn of the Welsh secretary, Mr Bill Clement, to issue a statement that read on similar lines to that made by Mr Law in Edinburgh. Wales offered to play the game in Cardiff or at a neutral venue. The IRFU, feeling that it was Dublin or not at all, rejected the proposal.

Even at the height of the political troubles and violence in Ireland after the 1914–18 war, the international rugby fixtures had been played. In this context, the failure of Scotland and Wales to come to Dublin occasioned great surprise and not a little resentment among Irish rugby supporters. For its part, the IRFU adopted a cool and dignified stance.

Friends are needed in times of stress, and in France Ireland found a friend with whom affinity had begun long after the forming of the old friendships between the home unions. France was willing to oblige one of the family of rugby nations and came to Dublin and met Ireland on 29 April, when the French team got the warm-hearted reception they deserved from the attendance of almost 30,000. It mattered little that Ireland won; it mattered a great deal that the game took place.

In view of the decisions of the Welsh and Scottish Unions and the refusal of British clubs to travel to Ireland, there was a lot of speculation about whether or not the Seventh All-Blacks would travel to Ireland for the four games that were on their itinerary in the 1972–73 season.

However, all doubts about the intentions of the New Zealanders were removed when their manager, Ernie Todd, announced that they intended to travel to Ireland and fulfil their programme, which was a two-part one, against Leinster and Ulster in November 1972 and against Ireland and Munster in January 1973.

The New Zealanders won a great match against Leinster in Dublin and the following day travelled to Belfast to prepare for the game against Ulster; if Ravenhill was forbidden territory to others, the New Zealanders saw no reason why they should not honour their commitment to play there. They duly arrived, were given a tremendous reception and won into the bargain.

They travelled back to the Republic in January, and Ireland achieved her best result against them by drawing 10–10 on 10 January. A draw was a fair result to a splendid game, but Ireland almost snatched an historic win in the closing minutes. Tom Grace scored a dramatic equalising try in the right-hand corner within no more than an inch of the dead ball line, and Barry McGann's conversion was off target by inches. Four days previously a penalty goal in injury time had given the New Zealanders a 3–3 draw with Munster at Musgrave Park.

The All-Blacks, like the Springboks before them, found rugby in the home countries a more highly organised exercise than at any time in history. In addition, they were perhaps not as good either as their illustrious predecessors, and their team had become noticeably unsettled by what they felt to be an unsympathetic attitude towards them during the early part of the tour. Ireland will, however, always remember the Seventh All-Blacks with affection and gratitude. They lived up to the principles on which rugby was nurtured and has prospered. They came, they saw, and they came back again.

The president of the Rugby Union, Dick Kingswell, made it clear in January 1973 that it was his union's intention to bring a team to Dublin to play Ireland on 10 February 1973. Some feelings were expressed in England that the example of Scotland and Wales should be followed, and it was rumoured that some players had expressed doubts about playing in Dublin. The English Union was, however, unanimous in its resolve to play the match unless the Irish Union advised them otherwise, and they duly arrived at Lansdowne Road with their chosen team.

For over a century the happenings on the field of international rugby have stirred men's emotions, but it is doubtful if there was ever a more moving or emotional scene than that at Lansdowne Road when the English side ran on to the field. The entire concourse to a man stood and applauded the English team for five minutes. It was a wonderful sight and a wonderful sound. It was a great occasion for Dick Kingswell and his committee and an even greater one for rugby football. It was hardly material that Ireland won a close match in which England missed more chances than they took.

The matches against Scotland and Wales took place according to plan in 1973. Ireland lost both games, but finished the season with a 6–3 win over France.

Syd Millar had taken over the position as coach to the Irish team at the start of the season, a season in which Tom Kiernan ended his international career after he won his fifty-fourth cap at Murrayfield. He left the international field with the dignity that he had always shown on it, and one of his last acts in an Irish jersey was to wave his right arm in the air to signal that the final Scottish drop at goal was good. It was the farewell of a great player and a great captain. Willie John McBride, who had won his fiftieth cap in the game against England, took over the leadership of the Irish side, and Tony Ensor replaced Kiernan in his position on the field.

Scotland celebrated their centenary and Ireland played a full part in the celebrations. There was a generous complement of Irish players in the combined Scotland-Ireland team that defeated England-Wales in the centrepiece of the celebrations. Mike Gibson and Tom Grace scored five tries between them.

In an international seven-a-side tournament at Murrayfield Ireland surprised not only the opposition but most observers by reaching the final in a form or rugby that is not widely practised in the country. England won the competition by beating Ireland in the closing seconds of a magnificent final.

The autumn of 1973 brought new and most welcome visitors in the Fijians and the Argentinians. The Fijians brought their own brand of fluent football to Lansdowne Road in September, where Leinster were hosts and victors in an attractive game. The Argentinians chose Ireland and Scotland for their first visit to Europe in Ocotber. They played four matches in Ireland. The tour opened with a game against Munster at Thomond Park and once again Munster drew with a touring team. Connacht entertained a touring side for the first time at the sports ground in Galway, and here the Argentinians recorded their only win of the four engagements they undertook in Ireland. It came as a welcome boost four days before the match against Ireland at Lansdowne Road, and in the aftermath of a defeat by Ulster at Ravenhill. Ireland, who had won one, drawn one and lost two of four Test matches against the Argentinians in their two visits to the country, evened the score by recording a convincing victory.

18

A dual triumph

Just as Ireland had won the title in 1935, but had to wait a few weeks before knowing that they had taken the championship, so history repeated itself in 1974.

Ireland had completed their programme with five points from four matches and that left them one point ahead of both Wales, who had to play at Twickenham, and Scotland who had to play against France at Murrayfield. This was a fortnight after Ireland had completed their four-match programme with a 9–6 win over Scotland in Dublin.

On 16 March 1974, Scotland lined out against France, who were warm favourites to win, while Wales went to London carrying the same burden. The situation was now out of Ireland's hands and the earnest hope was that Scotland would do Ireland the favour of beating France and that England would end a barren spell against Wales with victory at Twickenham. It was a rather tall order, and was put rather succinctly by one Irish player the week before the matches: 'One of the results might favour us, but surely it is optimism gone daft to think that both results will fall our way.'

Fall Ireland's way the results did for Scotland beat France and England, against the expectations of most and much to the annoyance of the big Welsh following at Twickenham, beat Wales.

So, at last, Ireland had regained the championship after a lapse of 23 years. One could argue that it was not a title won in the most exciting fashion, but it brought well earned success for some players who had served Ireland so admirably for so long. At the top of this list was Willie John McBride, who during the season had not only beaten Tom Kiernan's Irish cap record, but also set a world record of 57 caps, overtaking by two the mark set by his great New Zealand friend and playing adversary, Colin Meads. McBride captained the championship winning side, a fitting reward for a man who had rendered such magnificent service to his country. Ireland picked 19 players during the campaign adding some youthful zest to the great experience and skill of men such as Ray McLoughlin, Ken Kennedy and Mike Gibson; Gibson brought his caps total to 47, surpassing by one the number won by an illustrious predecessor Jack Kyle, a player to whom he had so often been compared. Kennedy became Europe's most capped hooker that season when he marked up 41 appearances.

McLoughlin, whose career had looked over when he was out of the national side from 1967 to 1971, must have got particular satisfaction from being part of a championship winning side. He had won 34 caps by the end of the 1974 campaign, the total would have been very much higher but for those four years in the wilderness with the knee injury that seemed likely to terminate his career.

Tony Ensor had been asked to fill the mantle of Tom Kiernan, no easy task, and he performed with distinction. The half-backs John Moloney and Mick Quinn performed very well, with Moloney playing probably the best rugby of his illustrious career. Quinn had come into the side in 1973. He was ever present in 1974 as was centre Dick Milliken, Sean Lynch, Kennedy, Terry Moore, and Fergus Slattery along with the captain McBride.

He was given yet another second-row partner in Moss Keane, a young man whose early sporting exploits had been confined to the Gaelic football fields in his native Kerry and with University College Cork; it was at University College that Keane was converted to the rugby code and he proved a most adept and willing pupil. He made his debut against France and then retained his place. He was to retain it for many years to come. Vinny Becker, an Irish sprint champion from the Lansdowne club, displaced Tom Grace against Wales and France, but Grace was back for the matches against England and Scotland. Wallace McMaster, from Ballymena, played in three games, being ruled out through injury for the match against Wales and replaced by Pat Lavery from London Irish. Paddy Agnew, a prop from the CIYMS club in Belfast was also a member of the team, if only fleetingly. He was called in as a replacement against France when McLoughlin was injured.

Stewart McKinney played three games on the flank, but did not play against Wales, being omitted for Shay Deering, from Garryowen, who, by his selection, maintained a great family tradition. His father Seamus, a splendid Irish forward of the 1930s, and his uncle Mark both played for Ireland. The young Deering had all the courage and skill associated with his father, but injury deprived him of many caps.

Ironically Ireland won the title after losing the opening match to

France at the Parc des Princes, the new headquarters of the French Federation following a long tenure at Stade Colombes. There followed a 9–9 draw with Wales in Dublin and Ireland had collected just one point from two matches, scarcely the kind of statistic to suggest impending glory. That draw enabled Ireland to maintain a ten-year unbeaten sequence against the Welsh in Dublin. Ireland then went to Twickenham and scored 26 points in a remarkable match won in the end 26–21, after leading at one stage 21–9. Gibson was brilliant that afternoon and scored 12 points on the ground where he had made so sensational a debut ten years previously. A feature of that win by Ireland was that it meant a hat-trick of wins over England and was also the only 'away' win recorded in the championship series for over two years by any country. It was to prove crucial in the final analysis.

There followed a 9–6 win over Scotland in Dublin, in what was not a match of quality, and one which Ireland were fortunate in the end to win.

So McBride had led the side to victory and thus enabled Ireland to start the centenary season as international champions. But further glory beckoned for McBride. He was named as captain of the Lions for the tour to South Africa that summer and had his great friend and clubmate Syd Millar as coach. By being named as captain, McBride became the latest in a long and distinguished line of his fellow countrymen similarly honoured. He had six other Irish players as team mates on that tour to South Africa. They were Grace, Milliken, Moloney, Kennedy, McKinney and Slattery. Had Gibson and McLoughlin not declared themselves unavailable, then the number would surely have been elevated by two.

McBride was making his fifth Lion's tour, a record, and by the time he and his team returned from South Africa, they had fashioned unprecedented glory. McBride led his side through 22 matches on that tour and came home with a record of played 21, drew one, lost none and won the Test series 3–0 with the final Test drawn.

They positively devastated the South Africans on their own soil. They won the first Test in Cape Town, the second in Pretoria and the third in Port Elizabeth in a manner that marked them down as team of exceptional talent. McBride, Milliken and Slattery played in all four Tests on the tour and the only one they failed to win was the last in Johannesburg. Slattery 'scored' what was generally considered to be the winning try in that game but, for some reason difficult to understand, the South African referee disallowed the score.

South African rugby had never had to endure similar torture and McBride and his fellow players returned home heroes to a man. Yet despite scoring deeds of record proportions, there were a few who sought to devalue the magnitude of the successes of that tour. Coming as it did in the aftermath of the Lion's success in 1971 in New Zealand, rugby in Britain and Ireland was now in the midst of a golden era. Unfortunately there was a failure to build on those achievements and, when the Lions went to New Zealand in 1977, they lost the series; the southern hemisphere had regained some measure at least of its previous superiority. Gibson joined the tour to South Africa as a replacement, but it speaks volumes for the play of Milliken and his young Scottish midfield partner Ian McGeechan that he could not make the Test side.

So it was against this background that Ireland set about celebrating the centenary season.

19

The centenary season

The most elaborate plans had been drawn up to mark the first century of the Irish Union. There had been suggestions that Sarsfield Hogan would be asked to take the presidency yet again, a task he had performed with distinction in 1949. But now, over seventy years of age, he declined the honour, feeling that it was a task for a younger man. There could not have been, as events proved, a happier choice for the task of leading the IRFU on the furious social round that season than Harry McKibbin. His great tact, vast experience and most pleasing manner saw him do a wonderful job at the helm in so demanding a season.

The action started early with Ireland playing against a President's XV at Lansdowne Road early in September. The President's XV was drawn from seven nations and, in a gesture to the players, the IRFU decided that caps would be awarded for the match. Nature was not in a bountiful mood on the afternoon of 7 September 1974 in the Dublin area. Perhaps it was a reminder to us all of the kind of conditions in which George Hall Stack and his pioneers had started it all on that afternoon in Kennington 100 years previously.

The ceremonies started with an ecumenical service with the flags of every club affiliated to the IRFU on view.

The match itself provided some excellent entertainment despite the heavy rain and treacherous surface and ended in an 18–18 draw.

There followed a tour by the Wolfhounds, the Irish equivalent of the Barbarians, who played in all four provinces. They had assembled a worthy collection of players drawn from the major rugby playing countries with the exception of New Zealand. They had their own special part in the centenary celebrations, a tour to Ireland which opened on 6 November at the Mardyke, Cork, and appropriately it opened against the Combined Universities, a fitting tribute to the universities, who have given, and still give, so much to Irish rugby. The All Blacks played against all four provincial sides, with the game against

Connacht in Galway on 20 November being especially significant, the first for Connacht against a major touring team.

The All Blacks, led by Andy Leslie, a back-row forward in the typical New Zealand mould, and with Noel Stanley as manager and J.J. Stewart as the coach, beat all four provinces and the Universities, who in fact, gave them their hardest match.

That was the record they took into the international on 23 November at Lansdowne Road and in that encounter they proved that their scrummaging, allegedly weak, had improved immeasurably and they proved much too good for an Ireland side which had to field without Mike Gibson, who was injured. His place was taken by James Crowe, a young student at UCD who, by his selection, was emulating a famous father, Morgan who had been capped in 1929. A student from UCC, Pat Parfrey, also won his first and as it transpired only cap that afternoon. All Ireland's experienced men were on hand in the pack, but they just could not cope with the All Blacks, who from start to finish were the better side.

So the hope that Ireland would mark their centenary season by beating the All Blacks for the first time perished.

The All Blacks were most worthy ambassadors for their country and took a full part in the celebrations, but, in typical manner, did not sacrifice anything on the field to the demands of the social whirl.

Despite the defeat, there was optimism that Ireland would do well in the championship and, for a while, hope flickered in that direction. But there were, too, ominous signs that the Irish players who had been through that hard tour of South Africa the previous summer were now showing that the tour had taken a lot out of them and they had not, because of the early start to the international season, been able to take the customary rest players take at the start of a season immediately following a Lion's tour.

England came to Dublin for the opening match of the championship in January; Ireland won by twelve points to nine but without ever looking convincing. That match marked the start of the international careers of number eight Willie Duggan, from Blackrock College, and Pat Whelan, a hooker from Garryowen. Whelan had thus taken over from Ken Kennedy and had been Kennedy's principal challenger over the previous seasons. Duggan that afternoon started what was to be a very distinguished and protracted international career. Sean Lynch had given way to Roger Clegg, a prop from the Bangor club, who had won a cap in 1973 and at outside-half Billy McCombe returned to the international scene to win his second cap seven years after he had made his only previous appearance for Ireland against France in 1968. There were distinct signs that some very illustrious careers were in their closing phase that centenary season. If England proved manageable, Scotland, at Murrayfield, did not and Ireland lost by 20 points to 13 with the Scottish pack doing a very good demolition job.

The visit of France to Dublin was next on the agenda and here the Irish gave their best display of the season winning by 25 points to 6. That was the highest total Ireland had scored against France and the occasion was made all the more memorable by the fact that McBride scored a try, the only occasion in his 63 appearances for Ireland that he had done so. The crowd came onto the pitch to acclaim the try. McCombe's recall had been a success and he was scoring liberally for Ireland. Ken Kennedy had been recalled for the match, and on the flank, Slattery was partnered by a new cap, Mick Sherry from the Lansdowne club.

So Ireland went to Cardiff in optimistic mood, but left chastened as no other Irish side in history had been at the famous shrine of Welsh rugby. Ireland got destroyed that afternoon as the brilliant Welsh backs ran riot and Ireland lost by 32 points to 4, with Duggan getting a late try as the only measure of consolation and a very minute one it was. Wales had played brilliantly and that total of 32 was a record by the Welsh against Ireland.

It was, as circumstances decreed, to be the last hurrah, too, for several of the great Irish players who had been on the scene around this period.

We were, in effect, witnessing the end of an era on that day of brilliant sunshine in Cardiff. We were also bearing witness to a Welsh side at the height of their powers and one that went on to fashion a string of victories unmatched in the annals of the game. Yet one felt the sadness not just of a heavy defeat, but of the belief that not again would we see some of the greats of Irish rugby in an Ireland jersey. The feeling was to be given substance within the next few months.

But the centenary celebrations were not yet done. On 19 April there was a four countries match at Lansdowne Road. Appropriately that ended in a win for Ireland-Scotland by 17 points to 10 over England-Wales. McBride led the Ireland-Scotland team and it was the last occasion we were to see him lead out a side at Lansdowne Road. There was a surprise in store for him as he left the field, for he was 'captured' by television personality Eamon Andrews and that evening was the subject of the 'This is your Life' programme.

What a rugby life it had been, too; 63 caps, an all time record for a forward, five Lion's tours, 17 Test appearances for the Lions and he had been part of those glorious successes in New Zealand in 1971 and the man at the heart of the success in South Africa in 1974.

Whatever the disappointments of the season on the international field, the centenary dinner in Dublin on the night of the Combined match was a marvellous affair. Personalities from the world of rugby assembled and an especially memorable part of the evening was a great speech from one of the legendary figures of rugby, England's Sir Wavell Wakefield.

The curtain came down on the centenary season at Thomond Park, Limerick when a special All Ireland competition was held. It was won by St Mary's College, then with a side blessed with an abundance of talent, including internationals Tom Grace, John Moloney and Denis Hickie. Now it was on to the next one hundred.

20
A lean period
1975–78

When the 1975–76 season started, it was very much a changed scene as far as the Ireland side was concerned. During the summer Willie John McBride decided that the time had come to stand down from the demands of the international game. He wrote to the secretary of the Ulster Branch, Frank Humphreys, informing him that he did not wish to be considered again for the Ulster team and that was its own declaration that he was no longer in the reckoning for the Ireland side. Gone, too, was Ray McLoughlin, who did not make any formal announcement about his retirement, just faded out of the game at representative level. The 1975 season was also to be the last for Ken Kennedy and, having served three years as coach, Syd Millar had surrendered that onerous position.

It was indeed changed times in Ireland. Millar was succeeded as coach by Roly Meates, a man who had been deeply involved on the coaching scene both with Trinity College and with the Leinster side. Meates' first assignment in his new capacity was to prepare the Ireland 'B' team for the match against France in Dublin on 6 December 1975. This was Ireland's first venture into the 'B' area of activity and it was not greeted with universal enthusiasm in Ireland. Some felt, and with justification, that Ireland just did not have the depth of resources to field two international teams at senior level.

But, in fact, Ireland won that afternoon, by 9 points to 6 with all the scores coming from penalty goals. It was a bad tempered affair that saw four players sent off the field by English referee Alan Welsby, two from each side. However welcome a win, it could not, in the circumstances, be classed as an auspicious start to this new area of international rugby for the Irish.

Meates, a former Leinster prop, then had the task of getting a side ready to meet Australia in January. With some of the great players gone and others of experience out of form, the selectors came up with a strange mix.

They brought back Mick Molloy to partner Moss Keane in the second-row. Molloy, a doctor in London, had last played in 1973 and was now very much in the veteran stages. At prop, Ray McLoughlin's older brother Fedhlim was given his first cap and his partner in the front-row was Paddy Agnew, from the CIYMS Club in Belfast. The age ratio of the Irish pack had certainly not been brought down. John Cantrell, a highly skilled hooker from UCD who had played in the 'B' match succeeded Kennedy. Gibson, who had taken over the captaincy, was partnered by Ian McIlrath, from Ballymena, and at half-back the selectors went for a youthful combination of Ollie Campbell, from Old Belvedere and John Robbie the Trinity scrum-half. Robbie displaced John Moloney, who had not had a good season.

Campbell and Robbie did reasonably well but laboured in difficult circumstances and Campbell, a place kicker of quality, missed several kicks at goal that afternoon when Ireland lost 20–10; they were the only one of the four home countries to lose to the Wallabies. That Campbell should have failed with the penalty chances was ironical, for a few years later, his exploits in that particular facet of the game would be of record breaking proportions.

At the start of the season, Ireland received a bad blow when Dick Milliken, who seemed set for a protracted career, sustained a very bad ankle injury and, while it was hoped he would recover, in fact it was of such a nature that he never again played representative rugby. His attempts at a comeback were invariably stifled by the ankle. Milliken, who had starred in South Africa, would have been an invaluable asset to Ireland at this particular time.

So Meates had got off to a rather disappointing start with his team and the season was a troubled one for him and for Ireland. Ireland's first match in the championship presented a forbidding prospect, a visit to Paris. The Irish were overwhelmed 26–3. The 23 points margin was the best France had ever enjoyed against the Irish. That afternoon, a prop from Old Wesley, Phil Orr made his debut, coming in as a late replacement for Agnew. He was one of the few successes in the side and was to have an international career of immense distinction, still being there ten years later in the heart of the Irish scrum.

Barry McGann had been restored to the outside-half berth, returning after a three year's absence. His form that season had merited his return and his experience and immense footballing skills got their due reward. Brendan Foley, a durable forward from the Shannon club, came in to partner Keane in the second row and Shay Deering was on the flank. Phil O'Callaghan, from Dolphin, was in the front row with Orr and Cantrell. O'Callaghan had last played in 1970. So if some of the old had gone, the selectors were intent on reverting to others who had served the cause in the past and had then been omitted.

Gibson's captaincy was not a success and he was never happy in the role. There was a suggestion that he would be relieved of the task for the next match, against Wales in Dublin, but before a decision was taken, he wrote to the chairman of selectors Joe Fanagan and informed him that he did not again want to be considered for the captaincy. In writing that letter, Gibson did no more than anticipate the selectors' minds; he would not in any case have led the side against Wales. The task was given to Tom Grace and the great St Mary's College wing was a happy choice for what was a difficult task at a very difficult time. He did it admirably, but Ireland lost 34–9 to Wales and had Donal Canniffe, from Lansdowne, at scrum-half for Robbie Canniffe, who had served much of his apprenticeship with the Constitution club had led the 'B' side against France.

Ireland went to Twickenham in search of a fifth successive win over England and a hat-trick of successes at Twickenham; they duly won 13–12. Ireland trailed 9–0 at one stage, but inspired by McGann, who scored nine points, they fought back to gain a most worthy and a very welcome win. There were two more newcomers in the threequarter line, Joe Brady, from Wanderers, and Steve Blake-Knox from NIFC. Harry Steele, another who had played in the 'B' match, won his first cap as deputy for Willie Duggan, who was injured.

Steele, from Ballymena, was a most accomplished and versatile forward who could play in the second- and back-rows with equal facility. There was some confidence that Ireland would beat Scotland in the last match in Dublin, but on a damp and dismal afternoon the Scottish pack ruled the day and their team won 15–6 in a match that did not produce a single try. It was Scotland's first away win for five years. John Moloney had been recalled to scrum-half for the match, but his recall did not herald either success for Ireland nor for the player, who had failed to recapture his great form of the mid-1970s. The match was notable for the fact that Harry McKibbin, from Instonians, son of the IRFU president of the centenary season, came on in the 73rd minute as a replacement for Gibson, thus emulating the achievement of his father in gaining international honours. It was, in fact, his only appearance in the national jersey.

That summer Ireland faced an awesome task, in the shape of a tour to

New Zealand and Fiji. It was felt that such a tour would do much to hasten the development of the young and inexperienced players in the Ireland side, but that in fact was not the end product, although, under the inspiring leadership of Tom Grace and the industry of Meates, the team did not do at all badly. The manager was Kevin Quilligan, from Garryowen, a man who, as player and administrator, had served the game well.

Ireland took twenty-five players on the tour with John Moloney being omitted, the selectors opting for Canniffe and Robbie as the scrum-halves. The tour opened with a win over South Canterbury at Timaru and there followed a very good win over North Auckland in Whangarei. Ireland lost the third match most unluckily to Auckland, being deprived of a try in the most controversial of circumstances that would have made all the difference as they lost 13–10. They then beat Manawatu in Palmerston North, but were overwhelmed by Canterbury at Lancaster Park. Deering was injured in that match and ruled out of further participation on the tour, a cruel blow. He was replaced by the veteran Jimmy Davidson, a man who had made his debut in the 1960s.

A win over Southland in Invercargill followed in a most unpleasant match, ruined by the petulance of the home players who seemed more intent on physical intimidation than football. Scrum-half Robbie McGrath, from Wanderers, who had been flown out as a replacement when Canniffe broke an ankle in training, was badly cut on the head in the match.

Ireland went into the Test match in Wellington with four wins and two losses and, although they played reasonably well, lost 11–3, paying a high price for a few missed chances that might, if taken, have turned the game.

On the way home Ireland played Fiji and won 8–0 in Suva on a ground quite unlike anything previously endured. There were heavy areas of the pitch and indeed frogs were jumping on the playing surface during the match.

They returned and prepared for the next season, when Dudley Higgins, a Triple Crown winner at full-back in the 1948 side, took over the presidency. He had accompanied the side to New Zealand and had, in fact, acted in the presidential capacity through the season as the man elected, Dr Jim Keane, had died within twelve days of his election. Keane had been a great servant to the game in Connacht and his untimely death deprived him of fulfilling a role to which he had been so eagerly looking forward.

If 1976 was one of problems, 1977 was a positive nightmare and Ireland lost every match played. A 25–9 defeat in Cardiff was an unhappy beginning and that match also saw two players sent from the field, Willie Duggan (Ireland) and Geoff Wheel (Wales). Duggan thus had the doubtful distinction of being the only Irishman sent from the field in a full international. His dismissal, and indeed that of Wheel, was by no means greeted with unanimous approval and the action of referee Norman Sanson came in for some severe criticism.

It was an Ireland side much altered. There was a new full-back in Frank Wilson, from CIYMS, who had been impressive in a 'B' international in Dijon against France, a match in which a young man named Tony Ward first wore the green jersey. Ward had been a soccer player of note, but while studying in Limerick had been prevailed upon to return to rugby by the Garryowen club. He had been an accomplished schools player with St Mary's College in Dublin. In fact Ward did not get into the Ireland side that season, when Ireland used twenty-seven players in four matches, but the signs were evident that his advent would not be long delayed.

The problems faced by the selectors in 1977 are amply demonstrated by the fact that only six players were in the side for all four matches, Grace, Gibson, Orr, Whelan, Keane and Duggan. Whelan had displaced Cantrell as hooker in New Zealand and had held onto the berth. Caps were handed out liberally and youth given its chance. Two nineteen-year-olds, Alistair McKibbin, another son of the cenentary year president, and Jim Bowen, from Constitution, both got selected. They were on the first Ireland schools side to play England in 1975. Gibson had two matches at outside-half, a position he had last occupied in 1969. Quinn was eventually restored to the position and Robbie took over again at scrum-half from Robbie McGrath who had been capped against Wales as had Tom Feighery from the St Mary's Club whose brother Con had been on the 1972 side. Ned Byrne, from Blackrock College, eventually won his way into the side and his selection enabled him to complete a unique double. He had won an All Ireland senior Hurling medal with Kilkenny and thus became the only man in history to reach the zenith at both sports.

An odd aspect of the season was that Ireland led at half-time in three of the four matches and against England were level at the interval; yet they lost all four. Fergus Slattery's return to the team after missing out in 1976 added much needed pace to the back-row and a young Wanderers' wing, Alfred McLennan, held out promise. But some of the younger element brought in just did not measure up to the required standard and it was, in all, a very disappointing season. The consequences of it were that Meates lost the coaching position for the 1978 campaign and the task was taken over by one of the selectors Noel Murphy, whose eminent career had ended in 1969 with 41 international caps. He had coached Munster with some success and brought an immense depth of experience to his task.

21

Glory down under

When the Lions went to New Zealand in 1977, the composition of the team accurately reflected the strength of the game in the four home unions. The original selection included no more than three Irishmen, Willie Duggan, Mike Gibson and Philip Orr. Prior to departure, Geoff Wheel, of Wales, withdrew and Moss Keane was called into the party. So four Irishmen set out on the adventure, destined to end in defeat for the Lions.

Duggan was the most successful of the Irish players and did extremely well. He was an automatic choice for the Tests. Keane and Orr both played in one each but Gibson, undertaking his fifth tour to equal McBride's record, had a most frustrating time and, in fact, played in only five matches and was never a serious contender for a Test place.

Noel Murphy, meanwhile, was faced with the task of restoring confidence in the Irish side. The selectors too had the task of getting things right, something they had patently failed to do the previous year, when they stumbled from error to error.

Ireland played Scotland in a 'B' international at Murrayfield and won the match with the Irish scores coming from the half-backs Ward and Colin Patterson, the latter a scrum-half from Instonians who was building a worthy reputation. He had been given the scrum-half berth on the senior side in the final trial, thus underlining the suggestion that his first cap beckoned. In fact he was injured in the trial and when the team to play Scotland in Dublin was announced, John Moloney had been restored to scrum-half and Ward was named for his first cap at outside-half. Paul McNaughton, like Ward an accomplished soccer player, was in the centre with Alistair McKibbin; Gibson was not available. Donal Spring, a student at Trinity College, and a member of a renowned sporting family from County Kerry, was named at second-row with Keane. John O'Driscoll from London Irish, a younger brother of Barry who had played at full back in 1971, was in the back-row.

Ireland won the match 12–9 and Ward made a memorable debut, scoring eight points with two penalty goals and a conversion. Scotland missed a great chance to equalise late in the game but elected to run a penalty from a very kickable position and failed to profit.

Noel Murphy made an auspicious start. Ireland went to France and on a pitch frozen solid in parts lost by 10 points to 9. Seldom can an Irish side have been so unlucky. The pitch, quite frankly, was not in a fit condition for a match. The Irish played heroically, none more so than Duggan, Moloney, Ward and Tony Ensor at full-back. Ward kicked three penalty goals. Harry Steele was, by now, Keane's second-row partner, and a good hand he made of it. He had been brought into the position on the morning of the match when the man chosen, Emmet O'Rafferty from Wanderers, had to cry off due to a leg injury. O'Rafferty was never to get another chance.

Ireland had made a surprising decision for that match by naming Gibson on the right-wing and omitting Grace. This was the third position in which Gibson had played for Ireland but his great football skills and considerable pace enabled him to play on the wing as well as he had played at outside-half and centre.

Ireland met Wales at Lansdowne Road with Wales going for a hat-trick of Triple Crowns and, in a memorable match, Wales won 20–16. The crucial try was scored in very doubtful circumstances and the great Welsh full back J.P.R. Williams incurred the wrath of the crowd by a very late charge on Gibson, an indiscretion compounded in the aftermath of the match when Williams described his action as 'a professional foul'. It was a foul not appreciated by the spectators that afternoon. Ward scored twelve of Ireland's points and Moloney got a try.

Ireland's last match was at Twickenham, where England won for the first time against the Irish since 1970, taking the match 15–9. Ward scored Ireland's nine points with a dropped goal and two penalty goals to bring his total for the season to a record 38 in four matches. He had made a tremendous impact and was named as 'European Player of the Year' for his exploits. Ireland seemed to have found a star to occupy a key position and he looked likely to hold down the position for years to come. 'The future of Irish rugby is in the hands of Tony Ward and some others,' said Noel Murphy, words that were to have a very hollow ring twelve months later.

Although there was only one win from four matches, Ireland had been very unfortunate against both Wales and France, and against

England it had taken a try by Mike Slemen in the second-half to see England to success. Things had taken a decided upturn and events in 1979 followed a course to give strength to that belief.

The All Blacks came to Britain in the autumn of 1978 with Graham Mourie as captain. They were scheduled for three matches in Ireland, against Munster at Thomond Park, against Ireland in Dublin and against Ulster.

Their first engagement was against Munster on 31 October. It was the fifth match of the visit and the New Zealanders went into it with a 100 per cent tour record.

Conscious of Munster's great record against touring teams, and their ability to raise their game on such occasions, the All Blacks selected what was almost a full strength Test side. Munster, coached by Tom Kiernan, made it implicitly clear from the outset that they were prepared to take the All Blacks on and this they did as never before. The ground was throbbing with excitement as Munster took the game to the visitors. The home team were well endowed with experience with internationals behind the scrum in full-back Larry Moloney and threequarter Seamus Dennison. Jimmy Bowen, Ward and Canniffe were the halves and in the pack Moss Keane, Brendan Foley, Donal Spring and Pat Whelan, internationals all, were accompanied by four players of quality, two of whom were later that season to play for Ireland, flanker Colm Tucker and prop Gerry McLoughlin. With the Munster forwards giving the visitors a torrid time, Ward controlled the play outside the scrum. He teased the All Blacks with some brilliant tactical kicking, ably served by Canniffee, and gave his side the lead with a dropped goal. He was to score eight points that afternoon with flanker Christy Cantillon getting the only try. Munster tackled like demons that memorable day and carried out Kiernan's instructions to the letter. He deserves immense credit for so historic a victory. When the final whistle blew, the ground positively erupted. The players were carried shoulder high from the field. Munster rugby had known no greater day or finer hour and how appropriate that this win should have come in the great rugby city of Limerick where there is an interest in and passion for the game that embraces all sections of society.

The following Saturday Ireland lost to the All Blacks with Ward having Patterson as his partner.

Ireland faced the 1979 campaign in reasonably confident mood and drew with France 9–9 in Dublin. As was now the general pattern, Ward accounted for all nine points. He could and should have won the match for Ireland in the closing stages. Ireland was awarded a differential penalty in front of the French posts, but unsure whether or not he could take the ball back as far as he liked for the drop at goal, he decided to take the kick, was too close, and the kick was blocked down.

Ireland, by now, had some more newcomers in their side including at full-back Dick Spring, whose younger brother Donal was an established international but ruled out through injury. Dick Spring, who won three caps, subsequently entered the political arena with great success and is currently deputy Prime Minister in the Republic government (1986). Politics were far from his mind when he lined out against Wales in Cardiff and was in an Ireland side that scored 21 points but still lost 24–21. Ireland paid heavily for mistakes, with Patterson making one in front of his own posts and Spring another near his own line which allowed Wales to score two crucial tries. Ireland had the frustration of attaining what was then their highest score against Wales, yet lost a match they should have won. Terry Kennedy, from St Mary's College, was on one wing. Colm Tucker and Gerry McLoughlin from the Munster side had won international recognition in the aftermath of the All Blacks match but Mike Gibson had gone. There was, however, another Michael Gibson in the side, a big forward from the Lansdowne club, and his line-out skills were invaluable. He did not have a long international career, as injury too often marred his chances but he performed with great distinction in 1979.

England came to Dublin and were well beaten, with Ward having one of his greatest games in the green jersey. So the Irish travelled to Murrayfield to meet Scotland in the final match and dramatic developments were at hand.

Mike Gibson had informed the selectors that he did not wish to be considered again before the start of the championships. There was a doubt about the fitness of Alistair McKibbin and so Gibson was summoned to the Irish practice session on the Thursday preceeding the match. By now he had already established a world record of 66 caps. That looked likely to be his total when he sent that letter to the selectors, but he was destined to earn three more.

McKibbin proved his fitness, but Terry Kennedy was suffering from influenza. He was forced to withdraw the day before the game and so Gibson was back to win his 67th cap, playing on the wing. Ireland, by now, had a new full-back in Ronnie Elliott, from Bangor, who had displaced Spring. Elliott won his only cap that afternoon and a difficult time it was for him and everyone else. A strong and capricious wind blew around Murrayfield and it ruined a match that ended in an 11–11 draw.

It had not been a bad season for Ireland, a win and two draws from four matches and, with any element of fortune, there would have been a win in Cardiff. Ireland's season was not, however, over for there was a tour to Australia in May and so preparations were in hand for that. Ward, meanwhile, had again been named 'European Player of the Year' and that was but one of the many awards made to him. He was now rated among the best in the game and, by the All Blacks, the very best. There were, however, a few in Ireland who did not see it that way and they were to wield a profound influence on coming events.

One was the man named as manager of the team to tour Australia, Jack Coffey. Coffey had made it clear that he was not among Ward's admirers even before the tour started and made some ominous comments to that effect.

There were some in Ireland among what one might loosely term 'the establishment' who thought Ward was getting far too much publicity. They seemed to fail to appreciate just what he had meant to, what he had achieved for, Ireland. He had come onto the international scene at a time when Ireland was firmly rooted at the bottom of the ladder having managed just one win in two seasons. They had been whitewashed in 1977, the year before Ward's arrival. He lifted the whole scene and generated attention and excitement among followers and even those whose support might be deemed tenuous. That did not apparently go down too well with some and certainly not with the tour manager.

Ollie Campbell, who had won his only cap against Australia in 1976, and who had been injured for much of the 1979 season returned, for the Leinster Cup campaign with his club Old Belvedere and played splendidly. He was chosen as the second outside-half to go to Australia. It was a wise and justified choice. Fergus Slattery had, by now, assumed the captaincy. A few players were forced to withdraw from the touring party including Donal Spring and the younger Michael Gibson. Willie Duggan, under something of a cloud for a time that season, had returned with some excellent displays and was duly chosen. John O'Driscoll, capped against Scotland, was also chosen and John Moloney, who had not played that season in the championship as Colin Patterson held down the scrum-half berth, was named as second scrum-half.

Ireland opened the tour in Perth and easily beat Western Australia. That afternoon Campbell was off form with his kicking, but it did not matter as Ireland won easily. The next match was against ACT in

Canberra and Ward scored 19 points, an all time record at the time for an Irish player in any match. The following Saturday he played brilliantly again as Ireland beat New South Wales in Sydney; Ward scored eight points in a 16–12 success. Ireland had been cruising to success when Mike Gibson, playing on the wing, made two uncharacteristic errors to allow the home team back into the match, but some brilliant defensive kicking by Ward kept Ireland in front.

The next match, and last before the first Test, was against Queensland in Brisbane and Campbell was named at outside-half. He marked the occasion by scoring all Ireland's 18 points in an 18–15 triumph. Campbell had played splendidly as Ward had done in the other matches and there was a suggestion that Campbell would make the Test side—in the centre.

Ireland had a problem in that area and Gibson, who had played on the wing early in the tour, was showing the weight of the years. Before the team was selected, the manager was making ominous sounds about who would play at outside-half and the indications did not look favourable for Ward. He was the man in possession, had played splendidly for Ireland in every international, had played near the peak of his form on the tour, yet inexplicably seemed destined to be dropped. That, after he had scored 19 points in a match just a week earlier to establish a record for Ireland.

The grapevine proved correct and, when the team was announced Ward was omitted, Campbell was outside-half, McNaughton and Gibson were in the centre and Kennedy and John Moloney were on the wings with a newcomer at full-back in Rodney O'Donnell from the St Mary's Club.

Moloney, a sprinter of considerable merit, had played on the wing against Queensland when McLennan was forced out, retained the berth to win his 24th cap, but the previous 23 had been at scrum-half. Ward was shattered when he heard the news and so were the people at home in Ireland when it was conveyed to them.

The team was announced after the squad travelled to Paradise Bay just outside Brisbane for a training session. Ward had got a tip off from his team mate Pat Whelan on the coach journey to Paradise Bay; Whelan had been told by a journalist who, the previous evening, had heard Coffey pronounce on the possible selection at outside-half.

Seldom, if ever, in history had a man been dropped in the aftermath of so many magnificent performances. Were any of us to be judged on similar lines in our chosen profession, then we all would have reason to fear the future. Perhaps it might all have been more understandable had

Ireland opted to play an expansive game, but, in fact, Ireland did nothing of the sort. It was ten-man rugby all the way and Campbell, brilliantly served by Patterson, and playing behind an Ireland pack that dominated the Australians, had a field day in the Test scoring 19 points with four penalty goals, a dropped goal and two conversions. That was a total of 19 points, ironically the figure Ward had set 12 days previously when he played against ACT.

It was hard on Ward and, in many respects hard on Campbell, who must have felt the pressure caused by the controversy. But he remained ice cool and all his immense footballing skills and splendid temperament were revealed. Ireland won 27–12, a magnificent victory with the Irish pack, Patterson, Campbell and full-back O'Donnell in majestic form. Yet one could not escape the conclusion that Ward had been extremely harshly treated and the management, in fact, gave contradictory accounts of the selection.

Noel Murphy said that senior players were not consulted in the selection, yet Fergus Slattery, who with Murphy and Coffey formed the selection committee, said they had been consulted, notably Mike Gibson, who had been extremely fortunate on his form to have got a Test place. Coffey went back on an agreement he had made with the touring Press prior to the tour when he refused to allow Ward to be interviewed. Coffey and Murphy had, at a meeting prior to that tour, assured those of us travelling with the party that, provided, the management was asked permission, players could be interviewed. Even a request that Ward be interviewed with the manager and coach present was rejected by Coffey, whose intransigence was not appreciated. His constant sniping at Ward prior to the tour, and indeed during the tour, was hard to fathom. Perhaps he felt justified in the aftermath of the match, one must hope he has not been subjected himself to judgement based on similar lines.

What Ward would have made of the chances Campbell took so brilliantly one cannot say. His career from that day on was to be constantly interrupted. In the fickle manner of the public mind, critics suddenly came forth to analyse his game and tell of his faults. Not too many would have offered similar judgements prior to the tour.

Noel Murphy was, quite frankly, much more forthcoming than Coffey and admitted he had grave reservations about omitting Ward and said he had a few sleepless nights wondering if he had made the right decision. 'I knew', said Murphy 'that if we lost, there would have been a terrific outcry at the dropping of Tony Ward.'

What those of us there still wonder, nonetheless, is just what powers of logic were used by Murphy, Coffey and Slattery, to justify the dropping of the player. Murphy and Slattery were both eminent internationals themselves. Had they been subjected to similar treatment then their cap collection would have been infinitely less.

Ireland went on to beat New South Wales Country Districts on that tour, lost to Sydney, when Campbell played at full-back with Ward at outside-half, and then came the second Test and last match of the tour.

Had Campbell been dropped to accommodate Ward, it would have been as unjust as was the dropping of Ward in the first instance. Campbell had taken his chance brilliantly and again in the second Test played well as Ireland won this time much more narrowly and less convincingly by 9–3. The Australians were much tighter in this game and, urged on by the partisan crowd at Sydney Cricket Ground, gave full vent to their feelings. Nonetheless it was a magnificent win for Ireland who thus took the series 2–0, the best result ever attained by one of the home countries in a Test series in the southern hemisphere, before or since.

Ireland returned home looking forward eagerly to the coming season. Murphy, it seemed, had built a side now capable of offering a really worthwhile challenge in the championship.

Ward was mystified by the whole sequence of events and was never given an explanation as to why he was dropped or what he had done wrong in his games for Ireland. Never again was he to be Ireland's regular choice at outside-half, but he would have many more hours when he underlined his great ability. So, too, would Campbell both for Ireland and the Lions. There are some who have profound regret that Ireland did see fit to play both together more often than the three occasions they did in 1981.

22

From whitewash to Triple Crown 1981–82

The promise of the 1979 tour to Australia was not maintained during the 1980 championship season and hopes of a Triple Crown for the first time since 1949 perished at the first hurdle when England scored a very comprehensive win at Twickenham. That was the prelude to a Grand Slam for an England side splendidly led by Bill Beaumont.

Ward had a knee injury which kept him inactive for much of the season and in any case Campbell was now firmly established at ouside-half and playing in a manner that justified his continued selection. Ward recovered midway through the championship and was called into the Ireland replacement panel as understudy for Campbell. Ireland lost to France as well as England, but beat Scotland and, in the final match of the campaign, played the best rugby of the season to overwhelm Wales in Dublin. Campbell's kicking skills earned him a record 46 points in the championship series.

Ciaran Fitzgerald, a hooker from St Mary's College, who had displaced Pat Whelan in Australia, and O'Donnell, a star at full-back on the tour, were now established members of the side. Moloney had played two more matches in the 1980 campaign on the wing and that marked the end of his long and very distinguished international career.

The selection of the Lions team to tour South Africa brought with it the usual chorus of protest about continuing links with South Africa. Some players were not available for the tour because of business commitments and some because they did not want to play in South Africa. Ireland had five players in the party. They were O'Donnell, O'Driscoll, Patterson, Campbell and Colm Tucker, from Shannon, who, although not able to command a regular place in the Ireland side was still deemed good enough to merit Lions selections. Events on the tour were to justify that choice. Ward was not even sent an availability card as Campbell and Gareth Davies of Wales were the outside-half choices.

The tour was plagued by ill luck in the matter of injuries from the outset. Quite apart from the playing representation, Ireland also had the singular distinction of providing both manager, Syd Millar and coach, Noel Murphy. They did not have an easy time.

With both Campbell and Davies injured, the Lions had a problem at outside-half just prior to the first Test and they asked for Ward to travel out. He did so with some reluctance, but eventually agreed to go. Within a week of his arrival he was selected for the first Test in Cape Town. He had not played an international for almost a year and a half, his last appearance being against Scotland in March 1979. He damaged a thigh during training prior to the Test, but that afternoon at Newlands scored 18 points for the Lions, an all time record for a Lions player in a Test match. Alas the team was not blessed with success and South Africa won the Test and indeed the series, 3–1, with the Lions winning only the last Test in which Campbell played.

In addition to Ward, both Orr and John Robbie were also called out as replacements on the tour, which was to end the representative careers of two of the Irishmen, O'Donnell and Patterson, who both received horrific injuries. O'Donnell cracked a bone in his neck that necessitated two operations, one which had proved unsuccessful in South Africa and another on his return. Patterson, in the second last match of the tour, sustained a knee injury that ended his career. It had proved a costly exercise for the Irish.

The 1980 championship marked the end of Noel Murphy's reign. He had served three years as Ireland coach. He was replaced by Tom Kiernan, his Constitution clubmate, and, indeed, his cousin; Kiernan was to have a torrid first year in office. Ireland lost all four championship matches in 1981 and, during the campaign, decided it was time for Ward and Campbell to be accommodated in the same side, this after Ireland lost the opening match against France by 19 points to 13 in Dublin.

Ireland had played Romania in the autumn in Dublin and drew 13–13. Ward that afternoon played at outside-half with Campbell in the centre, a selection not made originally, but which came about when one of the selected centres, McNaughton, withdrew. Ireland scored a brilliant try that afternoon, but nonetheless, when the championship came round, it was Campbell back at outside-half with McNaughton partnered by the young Queen's University medical student David Irwin in the centre. Irwin had gone to Australia and then came into the national side the following season. A young full back from Trinity,

Top: Kevin Flynn breaks down the England defence to score a famous match-winning try against England at Twickenham in 1972. Flynn won twenty caps for Ireland between 1959 and 1973 and was chairman of the Ireland selectors in 1982 when Ireland won the Triple Crown and Championship. Behind him in the photograph is Mike Gibson

Above: The most famous Munster side of all. Heroes to a man: the Munster team that beat New Zealand at Thomond Park on 31 October 1978. Munster won 12-0 and became the first and thus far only Ireland side to beat the All Blacks. *Back row, left to right:* S. Gavin (president Munster branch), J. Cole (touch judge), G. McLoughlin, L. White, M. Keane, D. Spring, C. Tucker, P. Whelan, B. Foley, C. Thomas (Wales) (referee), M. Walsh (touch judge). *Front row:* T. Ward, C. Cantillon, M. Finn, S. Dennison, D. Canniffe (capt), G. Barrett, J. Bowen, L. Moloney

Top left: George Scriven, president of the IRFU and captain of Ireland in the same year, 1882-83. International referee and uniquely twice president of the IRFU

Top right: H. W. D. Dunlop, the man who was responsible for the initial development of Lansdowne Road and the founder and first president of the Lansdowne club

Above: The committee of the IRFU 1985-86. *Back row, left to right:* P. McNamara, N. Henderson, P. Bolger, A. Browne, M. Cuddy, P. Boyle, J. Fahy, T. Kiernan, K. Reid, S. Millar, R. Fitzgerald (secretary treasurer). *Sitting:* P. Patterson, R. Dawson, J. Nelson, (honorary treasurer), Sir E. Bell (senior vice president), D. McKibbin (president), P. Madigan (junior vice president), M. Carroll, H. McKibbin, R. Deacy

Above: Eugene Davy, a great Ireland player in the 1920s and 1930s and president of the IRFU in 1967-68. He also captained Ireland and is still rated as one of the greatest backs to wear the green jersey. He once scored three tries for Ireland in the space of twenty minutes against Scotland at Murrayfield

Top left: G. P. S. 'Sarsfield' Hogan, arguably Ireland's greatest rugby legislator. Former final Irish trialist, he was a member of the IRFU committee from the mid 1930s until 1971. He was president of the IRFU in 1948-9, president of the Leinster branch, an Ireland selector and he represented Ireland on the International Board from 1946 until 1971. He was also manager of the Ireland side that toured Argentina and Chile in 1952

Top right: A great player and a great legislator, Harry Thrift. He captained Ireland in 1908, was president of the IRFU in 1923-24, on the International Board from 1931 to 1956 and honorary secretary of that body from 1933 to 1956

e: Ireland's contribution to international refereeing een immense. Kevin Kelleher, seen here, shares with n Walters (Wales) the distinction of having refereed ty-one internationals, a world record

This page and opposite: great Irish touring teams. *Top:* The Ireland team and officials that toured Australia in 1967. Ireland won the only Test match played on that tour and thus became the first of the home countries to win an international in the southern hemisphere. Team captain Tom Kiernan is third from left in centre row, seated next to Eugene Davy, who was manager, with assistant manager Des McKibbin on Davy's left

Above: New Zealand and Fiji, 1976. *Back row, left to right:* M. Quinn, J. Robbie, J. Cantrell, R. Clegg, P. Orr, P. Whelan, L. Moloney, S. Deering, T. Feighery. *Middle row:* I. McIlrath, J. Brady, H. Steele, R. Hakin, M. Keane, W. Duggan. E. O'Rafferty, B. Foley, D. Canniffe. *Sitting:* S. McKinney, A. Ensor, B. McGann, R. Meates (coach), T. Grace (capt), K. Quilligan (manager), M. Gibson, W. McMaster, P. O'Callaghan. *Insets:* R. McGrath, J. Davidson

half-century bridge. The Ireland team that won the Triple Crown, Championship and completed Ireland's only Grand Slam in 1948, forty-nine years after the previous Triple Crown success in 1899. *Back row, left to right:* . Crawford (selector), W. McKee, J. McCarthy, J. C. Daly, J. E. Nelson, C. Callan, D. O'Brien, W. McKay, . O'Hanlon, M. Allen (referee). *Sitting:* A. McConnell, B. Mullan, K. Mullen (capt), Dr T. McGrath (president RFU), D. Higgins, P. Reid. *Front:* E. Strathdee, J. Kyle. *Insets:* J. Mattsson (played against England), M. O'Flanagan (played against Scotland), H. De Lacy (played against England and Scotland)

he Greens become Whites. The Ireland side that played South Africa in Dublin in 1931. The picture includes some f Ireland's greatest players. *Back row, left to right:* M. Allen (referee), M. Crowe, L. McMahon, E. Lightfoot, . Russell, J. Egan, J. Siggins, H. Withers, N. Murphy, W. Clarke, (president IRFU). *Front row:* V. J. Pike, E. Davy, . Clinch, G. Beamish (capt), P. Murray, J. Farrell, J. Arigho

Lansdowne Road as it was in 1914. This group, volunteers from Leinster rugby clubs, were preparing to go to the Great War. The picture, taken in September 1914, shows the eastern side of the ground. The wooden structure in the background is a Press stand

Lansdowne Road, January 1984. The New East Stand, which can accommodate 13,400 people. It was built at a cost of over four million pounds and much of the revenue was raised by the sale of ten-year tickets at £500

yle was a hero of the Ireland teams that won the Triple Crown and Championship in the golden era between
nd 1951. Here he is seen making the break that led to his scoring a memorable try against France in Belfast in
Kyle was capped forty-six times for Ireland between 1947 and 1958 and captivated New Zealand on the
:our of that country in 1950

action shot of John O'Meara as he sends out a pass to Jack Kyle during the match against England at
:>wne Road in 1951, a season in which Ireland won the International Championship. O'Meara was capped on
-two occasions

Top: The first Ireland Schools side to play in an international, against England at Lansdowne Road in March 1975. No fewer than seven of this side went on to win full caps, while an eighth not in the photo — Ronan Kearney — came on as a replacement and was also capped at full level

Above: The first Ireland team to play in a 'B' international, against France at Lansdowne Road i December 1975. Ireland won a match in which fou players, two from each side, were sent off the field b referee Alan Welsby. *Standing, left to right:* D. Burn (touch coach), A. McLean, B. Smith, H. Steele, D. Dalton, E. Molloy, N. Byrne, A. Welsby (referee *Sitting:* T. Feighery, J. Cantrell, J. Foetune, D. Cann (capt), D. Higgins (president IRFU), R. Finn, J. Col M. Casserly. *Front:* L. Moloney, H. Condon

ow: Moss Finn scoring Ireland's second try in the match against Wales in Dublin in 1982. The try was brilliantly ceived and is rated among the best ever seen at Lansdowne Road

tom: Mike Gibson, arguably the greatest back to wear the Ireland jersey, launches yet another attack. On his right hil Orr, and on his left Pat Whelan from Garryowen, a hooker of great ability. On Whelan's left is Robbie McGrath, and's scrum half during the 1982 Triple Crown and Championship season. Gibson, with sixty-nine caps, is the ld's most capped player

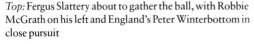

Top: Fergus Slattery about to gather the ball, with Robbie McGrath on his left and England's Peter Winterbottom in close pursuit

Above: Ready and waiting. The Irish forwards at a line-out against Scotland at Lansdowne Road in 1982: Moss Keane, Philip Orr, Donal Lenihan, John O'Driscoll, Willie Duggan and Fergus Slattery

Above: Donal Lenihan, capped twenty-two times as a second row forward, demonstrates his ability to go high in the line-out in this match against England. The England player awaiting developments is Phil Blakeway and the player giving Lenihan a 'helping hand' is Des Fitzgerald

Below: Tony Ward made a huge impact when he came into the Ireland side in 1978. A brilliant place kicker, Ward was twice named 'European Player of the Year'. His career has been marked by controversy, but he made a great comeback to the Ireland side against Scotland at Lansdowne Road in 1986

Record maker: Philip Orr leads Ireland out at sdowne Road in March 1986 against Scotland. Orr winning his fiftieth cap to equal the world record for op forward held by Sandy Carmichael (Scotland). Orr capped initially in 1976 and played forty-nine secutive matches for Ireland before being dropped for natch against Wales in 1986. He was subsequently led for the last match of the 1986 championship

Above: Michael Kiernan, with scrum-half Robbie McGrath on his right and Fergus Slattery behind, makes a typical break during Ireland's Triple Crown-winning season in 1982. In 1985 Kiernan took over the kicking duties and played a central role in another Triple Crown and Championship triumph

Ollie Campbell, whose magnificent kicking enabled Ireland to win the Triple Crown and Championship in 1982 and share the title in 1983, sends yet another on the way to its target. He is the highest points scorer for Ireland in history with 217 from twenty-two appearances between 1976 and 1984

Hugo MacNeill, had forced his way into the team and John Robbie was Campbell's partner at half-back. The pack was an experienced outfit with Whelan back as hooker due to an injury to Ciaran Fitzgerald.

After losing to France, Ireland chose Ward at outside-half for the visit to Wales with Campbell in the centre. Ireland scored two memorable tries against the Welsh with Ward the creator of both. On a very blustery day Wales won 9–8, with a last minute dropped goal giving them an undeserved victory. Ironically, both Ward and Campbell found the wind impossible to judge, but Ward hit an upright with a conversion attempt that, had it gone over, would have given Ireland a win.

The experiment was continued against England in Dublin when Ireland lost 10–6. Then, in the final match, they went down most unluckily to Scotland 10–9 at Murrayfield; Scotland won the match with an interception. So Tom Kiernan had got a whitewash in his first season as coach and how unlucky he and Ireland had been. Two matches lost by a point.

That summer Ireland travelled to South Africa, a tour that was marked by tremendous controversy. The visit of the Lions the previous season had exposed South African claims about multi-racial rugby as spurious. Several Irish players refused to go to South Africa and some others could not get time off work. It was, consequently, a weakened Ireland party that travelled to South Africa with Kiernan as coach, Paddy Madigan, an IRFU committeeman as manager, and Malcolm Little from Galway, as medical officer. Ward was one of those who refused to travel and his absence was compounded by a wrist injury to Campbell in the first Test. Keane, MacNeill and Donal Spring had, like Ward, refused to travel. McNaughton, Mick Fitzpatrick and Ciaran Fitzgerald were unavailable for business reasons. Jerry Holland, from Wanderers, was called into the party and won two caps in Keane's absence.

Ireland played magnificently in the two Tests. Ironically Campbell was not selected at outside-half for the first Test, the selectors opting for the St Mary's College player Paul Dean, who won his first cap. A former schools international, Dean was a fine distributor of the ball. Yet it seemed strange that, here, we had Campbell being selected in the centre, a decision Ireland selectors had been so reluctant to make to accommodate both he and Ward until a few months previously. Campbell, a lovely footballer, devastating tackler and great defensive reader of the game, had all the attributes to make a centre of the highest class and he proved that in the few games he played in the position.

The constant controversy, Ward or Campbell, was totally unnecessary. Ireland had two of the best backs in the game in these two men and there should not have been a question of one or the other. It should have been both. In a four countries match, just prior to the tour, Ward had kicked 15 points, the highest total by an individual in such a match when playing for Ireland-Scotland against England-Wales as part of the Welsh centenary celebrations. Now it was Dean at outside-half at Newlands, but the match, a most exciting affair, went to the South Africans. In the second Test at Durban, Ireland lost by a point with the Springboks outside-half Naas Botha kicking South Africa to victory. Ireland played that Test without Campbell, without full-back John Murphy from Greystones and without John Robbie. Murphy had made his debut at Newlands and played magnificently but was, like Campbell, injured. Robbie too was ruled out of both tests and it was Robbie McGrath, who played at scrum-half. McGrath had first been capped three years previously and he had a great tour. The veteran Mick Quinn had been summoned when Campbell was injured and he played in the second Test with Dean in the centre and John Hewitt, from the NIFC club, had the distinction of winning two caps on the tour, both as a replacement. The provincial matches on the tour were most disappointing and some of the opposition provided by the South Africans was ludicrous. Such opposition as the South African Mining team, the Gold Cup selection and The President's Cup selection were supposed to emphasise the multi-racial nature of South African rugby. All they did was underline what a sham it was.

For Kiernan, it was a season that had seen six losses from six full internationals. Yet that hardly reflected the true worth of the side and he was to prove the point within a matter of months.

The Australians came in the autumn of 1981 and again beat Ireland who had Ward as outside-half in Campbell's absence through injury. Ward, meanwhile, the previous Tuesday, had destroyed the Australians in Cork as Munster again managed a great win over a major touring side.

It was an unlikely background against which to fashion a Triple Crown and championship success, but that is exactly what Kiernan achieved when Ireland took the Triple Crown for the first time since 1949 and had the great joy of doing it at Lansdowne Road for the first time in history.

Campbell, unavailable against Australia, did not return to the game until a few days after Christmas and, after playing in one club match, was selected for the opening international of the championships, against Wales in Dublin. Ward had again been discarded and indeed the selection committee, under the chairmanship of Kevin Flynn, did not deem Ward good enough even for a place on the replacement panel. Despite Campbell's late return, he played magnificently. Ireland beat Wales in the opening match in Dublin, a match which had to be postponed originally because of a heavy snow fall.

Robbie and McLennan were now no longer available as both had opted to settle in South Africa, but many of the old guard remained. There had been some disturbing aspects of the performance against Australia, but, nonetheless, the selectors opted to stick substantially with the men who played in that game. Ward was an exception. Despite his performance for Munster, described by Flynn thus: 'I have never seen him play better and his kicking was of the highest class', he was now firmly consigned to the outside.

The Irish trial, just before Christmas 1981, saw some eminent names in the junior side, men such as Moss Keane and Fergus Slattery. Ward was outside-half for the senior side and returned a 100 per cent record with his kicking. All to no avail however. The old hands who had been relegated to the Possibles proved their point in the most convincing manner.

Trevor Ringland, a wing from Queen's University, had made his debut against Australia and Donal Lenihan, a second row from UCC, who had also won his first cap that day, were both chosen for the match against Wales. There were two alterations behind the scrum, with Campbell in for Ward and Moss Finn, from Constitution, in for Terry Kennedy, who had broken a leg. Finn had won one cap in 1979 while a member of the UCC club.

Ciaran Fitzgerald was recalled as hooker, Gerry McLoughlin came in at tight-head prop for Mick Fitzpatrick. Keane, who was unavailable for the match against Australia, returned to partner Lenihan and the back-row was the old reliable trio of Slattery, Duggan and O'Driscoll.

Fitzgerald was given the captaincy, an inspired choice by Kevin Flynn and his selection colleagues. Fitzgerald, in some respects, had been fortunate to oust Cantrell from the hooking berth for the latter had played well against Australia and that could not be said of too many of the Ireland side that afternoon.

But his qualities of leadership, already demonstrated with Connacht and the Ireland 'B' side, were needed when Slattery informed the selectors that he did not wish to continue as captain after the defeat by

Australia. After making a very uneasy start against the Welsh, Ireland were 9–8 down in the first half, the trend of the match altered dramatically after Wales had failed to take a great chance of a try.

Ringland had scored Ireland's try, but Terry Holmes (try) and Gwyn Evans (penalty goal and conversion) had appeared to put Wales on the road to victory and Ireland faced a seventh successive international defeat. But inspired by Fitzgerald, the Irish forwards improved dramatically and proceeded to play Wales off the field and Campbell responded in his own brilliant manner to the service laid on for him. Not even injuries to two Irish players, both the centres, could halt the impetus. Dean and David Irwin were both injured, with Irwin having broken a leg. Michael Kiernan, a nephew of the coach, and John Murphy, the reserve full-back, took over as the midfield players and were as inspired as their colleagues.

A glorious break by Campbell opened the way for a try by Finn, then Finn scored another try, rated by many among the best ever seen at the venue, and Ireland won 20–12. The win was greeted with tremendous enthusiasm. Now thoughts turned to Triple Crown possibilities; the gloom engendered by recurring defeat was lifted that afternoon when Ireland won on home soil for the first time in two years.

The next assignment was against England at Twickenham and that was a formidable assignment against a country that still had many of the men who two years previously had won the grand slam.

Kiernan was very careful to kill any talk of Triple Crowns and championships. It was to him a philosophy of one step at a time. He, better than most, knew just how unpredictable the international game could be, the narrow line between victory and defeat. His cautious optimism was undoubtedly the right attitude to instil into his players.

Although through the years, well treated himself by the Press, he was a noted critic of the news media, never losing the chance to knock the rugby writers. He told his players to ignore what they read. In fact, he might have directed that caution towards the public, rather than the Press, most of whom were, like Kiernan, no more than cautiously optimistic.

England lost their great captain Bill Beaumont a few days before the game when he was forced into retirement due to a head injury. England, who came into the match against the background of a draw with Scotland at Murrayfield, were favourites, but Ireland won the match and thoroughly deserved to do so. The Irish pack again played well, notably in the loose, with a team that saw Dean back at centre as partner to Kiernan, the latter who had taken over from the injured Irwin.

Ireland did well in the line-outs and managed to stand up to the demands in the tight; they also revealed the right level of opportunism behind the scrum inspired by a fine display from Campbell in the key position of outside-half. MacNeill scored a try, his third for his country, and Gerry McLoughlin got another after he was driven over the line by the sheer weight of Irish players who were up in support. McLoughlin, who had resigned his post as a school teacher to go to South Africa in 1981, maintains to this day that he pulled the other players over with him. Whatever the method, it was a memorable and invaluable score.

Although Ireland did not mark the occasion by scoring tries of the calibre they had attained against Wales, they scored a most worthy win by 16–15, with England getting a late try to make the score much closer than the general trend of the match warranted. Campbell had kicked a conversion and two penalty goals to supplement the two tries.

So now Scotland alone stood between Ireland and the Triple Crown and no match in recent history captured the imagination of the Irish public as did this one scheduled for Lansdowne Road on 20 February. The clamour for tickets was unprecedented but only about 50,000 lucky souls could be accommodated in Lansdowne Road that afternoon. It was a dull day and in many respects a rather dull match in terms of the quality of the fare, but it was a wonderful occasion as Ireland swept to victory by 21–12. Campbell scored all Ireland's points, six penalty goals and a dropped goal. Scotland got the only try and a good one it was, but they never really looked likely to spoil the party.

So Ireland had won the Triple Crown for the first time since 1949 and in front of the home crowd at Lansdowne Road at that. The crowd went wild and Campbell was a national hero. No more modest man could have so severe a burden placed upon him as hero worship.

The team that fashioned that win was H. MacNeill; M. Finn, M. Kiernan, P. Dean, K. Crossan; O. Campbell, R. McGrath; P. Orr, C. Fitzgerald (capt.), G. McLoughlin, D. Lenihan, M. Keane, F. Slattery, W. Duggan, J. O'Driscoll.

There had been one alteration from the side that beat England. Trevor Ringland was forced out through injury and he was replaced by his Ulster colleague Keith Crossan who won his first cap.

Ireland also won the championship that afternoon with six points from three games, but now a Grand Slam beckoned and the last match was against France in Paris on 20 March, a month after the win over

Scotland. Whether it was the fact that four weeks separated the matches or that Ireland may have had an element of complacency, the team just did not play with anything like the spirit and confidence that had marked the Triple Crown series. France, that season, had lost all three matches prior to the game against Ireland and had refashioned their side. Ireland went to Paris as warm favourites and returned comprehensively beaten by 22–9.

But it had been a great season for all that, and Kiernan deserves the utmost credit for lifting the side. Campbell's play had been crucial and Fitzgerald's leadership invaluable. The road ahead looked to be smooth, and, indeed, in 1983, with a side built on substantially the same lines to the previous season, Ireland again won three out of four matches, but this time, not the Triple Crown as the game lost was to Wales in Cardiff. In the end, they shared the championship with France and that was to be the end of Kiernan's tenure of office as Ireland's coach. He had started with a whitewash, gone to a Triple Crown and Championship and ended by sharing the championship. Not a bad return for the players and the coach.

23

No joy for McBride

Just as the team of 1982 had been led by Ciaran Fitzgerald, so also was the team in 1983 and his track record was now such that he was the warm favourite to lead the Lions to New Zealand in the summer of 1983. The choice of captaincy for that tour was the subject of animated debate in the British Press with many advocating the case for Peter Wheeler, the England hooker. Ironically that support came for Wheeler, even though he had been consistently overlooked by the England selectors, who, when Beaumont went, turned to scrum-half Steve Smith to lead the team.

There was a strange apathy towards the choice of Fitzgerald and some grossly unfair and unjustifiable criticism. The team he had led in 1983 had, in fact, enjoyed exactly the same ratio of success as the 1982 side, which had also won three matches. Indeed in some respects the Ireland side of 1983 played better than the Triple Crown side and in personnel was almost identical. David Irwin had returned after recovery from a broken leg and replaced Dean in the centre and that was basically the only alteration. The pack was the same and had earned the affectionate appellation of 'Dad's Army' because it contained so many of the old brigade in Keane, Orr, Slattery, Duggan and O'Driscoll. Furthermore it was to Fitzgerald's credit that he could manage to get so many good performances out of his old warriors. His credentials to lead the Lions were, in the view of many, impeccable. Some believed that he was not good enough to merit a Test place, but that argument, too, scarcely stood up to investigation. Strangely when Wheeler, a fine player and excellent hooker, failed to get into the side at all, the anti-Fitzgerald element in the Press turned to Colin Deans as the man with which to beat Fitzgerald's back. It was all rather odd, for there was scarcely a word about Deans when the case for Wheeler was being propagated.

Whatever the views of the rugby writers, the selectors saw it otherwise and Fitzgerald was duly chosen to lead the Lions. Willie John

McBride had been appointed manager and Jim Telfer of Scotland was coach.

Fitzgerald was not short of Irish company. Ringland, Kiernan, Irwin, Campbell, Lenihan and O'Driscoll were all chosen for the tour. On the eve of departure, Lenihan was ruled unfit by the team doctor and so he had to return from London to Cork rather than fly from London to Auckland with the party.

In truth the Lions were just not good enough to meet the challenge of a most accomplished New Zealand side and it is doubtful whether any combinations of players chosen from Britain and Ireland would have fared any better than Fitzgerald's side did. They were beaten in all four Tests, comprehensively so in the final Test in Auckland.

The first Test could well have been won and would, I believe, but for an injury to Terry Holmes and a very bad refereeing decision. Once again Fitzgerald came under attack, this time for his alleged inability to throw the ball into the line-out accurately. Yet line-out play had been a feature of Ireland's championship winning sides and Lenihan had emerged as a line-out player of the highest quality, with Fitzgerald as the man throwing in to him. Injuries were another factor that hindered the Lions and indeed, towards the end of the tour, Lenihan and Gerry McLoughlin were both summoned to the aid of the party.

The critics of Fitzgerald had a field day in the aftermath of the whitewash and McBride, too, came in for severe criticism. Strangely, the coach, Jim Telfer, got off relatively easily although his methods were less than successful and his approach to his sessions often severely criticised by his players. Furthermore, Telfer never really allowed Fitzgerald to lead that side and assume the full responsibilities a captain should have on a tour. But all that having been said, it was not Fitzgerald's fault or Telfer's fault or McBride's fault that the Lions were so comprehensively beaten. One can but wonder if another management structure would have done any better.

Some of the Irish players on the tour did not play as well as they can, notably Campbell who was not the force expected in the Tests. I think it would be right to say that Ringland alone of the Irish enhanced a reputation on that tour.

It was against that background that McBride returned, and shortly after his return, he was elected as coach to the Ireland side to succeed Tom Kiernan. The choice of McBride was a split decision among the national selectors. He beat Mick Doyle, the former international and Leinster coach, in the vote.

From the outset, he inherited some problems and, as the season progressed, these problems were to be compounded by injuries and other factors. Many of the Ireland forwards were nearing the end of the international line and some of the backs, notably those who had been to New Zealand, were finding a return to form an elusive target. Nonetheless, there was reason to believe that Ireland would have a reasonable season. The foundation for a good side seemed on hand, but what was missing was the vital element of good fortune that any side needs and especially a side under new direction.

Campbell was out of action early in the season, struck down by illness. Ward was still on hand, but his only appearance in 1983 had been of a few minutes duration when he came on in the final match of the season against England in the closing stages as a replacement for Campbell.

The opening assignment for Ireland was against France in Paris, just about the hardest possible start for McBride and his side. Kiernan had been dropped for the match and replaced by a new cap in Rory Moroney from Lansdowne. Keith Crossan replaced Finn on the wing and that was the sum total of the alterations behind the scrum from 1983. The pack was identical and perhaps here was the first error as evidence that the years were taking toll was ignored by the selectors in the belief that they could get another year out of the old guard. But two years when a player is over thirty can be a lifetime and so it proved for many of the Irish that season. Once more Ireland lost, this time 25–12 and that score was representative of the general trend of the match.

The next task was Wales in Dublin and Ireland, despite the defeat in Paris, were favourites for this against a Welsh side less than settled and under new leadershp in Mike Watkins and minus Terry Holmes. There were two changes in the pack. McLoughlin was dropped and replaced by Jim McCoy, a prop from Dungannon, and Slattery withdrew from the side due to illness giving a first cap to Willie Duncan, a flanker from Malone. The match was in the balance until Wales scored a try in the closing quarter to gain a merited win. Ireland now had two defeats from two matches and it was clear that they had major problems.

Changes were made for the match against England. Kiernan was recalled to the centre as was Moss Finn as his partner. McGrath was dropped and replaced at scrum-half by Tony Doyle from Greystones and the most sensational decision of all was that Ciaran Fitzgerald was dropped and replaced by the Bective hooker Harry Harbison. That caused major controversy, especially bearing in mind the background.

Fitzgerald had been injured in the early stages of the match against Wales and replaced by Harbison. He therefore bore no culpability for the defeat, having been on the field only a matter of a few minutes. The selectors stated they had dropped Fitzgerald as they feared the head injury he sustained against Wales might reopen. But they came to that decision despite medical advice that Fitzgerald would be fit to play. He proved that point, too, by playing for his club the same afternoon Ireland played England in Twickenham and lost.

But the omission of Fitzgerald was not the only sensation. As the team assembled on the Thursday before the match, Campbell withdrew due to illness and the selectors called up Tony Ward to replace him. So Ward was back again on the international scene, a stage on which he had performed for five minutes twelve months earlier and prior to that not since the autumn of 1981. The captaincy was given to Willie Duggan; despite his vast experience and unquestioned ability, he would not by any means have been the unanimous choice of the public. He would not have been too many players' choice either! Duggan was just not captaincy material however admirable his many other qualities. The decision to drop Fitzgerald was a bad one from every point of view and clearly seen to be that. Two of the men who were among the most notable advocates of dropping him, selector Mick Cuddy and Mick Doyle then a substitute selector, were, within less than twelve months, as chairman of selectors and coach respectively, to turn to Fitzgerald to lead Ireland out of the wilderness again in 1984–85. Victory then helped erase the memories, but in the midst of the 1984 campaign, Fitzgerald was to be the sacrificial lamb. Ireland lost to England by 12–9 in a match that was highly entertaining and one that Ireland might have won. Ward kicked three great penalty goals, but it was not enough as Dusty Hare kicked three for England, and outside-half Les Cusworth dropped a goal.

So Ireland now faced the task of avoiding a whitewash in the final match against Scotland in Dublin. What a contrast to the background when the sides had last met at the venue. Then Ireland were in sight of the Triple Crown, now it was Scotland who came in pursuit of that objective. MacNeill was dropped and replaced by John Murphy, and Derek McGrath, from the UCD club, was named on the flank for Duncan. Des Fitzgerald, who had come into the side for McLoughlin after the defeat by Wales, retained his place and Duggan retained the captaincy.

That afternoon a gale was blowing in Dublin and Duggan, after winning the toss, scorned the use of the wind in the first half. It was to prove a disastrous decision. Within a few minutes, Scotland were twelve points up; then Ireland conceded a penalty try. The match was over almost as soon as it had started and Scotland turned on the style to win the Triple Crown for the first time in forty-six years and beat Ireland by a record margin, 32–9. In the midst of Ireland's troubles, Ward was concussed and had to leave the field. He was replaced by Hugh Condon, a London Irish player, who had won a 'B' cap in 1975. So the glories of the previous two years were now gone and Ireland were back at the bottom of the ladder in every sense.

Slattery and Campbell, as circumstances transpired, never again played for Ireland. Illness struck both down and indeed the appearances of both men since have been infrequent, but Slattery did return to his club's senior side late in 1986.

For McBride, who had known such success as a player with Ireland and the Lions, it was the other side of the coin now. He witnessed failure in New Zealand as the manager of the Lions and now a whitewash in his first year as national coach. He was about to pay the ultimate price, too, for that failure and was subjected to criticism of the most virulent kind, sadly his most potent critics being some of the selectors with whom he had served. Ireland's problems that season were of a many sided nature; to blame McBride for them was as unjust as it was unfair. The knives, however, were being sharpened and within a few months McBride was to be subjected to indignity that did not serve the cause of Irish rugby in a very worthy manner, nor was it any advertisement for the alleged democratic process.

24
Triumph and trouble
1983–86

When in the mid 1970s, the IRFU decided to alter the method by which the selectors would be appointed and gave to the selectiom committee the right to select their own coach for the national side, it seemed a step in the right direction. But the system had built into it the possibilities of embarrassment.

Briefly, the method by which the selectors were chosen was that each province nominated three men, and a sub-committee of the IRFU then chose five selectors and two substitute selectors with the proviso that Leinster, Munster and Ulster had to have at least one representative each on the committee and not more than two. Connacht, in the wilderness for so long as regards selection, now had a chance to get representation; in fact P.J. Dwyer was made a selector in 1981.

The selectors met in the aftermath of the annual general meeting each season to select a chairman and to pick the coach from a panel nominated to the IRFU coaching sub-committee. All fair and above board, one might say, but in fact with some selectors also deeply involved in coaching, the possibility was always there that two of the selection committee could be contenders for the task of coaching the national side. That is exactly what happened in the summer of 1984. McBride, who had been made a selector the previous season as well as being appointed coach, had beaten Mick Doyle, the former Ireland and Lion's flanker for the coaching position. Doyle had come with very impressive credentials following a highly successful spell with Leinster during which the province won the Interprovincial title four times in five years, including a hat-trick between 1979–80 and 1981–82.

McBride, too, had performed very well with a young and inexperienced Ulster side and it was against that background that he had been named as coach to the national team.

Despite the whitewash endured by Ireland in the 1983–84 campaign, it was felt that McBride would get another chance to reveal his ability for the season 1984–85, but there were rumblings that he might lose out to Doyle, now a selector, the latter having moved up from the substitute's bench to replace Roly Meates on the committee.

There was one other alteration on the selection committee with Jim Kiernan, brother of the illustrious Tom and father of Michael, elected to succeed Brian O'Brien as Munster's representative.

Mick Cuddy, who was serving his third year on the committee made no secret of his preference for Doyle over McBride and indeed had proposed Doyle for the job the previous season, but failed to get the necessary support.

By a majority 3–2 vote Doyle beat McBride for the coaching position and so McBride was out after just one year. It caused major controversy, not least because so many felt it unfair that McBride should have been asked to bear full responsibility for what happened the previous season, and also that he had not been given a reasonable chance.

Not everyone was happy about the background to the meeting with a firm belief prevalent that McBride had been the victim of a previously arranged coup involving Cuddy, Doyle and Kiernan. There was talk about McBride and his Ulster selectorial colleague Jim Donaldson resigning from the selection committee, a happening, had it taken place, that would have put the whole selection process into chaos. Eventually McBride decided to stay on the committee as did Donaldson, and Ireland set about rectifying the sad state of affairs that was the position at the end of the previous season. They were to succeed admirably, indeed beyond the expectations of most.

From this situation the IRFU had learned a very important lesson about the election of a coach. At the time the coach was chosen by the selectors and the decision had to be ratified by the full IRFU executive. While the IRFU does have the power of veto, in reality, should they reject the nomination of the selectors, then they are giving a vote of no confidence in the selection committee. That was the position the IRFU was in when Doyle beat McBride and, however unhappy some were about the matter, the IRFU did ratify the appointment of Doyle. It was not that anyone really doubted Doyle's credentials, rather the feeling was that the manner and method by which he had been chosen left much to be desired.

At the annual general meeting in June of 1985, it was decided that never again would the union be subjected to so embarrassing a position. From the season 1986–87 onwards, the IRFU decided that a sub-committee would pick the coach and chairman of selectors, thus avoiding in the future the ludicrous position of two selectors opposing each other for the coaching position and, in effect, voting for themselves. It was divisive and seen to be divisive.

Not daunted by the wave of controversy, Doyle set about his task and issued a declaration of intent. The Irish approach was based primarily on forward strength, that being a more notable characteristic of the game here than consistently fluid back play, however distinguished some Ireland backs. Doyle said that his approach would be to run the ball at every opportunity.

'We will not get involved in any macho scrums. The talent at our disposal now is good enough behind the scrum to adopt an open approach. As far as I am concerned the scrum is no more than a means of restarting the game,' said Doyle. Doyle was right when he added that Ireland just did not have the men of sufficient power and experience to play a game based on the forwards. But his statement that the scrum was no more than a means of restarting the game most certainly did not stand up to investigation and those words were to rebound on him in the most telling manner. But not immediately, for glory based on the philosophy was at hand.

Doyle said he was confident Ireland would be able to win their own ball readily enough in the scrums and do reasonably well in the line-out and that would be sufficient to give his talented backs a chance. His first test came against Australia on 10 November 1984 at Lansdowne Road. It was the ideal preparation for the forthcoming championship and Australia had the best side ever to come to these shores. They proved the point by doing the grand slam and beating Ireland 16–9. Ireland did not threaten to win against the Wallabies but did play with sufficient flair to give hope for the days ahead.

It was a much changed Ireland side. Willie Duggan and John O'Driscoll had gone and Ciaran Fitzgerald was recalled to lead a team that now included new caps in centre Brendan Mullin from Trinity and scrum-half Michael Bradley from the Constitution club. Bradley had served some apprenticeship as a replacement. In the pack Jim McCoy was recalled at tight-head prop and Willie Anderson, a tall back-row forward from the Dungannon club whose representative career had been as a number eight with Ulster, was brought into the second-row to partner Donal Lenihan. Philip Matthews, from Ards, and Willie Sexton, from Garryowen, were on the flanks, both new caps and Ronan Kearney, who had played against France in Paris in 1982, was at number eight. The outside-half berth had been given to Paul Dean, from St

Mary's College, with Tony Ward overlooked, the view having been taken that Dean would co-ordinate the attacking back line more effectively than Ward. But Dean, who had won all but one of his seven previous capts at centre, was not a good tactical or defensive kicker. Doyle and his colleagues were prepared to accept that to accommodate a man they believed would get the best out of the attacking skills of his threequarters.

Dean in that respect did the job and did it well in a position that remarkably he could not hold down for Leinster on any kind of regular basis during Doyle's tenure of office as coach for that side.

Although Ireland called in five new caps against Australia, Mullin, Bradley, Anderson, Matthews and Sexton, the pattern was not complete. With the front five having limitations, the back-row was crucial and here fortune favoured Ireland in a quite remarkable manner.

Since Fergus Slattery had gone, Ireland badly needed an open side flanker, Matthews being the ideal man on the blind side. The answer came in the shape of Nigel Carr, Matthews' Ards' clubmate. The pair had been together at Regent House school, at Queen's University and now at Ards. Carr was a player of immense potential, but had consistently been dogged by a knee injury. Indeed in 1984 it looked as if he would not play rugby again. But he fought his way back to fitness, a fact he proved when he helped Ulster beat Australia at Ravenhill a few days after the international in a memorable encounter. It was Ulster's first win over a major touring side and Carr had played magnificently in helping to fashion the success, with Ulster winning 15–13. He then played for Ireland in a 'B' international against Scotland in Galway proving beyond doubt that he was ready to win his first cap.

Fortunate disposition of circumstances also brought forward an unlikely number eight. Brian Spillane, a young medical doctor in Limerick, had played for Munster, but in the second-row. Like Carr he had been troubled by injury, but Munster selected him at number eight and he gave some great displays in the position. Thus Spillane and Carr were both named in the Ireland side for the international against England due to take place at Lansdowne Road on 19 January. Keith Crossan, who had missed the match against Australia due to illness, was back on the left wing and Michael Kiernan was restored to centre at the expense of Moss Finn. Kiernan had played on the wing against Australia and played extremely well in Crossan's absence. He had also been given the place kicking duties in rather exceptional circumstances. When Doyle and his colleagues decided to leave Ward out against Australia, they went into the match without a specialist place kicker, a very great chance to take bearing in mind the importance of penalty kicking in internationals. In that, as in much else, the gamble was to pay off.

Finn in fact was nominated place kicker against Australia, but after he sustained an injury during the match, Kiernan was pressed into service and kicked three penalty goals in Ireland's 16–9 defeat. No tries had come from the new found confidence in the running game against Australia but there had been no lack of initiative. With the back-row now reconstructed, the trio of Matthews, Spillane and Carr were to have a profound influence on Ireland's success.

They did much to make up for deficiencies in the tight five. They were tremendously effective in the open and in getting to the loose ball and Carr was a scourge to any opposing outside-half.

With Dublin enveloped in snow, the match against England scheduled for 19 January had to be postponed and so it was against Scotland, the reigning grand slam champions, that Ireland opened their campaign in February. It was a daunting task for a side relatively untried and the early indications in the match were that Ireland would pay the penalty for not selecting a specialist place kicker as Kiernan missed three attempts at goal. But, despite that, the Irish side were playing well and giving Scotland a lot of trouble behind the scrum. With the game approaching injury time, Ireland trailed and then in the 79th minute, Ringland scored a magnificent try after a great back movement, Kiernan converted and Ireland won 18–15. Ringland had scored two tries, and Kiernan's kicking had come good in the second-half. Kiernan scored two penalties and a conversion and had also dropped a goal in the first-half.

The enthusiasm generated by the win, and the manner of its attainment, were immense and Doyle took the mantle of a Messiah.

France provided the next obstacle in Dublin. The visitors were favourites to win but, as so often in the past, an intemperate approach did much to blunt their skills and Ireland got a draw at 15–15 in what was an ill tempered affair that did nothing for the image of the game. It proved, too, a costly exercise for the Irish who lost two players through injury; Spillane was the victim of a totally unnecessary kick in the head early in the game and Matthews suffered a shoulder injury; Spillane was replaced by Brian McCall, a second-row forward who played with London Irish and who had been at Queen's University. McCall had served a very worthy apprenticeship having been capped for Ireland at schools, 'B' and under-23 levels and so he joined the illustrious band who had been similarly honoured. The veteran prop Mick Fitzpatrick replaced Matthews.

There had been only one change from the side that beat Scotland and that was the inclusion of Rory Moroney for Mullin, who was ruled out by an injury. Moroney had been capped the previous season.

The next match was against Wales in Cardiff, scarcely a happy hunting ground for the Irish, the last win there having been achieved as far back as 1967. Mullin returned for the game and Ireland gave a five star performance, destroying the Welsh by 21 points to 9. The back-row was superb in that match during which Ireland struggled at times for set piece possession but more than made up for it with their general industry around the field and the eagerness with which the backs responded. With Wales missing several likely kicks at goal and their confidence beginning to wane, Ireland grew by the minute and the second-half saw the team play some great rugby. Ireland scored two tries, one by left-wing Crossan who was now playing so well that many rated him the best wing in the championship. He played brilliantly in Cardiff and was rewarded with his first try for his country. Ringland got the other try to bring his total to four in the Ireland jersey. Kiernan kicked three penalty goals and two conversions. The gamble of giving him the place kicking duties certainly was paying the most handsome dividends.

So Ireland faced the last match, against England in Dublin, on the afternoon of 30 March. The Triple Crown and championship were the prizes on offer. England, too, came to the match with hopes high of attaining a similar double. Their programme, disrupted by the postponement of the match against Ireland in January left them with another game after the match in Dublin against Wales in Cardiff a fortnight later. Having beaten Scotland and drawn with France, they had much to play for.

The match started sensationally with Ireland trailing by three points after England's outside-half Rob Andrew had kicked a penalty goal. But then Mullin got a try for Ireland after he blocked down a relieving kick by the England full-back. The capacity crowd gave Ireland tremendous support, but they had to endure many anxieties for this was not the Ireland of the fluent style that had crushed Wales. The England pack did very well in the set pieces and Ireland, at times, struggled.

By the final quarter Ireland trailed by three points, before Kiernan kicked a penalty to leave the sides level at 10–10, and that was how it stayed until the last minute. Then Ireland drove forward after Spillane won a line-out. Lenihan was in the van as the ball was won in a ruck and Kiernan dropped a goal. It was to prove crucial as the minutes of injury time that remained were played to a crescendo of sound coming up from stand and terrace.

Ireland won 13–10 and, for the second time in three years, had won the Crown and the championship before the faithful at Lansdowne Road.

From whitewash to champions again just as in 1982 and, for Ciaran Fitzgerald, a personal triumph. His powers of leadership were never more tellingly demonstrated as he urged the Irish on in those final pulsating and unforgettable minutes.

So Doyle had proved his point and led Ireland out of the wilderness and done it in the manner he had promised. He readily admitted that he had not expected Ireland to win the championship but, having done so, he and the Irish public generally were, I believe, lulled into a false sense of security. The problems in the set pieces had been disguised. The team had immense character, a brilliant back-row, in Kiernan a man who kicked the goals and backs capable of taking even the half chance. They also had a considerable amount of luck, but few in the capacity crowd that shouted in acclamation that afternoon were giving any consideration to such factors. Ireland had won and all was right with the world.

Ireland had a scheduled tour to Japan in May, a tour arranged after the proposed visit to Argentina had been cancelled in the aftermath of the Falklands war. Argentina was not able to guarantee the safety of the Irish players and, quite correctly, the IRFU cancelled the tour.

The Japanese, who had been very anxious for a tour from the Irish, readily stepped in and Ireland set off in May for a five match visit that embraced two Tests. All the Triple Crown heroes were in the party and, as expected, Ireland came back with a 100 per cent record. Ireland won both Tests, the first in Osaka easily, the second in Tokyo, 33–15; but this second win was not attained without anxiety. The Japanese played very well for a long period and Ireland had to revert very much to a 10-man game in the second-half. They had lost Dean and Bradley by the interval and they were replaced by the men who had been in the replacement panel for the championship, the young Ballymena scrum-half Rab Brady and Ralph Keyes, from the Constitution club. Keyes had been preferred to Tony Ward as the replacement, but had failed to dislodge Ward from the Munster team. Carr did not play in either Test as he damaged a knee in the second match of the tour and Paddy Kenny, from Wanderers, played in both Tests in Carr's absence.

So Ireland returned home and the glories of the Championship and the success in Japan seemed to form a sound base on which to build for the year ahead. But there was to be no glory in the 1985–86 season and reality was forced on Ireland in the form of four championship defeats. It was back to the whitewash again. Ireland's forwards just were not good enough and had tremendous problems in the scrums. Furthermore an injury sustained playing for Ulster against Queensland ruled Matthews out of the games, while Crossan missed the first two games due to a broken cheekbone.

The programme opened against France and Ireland lost comprehensively, being badly beaten in scrum and line-out. Orr played his 49th consecutive match that afternoon, but was then dropped, one short of equalling the world record of 50 for a prop, held by Scotland's Sandy Carmichael.

The side was altered for the match against Wales in Dublin and, for a while, Ireland looked as if they would win. But Wales hit a golden spell early in the second half to erase an interval deficit of eight points and Ireland lost again. Dean was injured in that match and ruled out for the rest of the season. Now faced with a problem, the selectors recalled Ward to the panel for the visit to Twickenham, but opted for Keyes at outside-half. Orr was still ruled out and Paul Kennedy, from London Irish, who had replaced him against Wales was retained in the side in which Crossan, now recovered, played his first match of the campaign.

The Irish were destroyed in the scrum and conceded two push over tries and a penalty try as a direct result of the scrummaging problems on a pitch which had been passed fit for play only the previous afternoon having been subjected to heavy frost for a long period. While the surface was hard in places, that scarcely accounted for Ireland's problems and there was general amazement when Doyle and his captain Fitzgerald said after the game that they felt Ireland had done reasonably well in the scrum. Now Doyle knew that the scrum was far from being only a means of restarting the game. As if to mock his assessment, there were in fact no fewer than 52 scrums in that match.

The last match for Ireland was at home against Scotland and after Keyes was again picked at outside-half he was forced to withdraw. Ward was recalled for his first international in two years. Orr was to win his 50th cap and, in a realigned side, Anderson was picked at number eight with McCall partnering Lenihan in the second-row. Ireland played splendidly but lost most unluckily by a point, with Kiernan missing a penalty from almost in front of the posts in the last minute, a kick that, had it been successful, would have won the match for Ireland. Ward seldom played better for Ireland than that afternoon and Ireland can never have played so well and lost, a fact freely acknowledged by the gracious Scots after the match.

It had proved a remarkable season and in the sharpest possible contrast to the previous year. Now Doyle knew what it was like to coach a team whitewashed just as McBride had in 1984.

The danger signs had been hoisted early for Ireland, even before the championship, for Ireland played Fiji who came on a three match tour. Despite having the vast majority of the Triple Crown side of the previous year in the team, the Irish were very fortunate to scrape a narrow win. Fiji also played Ulster and Connacht, the latter having this match as part of their centenary celebrations. The milestone was suitably celebrated and nothing gave more satisfaction than victory over Leinster at Lansdowne Road in the Interprovincial series, their first win over Leinster for thirty years. Ulster, meanwhile, retained the title they had won the previous season and were in the process of establishing an all time record of seventeen consecutive victories over opposition ranging from the other provinces to the Wallabies. The sequence came to an end on a wet night in Belfast in January when Queensland beat a depleted Ulster side.

As Ireland face into the 1987 campaign, there is no doubt that much work requires to be done with the forwards, but backs of real quality are on hand. Indeed, one might say that seldom in history has Ireland been so well served in this department.

The 1980s were following a truly remarkable course for the Irish. Whitewashed in 1981, Triple Crown and International champions in 1982, joint champions in 1983, whitewashed in 1984, Triple Crown and International Champions in 1985 and whitewashed in 1986. It was certainly a sequence to give value to those who assert that the Irish are unpredictable.

25

The schools

In Ireland, there is no room for any argument that, were it not for the schools with their successive generations of dedicated teachers, lay and religious, the game could not, and would not, have progressed as it has done. It would not have developed into the wide area it now embraces in Irish society. For a long time very little rugby was played by youths other than that played in the schools. The schools were the nursery, the great area of development, from which the clubs drew their players. One could say that in places such as Limerick, clubs did cater for boys who went to non rugby-playing schools and, in more recent years, clubs in the provinces have done much to encourage boys, but generally the schools are still the main source from which the clubs get their players.

When the IRFU was founded the men at the heart of the foundation were all young and had been influenced by what they had played at school. Barrington and Wall, and others of their kind, brought with them the influences of their schooldays. Once the parent body had been established it was in many respects in the schools rather than the clubs that the spread and development was most pronounced. Certainly at the time of the foundation rugby was being played in several schools and by 1876 the first official schools cup competition had started.

The inaugural schools cup competition took place in Ulster in 1876 and since then cups in all four provinces have been an integral part of the rugby year and, apart from the internationals, they are the competitions that hold most appeal for the generality of the public.

St Patrick's day has been long established on the calendar as the day for the senior cup finals in Leinster, Munster and Ulster and it is not unusual to find as many as 50,000 people patronising those three finals. That is a remarkable tribute to the schools and the kind of rugby they have offered in reward for patronage.

But it is not just the finals that draw the crowds. In Leinster, for example, the schools cups senior (under-18) and junior (under-15) draw huge crowds throughout the competitions and it is commonplace for the branch ground at Donnybrook in the southern suburbs of Dublin to be packed to capacity for a first round schools cup tie. In Munster, too, even the early rounds draw big crowds as will the semi-finals and finals in Ulster and Connacht; the earlier rounds in Ulster are played on school grounds which tend to limit attendance, if not interest.

The inaugural Ulster Schools Senior Cup saw four schools contest the competition in 1975–76. They were Methodist College Belfast, Royal Belfast Academical Institute, Armagh Royal School and The Royal School Dungannon. How very appropriate that Dungannon should have been there for, of course, they were in at the foundation of the old Irish Football Union.

The Ulster Schools Senior Cup is not only the oldest competition in Irish rugby, but the second oldest in the world, being predated by only the London Hospitals Cup. Unlike that great old competition, not now graced by the huge array of internationals that sides could once call upon, the Ulster Schools Cup has gone from strength to strength. The first final was contested between Armagh Royal and RBAI, or as it was then, Royal Academical Institution. The level of competitiveness and the total commitment that marks the schools game was well demonstrated in that year now well over a century ago. It took three matches to decide the winners, with Armagh prevailing by a dropped goal to nil after two draws.

Indeed Armagh proved to be the dominant force in the early days, winning the cup again the following season, this time beating Methodist in the final before Methodist engraved their name for the first time in 1878, the first of no fewer than twenty-four occasions when the great rugby school has won the province's premier schools trophy. But four times within the next five seasons, it was Armagh who took the cup with Methodist again breaking the sequence by winning in 1882.

The competition has prospered through the years, but, remarkably, Dungannon, one of the four original entrants, have won it but once, in 1907. Armagh, winners seven times in the first decade of the competition had to wait until 1977 to win it for the eighth, but how good it is to see that all the original entrants for the cup in Ulster are still at the heart of the schools scene, still making major contributions. Some new names were engraved on the cup in recent times, too, including Grosvenor High School from Belfast, Rainey Endowed, Ballyclare High School and Ballymena Academy. Others such as Campbell College Portora, and Foyle College have long and distinguished connections with the cup.

In 1910, the Schools Medallion was inaugurated for boys of under 16 years. Methodist, or to give the school its popular name 'Methody' were the inaugural winners and, the trophy has adorned the trophy cabinet in RBAI, Dungannon, Coleraine Academical Institute, Ballymena, Belfast Royal Academy, Regent House, Annadale Grammar School, Campbell and Bangor Grammar School. Indeed Bangor brought off the senior and medallion double in 1985, and last (1985–86) season won the senior cup yet again. Here is a school that has become a real power in recent years, up there with RBAI, Methody and Campbell.

If the Leinster branch was a decade behind their Ulster counterparts in starting a cup, the success of the competition has been nothing short of remarkable. The schools cups at senior and junior (under-15 years) are eagerly looked forward to by young and old alike.

The Leinster Senior Schools Cup is a magnificent old trophy, brought as a result of a collection made by the branch with the schools contributing £5 each plus an entry fee of two shillings and six pence. The branch added to the collection by giving £10 and the honorary treasurer of the branch, Harry Shepherd, gave £10 to the cup fund and the trophy was purchased. The actual cup is a composite of an old hunting trophy and one other trophy with the foot of the cup being fifty years older than the bowl. The competition was a great success from the outset and remains so to this day. The entrants for the inaugural competition were Blackrock College, The High School, Wesley College, Farra, Santry School, Rathmines School and Corrig. That was in 1887.

Blackrock and The High School contested the first match in the competition and Blackrock won by a dropped goal to nil. Contemporary reports suggest that over 2000 attended that match. The result certainly set a trend maintained to this day, a victory for Blackrock who have been the most renowned of all schools on the rugby scene in Ireland.

Blackrock won the inaugural competition as they won the cup again this year and, in all, have captured the trophy on 57 occasions in the 100 times it has been contested. Happily Wesley and The High School of the original entrants are still thriving and still participate on an annual basis. Sadly such schools as Farra, beaten in the inaugural final by Blackrock, Santry, Corrig and Rathmines have long since disappeared.

As the years went by, so the popularity of the competition increased and, if some old schools went by the wayside, so others emerged and have long histories of participation to this day. In this category one must place such as St Columba's, Castleknock, St Andrew's, St Mary's College, Mountjoy, Clongowes Wood College, Dominican College

Newbridge, Presentation Bray, The Cistercian College Roscrea, Belvedere College and The King's Hospital. Other schools of more recent times who have made an impact include such as Terenure College, Christian Brothers College Monkstown, St Paul's Raheny and De La Salle Churchtown. The latter won the cup in 1983 for the first time, having been finalists in 1968 and again in 1975. De La Salle also captured the trophy in 1985 and were beaten in the final by Blackrock in 1986. Terenure, too, after emerging as a real force in the 1950s, when they captured the trophy for the first time (in 1952) and took it again in 1958, have been regular participants in the closing stages since. They had their golden spell between 1978 and 1983 winning the cup three times in that period. CBC Monkstown won it for the first time in 1976.

So popular did the competition become in the early 1930s, that it was necessary for the Leinster branch to have two sections with the weaker schools contesting section 'A' and two schools from that section then qualified for section 'B' to compete with the stronger schools. That principle holds good to this day and at times some of the qualifiers from the weaker section have made a great impression on the scene.

As in Ulster, the Leinster branch started a Junior Cup, this one for under 15s. St Andrew's won the inaugural competition in 1909, beating Belvedere in the final. As with the Senior Cup, it was also necessary to run two sections in the Junior Cup and that position has obtained since 1933.

Blackrock have been the dominant force at junior level as well as senior level, capturing the cup on thirty-five occasions, and they have completed the senior-junior double on nineteen occasions, the most recent being last season. Belvedere have a fine record at junior level, as have Castleknock and Terenure.

While developments in Munster and Connacht at schools level came much later than in Ulster and Leinster, the schools competitions in these provinces have been of immense value. Schools in Munster such as Rockwell, Presentation College Cork, Christian College Cork, Crescent and St Munchin's Limerick have for long been major forces on the scene as was Mungret College in Limerick. Mungret College unfortunately closed down in the 1970s and was a sad loss to the scene. The name of the school appears on both Senior and Junior Cups and several internationals were pupils there.

It is good to see new forces emerging, too, in the provinces such as St Clement's and St Endas while Midleton College, Waterpark College Waterford and a few others, while not as strong as such as Rockwell,

PBC, CBC, Crescent and St Munchin's have never lost the will to compete. Into this category come Glenstall Abbey who lost the 1970 final after a replay to Rockwell.

CBC Cork won the inaugural Munster Schools Senior Cup in 1909 and are still a major force on the scene having their most productive period in the 1970s when they won the cup eight times in the space of nine years, with their great Cork rivals, PBC breaking the sequence in 1975. Rockwell had been the main force in the early years, recording their initial win in 1910 and having five wins in the following six years.

The first victory for Presentation College Cork came in 1918 and that was to be the first of many. Schools such as Abbey also won the trophy, but Abbey unfortunately has long since closed down.

Limerick CBS were also a force for a while, but the school stopped playing rugby. Crescent College made the big breakthrough in 1947 and in recent seasons have been particularly powerful and are the current holders, while St Munchin's won it in 1968 and again in 1982. Rockwell lead the honours list with twenty-two wins followed by CBC Cork with twenty-one titles and just behind come PBC Cork. The Presentation sister College in Cobh, a town at the mouth of Cork Harbour, won the cup for the only time in 1938, a result at the time deemed to be sensational.

The Junior Cup was started in 1932 and Limerick CBS won the inaugural competition. It was, however, Rockwell who set the early pace and that great school, a sister College to Blackrock in Dublin, and run by the Holy Ghost Fathers, have since been overtaken by PBC Cork, who have a magnificent record at junior level in recent years. They won it last season for the fourth consecutive season and in all have captured the trophy a record twenty-one times.

Schools rugby in Connacht has a more erratic history and has followed a less even path than in the other provinces. The West of Ireland is traditionally Gaelic games territory, but the Senior and Junior Cup competitions in Connacht are now firmly established and organised on a proper basis. Compared with the other provinces, there are only seven rugby playing schools in the province, but the competitive nature of the cups is no less concentrated. Marvellous work has been, and is still being, done in the west by teachers and the branch executive in Connacht to promote the game in the schools.

Ironically, it was a Galway school, the now defunct Galway Grammar School who helped establish the Connacht branch of the IRFU which was 100 years old last season. It is also pertinent to point out that, so anxious were the authorities in Galway to have the school in competition, that in the early years, Galway GS actually entered for the Leinster Schools Cup.

No such expedient is now necessary for the Connacht schools to get competitive rugby, but as in other provinces, some of the pioneers on the schools scene have gone. Galway Grammar School and Renelagh Athlone for instance are no longer on the scene, but made major contributions. The name Ranelagh does appear on the Connacht Schools Senior Cup, a competition started in 1913. The first winners were St Joseph's College, Garbally Park from Ballinasloe, and that great college is still at the forefront of affairs winning the cup on twenty-six occasions. They contested the final last season against St Ignatious College Galway, popularly known as 'The Jes', being run as it is by the Jesuit Fathers.

St Ignatious were a force in the early days, but then the game was banned in the school for over forty years. But they came back in the 1970s and immediately made their mark again. They won the cup in 1985 and contested last season's final against 'Garbally'. The first match was drawn and the reply won by St Joseph's.

St Joseph's Galway are another lively force and perhaps it is indicative of the spread of the game that, out in the depths of Connemara, the Clifden Community School stands able to compete with the best. Indeed Clifden recorded an historic win in 1975 in the Senior Cup. Sligo Grammar School is also long established and thriving. It would be nice to see more schools take up the game west of the Shannon, and hopefully that will happen.

While in the early days the branch executive committees ran the schools cups, the administrative set up is now much more elaborate. All the provinces have their own schools committees, who run the game at this level but are of course, under the jurisdiction of the branch executive committees. It is hard to quantify the contributions made by so many individuals to the growth of the schools game and perhaps future generations who study the history of the game in Ireland may well wonder why it was that Ireland did not compete at international level on the schools scene until 1975. That is a pertinent question, especially when one realises that, as at senior level, schools interprovincials have a long history.

For instance, the first schools interprovincial match took place between Leinster and Ulster in 1887 and the provinces have met on a regular basis since then. Munster soon entered the fold and, before the last century had run its course, were also competing on the interprovicinal scene even though at that time there was no established competition for the Munster Schools. Connacht, too, came on the scene in the 1920s and, although for a while they tried to compete with the other provinces, it was an unfair situation for they just did not have the depth of resources to compete. But the situation that now obtains is more satisfactory. All the other provinces now meet Connacht annually but field what amounts to second strength sides.

But one must return to the question of Irish participation in schools internationals. Several views have been expressed on this important matter and several reasons given through the years for the fact that Ireland alone of the home countries stood aside from the schools international arena. Traditionally the schools cups are run from January to March, and, of course, the schools examinations take place in June, thus there is not a lot of time left for students to apply their minds to the main purpose of their academic careers in the schools.

There was also a view that, to give schools players international caps, might give them an inflated idea of their own importance and not be conducive to their best interests. Such arguments are hard to follow, for surely the very nature of international rugby and interprovincial rugby could have the very same effect, especially bearing in mind the value put on schools cup medals and the huge attendances that patronise the schools game. Whatever the reason for keeping Ireland out of the schools international arena, the position changed dramatically in 1975. The alteration came about because of the centenary celebrations of the Union. It was decided that the schools would have to be honoured in an appropriate manner and so it was that an international was arranged for the Ireland schools, and in the natural order of things, the first match was arranged against England, Ireland's first opponents in the international field in those long ago days of 1875.

That match played at Lansdowne Road on the afternoon of 29 March 1975 was to be highly significant in putting Ireland in her rightful place in the schools international scene. Bearing in mind the standard of schools rugby that had obtained in Ireland, it was a reasonable belief that Ireland would hold her own with any opposition at under age level, even if the playing population relative to the other home countries was smaller. The very same argument could be made about the full Ireland side, which is chosen from a much smaller pool of senior players than in any of the other countries competing in the championship.

There was a problem about age qualification and in this respect Ireland was at a disadvantage relative to the other home countries with the Irish players all being basically under-18 at the start of their school year. Initially the other countries had a higher age limit, that may, or may not, have had a bearing. In any case the position that now obtains is thoroughly satisfactory to all.

Having at last made the big decision to enter the international arena, that inaugural match in Dublin in 1975 opened the way for regular Irish participation since. The following year, Ireland played two schools internationals, against Scotland and Wales and every season since the Irish schools side has played two internationals, alternating the fixtures. It was hoped that Ireland could manage to play the other three home countries on an annual basis but this has not proved viable.

Ireland does, however, play Australian schools and New Zealand schools when those countries tour in this part of the world and indeed, in the summer of 1980, there was an historic tour to Australia made by the Ireland side.

There is evidence, too, of the very strongest nature, to suggest that the decision taken in 1975 was extremely wise and beneficial to the game in Ireland for no fewer than nineteen boys capped at schools level since 1975 have subsequently been capped at senior level. That is a remarkable number, bearing in mind that Ireland has been in the schools international arena for only twelve years and that those capped over the last few years would not, as yet, have reached a sufficient level of maturity and experience to be contestants for full caps.

A very relevant statistic in relation to the first Ireland schools side is that no fewer than eight of the players who represented Ireland that afternoon went on to win full caps, a few of them within a matter of two years after playing in that match. A full list of schools internationals is in the appendix to this book and it makes interesting reading, for, apart from those who have been capped at full and schools levels, many others have also played for the Ireland 'B' side.

The game is extremely well organised within the country at schools level and the IRFU now has a schools standing committee to attend to the needs and to legislate for and watch over the schools game. It is currently under the chairmanship of former eminent international Noel Henderson.

Through the years all the branches have been admirably served by their own schools committees and many have given long and very distinguished service to the game. One man is unique in that he has served as honorary secretary to both the Leinster and Munster schools committees: the late Tim West, a school teacher who ended his involvement professionally as headmaster of Midleton College. He was to live to see his son John become one of the most respected of international referees.

Another very eminent referee, Kevin Kelleher, who in fact shares with Gwyn Walters of Wales the record number of appearances for an international referee, has rendered magnificent service to the game in Leinster at schools level. He has been honorary secretary of the Leinster Schools for the last thirty-one years.

All the provinces have been fortunate in their officials through the years, men of the utmost dedication. For instance when the schools team toured Australia in 1980, the three officials that went with the team can all be put in the forefront of schools legislators. There could not have been a happier choice for manager of that team that Roy Loughead, of Ulster. He was an outstanding success on that tour as was the coach Caleb Powell, a man whose involvement with the Leinster and Irish schools in the modern era has brought great benefits. A teacher at The Kings Hospital, in Dublin, he has also made a major contribution to the progress of the game in that particular academy and during his tenure as coach to the schools national side worked with great industry and no little effect.

The third official on that Australian mission was Brother Philip O'Reilly, and he was the man who had piloted the CBC team in Cork to that magnificent run of success in the schools cups. He has done great work for his school, his province Munster and the Ireland schools.

With the schools team now competing internationally it is natural that the officials involved would have more attention focussed on them than the many who had done great work in the past for both schools and provinces. Some of these men would not have been well known outside the confines of their own provincial areas, but one must not forget successive generations of such dedicated men; the debt owed to them by Irish rugby is immense.

Ken Armstrong and Noel Turley from Ulster and Leinster respectively are two who have been involved in coaching Ireland schools sides. Many is the tale told about famous school coaches, the favourite of course being dependent on what particular school the teller comes from. Yet there have been some schools coaches whose achievements are legendary throughout the whole of the country and in this regard the work of Father Hampson and Father Walter Finn, from Blackrock

College in Dublin is known and appreciated across the whole country. One must mention Noel Carpenter from Connacht, currently, and for quite some time, a member of the schools international selection committee.

With the structure of the game being as it is in Ireland, the welfare of the game, its future development and evolution is dependent, as it always has been, on the schools scene being vibrant. The IRFU is well aware of the necessity for a healthy schools game. Happily, too, it is aware that more needs to be done for boys from non rugby-playing schools and every encouragement must be given to clubs who devote time to developing such talent. Magnificent is not too strong a word to use to sum up the schools contribution to Irish rugby.

26

The legislators

Players, as a general rule, and most spectators, other than those directly involved in club administration, do not, I believe, take an interest of any real consequence in the legislation of their particular sport. Perhaps some contentious issue comes up and then the attention is focussed on the men in the corridors of power. The day to day running of the game is not, however, of any real concern. There is one notable exception in this particular field of activity and that is the question of team selection at international and interprovincial level. For a period each season the selectors are constantly in the news and each season there is considerable interest in the composition of the Ireland international selection committee and in those who select the four provincial sides.

It has been said, and probably with some truth, that no one is forgotten as quickly as the previous year's union president. For twelve months he is the centre of attraction and then becomes no more than another former president.

In modern times, the IRFU has adopted a policy that the president sits for one year on the IRFU committee following his year of presidency and that is, I believe, a wise course.

There are and have been, of course, exceptions to this principle and indeed last season, for instance, two former presidents of the union, in addition to the immediate past president, sat on the committee.

Throughout the pages of this book the names of many men who have made remarkable contributions to the running of the game in Ireland are mentioned, some more frequently than others. Whatever the casual nature of public interest and concern, I have no doubt that the game in Ireland has been admirably served by many—some have left a mark, not only in the immediate confines of the country, but on the administration of the game on a worldwide basis.

I do not think that many will offer an argument when I suggest that the first of the really notable Irish administrators was R.M. Peter. His tenure of office as honorary secretary of the IRFU was of comparatively short duration, but he was the man in that onerous position when the two Unions amalgamated to form the IRFU and was a central figure in the delicate negotiations that ensued in that happy union. Contentious, perhaps, but his interest was total and extended to producing a football annual that was a testimony to his industry and to his knowledge.

Sir William Goulding was another from the early days. He was a man who did so much to promote the game in his native Munster.

Contributions to any organisation cannot be measured by time alone, for it must be stressed that for quite a long period there were many in positions of power, who might well have stepped aside to leave more enlightened minds get to work.

As already outlined, the problems of the 1930s underlined this contention. The IRFU badly needed a shake up and the evidence is very strong that when it came, it was greatly beneficial to the game. The selection committee, for instance, was quite a remarkable body for a long time with some men on that august body for a quarter of a century and more. However acute the minds of such men, and however avid their interest, it is difficult to accept that so long a tenure of office in such a position can have been fruitful.

One such man was John Macaulay from Munster, who had been capped in 1877. He was obviously very partial to the job of selecting the national team for he sat on the committee of selection first in 1895, had two brief breaks and was still there in 1930. Yet he was a remarkable man and gave tremendous service to the game in Ireland and in Munster, being honorary treasurer of the Munster Branch for the better part of half a century. He was, too, president of the IRFU 1894–95 and altogether must be put in with the more eminent of Irish rugby legislators.

George Scriven holds a unique place in the annals of the game in Ireland, the only man to have been president of the IRFU twice with a break in between his terms of office. He was president in 1882–83 and again in 1885–86. While he held that office, it is a notable fact that he also played for Ireland in 1882–83 when he captained the side. As president of the union in those days, he would also have been, in effect, chairman of the selection committee. He achieved the quite astonishing feat of being union president, chairman of the selection committee and captain of the national side at the same time. He was also, of course, an international referee as has already been outlined previously in this book.

The formation of the International Board on the Irish initiative in 1885–86 was to bring a new concept to the game, and last season the Board celebrated its centenary. Two special matches were arranged to mark that great occasion, yet sadly neither was held at an Irish venue. There is no doubt that, when one looks at the men who have represented Ireland on the Board, then in that comparatively small body we find undoubtedly some of the truly great Irish rugby legislators. Sir Frederick Moore, capped for Ireland as were two of his brothers, was a most able administrator and outstanding IRFU president (1889–90). He and Robert Warren were very influential in setting up a separate committee for international team selection.

The first honorary secretary of the International Board was Eddie McAlister and he held that position from 1887–1897. He was followed into the office by another remarkable man, Robert G. Warren. Robert Warren sat on the IRFU committee for over fifty years. An eminent player with the Lansdowne Club, he had captained Ireland in the 1880s and immediately took up the responsibility of administration when his playing days were over.

He was elected as one of the IRFU Board representatives in 1887 and served in that capacity until 1938. He had the dual responsibility of being a Board representative and honorary secretary of the Board, for he held that office from 1897 until 1933. He had succeeded McAlister as honorary secretary and when he laid down the burden it was to yet another Irishman that the Board turned to act as honorary secretary, Harry Thrift.

Here is another worthy to rank with the great administrators. A product of Trinity College, Harry Thrift was IRFU president in 1923–24. Eminent international, one time Ireland selector, he also captained Ireland in 1908 against England. He was on the board from 1931 to 1956 and, for a period during that term of office, he had as his International Board colleague, Sarsfield Hogan.

Sarsfield Hogan had been a player of great ability and was a member of the University College Dublin Club in its early years. He had played on the first UCD team to win the Leinster Senior Cup in 1924 and then gave great service to Lansdowne as a player. He was most unlucky not to have won an international cap. He was also a sportsman of the most rounded skills. Rugby, cricket, athletics, tennis and golf were all mastered by a man who was also to achieve great academic distinction. He was the man who, in the 1930s, had seen that remedial action needed to be taken in the field of Irish rugby administration, and he did what was necessary.

Still hale and hearty, he retains to this day a truly remarkable memory and sharpness of intellect. He gave magnificent service to the game at every level. His contribution to university rugby was immense. He served the Leinster branch with distinction and the IRFU equally so, but it was as a member of the International Board that he achieved a reputation across the rugby world as being arguably the most able and astute legislator of his era. Greatly respected in all corners of the rugby world, he was on the Board from 1946 until he retired in 1971. In that period he was to help legislate for the game in an era when it underwent immense change, both in law and in attitude. As a law maker, he was among the very best and the combination he formed with Harry Thrift between the years 1946 and 1956 was in the opinion of many who sat with them on the governing body, arguably the best team any country ever had on the Board.

J.B. Moore, who sat on the Board between 1892 and 1927, was another astute man and assiduous worker for the game as was A.D. 'Coo' Clinch. An international of great ability, he was also a long time member of the national selection committee and on the International Board from 1928 until 1936. His son 'Jammie' was one of Ireland's greatest forwards in the period between the wars.

Harry Sheppard's contribution to Irish rugby is dealt with to a large extent in the chapter on Lansdowne road, but he was another of Ireland's Board representatives in the early days.

When Harry Thrift relinquished the honorary secretaryship of the Board in 1956, it was yet another Irishman Eddie Kirwan who took up the burden of office and held the position until 1971, retiring at the same time as his great friend and colleague Sarsfield Hogan. He, like Hogan, had also been president of the IRFU; Kirwan was a leading light in the Palmerston club in Dublin.

Jack Siggins, another still happily with us and still with a deep interest in the game, was a distinguished Board member and IRFU committee man for a number of years. Another former Ireland player and captain, he was a stalwart of the Ulster branch and served on the Ireland selection committee and as a manager of the Lions in 1955. Like those of the previous generation, the men who have served Ireland on the governing body in modern times have maintained high standards. Harry McKibbin has been a Board member for almost twenty years. He comes from a family that has given an immense amount to the game. A former international, he was with the Lions in South Africa in 1938 and like many another missed a host of international caps because of the 1939–45 war.

He was an outstanding president of the IRFU in the centenary year and is one of the former presidents who stayed on the committee long after his year of office. His brother Des was president of the IRFU last season and was manager of the Ireland tour to Japan in the summer of 1985. Like Harry, he too played for Ireland. Harry's two sons, Harry junior and Alistair, maintained the great family playing tradition and were both capped, while another son Roger was a final trialist whose career was restricted by injury. Des's son Brian won two caps for Ireland at schools level.

The McKibbins from Belfast rank among the great Irish rugby families. Harry and Des McKibbin have the unique distinction of being the only brothers to have been IRFU presidents.

There have been two instances of father and son. J.J. Coffey, another very distinguished legislator was president in 1924–25 and his son Jack held the same office in 1977–78. Both were stalwarts of the Lansdowne club. Jack Coffey was manager of the Ireland side that toured Australia with such success in 1979.

The Irwins from Belfast were the first father and son to be elected IRFU presidents. Sir S.T. Irwin held the office in 1935–36 and his son Sinclair was president in 1969–70 and briefly on the International Board.

As circumstances should have it, Des McKibbin has been succeeded as IRFU president by another Ulsterman, Sir Ewart Bell. He is the latest of the many able administrators to come from Ulster to serve the IRFU in the highest office. An eminent civil servant and a former Ireland international, he has been at the forefront of the endeavours to lift the game in Ireland into a new competitive structure. A profound thinker, he will assuredly mark his year of office with great distinction.

He is surrounded by a lot of experience and has, as his senior vice president, Paddy Madigan who will be the first man from the Old Belvedere club to take up the presidency of the IRFU in 1987–88, a fitting tribute to a great club and indeed to a man who has given immense service both to Leinster and Irish rugby. He toured Argentina with Ireland in 1970 and was one of those extremely unlucky not to win an international cap. The honorary treasurer of the IRFU, Jimmy Nelson, has, as so many of his predecessors have done, managed the finances of the IRFU with great wisdom.

Nelson is another who holds a unique place in the IRFU. He

succeeded Tommy O'Reilly as honorary treasurer in 1976 and on the insistence of his colleagues, but with some personal reluctance, he held the dual office of president of the union and honorary treasurer in 1983–84.

He has been an outstanding success in his capacity as honorary treasurer, not least in the way the financing of the new East stand at Lansdowne Road was handled.

The present committee of the IRFU embraces wide experience and that will be needed in the face of the huge challenge the amateur ethic has to withstand.

The main income is derived from the gate receipts for the home internationals. The calls on the union's resources are many and, in this respect, it has been immensely gratifying to see so many new clubs and grounds throughout the country benefitting from the union offering generous assistance to the clubs. But finance is but one of the many issues on which the IRFU, in common with all sporting bodies, must address itself.

The amateur ethic of rugby football has never been more seriously under threat than at present and the International Board, 100 years after its foundation now must meet the most severe challenge in its history. Sponsorship, advertising, the World Cup, and payment to players are all issues now occupying the time and effort of the International Board.

Ronnie Dawson, one time Ireland and Lions captain has been one of the Irish Board members since 1975 and he has consistently laid out Ireland's attitude to these matters. He brings to his task on the Board a volume of great experience as player and legislator and has a great care for the amateur ethic. He is the latest in a long line of worthy men who have served Irish interests at the highest level of administration.

But if the Board is the centre of the stage, as it were, so too the union must be run on a day to day basis.

The days when an honorary secretary sufficed to carry that task have long gone and in 1925 it was decreed necessary that Ireland have a fulltime official in that office.

They turned to R.W. 'Rupert' Jeffares and he held the position until 1951 with the office of joint secretary-treasurer being instituted in 1947. In 1951, he was succeeded by his son Billy, who bore the same initials. They were at the heart of many changes in the day to day running of the union as the game expanded and when Billy Jeffares died in 1964, he was succeeded by Bob FitzGerald, who held the office until he retired last June.

Bob FitzGerald was to see vast changes during his period in the union office at Lansdowne Road and none more so than the great increase in the number of players involved in the game in Ireland. The representative programme expanded as well with 'B' internationals and schools internationals becoming part of the rugby calendar as well as more regular overseas tours by Ireland and the other home countries.

He ran the union office with immense efficiency, dedication and integrity. A player of note in his days with the Palmerston club, he had served as president of the Leinster branch and honorary treasurer of that body before taking up the secretaryship of the IRFU. He was succeeded last July by Patrick Moss, a former player with Trinity, and Wanderers, who inherits an onerous office.

As has been obvious in the preceeding pages, the game in Connacht went through many difficult periods but is now firmly established. A fortunate disposition of circumstances ordained that the game in the west was, at crucial times, to be served by men of great dedication. Foremost in this respect one must mention the late Henry Anderson, who was president of the Connacht branch from 1920 to 1949 when he died suddenly. He had also been president of the IRFU and, by taking that office in 1945–46, bridged a long gap since the previous Connacht man had held the position. He gave Connacht rugby incredible service as did another later to gain the IRFU presidency, Galway solicitor Chris Crowley, a man in the mould of Henry Anderson.

Rugby legislation, of course, is about people other than those who guide the affairs of the parent union. In Ireland for instance, the four constituent branches, Connacht, Leinster, Munster and Ulster, all have their own committees and all have been admirably served through the years by men of the utmost dedication. Some have been mentioned already in this book, but others who did not ever sit on the IRFU committee are worthy of mention for their work has been central to the propagation and welfare of the game. In Munster, for instance, Bill O'Brien was honorary secretary of the branch for over forty years before he relinquished the post in the early 1980s. Indeed Bill had succeeded his father as honorary secretary of the branch. A Corkman of outstanding quality, he had some able allies at his side. The name of Murphy has long been synonymous with the Constitution Club and Noel Murphy senior was another who, after a long and distinguished career, gave years of wonderful service to the game. He was president of the IRFU in 1960–61 and was manager of the Ireland team that toured South Africa in 1961. His son, Noel A., like his father an international, has followed a similar path on the legislative side and is currently vice president of the Munster Branch. Tom Kiernan can lay claim to have been one of the youngest men to hold the office of Munster president, not long after he retired as a player. On the coaching, playing and administrative sides, his contribution has been considerable; he was elected junior vice president of the IRFU last June.

Then one must not forget the name of Moss Scanlan. He has been the honorary secretary of the South Munster sub-committee for fifty years and still retains the post and all his old enthusiasm.

Men like Scanlan are the life's blood of the game and every province has been fortunate in this regard. Eddie Taylor (Leinster), Frank Humphreys (Ulster), Judge Charlie Conroy (Leinster) and Des Scaife (Leinster) are all owed an immense debt.

It is not easy to quantify all the great individual contributions, suffice to say that Irish rugby has, generally, been excellently served since the first administrative body and subsequently the four constituent branches were established.

There have been occasions through the years when the IRFU and the branches have all been accused of intransigence and, to some extent, the charges have been valid. Possibly the same can be said of every legislative body. Yet if this book has not conveyed, on a general basis, just how well the game has been run, then it has failed in a primary purpose.

The IRFU has, for over 100 years, brought Irishmen and Irish women from the four corners of the country together, united in a common cause, the greater good of the game. It has succeeded admirably where successive generations of politicians have failed miserably. Its success and the great development of the game in Ireland, notably in recent years, has been one of the more satisfactory sociological elements of Irish life.

That is not bad testimony to the men who, in the midst of the Victorian era, formed the first legislative body for rugby in Ireland. Rugby football in Ireland in 1986, is a fitting monument to those students at Trinity College and those who allied themselves to the students to put Ireland into the field of international rugby competition. Not the least tribute to their vision is that through over a century of time, countless thousands have derived immense pleasure from the rugby game.

27

Lansdowne Road

There is much that can be read into the character of a ground and the great sporting stadia of the world all have their own defined atmosphere. The Arms Park, is the shrine to which they come from the Valleys to worship and to exhort as only the Welsh can. 'Bread of Heaven' comes up from the terraces and nowhere can one hear singing to compare with the Welsh when they render 'Land of my Fathers'. It is awesome in power, intimidating and yet wonderfully beautiful.

The atmosphere at Twickenham is infinitely more staid, yet in its own way captivating with the trip to the ground through the London suburbs, the lunch baskets out in the car parks and the ample stands now rising from all four sides. Murrayfield, which recently underwent a major rebuilding programme, has perhaps lost some of its own character by the building of a huge stand down the side where the open banking invariably drew the greatest level of support for the Scots. And what of Parc des Princes, with the men from the South West up in the capital for the day? An international there is a glimpse of life as it is lived in France.

Newlands, Eden Park, Lancaster Park, King's Park, Loftus Versfeld and Ellis Park. They are all part of the tradition of international rugby. There are grounds readily associated in the minds of countless thousands who have never sat in their stands or stood on their terraces. And there is Lansdowne Road, the grand aristocrat of them all, the oldest international rugby ground where, since an afternoon in 1878, the tumult and the shouting have split the skies in Dublin's southern suburbs. There is something special about Dublin on the day of a rugby international. Good humour seems to pervade the whole city and there are many who have undergone a ritual unaltered through the years on the day the Irish are playing at Lansdowne Road. For some it is the walk from the city centre, easily attained in twenty minutes. For others the trip from Cork and Limerick and Galway and Belfast.

Ask the visitor to Lansdowne Road, what is it about a match at the ground that makes it different? Usually one gets the answer about the 'easy' atmosphere that obtains. Here it does not seem to matter quite so much if the home side loses as at other venues. The support and enthusiasm is no less ardent for Ireland than it is for other countries on their own heath, but defeat is not a national disaster. Perhaps the happenings through the years have conditioned such an attitude, and I believe that nowhere is Irish rugby better assessed than at Lansdowne Road on the occasion of an international.

It grows old with dignity, bearing as it does the marks of its long history and great tradition, but never less than immaculate for the big day. Modern amenities in an old world setting on three sides, with the concession to the 1980s now on the eastern side of the ground.

What Henry Wallace Doveton Dunlop would make of it all now it is hard to imagine, but he was nothing if not forward thinking, as he proved by taking a lease on the ground from the Pembroke Estate in the early 1870s.

Dunlop, an athlete of note in his day, laid his plans carefully as he set about designing what one might term in the modern idiom, a sports complex. He was certainly ahead of his time as well as a gentleman of the most rounded sporting interest. Not alone did he lay a cinder track for his beloved athletics, but also tennis courts, a cricket square and he started a rugby club now and long since among the very best in the land, Lansdowne Football Club.

Dunlop was the man who founded the Irish Champion Athletic Club and Lansdowne Road, in the natural order of things was the headquarters. In those early days the pitch ran from east to west, not as now from north to south. Dunlop was a man of practical application, too, for in the early days when there was trouble from flooding, he lifted the surface of the pitch by moving 300 cart loads of soil from a trench along the railway line that runs behind the west side of the ground.

When the Irish Football Union, as it then was, rejected the suggestion of playing against England in Dublin in December 1875, Dunlop made no secret of his disappointment, but he would later have the satisfaction of seeing his ground established as the headquarters of the game in Ireland.

The sporting history associated with the ground is by no means exclusive to rugby football and indeed the first international to take place there was an athletics international between Ireland and England. That meeting, held on 5 June 1876 was, in fact, the first athletics international in history. Over seventy years later, and long after the cinder track that Dunlop had laid down in the early years had disappeared, the ground was packed to its capacity to see a great Irish athlete Ronnie Delany, the Olympic 1500 metres champion in 1956 and no mean rugby player, take on the best from abroad and win. It has also been the location for soccer internationals on a regular basis for the past fifteen seasons, has housed European Cup ties and, of course, was the venue for the Irish Lawn Tennis Championships before the Fitzwilliam Club became the venue.

The first pavilion built on the ground by Dunlop was on the site of the building now adjacent to the west stand at its northern end, a structure that for a long time was the Lansdowne headquarters before they built the more elaborate clubhouse they now occupy at the side of the back pitch. The original pavilion was burned down, and Lansdowne and Dunlop moved to the opposite corner, the north-east, before moving back again.

The first rugby international played at the ground was on the afternoon of 11 March 1878 and never since that day has an international rugby match been played in Dublin at any other venue. Dunlop, who had earlier persuaded the rugby union that Lansdowne Road was a fit location for representative matches by staging interprovincials there, now saw yet another dream realised. As he developed and improved facilities at the ground, so also he surrendered his interest in the lease and sold it to Harry Sheppard, the honorary treasurer of the IRFU.

With Sheppard, and his close associations with rugby, now in possession the IRFU felt secure in their tenancy, but then in December 1906 there was a very unfortunate and sad development. Sheppard died in unexpected circumstances and that of course presented its own difficulties to the IRFU.

With commendable wisdom, and revealing a capacity for a clever business deal, they decided at a meeting in January 1907 to offer £200 to the representatives of the late Harry Sheppard for their interest in the lease. The offer was accepted. There followed negotiations with the Pembroke Estate, they negotiated a new lease, fifty years in duration at an annual ground rent of £50 per year.

With their tenancy now absolutely secure and the financial position of the union relatively strong, they set about a major development programme. They decided to alter the layout and it was at this time the playing pitch was altered to its present north-south alignment. They decided to build a covered stand on the west side of the ground and an uncovered stand to the left of that structure. The project was completed at a cost of over £6000 in time for the match against Scotland in 1908; Ireland marked the occasion with a victory!

The only building on the eastern side of the ground was a small wooden structure that served as a 'Press Box', but twenty years after what can be termed the IRFU's first major development programme, they dug into their resources again and built a stand on the east side that was first used for the match against Scotland in 1927. The building had not been completed in so far as the roof had not been put on to a structure that had standing accommodation underneath. Those who stood under the new building that afternoon in 1927 were much better served than those who had possession of the much prized stand tickets. The heavens opened all afternoon and the prolonged downpour soaked those in the stand. To this day those who were in the stand that afternoon vividly recall their experience. But the position was soon remedied and the roof affixed to a structure that stood until demolished at the end of the 1982–83 season. Meanwhile there was another major development in 1955 when it was decided to demolish the west stand, built in 1907, and replace it with a two tier structure. That stand was built across the railway line that serves the suburbs of such places as Blackrock, Dun Laoghaire, Monkstown, Dalkey and Bray and is the main line for towns in the south-east of Ireland.

By now the capacity of the ground was in the region of 50,000 but as demands for international tickets grew, and the interest in the game spread, the IRFU decided to undertake another major bulding programme in 1976.

Under the guidance of Ronnie Dawson, an architect by profession, the bottom tier of the West stand was taken out and a new and more spacious one put in its place. With inflation elevating costs and the interest rates for borrowing prohibitive, the union decided to raise some of the capital for the new structure by selling 2000 ten-year tickets for £150 each and launched 'The IRFU Fund Club'.

The money that came in from this scheme helped considerably towards the cost of the building and those who purchased the ten-year tickets got the 'bargain' of a lifetime. The tickets guaranteed a seat for every international for ten years at the ground and were based on the price of a stand ticket at the time. Those who purchased them were to see ticket prices mount considerably and their initial investment paid a handsome return. Those tickets will expire next year, but plans are afoot to give those who purchased them first option on renewal, a very fair decision and its own gesture of thanks by the IRFU to those who had put the money up ten years previously. One thing is for sure, the holders of those ten-year tickets for the bottom tier in the west stand will not be getting renewal terms on the same price of £150.

The most recent development at the ground was to prove not only the most ambitious but also the most costly. In 1982, in the aftermath of a Triple Crown win for Ireland, it was decided that the old east stand had had its day. A few years earlier the old uncovered stand in the north-east corner had been demolished as the cost of renovation would not have been worthwhile. Close inspection of the east stand, built in 1927, underlined that, if the building was to be preserved, it would require the expenditure of a lot of money and it would not have been worthwhile. So again taking their courage in their hands, the union decided to build a structure that would increase the seating to 13,400 by demolishing the stand and building a new and much more elaborate one in its place. It meant, among other things, of course, that spectators would no longer be able to stand on terraces underneath. But, with a fine regard for tradition, the union settled on a plan that allowed for spectators to stand in front of the new structure.

The cost of the new building might have frightened less courageous souls than those in the IRFU. The sum involved came to over four million pounds and raising that kind of capital presented its own problems.

Yet again the union opted for a ten-year ticket scheme, this time the cost being £500 per ticket.

They launched the scheme in an economic climate anything but favourable, but at a time when enthusiasm for the game in Ireland had reached a new peak, fanned by the Triple Crown and championship success in 1982. Within a matter of a fortnight, the scheme was over subscribed and so great was the demand that it was decided to extend the offer still further. Eventually 5,800 ten-year tickets were sold to bring in almost three million pounds. It demonstrated as well as anything could just how great the demand is for stand tickets for the rugby internationals. The new stand can seat 13,400 people and, if it is not everyone's ideal structure, its construction has been thoroughly vindicated as its need was great.

As well as being the venue for all of Ireland's home rugby internationals, it is now also the home ground for the Republic of Ireland soccer matches by agreement between the IRFU and the Football Association of Ireland. Henry Wallace Doveton Dunlop was unquestionably a man ahead of his time.

28

Game development

The coaching concept having been firmly established in all the major rugby playing countries by the 1970s, at least where the national teams were concerned, the feeling within the IRFU was that they needed something more than just a coaching structure and that 'game development' and all this embraced was a necessity.

They had been looking carefully at the problems within the country and it was decided the union would appoint a Game Development Officer. This was to put the position on a proper footing and to have someone on hand on a day to day basis to whom clubs and branches could turn for advice and assistance. There was considerable anxiety that the game should prosper in the schools and that every possible assistance should be given both to schools that wanted to take up the game and to schools and clubs who were having problems.

Thus in January 1979, the IRFU took the unprecedented step of appointing a full-time Game Development Officer. The position had been advertised in the national press and interviews were held, the aim being that the best possible candidate would fill this vitally important post. It was stressed that the Game Development Officer would be accountable to a development committee which had been set up under the chairmanship of Sir Ewart Bell, a man committed to this concept and one of the most profound rugby thinkers on the IRFU Executive. He was a happy choice to lead this committee.

The union had assembled a worthy body to act on the game development committee, drawn from a wide cross-section of the game in Ireland. Schools representatives, referees, former eminent players and experienced administrators formed the committee.

The Game Development Officer chosen by the IRFU was a man who had a long association with the sport and one who had played it at senior representative level, George Spotswood from Ulster. He brought to his onerous task a great interest in the game. He had played for

Dugannon and Malone and had worn the Ulster jersey with distinction. Professionally, he was a teacher at the Regent House School and, during his distinguished tenure at the school, he coached the 1st XV and with some success. He was to have the great satisfaction of seeing some of those he had coached later progress to the Irish national side.

George Spotswood took up his duties in January 1979 and immediately set about a deep study of the game in Ireland, where it was going and what was needed to maintain progress. Of equal importance was the question of how to channel effort into the areas that would yield the later dividend.

One of the results of the early days in his new capacity was a realignment of the long established interprovincial series. It was decided that, instead of the championship being spread over six weeks, in fact it would be a double programme confined to three weeks. Thus each Saturday it was a double programme of matches with all four provinces involved. This had a two-fold effect, one beneficial, the other more controversial. On the credit side, by reducing the championship to three Saturdays, it helped the clubs who had players on the provincial sides and this was probably more beneficial to Leinster than any other province. Invariably players from Leinster clubs not only played for the Leinster provincial side, but many also played for Munster and Connacht and indeed in a few cases for Ulster. But the national selectors were not especially happy with the arrangement, which still obtains. The interprovincials have always been fundamental to the construction of the national side, the step up from club level to the representative arena, and, at the same time highly competitive, being a championship.

It is a series that has, through the years, come in for some criticism. Some have argued that the competitive nature of the series at times imposed its own demands and that provinces do not play the open type of rugby some would like to see, being hidebound by fear of making errors. There is some truth in this assertion, but I have yet to meet a national selector who favours the discontinuance of the inter-provincials. Year after year they bring players forward for the national side. On the other hand they also reveal flaws in the temperament of players when they have been asked to take the step up from outside the confines of their own clubs. Thus it can be argued it has a very positive, as well as negative, value.

The development committee also conceived the idea of an under-20 interprovincial series and the feeling was that there was a great need for this. It was presented as an incentive for players not long out of school to gain representative honours within an age grouping and would help in the development of the more promising players in the country. To that end, it has served an admirable purpose, providing an ideal stepping stone from schools to senior representative levels.

Unfortunately, the original idea was not maintained for various reasons. The basic belief was that the under-20 matches should be played on the mornings of the senior interprovincials between the same provincial sides at the same venues as the senior games, allowing the senior selectors to watch the under age games and keep a sharp eye on the talent evident and emerging.

Alas for good intentions, the series, although having proved valuable, was not maintained in the form originally conceived. For a period, it was decided to reverse fixtures, thus when Leinster played Munster in Dublin at senior level, on the same afternoon, the two under-20 sides from the same provinces would meet at a Munster venue. That proved totally unsatisfactory and, in so far as it proved possible, the union went back to the original concept of the senior and under-20 games being played between the same provinces on the same day and in the same city. However, too often the under-20 matches, notably in Leinster, have been put on in direct opposition to the senior games with the same kick-off times at different locations. That is a practice that many want to see stopped as soon as possible. Not only has it meant the under-20 teams playing to sparse audiences, but it basically devalues the series and also deprives the senior selectors of seeing the emerging talent.

The idea of an under-19 side at provincial level was brought to fruition by Leinster initially and proved very successful and for a decade the Leinster under-19 team went unbeaten. But the other provinces did not have the same element of enthusiasm for the under-19 idea and, consequently, when the IRFU took a hand they opted for the under-20s. The Leinster under-19 team played many of their matches against outside opposition, notably in Wales, and many of the youngsters who had cut their teeth at this level of the representative game after leaving school, went on to earn Ireland caps.

One of the issues to which the Game Development Officer and his committee devoted a lot of attention was the senior club scene. Almost since the start of organised rugby in Ireland the game has been based on a competitive premise, with the Leinster, Munster and Ulster senior cups having histories that date back over a century. The Connacht Senior Cup is of more recent vintage, but is also a very old established competition. The Leinster Senior Cup was started in 1882, the Ulster counterpart just three years later. Munster followed in 1886 and Connacht in 1896. Those competitions, played annually in the closing months of the season, are highly prized and fought out with great intensity.

The provincial senior leagues, although to an extent fulfilling a useful purpose, were deemed unsatisfactory by the game development committee and quite correctly so. The Ulster Senior League was started in 1891, the Munster Senior League in 1903, and Connacht followed suit in 1926. But the leagues have a rather erratic history and it was not unknown for the competitions to remain unfinished; this certainly happened several times in Munster. Leinster did not have a senior league until 1971 and, when the competition was inaugurated, it did help fill a void but has never been considered remotely satisfactory.

It has been, for a start, extremely limited in its scope in what is the biggest provincial unit of the IRFU. It has been run in four sections and to a great extent has been more like a knock-out competition than a league, with clubs not playing any more than four games in their sections and, indeed, in the case of three of the four sections, the clubs play only three sectional games, the winners of each section qualify for the semi-final knock-out stages. Attempts to broaden the scope of the Leinster Senior League were met with considerable resistance and indeed, sad to relate, organised opposition from some clubs.

Although the leagues are competitive in the various provinces one must doubt that they have proved really beneficial. The Ulster Senior League has been run in different forms through the years. In the 1970s Des McKibbin, President of the IRFU last season, produced a most commendable report that led to a format being introduced that embraced promotion and relegation. But unfortunately it perished after a short period because clubs were opposed to it. No club wanted relegation, rather permanent senior status irrespective of their records on the field. There has not ever been a satisfactory system devised for progressive junior clubs to win senior status in their own right. McKibbin sought to remedy these failings, but his admirable ideas did not get the support they so richly deserved.

Having studied the club structure in great depth, the game development committee of the union produced a document for consideration by clubs and branches. Central to the recommendations was that there was a need, and a very important one, for a national competition. The members of that committee in the early 1980s saw what was needed and produced the most convincing arguments to support their contention. They laid out all the different options for clubs, produced several different formats for either a national knock-out competition or alternatively a national league.

After weighing all the considerations and listening to the advice and opinions sought and received from throughout the country, the game development committee finally concluded that the game in the country would be best served by starting an all-Ireland league.

There were several ideas behind this concept and foremost was that, in the opinion of the committee, a five division league with promotion and relegation operating, would not alone lift playing standards, but would bring in added revenue to the game, give the proper reward for performances and generally have the best players and clubs playing each other with something important at stake on a regular basis, rather than engage, as too many have done for too long, in a lot of meaningless friendly fixtures.

Some senior fixtures, involving clubs from Ireland against clubs from Britain are long established and valuable both from playing and social viewpoints. The idea of an all-Ireland league was not to kill off such fixtures; the aim was the highly noble concept of making the game better for the players and for the clubs. Indeed it was stressed in the report that fixtures involving club sides from other countries had a part to play. It was equally stressed that the various cup and league competitions in the provinces had served the game well, but it was time to change and to keep pace with what was happening in other countries.

The irony of the whole affair was that, while Ireland had led the way in the matter of club competitive football among the home countries, now Ireland had been left behind, the only one of the four not to have a national competition. The arguments were answerable, the evidence of the strongest possible fibre.

With Sir Ewart Bell having taken over as junior vice-president of the IRFU, chairmanship of the game development committee had been handed over to Tom Kiernan, one of the Munster representatives on the IRFU executive. Like his predecessor in the chair, Kiernan was another steeped in the game, one of the most distinguished players ever to grace the international scene and a man who had a great care for and understanding of the game and its ethos. He was a very good choice in a key position and he presided over a committee of men who encompassed great experience across the whole structure of the game. They decided late in 1984, after the most careful study and preparation, to recommend an all-Ireland league, based on five divisions with promotion and relegation between them. Initially it was decided that the clubs with the best records in the various provincial leagues would fill the top division of nine clubs with three clubs from Leinster, three from Ulster, two from Munster and one from Connacht forming the initial first division. The other divisions were to be constructed along similar lines.

They circularised the various clubs and branches with their recommendations which had the unanimous support of the IRFU executive, now under the presidency of Michael Carroll, from the Terenure Club. Carroll has been an Ireland selector and indeed chairman of that body in the 1970s. He had been president of the Leinster branch, of his club and a member of the IRFU executive for several years before he took over the union presidency.

Meetings were held throughout the country and Kiernan and his fellow game development committee members took the trouble to travel around the provinces explaining the league, its concept and assuring clubs that they would not lose senior status. They outlined the value of the league and gave assurances about finance.

The clubs were asked to reply to the recommendations and to give their opinions on the league and what form they wanted any amendments to take. Just prior to the end of the 1984–85 season, the clubs replied to the Game Development Officer, who was the central co-ordinating figure in the plan for a senior national league.

Almost two-thirds of the clubs voted in favour of the concept of an all-Ireland league, but there was general agreement that some amendments needed to be made. Foremost in this respect was the desire to see a system of two-up and two-down throughout all five divisions; there was also strong support for financial subsidy by the union towards travelling and accommodation costs. One could argue that the union had a strong mandate now to go ahead with the league, by just agreeing to the two-up and two-down principle and giving assurance of financial support.

They went back to the clubs again with the new proposals, now much more in line with what the generality had asked for. They gave the financial guarantees, agreed to the two-up and two-down proposal and asked the clubs to vote again on the issue. With two-thirds having already supported the idea before the union had agreed to the amendments, and before having been given generous financial support, it seemed certain that the all-Ireland league would start as the IRFU has envisaged in the season 1987–88.

There followed what can only be described as an unedifying exercise
in self preservation by some clubs and individuals. Some old established
clubs, knowing that their record in recent seasons would mean being in
the lower divisions, waged considerable campaigns to kill the all-
Ireland league. Caucus meetings were held and even a few individuals on
the IRFU executive, although that body had given the league concept
unanimous support, were at the forefront of the opposition to the
league.

It must be stressed, however, that strong and organised as the
opposition was, several of the best clubs in the country stood firm in
their support. Clubs such as Lansdowne, Wanderers, Blackrock College,
St Mary's College, Greystones Old Wesley and the newly formed De La
Salle Palmerston club in Leinster supported the league, despite all
opposition and some of the selfish and spurious arguments against it.
All the Connacht clubs supported the league except University College
Galway. In Ulster such as Ballymena, Ards and Malone gave it full
support; in Munster, Constitution Garryowen, University College Cork
and Dolphin were all in favour. Eventually, when the replies were sent
to the IRFU Game Development Officer, the issue had proved divisive.
Twenty-three of the forty-eight senior clubs supported the league,
twenty-three opposed it and two clubs had not replied.

Those two clubs, Ballinasloe and Westport, had however taken
decisions to support the league, but had not notified the IRFU
accordingly. It would have meant a majority for the league, but it would
not have made a difference. The IRFU felt they did not have a mandate
to start the league and this was announced following a meeting of the
IRFU executive in Galway just near the end of 1985.

It was a crushing blow to those clubs who wanted to do what was
right and very meagre reward indeed for the men on the game
development committee who had worked so very hard to produce an
acceptable format. The IRFU announced that day in Galway that,
despite the setback, the idea of an all-Ireland league was not killed for
good. They also instructed the four branches to come up with proposals
about their own provincial leagues that would help improve standards
and asked that they report their findings to the union executive.

Leinster, the province with the most unsatisfactory league of all,
certainly took that union directive seriously and immediately set about
restructuring their league to take effect from the start of season
1987–88. Ulster, too, have opted for a merit league to start in 1986–87.

Leinster's broad concept was that the league consist of two divisions with promotion and relegation in operation. The remarkable aspect of that decision was that Leinster had rejected this same proposal a decade earlier after the branch executive had agreed to bring such a concept about. Then, as was the case in relation to the national league, the proposal was killed by the clubs, with some working assiduously in the cause of halting the new idea.

Hopefully the new Leinster and Ulster set-up will prove successful and the forerunner to the badly needed, but thus far ill-fated, all-Ireland concept.

The club structure was but one of the matters within the ambit of the Game Development Officer. As his responsibilities grew and became more onerous, the IRFU decided in 1984 to change the set-up within their own administration with regard to game development.

George Spotswood changed positions, as it were, and became Technical Director and got a new assistant in John Murphy, like Spotswood a former school teacher and like his immediate boss, a man with a long involvement in the game. He played at senior level for the Skerries club, who were promoted to senior status in the mid 1970s after a distinguished run of success at junior level. Spotswood and Murphy are responsible on a day to day basis for the actual rugby aspects of the union and among their tasks is to make arrangements for Ireland training sessions and generally keep a sharp eye on developments at playing level within the game in Ireland. Schools rugby is a major concern for them. They have important roles to play.

The question of fixtures for Ireland, is of course, a matter for the IRFU executive and decisions on Ireland's participation at whatever level is their responsibility. On the morning that the decision on the all-Ireland league was announced in Galway, it was also announced that Ireland would enter for the World Cup in Australia and New Zealand in 1987.

That was not an unanimous decision and it was a very contentious issue. When the World Cup was proposed at the meeting of the International Board in Paris at the end of the 1984–85 season, it did not have Ireland's support. Indeed at the annual general meeting of the IRFU in June of 1985, Ronnie Dawson stated quite clearly that Ireland was against the World Cup and gave three specific reasons: the danger of professionalism, the added pressure on players and the disruption to tours already scheduled.

But despite that, Ireland eventually decided to enter the inaugural tournament for what is called the 'The Webb Ellis Trophy' but is, of course, a World Cup. The majority feeling within the IRFU, and I stress it was a majority verdict, was that it would be better for Ireland to participate, for in that way a ready eye could be kept on the matters about which the Irish Union felt concern. Not everyone agreed with that decision, but one could see the reasoning behind it. Yet there was, and still is, a feeling that, had Ireland stood firm on the stated principles, it might have served their beliefs to a better degree than taking part in the tournament. The draw for that brings Ireland in against Tonga, Canada and Wales in the group stage and Ireland will play in Wellington, Dunedin and Brisbane.

In 1975 Ireland played at 'B' level for the first time, against France in Dublin and an unedifying match it was with four players sent off the field by the referee Alan Welsby (England). Ireland continued to play at 'B' level until 1984, but it was felt that 'B' internationals do not basically best serve the Irish as a means of progression to the full international stage. Some would like under-23 matches, or something on the under age basis, but such fixtures have proved elusive. Ireland did play one under-23 match, against Holland in Hilversum in October 1979 and won it comprehensively.

International competitions below the level of the full grade are imperative towards game development, especially in a country such as Ireland with a limited playing population relative to most opponents.

World Cups and their attendant dangers brought further into focus the question of sponsorship. For a long time this was resisted in the most steadfast manner by the International Board and particularly by the four home unions. But necessity, or so the advocates of sponsorship told us, eventually saw the sponsor become an integral part of the game in Ireland as elsewhere.

Time was when Lansdowne Road did not carry advertisement hoardings; now space is at a premium. The various cup and league competitions in the provinces are all now sponsored as indeed are the schools cups. The interprovincial championship, too, is also sponsored as it has been for five of the last seven years.

In 1984 an international at Lansdowne Road was sponsored for the first time when the Digital Equipment Company sponsored the match against Scotland. The same firm also sponsored Ireland's two championship matches in Dublin in 1985 and, prior to last season's internationals, it was announced that Digital had signed a contract with the IRFU to sponsor all home matches for a three-year period with a sum of £300,000 being involved.

That kind of money in times of recession and inflation does much to help the game and the Digital sponsorship has the virtue of being extremely dignified with none of the pressure too often associated with this new element apparent. But there is danger in sponsorship and it is present on many levels. Far too many sports have found that sponsors were having far too much say in the administration of their sports with television inevitably a key factor in this area. There is the danger that unions, branches and indeed clubs can commit themselves to a level of expenditure based on the expectation of sponsorship money that, at times, does not materialise.

The IRFU has walked a careful enough path in this respect and every sponsorship deal by club and branch must be first passed by the union before being accepted. This is essential vigilance.

The IRFU will not accept sponsorship from any firm involved in the tobacco industry on the grounds that it is not conducive to health. It is very hard to argue against that stand. For a while there was also a ban on sponsorship and advertising from firms manufacturing alcoholic spirits but that was relaxed in 1985.

Sponsorship, it seems, is now firmly entwined in the development of the game.

Not the least important part of the duties of Spotswood and Murphy is the co-ordination of statistics in relation to injuries. All injuries sustained in the game are reported to the IRFU and monitored in the most careful manner. This is an aspect of the game now quite correctly deemed of great importance and the advances made with regard to medical care have been rapid and essential.

Neck injuries in particular have caused immense concern and, while the number of serious injuries relative to the number playing the game in Ireland is very small, that is not a reason for complacency; on the contrary the view is that one serious injury is one too many.

In an effort to help players permanently disabled by paralysis, the IRFU set up a charitable trust. It has been a great success and has helped alleviate financial strain on the injured, their dependants and their relatives. Doctors are on hand at all major matches and at all schools matches. There are medical centres at several grounds and arrangements made for doctors to be on call to deal with any injuries needing their attention. The laws in relation to the scrum have been amended to cut down the possibility of injuries as well as the laws in relation to ruck and maul. Referees are under strict instructions to apply the laws.

At schools level, the laws in relation to replacements are wide embracing to try to make sure that injured players do not stay on the field; the IRFU do not allow extra time to be played in schools cup matches.

The medical officer is now a fundamental part of the scene at club, branch and union level and, unlike former times, a doctor now travels with all teams at representative level, even on overseas tours.

In this regard two men who gave devoted attention to Ireland teams were the late Dr Jamesy Maher and the late Bob O'Connell. These men are owed an incalculable debt for the service they rendered to Ireland and to the development of the game. Even before the medical officer was part of the touring set-up both Jamesy Maher and Bob O'Connell travelled abroad with Ireland at their own expense. Such dedication and unstinting service is worthy of a high place for both in the history of the Irish game. Now Joe Gallagher and Dr Mick Molloy, the former Ireland second-row, are the medical officers to the IRFU. Game development has come a long way since those humble beginnings in the long ago at Trinity College, but there can be no complacency and no standing still. Ireland has reason to look to the future with hope, to look on the past with pride, to see visions of the days ahead and to plan carefully for the future generations of rugby men who will take up the torch set alight in those days of long ago in the Victorian era.

In the past challenges were met, as they can be again now. Now the challenge comes from rebel tours to South Africa in open defiance of the game's authorities. Professionalism has no part to play in the game in Ireland and could not be sustained. The principles of the amateur game are under threat—that is the task facing those who guide Irish rugby destiny.

APPENDIX 1
IRISH NATIONAL AND INTERNATIONAL OFFICERS AND REPRESENTATIVES

IRISH RUGBY FOOTBALL UNION OFFICERS

Presidents

1874–76 Duke of Abercorn
1876–79 Duke of Marlborough
1879–80 Dr W.C. Neville
1880–81 Sir W. Goulding
1881–82 R.B. Walkington
1882–83 G. Scriven
1883–84 A.R. McMullen
1884–85 R.E. McLean
1885–86 G. Scriven
1886–87 W.L. Stokes
1887–88 J. Chambers
1888–89 Dr R. Biggs
1889–90 Sir F.W. Moore
1890–91 M.H. Tumbrill
1891–92 H. Hook
1892–93 J.R. Blood
1893–94 R. Garrett
1894–95 J. Macaulay
1895–96 R.G. Warren
1896–97 J. Dodds
1897–98 J.P. Maguire
1898–99 J.B. Moore
1899–1900 S. Lee
1900–01 J. O'Sullivan
1901–02 T. Thornhill
1902–03 J. Johnston
1903–04 V.J. Murray
1904–05 Dr A.D. Clinch
1905–06 F.M. Hamilton
1906–07 J. Flynn
1907–08 G.H.B. Kennedy
1908–09 A. Barr
1909–10 C.W.L. Alexander
1910–11 Dr F.C. Purser
1911–12 J.H. O'Conor
1912–13 Major R. Stevenson
1913–16 F.H. Browning
1919–20 A. Tedford
1920–21 W.P. Hinton
1921–22 R.W. Magrath
1922–23 G.G. McCrea
1923–24 H. Thrift
1924–25 J.J. Coffey
1925–26 F.J. Strain
1926–27 G.T. Hamlet
1927–28 Judge J. Sealy
1928–29 H.J. Millar
1929–30 T.J. Greeves
1930–31 J.G. Musgrave
1931–32 W.A. Clarke
1932–33 C.S. Neill
1933–34 S.E. Polden
1934–35 Dr J. Wallace
1935–36 Sir S.T. Irwin
1936–37 Judge C. Davitt
1937–38 Dr H. Emerson
1938–45 J.J. Aarren
1945–46 H.J. Anderson
1946–47 W.A.B. Douglas
1947–48 Dr T.M. McGrath
1948–49 G.P.S. Hogan
1949–50 W.G. Fallon
1950–51 Sir W. Tyrrell
1951–52 D.J. O'Connell
1952–53 V.E. Kirwan
1953–54 J.B. O'Callaghan
1954–55 C.J. Hanrahan
1955–56 H.M. Read
1956–57 J.R. Ramsey
1957–58 W.E. Crawford
1958–59 J.J. Glynn
1959–60 J.R. Wheeler
1960–61 N.F. Murphy
1961–62 L.B. McMahon
1962–63 J.A.E. Siggins
1963–64 T.A. O'Reilly
1964–65 C.C. Harte
1965–66 Dr P.F. Murray
1966–67 D.G. O'Donovan
1967–68 E.O'D. Davy
1968–69 C.P. Crowley
1969–70 J.W.S. Irwin
1970–71 E. Patterson
1971–72 D.A. Dineen
1972–73 Judge J.C. Conroy
1973–74 I.F. Mahony
1974–75 H.R. McKibbin
1975–76 Dr J. Keane
1976–77 J.A.D. Higgins
1977–78 J.E. Coffey
1978–79 K.J. Quilligan
1979–80 J. Montgomery
1980–81 R. Ganly
1981–82 J.J. Moore
1982–83 J.E. Nelson

1983–84 G.F. Reidy
1984–85 M.H. Carroll
1985–86 D. McKibbin
1986–87 Sir E. Bell

Honorary secretaries

1874–76 H.D. Walsh
1876–78 W. Wilson
1878–79 W.C. Neville
1879–82 R.M. Peter
1882–86 H.G. Cook
1886–97 E. McAlister
1897–1925 C.F. Ruxton

Secretaries

1925–47 R.W. Jeffares Sr.
1951–64 R.W. Jeffares Jr.

Honorary treasurers

1875–79 R.M. Peter
1879–80 E. Hughes
1880–81 C.B. Croker
1881–82 J. Atkinson
1882–86 W.J. Goulding
1888–92 J.R. Blood
1892–94 E.L. Maunsell
1895–1906 H.C. Shepperd
1907–16 F.H. Browning
1920–45 W.A. Clarke
1945–47 J.R. Ramsey
*1964–76 T.A. O'Reilly
1976–   J.E. Nelson

*Honorary treasurer of the Union
restored as a separate office from that of
treasurer in 1964.

Joint secretary-treasurers

1947–51 R.W. Jeffares Sr.
1951–64 R.W. Jeffares Jr.
1964–86 R. FitzGerald
1986–   P. Moss

IRISH INTERNATIONAL BOARD REPRESENTATIVES

1886–92 T.R. Lyle
1886–97 E.A. McAlister
1887 W. Hogg*
1887 – Kirkpatrick*
1887–1938 R.G. Warren
1888–91 J. Chambers
1889 – Asher*
1892–1927 J.B. Moore
1893 J. Stewart*

1896 W. Ayres*
1897–1906 H.C. Sheppard
1898 J. Dodds*
1899 C.F. Ruxton*
1928–36 Dr A.D. Clinch
1931–56 H. Thrift
1932–46 F. Strain
1945 Judge C. Davitt
1946–71 G.P.S. Hogan
1948 J.R. Ramsey*
1957–71 J.A.E. Siggins
1967– H.R. McKibbin
1971–73 J.W.S. Irwin
1973–75 D.A. Dineen
1974– A.R. Dawson*
1975– A.R. Dawson

* Substituted for elected member

APPENDIX 2
IRISH SELECTORS AND COACHES

IRISH SELECTION COMMITTEES

1893–94 J.R. Blood, R.G. Warren, R. Garrett, R. Stevenson, J. Hook, H. McOstrich
1894–95 W. O'Conor, R.G. Warren, R. Garret, J. Dodds, J. Hook
1895–96 T. Thornhill, R.G. Warren, R. Garret, J. Chambers, J. Macaulay
1896–97 T. Thornill, R.G. Warren, J. Dodds, C. Le Fanu, J. Macaulay
1898–99 T. Thornhill, L.H. Gwynn, R. Stevenson, S. Lee, J. Macaulay
1899–1900 T. Thornhill, L.H. Gwynn, C.S. Harden, S. Lee, J. Macaulay
1900–1901 T. Thornhill, J. Sealy, C.S. Harden, J.J. Ferris, G.D. Bateman
1901–02 T. Thornhill, C.V. Rooke, C.S. Harden, F.M. Hamilton, J. Macaulay
1902–03 H.W. Jones, J. Sealy, C.S. Harden, A. Barr, J. Macaulay
1903–04 A.D. Clinch, J. Sealy, C.D. Neill, W.G. Macome, J. Macaulay
1904–05 A.D. Clinch, J. Sealy, J. Fulton, A. Barr, J. Macaulay
1905–06 A.D. Clinch, J. Sealy, A.F. Clarke, S.T. Irwin, J. Macaulay
1906–07 A.D. Clinch. C.B. Cullinan, A.F. Clarke, F. Gardiner, J. Macaulay

1907–08 A.D. Clinch, F.C. Purcer,
A. Barr, F. Gardiner, J. Macaulay

1908–09 A.D. Clinch, J.J. Rowland,
A. Barr, J. Fulton, J. Macaulay

1909–10 A.D. Clinch, F.C. Purcer,
A. Barr, F. Gardiner, J. Macaulay

1910–11 A.D. Clinch, F.C. Purcer,
T.N. Heron, F. Gardiner, J. Macaulay

1911–12 A.D. Clinch, B. Solomons,
T.N. Heron, A. Tedford, J. Macaulay

1912–13 A.D. Clinch, J.J. Coffey,
S. Lee, F.G. Strain, J. Macaulay

1913–14 A.D. Clinch, J.J. Coffey,
C.S. Neill, F.G. Strain, J. Macaulay

1915–18 No Selection committees
appointed.

1919–20 B.R. Doran, B. Solomons,
S.B. Campbell, F.G. Strain,
J. Macaulay

1920–21 B.R. Doran, W.A. Daish,
S.B. Campbell, F.G. Strain,
J. Macaulay

1921–22 H. Thrift, W.A. Daish,
Dr H. Emerson, F.J. Strain,
M.F. Landers

1922–23 S.E. Polden, J. Warren,
A.R. Foster, A. Tedford, M.F. Landers

1923–24 S.E. Polden, J. Warren,
A.R. Foster, A. Tedford, J. Macaulay

1924–25 S.E. Polden, J. Warren,
A.R. Foster, Dr H. Emerson,
J. Macaulay

1925–30 S.E. Polden, J. Warren,
T.J. Greeves, Dr H. Emerson,
J. Macaulay

1930–31 S.E. Polden, J. Warren,
T.J. Greeves, Dr H. Emerson,
J.G. Musgrave

1931–32 A.D. Clinch, J. Warren,
T.J. Greeves, J. Gillespie,
J.G. Musgrave

1932–33 S.E. Polden, J. Warren,
T.J. Greeves, J. Gillespie,
J.G. Musgrave

1933–34 S.E. Polden, J. Warren,
T.J. Greeves, Dr F.P. Montgomery,
J.G. Musgrave

1934–36 Dr P.F. Murray, G.P.S. Hogan,
T.J. Greeves, Dr F.P. Montgomery,
J.G. Musgrave

1936–37 W.P. Collopy, G.P.S. Hogan,
F.J. Greeves, R. Hamilton,
J.G. Musgrave

1937–38 W.P. Collopy,
Comdt. J. Gleeson, F.J. Greeves,
R. Hamilton, J. Quilligan

1938–40 N.M. Purcell, G.P.S. Hogan,
T.J. Greeves, R. Hamilton,
J. Quilligan

1940–41 N.M. Purcell, Dr H. Michael,
T.J. Greeves, R. Hamilton,
J. Quilligan

1941–42 E.C.G. Mulhern,
G.P.S. Hogan, T.J. Greeves,
R. Hamilton, J. Quilligan

1942–43 Dr H. Michael, L.B. McMahon,
T.J. Greeves, R. Hamilton,
C. Hanrahan

1943–44 G.P.S. Hogan, L.B. McMahon,
T.J. Greeves, W.E. Crawford,
C. Hanrahan

1944–46 G.J. Morgan, E.C.G. Mulhern,
W.E. Crawford, E.B.I. Goldsborough,
C. Hanrahan

1946–47 G.J. Morgan, L.B. McMahon,
W.E. Crawford, E.B.I. Goldsborough,
C. Hanrahan

1947–49 E.J. Lightfoot, L.B. McMahon,
W.E. Crawford, J.A.E. Siggins,
C.J. Hanrahan

1949–50 E.J. Lightfoot, C.R. Graves,
W.E. Crawford, J.B. O'Callaghan,
D.B. O'Loughlin

1950–51 J.J. Winters, C.R. Graves,
W.E. Crawford, J.B. O'Callaghan,
D.B. O'Loughlin

1951–52 J.J. Winters, C.R. Graves,
C.C. Harte, J.B. O'Callaghan,
N. Murphy

1952–53 J.J. Winters, P. Tighe,
C.C. Harte, J.B. O'Callaghan,
N. Murphy

1953–54 G.J. Quinn, P. Tighe,
C.C. Harte, J.W.S. Irwin, N. Murphy

1954–55 G.J. Quinn, P. Tighe,
C.C. Harte, J.A.D. Higgins,
D.B. O'Loughlin

1955–56 G.J. Quinn, C.A. Boyle,
W.E. Crawford, O.B. Glasgow,
D.B. O'Loughlin

1956–57 M.P. Crowe, C.A. Boyle,
W.E. Crawford, O.B. Glasgow,
D.B. O'Loughlin

1957–58 M.P. Crowe, C.A. Boyle,
J.A.D. Higgins, O.B. Glasgow,
D. Barry

1958–59 L. Lysaght, C.A. Boyle,
 J.A.D. Higgins, O.B. Glasgow,
 D. Barry
1959–60 L. Lysaght, C.R. Graves,
 J.A.D. Higgins, O.B. Glasgow,
 D. Barry
1960–61 C.R. Graves, D.P. Smyth,
 O.B. Glasgow, H.R. McKibbin,
 C. St George
1961–62 Dr K. Mullen, Dr G. O'Reilly,
 J.A.D. Siggins, H.R. McKibbin,
 C. St George
1962–63 Dr K.D. Mullen,
 Dr G. O'Reilly, H.R. McKibbin,
 J.E. Nelson, C. St George
1963–64 Dr K.D. Mullen,
 Dr G. O'Reilly, D. McKibbin,
 J.E. Nelson, M. Powell
1964–65 J.F. Coffey, Dr G. O'Reilly,
 D. McKibbin, J.E. Nelson, M. Powell
1965–66 J.F. Coffey, D.P. Smyth,
 D. McKibbin, J.E. Nelson, M. Powell
1966–67 J.F. Coffey, D.P. Smyth,
 D. McKibbin, W.E. Bell, J. Roche
1967–68 D. O'Leary, D.P. Smyth,
 W.E. Bell, D. McKibbin, J. Roche
1968–69 D. O'Leary, N. McConnell,
 W.E. Bell, N.J. Henderson, J. Roche
1969–70 D. O'Leary, A.R. Dawson,
 W.E. Bell, N.J. Henderson,
 Dr. D. Gleeson
1970–72 A.R. Dawson, M. Carroll,
 N.J. Henderson, J. Hewitt,
 Dr D. Gleeson
1972–73 M. Carroll, F. McMullen,
 J. Hewitt, S. Millar, P. O'Callaghan
1973–74 J.P. Fanagan, F. McMullen,
 W.J. Hewitt, S. Millar,
 P. O'Callaghan
1974–75 J.P. Fanagan, F. McMullen,
 S. Millar, R. Saunders, P. O'Callaghan
1975–76 J.P. Fanagan, N.H. Brophy,
 K.E. Reid, S. Millar, N.A. Murphy
1976–77 N.H. Brophy, R. Carroll,
 K.E. Reid, R. Saunders, N.A. Murphy
1977–78 N.H. Brophy, R. Carroll,
 K.E. Reid, R. Saunders, N.A. Murphy
1978–79 R. Carroll, P.F. Madigan,
 K.E. Reid, J. Lapsley, N.A. Murphy
1979–80 P.F. Madigan, M.K. Flynn,
 J.C. Lapsley, N.A. Murphy,
 B.P. O'Brien

1980–81 P.F. Madigan, M.K. Flynn,
 J.C. Lapsley, D.C. Glass, P.J. Dwyer
1981–82 M.K. Flynn, T.W.R. Meates,
 D.C. Glass, P.J. Dwyer. B.A. O'Brien
1982–83 T.W.R. Meates, M. Cuddy,
 D.C. Glass, P.J. Dwyer, B.A. O'Brien
1983–84 T.W.R. Meates, M. Cuddy,
 B.A. O'Brien, J. Donaldson,
 W.J. McBride
1984–85 M. Cuddy, M.G. Doyle,
 J.A. Donaldson, W.J. McBride,
 J. Kiernan
1985–86 M.G. Doyle, E. Coleman,
 W.J. McBride, J.A. Donaldson,
 J. Kiernan

COACHES TO THE IRELAND TEAM

(First appointed 1969–70)
1969–70 to 1971–72 A.R. Dawson
1972–73 to 1974–75 S. Millar
1975–76 to 1976–77 T.W.R. Meates
1977–78 to 1979–80 N.A. Murphy
1980–81 to 1982–83 T.J. Kiernan
1983–84 W.J. McBride
1984–85 to – M.G. Doyle

APPENDIX 3
PLAYERS CAPPED FOR IRELAND AT ALL LEVELS

CAPPED PLAYERS AT FULL INTERNATIONAL LEVEL

The following have been capped for Ireland at full international level.

Legend: *A* – Australia; *E* – England; *F* – France; *M* – Maoris; *NZ* – New Zealand; *S* – Scotland; *SA* – South Africa; *NSW* – New South Wales. (R) denotes came in as a replacement. Where a player played against the same country more than once in a season the number of times is given in brackets.

Abraham, M. (Bective Rangers) 1912 *E*, *S*, *W*, *SA*, 1914 *W*
Adams, C. (Old Wesley) 1908 *E*, 1909 *E*, *F*, 1910 *F*, 1911 *E*, *S*, *W*, *F*, 1912 *S*, *W*, *SA*, 1913 *W*, *F*, 1914 *F*, *E*, *S*
Agar, R.D. (Malone) 1947 *F*, *E*, *S*, *W*, 1948 *F*, 1949 *S*, *W*, 1950 *F*, *E*, *W*

Agnew, P.J. (CIYMS) 1974 *F* (R), 1976 *A*

Ahearn, T. (Queen's Coll, Cork) 1899 *E*

Alexander R. (NIFC, Police Union) 1936 *E, S, W*, 1937 *E, S, W*, 1938 *E, S*, 1939 *E, S, W*

Allen, C.E. (Derry, Liverpool) 1900 *E, S, W*, 1901 *E, S, W*, 1903 *S, W*, 1904 *E, S, W*, 1905 *E, S, W, NZ*, 1906 *E, S, W, SA*, 1907 *S, W*

Allen, G.G. (Derry, Liverpool) 1896 *E, S, W*, 1897 *E, S*, 1898 *E, S*, 1899 *E, W*

Allen, T.C. (NIFC) 1885 *E, S*

Allen, W.S. (Wanderers) 1875 *E*

Allison, J.B. (Edinburgh U) 1899 *E, S*, 1900, *E, S, W*, 1901 *E, S, W*, 1902 *E, S, W*, 1903 *S*

Anderson, F.E. (Queen's U, Belfast, NIFC) 1953 *F, E, S, W*, 1954 *NZ, F, E, S, W*, 1955 *F, E, S, W*

Anderson, H.J. (Old Wesley) 1903 *E, S*, 1906 *E, S*

Anderson, W.A. (Dungannon) 1984 *A*, 1985 *S, F, W, E*, 1986 *F, S*

Andrews, G. (NIFC) 1875 *E*, 1876 *E*

Andrews, H.W. (NIFC) 1888 *M*, 1889 *S, W*

Archer, A.M. (Dublin U, NIFC) 1879 *S*

Arigho, J.E. (Lansdowne) 1928 *F, E, W*, 1929 *F, E, S, W*, 1930 *F, E, S, W*, 1931 *F, E, S, W, SA*

Armstrong, W.K. (NIFC) 1960 *SA*, 1961 *E*

Arnott, D.T. (Lansdowne) 1876 *E*

Ash, W.H. (NIFC) 1875 *E*, 1876 *E*, 1877 *S*

Aston, H.R. (Dublin U) 1908 *E, W*

Atkins, A.P. (Bective Rangers) 1924 *F*

Atkinson, J.M. (NIFC) 1927 *F, NSW*

Atkinson, J.R. (Dublin U) 1882 *W, S*

Bagot, J.C. (Dublin U, Lansdowne) 1879 *S, E*, 1880 *E, S*, 1881 *S*

Bailey, A.H. (UC Dublin, Lansdowne) 1934 *W*, 1935 *E, S, W, NZ*, 1936 *E, S, W*, 1937 *E, S, W*, 1938 *E, S*

Bailey, N. (Northampton) 1952 *E*

Bardon, M.E. (Bohemians) 1934 *E*

Barlow, M. (Wanderers) 1875 *E*

Barnes, R.J. (Dublin U, Armagh) 1933 *W*

Barr, A. (Methodist Coll, Belfast) 1898 *W*, 1899 *S*, 1901 *E, S*

Beamish, C.E. St J. (RAF, Leicester) 1933 *W, S*, 1934 *S, W*, 1935 *E, S, W, NZ*, 1936 *E, S, W*, 1938 *W*

Beamish, G.R. (RAF, Leicester) 1925 *E, S, W*, 1928 *F, E, S, W*, 1929 *F, E, S, W*, 1930 *F, S, W*, 1931 *F, E, S, W, SA*, 1932 *E, S, W*, 1933 *E, W, S*

Beatty, W.J. (NIFC, Richmond) 1910 *F*, 1912 *F, W*

Becker, V. (Lansdowne) 1974 *F, W*

Beckett, G.G.P. (Dublin U) 1908 *E, S, W*

Bell, R.J. (NIFC) 1875 *E*, 1876 *E*

Bell, W.E. (Belfast Collegians) 1953 *F, E, S, W*

Bennett, F. (Belfast Collegians) 1913 *S*

Bent, G.C. (Dublin U) 1882 *W, E*

Berkery, P.J. (Lansdowne) 1954 *W*, 1955 *W*, 1956 *S, W*, 1957 *F, E, S, W*, 1958 *A, E, S*

Bermingham, J.J. (Blackrock Coll) 1921 *E, S W, F*

Blackham, J.C. (Queen's Coll, Cork) 1909 *S, W, F*, 1910 *E, S, W*

Blake-Knox, S.E.F. (NIFC) 1976 *E, S*, 1977 *F* (R)

Blayney, J. (Wanderers) 1950 *S*

Bond, A.T.W. (Derry) 1894 *S, W*

Bornemann, W.W. (Wanderers) 1960 *E, S, W, SA*

Bowen, D. St J. (Cork Const) 1977 *W, E, S*

Boyd, C.A. (Dublin U) 1900 *S*, 1901 *S, W*

Boyle, C.V. (Dublin U) 1935 *NZ*, 1936 *E, S, W*, 1937 *E, S, W*, 1938 *W*, 1939 *W*

Brabazon, H.M. (Dublin U) 1884 *E*, 1886 *E*

Bradley, M.J. (Dolphin) 1920 *W, F*, 1922 *E, S, W, F*, 1923 *E, S, W, F*, 1925 *F, S, W*, 1926 *F, E, S, W*, 1927 *F, W*

Bradley, M.T. (Cork Constitution) 1984 *A*, 1985 *S, F, W, E*, 1986 *F, W, E, S*

Bradshaw, G. (Belfast Collegians) 1903 *W*

Bradshaw, R.M. (Wanderers) 1885 *E, S*

Brady, A.M. (UC Dublin, Malone) 1966 *S*, 1968 *E, S, W*

Brady, J.A. (Wanderers) 1976 *E, S*

Brady, J.R. (CIYMS) 1951 *S, W*, 1953 *F, E, S, W*, 1954 *W*, 1956 *W*, 1957 *F, E, S, W*

Bramwell, T. (NIFC) 1928 *F*

Brand, T.N. (NIFC) 1924 *NZ*

Brennan, J.I. (CIYMS) 1957 *S, W*

Bresnihan, F.P.K. (UC Dublin, Lansdowne, London Irish) 1966 *E, W,* 1967 *A1, E, S, W, F,* 1968 *F, E, S, W, A,* 1969 *F, E, S, W,* 1970 *SA, F, E, S, W,* 1971 *F, E, S, W*

Brett, J.T. (Monkstown) 1914 *W*

Bristow, J.R. (NIFC) 1879 *E*

Brophy, N.H. (Blackrock Coll, UC Dublin) 1957 *F, E,* 1959 *E, S, W, F,* 1960 *F, SA,* 1961 *S, W,* 1962 *E, S, W,* 1963 *E, W,* 1967 *E, S, W, F, A2*

Brown, E.L. (Instonians) 1958 *F*

Brown, G.S. (Monkstown, United Services) 1912 *S, W, SA*

Brown, H. (Windsor) 1877 *E*

Brown, T. (Windsor) 1877 *E, S*

Brown, W.H. (Dublin U) 1899 *E*

Brown, W.J. (Malone) 1970 *SA, F, S, W*

Brown, W.S. (Dublin U) 1893 *S, W,* 1894 *E, S, W.*

Browne, A.W. (Dublin U) 1951 *SA*

Browne, D. (Blackrock Coll) 1920 *F*

Browne, H.C. (United Services and RN) 1929 *E, S, W*

Browne, W.F. (United Services and Army) 1925 *E, S, W,* 1926 *S, W,* 1927 *F, E, S, W, NSW,* 1928 *E, S*

Browning, D.R. (Wanderers) 1881 *E, S*

Bruce, S.A.M. (NIFC) 1883 *E, S,* 1884 *E*

Brunker, A.A. (Lansdowne) 1895 *E, W*

Bryant, C.H. (Cardiff) 1920 *E, S*

Buchanan, A. McM. (Dublin U) 1926 *E, S, W,* 1927 *S, W, NSW*

Buchanan, J.B. (Dublin U) 1882 *S,* 1884 *E, S*

Buckley, J.H. (Sunday's Well) 1973 *E, S*

Bulger, L.Q. (Lansdowne) 1896 *E, S, W,* 1897 *E, S,* 1898 *E, S, W*

Bulger, M.J. (Dublin U) 1888 *M*

Burges, J.H. (Rosslyn Park) 1950 *F, E*

Burgess, R.B. (Dublin U) 1912 *SA*

Burkitt, J.C.S. (Queen's Coll, Cork) 1881 *E*

Burns, I.J. (Wanderers) 1980 *E* (R)

Butler, L. (Blackrock Coll) 1960 *W*

Butler, N. (Bective Rangers) 1920 *E*

Byers, R.M. (NIFC) 1928 *S, W,* 1929 *E, S, W*

Byrne, E.M.J. (Blackrock Coll) 1977 *S, F,* 1978 *F, W, E, NZ*

Byrne, F. (UC Dublin) 1962 *F*

Byrne, S.J. (UC Dublin, Lansdowne) 1953 *S, W,* 1955 *F*

Byron, W.G. (NIFC) 1896 *E, S, W,* 1897 *E, S,* 1898 *E, S, W,* 1899 *E, S, W*

Caddell, E.D. (Dublin U, Wanderers) 1904 *S,* 1905 *E, S, W, NZ,* 1906 *E, S, W, SA,* 1907 *E, S,* 1908 *S, W*

Cagney, S.J. (London Irish) 1925 *W,* 1926 *F, E, S, W,* 1927 *F,* 1928 *E, S, W,* 1929 *F, E, S, W*

Callan, C.P. (Lansdowne) 1947 *F, E, S, W,* 1948 *F, E, S, W,* 1949 *F, E*

Cameron, E.D. (Bective Rangers) 1891 *S, W*

Campbell, C.E. (Old Wesley) 1970 *SA*

Campbell, E.F. (Monkstown) 1899 *S, W,* 1900 *E, W*

Campbell, S.B.B. (Derry) 1911 *E, S, W, F,* 1912 *F, E, S, W, SA,* 1913 *E, S, F*

Campbell, S.O. (Old Belvedere) 1976 *A,* 1979 *A 1,2,* 1980 *E, S, F, W,* 1981 *F, W, E, S, SA1,* 1982 *W, E, S, F,* 1983 *S, F, W, E,* 1984 *F, W*

Canniffe, D.M. (Lansdowne) 1976 *W, E*

Cantrell, J.L. (UC Dublin, Blackrock Coll) 1976 *A, F, W, E, S,* 1981 *S, SA, 1,2, A*

Carpendale, M.J. (Monkstown) 1886 *S,* 1887 *W,* 1888 *W, S*

Carr, N.J. (Ards) 1985 *S, F, W, E,* 1986 *W, E, S*

Carroll, C. (Bective Rangers) 1930 *F*

Carroll, R. (Lansdowne) 1947 *F,* 1950 *S, W*

Casement, B.N. (Dublin U) 1875 *E,* 1876 *E,* 1879 *E*

Casement, F. (Dublin U) 1906 *E, S, W*

Casey, P.J. (Lansdowne) 1963 *F, E, S, W, NZ,* 1964 *E, S, W, F,* 1965 *F, E, S*

Casey, T.C. (Young Munster) 1930 *S,* 1932 *E*

Chambers, J. (Dublin U) 1886 *E, S,* 1887 *E, S, W*

Chambers, R.R. (Instonians) 1951 *F, E, S, W,* 1952 *F, W*

Clarke, J.A.B. (Bective Rangers) 1922 *S, W, F,* 1923 *F,* 1924 *E, S, W*

Clegg, R.J. (Bangor) 1973 *F,* 1975 *E, S, F, W*

Clifford, T. (Young Munster) 1949 *F, E, S, W,* 1950 *F, E, S, W,* 1951 *F, E, SA,* 1952 *F, S, W*

Clinch, A.D. (Dublin U, Wanderers) 1892 *S,* 1893 *W,* 1895 *E, S, W,* 1896 *E, S, W,* 1897 *E, S*

Clinch, J.D. (Wanderers, Dublin U) 1923 *W,* 1924 *F, E, S, W, NZ,* 1925 *F, E, S,* 1926 *E, S, W,* 1927 *F,* 1928 *F, E, S, W,* 1929 *F, E, S, W,* 1930 *F, E, S, W,* 1931 *F, E, S, W, SA*

Clune, J.J. (Blackrock Coll) 1912 *SA,* 1913 *W, F,* 1914 *F, E, W*

Coffey, J.J. (Lansdowne) 1900 *E,* 1901 *W,* 1902 *E, S, W,* 1903 *E, S, W,* 1905 *E, S, W, NZ,* 1906 *E, S, W, SA,* 1907 *E,* 1908 *W,* 1910 *F*

Cogan, W. St J. (Queen's Coll, Cork) 1907 *E, S*

Collier, S.R. (Queen's Coll, Belfast) 1883 *S*

Collis, W.R.F. (KCH, Harlequins) 1924 *F, W, NZ,* 1925 *F, E, S,* 1926 *F*

Collis, W.S. (Wanderers) 1884 *W*

Collopy, G. (Bective Rangers) 1891 *S,* 1892 *S*

Collpy, R. (Bective Rangers) 1923 *E, S, W, F,* 1924 *F, E, S, W, NZ,* 1925 *F, E, S, W*

Collopy, W.P. (Bective Rangers) 1914 *F, E, S, W,* 1921 *E, S, W, F,* 1922 *E, S, W, F,* 1923 *S, W, F,* 1924 *F, E, S, W*

Combe, A. (NIFC) 1875 *E*

Condon, H.C. (London Irish) 1984 *S* (R)

Cook, H.G. (Lansdowne) 1884 *W*

Coote, P.B. (RAF, Leicester) 1933 *S*

Corcoran, J.C. (London Irish) 1947 *A,* 1948 *F*

Corken, T.S. (Belfast Collegians) 1937 *E, S, W*

Corley, H.H. (Dublin U, Wanderers) 1902 *E, S, W,* 1903 *E, S, W,* 1904 *E, S*

Cormac, H.S.T. (Clontarf) 1921 *E, S, W*

Costello, P. (Bective Rangers) 1960 *F*

Cotton, J. (Wanderers) 1889 *W*

Coulter, H.H. (Queen's U, Belfast) 1920 *E, S, W*

Courtney, A.W. (UC Dublin) 1920 *S, W, F,* 1921 *E, S, W, F*

Cox, H.L. (Dublin U) 1875 *E,* 1876 *E,* 1877 *E, S*

Craig, R.G. (Queen's U, Belfast) 1938 *S, W*

Crawford, E.C. (Dublin U) 1885 *E*

Crawford, W.E. (Lansdowne) 1920 *E, S, W, F,* 1921 *E, S, W, F,* 1922 *E, S,* 1923 *E, S, W, F,* 1924 *F, E, W, NZ,* 1925 *F, E, S, W,* 1926 *F, E, S, W,* 1927 *F, E, S, W*

Crean, T.J. (Wanderers) 1894 *E, S, W,* 1895 *E, S, W,* 1896 *E, S, W*

Crichton, R.Y. (Dublin U) 1920 *E, S, W, F,* 1921 *F,* 1922 *E,* 1923 *W, F,* 1924 *F, E, S, W, NZ,* 1925 *E, S*

Croker, E.W.D. (Limerick) 1878 *E*

Cromey, G.E. (Queen's U, Belfast) 1937 *E, S, W,* 1938 *E, S, W,* 1939 *E, S, W*

Cronyn, A.P. (Dublin U, Lansdowne) 1875 *E,* 1876 *E,* 1880 *S*

Crossan, K.D. (Instonians) 1982 *S,* 1984 *F, W, E, S,* 1985 *S, F, W, E,* 1986 *E, S*

Crowe, J. (UC Dublin) 1974 *NZ*

Crowe, L. (Old Belvedere) 1950 *E, S, W*

Crowe, M.P. (Lansdowne) 1929 *W,* 1930 *E, S, W,* 1931 *F, S, W, SA,* 1932 *S, W,* 1933 *W, S,* 1934 *E*

Crowe, P. (Blackrock Coll) 1935 *E,* 1938 *E*

Cullen, T.J. (UC Dublin) 1949 *F*

Cullen, W.J. (Monkstown and Manchester) 1920 *E*

Culliton, M.G. (Wanderers) 1959 *E, S, W, F,* 1960 *E, S, W, F, SA,* 1961 *E, S, W, F,* 1962 *S, F,* 1964 *E, S, W, F*

Cummins, W.E.A. (Queen's Coll, Cork) 1879 *S,* 1881 *E,* 1882 *E*

Cunningham, D.McC. (NIFC) 1923 *E, S, W,* 1925 *F, E, W*

Cunningham, M.J. (UC Cork) 1955 *F, E, S, W,* 1956 *F, S, W*

Cunnigham, W.A. (Lansdowne) 1920 *W,* 1921 *E, S, W, F,* 1922 *E,* 1923 *S, W*

Cuppaidge, J.L. (Dublin U) 1879 *E,* 1880 *E, S*

Currell, J. (NIFC) 1877 *S*

Curtis, A.B. (Oxford U) 1950 *F, E, S*

Cuscaden, W.A. (Dublin U, Bray) 1876 *E*

Cussen, D.J. (Dublin U) 1921 *E, S, W, F,*
1922 *E,* 1923 *E, S, W, F,* 1926 *F, E, S,*
W, 1927 *F, E*

Daly, J.C. (London Irish) 1947 *F, E, S,*
W, 1948 *E, S, W*

Daly, M.J. (Harlequins) 1938 *E*

Dargan, M. (Old Belvedere) 1952 *S, W*

Davidson, C.T. (NIFC) 1921 *F*

Davidson, I.G. (NIFC) 1899 *E,* 1900 *S,*
W, 1901 *E, S, W,* 1902 *E, S, W*

Davidson, J.C. (Dungannon) 1969 *F, E,*
S, W, 1973 *NZ,* 1976 *NZ*

Davies, F.E. (Lansdowne) 1892 *S, W,*
1893 *E, S, W*

Davis, J.L. (Monkstown) 1898 *E, S*

Davis, W.J.N. (Edinburgh U, Bessbrook)
1890 *S, W, E,* 1891 *E, S, W,* 1892 *E, S,*
1895 *S*

Davison, W. (Belfast Academy) 1887
W

Davy, E.O'D. (UC Dublin, Lansdowne)
1925 *W,* 1926 *F, E, S, W,* 1927 *F, E, S,*
W, NSW, 1928 *F, E, S, W,* 1929 *F, E,*
S, W, 1930 *F, E, S, W,* 1931 *F, E, S, W,*
SA, 1932 *E, S, W,* 1933 *E, W, S,* 1934
E

Dawson, A.R. (Wanderers) 1958 *A, E, S,*
W, F, 1959 *E, S, W, F,* 1960 *F, SA,*
1961 *E, S, W, F, SA,* 1962 *S, F, W,*
1963 *F, E, S, W, NZ,* 1964 *E, S, F*

Dean, P.M. (St Mary's Coll) 1981 *SA,*
1,2, *A,* 1982 *W, E, S, F,* 1984 *A,* 1985
S, F, W, E, 1986 *F, W*

Deane, E.C. (Monkstown) 1909 *E*

Deering, M. (Bective Rangers) 1929 *W*

Deering, S.J. (Bective Rangers) 1935 *E, S,*
W, NZ, 1936 *E, S, W,* 1937 *E, S*

Deering, S.M. (Garryowen, St Mary's
Coll) 1974 *W,* 1976 *F, W, E, S,* 1977
W, E, 1978 *NZ*

de Lacy, H. (Harlequins) 1948 *E, S*

Delaney, M.G. (Bective Rangers) 1895
W

Dennison, J.P. (Garryowen) 1973 *F,*
1975 *E, S*

Dick, C.J. (Ballymena) 1961 *W, F, SA,*
1962 *W,* 1963 *F, E, S, W*

Dick, J.S. (Queen's U, Belfast) 1962 *E*

Dick, J.S. (Queen's Coll, Cork) 1887 *E,*
S, W

Dickson, J.A.N. (Dublin U) 1920 *E, W,*
F

Doherty, A. (Old Wesley) 1974 *P* (R)

Doherty, W.D. (Guy's Hospital) 1920 *E,*
S, W, 1921 *E, S, W, F*

Donaldson, J.A. (Belfast Collegians)
1958 *A, E, S, W*

Donovan, T.M. (Queen's Coll, Cork)
1889 *S*

Dooley, J.F. (Galwegians) 1959 *E, S, W*

Doran, B.R.W. (Lansdowne) 1900 *S, W,*
1901 *E, S, W,* 1902 *E, S, W*

Doran, E.F. (Lansdowne) 1890 *S, W*

Doran, G.P. (Lansdowne) 1899 *S, W,*
1900 *E, S,* 1902 *S, W,* 1903 *W,* 1904 *E*

Douglas, A.C. (Instonians) 1923 *F,* 1924
E, S, 1927 *NSW,* 1928 *S*

Downing, A.J. (Dublin U) 1882 *W*

Dowse, J.C.A. (Monkstown) 1914 *F, S,*
W

Doyle, J.A.P. (Greystones) 1984 *E, S*

Doyle, J.I. (Bective Rangers) 1935 *W*

Doyle, M.G. (Blackrock Coll, UC
Dublin) 1965 *F, E, S, W, SA,* 1966 *F,*
E, S, W, 1967 *A* 1, *E, S, W, F, A* 2,
1968 *F, E, S, W, A*

Doyle, T.J. (Wanderers) 1968 *E, S, W*

Duggan, A.T.A. (Lansdowne) 1963 *NZ,*
1964 *F,* 1966 *W,* 1967 *A* 1, *S, W, A* 2,
1968 *F, E, S, W,* 1969 *F, E, S, W,* 1970
SA, F, E, S, W, 1971 *F, E, S, W,* 1972
F 2

Duggan, W. (UC Cork) 1920 *S, W*

Duggan, W.P. (Blackrock Coll) 1975 *E,*
S, F, W, 1976 *A, F, W, S, NZ,* 1977 *W,*
E, S, F, 1978 *S, F, W, E, NZ,* 1979 *E, S,*
A 1,2 1980 *E,* 1981 *F, W, E, S, SA* 1,2,
A, 1982 *W, E, S,* 1983 *S, F, W, E,*
1984 *F, W, E, S*

Duncan, W.R. (Malone) 1984 *W, E*

Dunlop, R. (Dublin U) 1889 *W,* 1890 *S,*
W, E, 1891 *E, S, W,* 1892 *E, S,* 1893
W, 1894 *W*

Dunn, P.E.F. (Bective Rangers) 1923 *S*

Dunn, T.B. (NIFC) 1935 *NZ*

Dunne, M.J. (Lansdowne) 1929 *F, E, S,*
1930 *F, E, S, W,* 1932 *E, S, W,* 1933 *E,*
W, S, 1934 *E, S, W*

Dwyer, P.J. (UC Dublin) 1962 *W,* 1963
F, NZ, 1964 *S, W*

Edwards, H.G. (Dublin U) 1877 *E,* 1878
E

Edwards, R.W. (Malone) 1904 *W*

Edwards, T. (Lansdowne) 1888 *M,* 1890
S, W, E, 1892 *W,* 1893 *E*

Edwards, W.V. (Malone) 1912 *F, E*

Egan, J.D. (Bective Rangers) 1922 *S*

Egan, J.T. (Cork Constitution) 1931 *F, E, SA*

Egan, M.S. (Garryowen) 1893 *E*, 1895 *S*

Ekin, W. (Queen's Coll, Belfast) 1888 *W, S*

Elliott, W.R.J. (Bangor) 1979 *S*

English, M.A.F. (Lansdowne, Limerick Bohemians) 1958 *W, F*, 1959 *E, S, F*, 1960 *E, S*, 1961 *S, W, F*, 1962 *F, W*, 1963 *E, S, W, NZ*

Ennis, F.N.G. (Wanderers) 1979 *A* 1 (R)

Ensor, A.H. (Wanderers) 1973 *W, F*, 1974 *F, W, E, S, P, NZ*, 1975 *E, S, F, W*, 1976 *A, F, W, E, NZ*, 1977 *E*, 1978 *S, F, W, E*

Entrican, J.C. (Queen's U, Belfast) 1931 *S*

Fagan, C. (Wanderers) 1956 *F, E, S*

Fagan, G.L. (Kingstown School) 1878 *E*

Farrell, J.L. (Bective Rangers) 1926, *F, E, S, W*, 1927 *F, E, S, W, NSW*, 1928 *F, E, S, W*, 1929 *F, E, S, W*, 1930 *F, E, S, W*, 1931 *F, E, S, W, SA*, 1932 *E, S, W*

Feddis, N. (Lansdowne) 1956 *E*

Feighery, C.F.P. (Lansdowne) 1972 *F* 1, *E, F* 2

Feighery, T.A.O. (St Mary's Coll) 1977 *W, E*

Ferris, J.H. (Queen's Coll, Belfast) 1900 *E, S, W*, 1901 *W*

Finlay, J.E. (Queen's Coll, Belfast) 1913 *E, S, W*, 1920 *E, S, W*

Finlay, W. (NIFC) 1876 *E*, 1877 *E, S*, 1878 *E*, 1879 *S, E*, 1880 *S*, 1882 *S*

Finn, M.C. (UC Cork, Cork Constitution) 1979 *E*, 1982 *W, E, S, F*, 1983 *S, F, W, E*, 1984 *E, S, A*, 1986 *F, W*

Finn, R. (UC Dublin) 1977 *F*

Fitzgerald, C.C. (Glasgow U, Dungannon) 1902 *E*, 1903 *E, S*

Fitzgerald, C.F. (St Mary's Coll) 1979 *A* 1,2, 1980 *E, S, F, W*, 1982 *W, E, S, F*, 1983 *S, F, W, E*, 1984 *F, W, A*, 1985 *S, F, W, E*, 1986 *F, W, E, S*

Fitzgerald, D.C. (Lansdowne) 1984 *E, S*, 1986 *W, E, S*

Fitzgerald, J. (Wanderers) 1884 *W*

Fitzpatrick, M.P. (Wanderers) 1978 *S*, 1980 *S, F, W*, 1981 *F, W, E, S, A*, 1985 *F* (R)

Fletcher, W.W. (Kingstown) 1882 *W, S*, 1883 *E*

Flood, R.S. (Dublin U) 1925 *W*

Flynn, M.K. (Wanderers) 1959 *F*, 1960 *F*, 1962 *E, S, F, W*, 1964 *E, S, W, F*, 1965 *F, E, S, W, SA*, 1960 *F, E, S*, 1972 *F* 1, *E, F* 2, 1973 *NZ*

Fogarty, T. (Garryowen) 1891 *W*

Foley, B.O. (Shannon) 1976 *F, E*, 1977 *W* (R), 1980 ,*F, W*, 1981 *F, E, S, SA*, 1,2, *A*

Forbes, R.E. (Malone) 1907 *E*

Forrest, A.J. (Wanderers) 1880 *E, S*, 1881 *E, S*, 1882 *W, E*, 1883 *E*

Forrest, E.G. (Wanderers) 1888 *M*, 1889 *S, W*, 1890 *S, E*, 1891 *E*, 1893 *S*, 1894 *E, S, W*, 1895 *W*, 1897 *E, S*

Forrest, H. (Wanderers) 1893 *S, W*

Fortune, J.J. (Clontarf) 1963 *NZ*, 1964 *E*

Foster, A.R. (Derry) 1910 *E, S, F*, 1911 *E, S, W, F*, 1912 *F, E, S, W*, 1914 *E, S, W*, 1921 *E, S, W*

Franks, J.G. (Dublin U) 1898 *E, S, W*

Frazer, E.F. (Bective Rangers) 1891 *S*, 1892 *S*

Freer, A.E. (Lansdowne) 1901 *E, S, W*

Fulton, J. (NIFC) 1895 *S, W*, 1896 *E*, 1897 *E*, 1898 *W*, 1899 *E*, 1900 *W*, 1901 *E*, 1902 *E, S, W*, 1903 *E, S, W*, 1904 *E, S*

Gaffikin, W. (Windsor) 1875 *E*

Gage, J.H. (Queen's U, Belfast) 1926 *S, W*, 1927 *S, W*

Galbraith, E. (Dublin U) 1875 *E*

Galbraith, H.T. (Belfast Acad) 1890 *W*

Galbraith, R. (Dublin U) 1875 *E*, 1876 *E*, 1877 *E*

Ganly, J.B. (Monkstown) 1927 *F, E, S, W, NSW*, 1928 *F, E, S, W*, 1929 *F, S*, 1930 *F*

Gardiner, F. (NIFC) 1900, *E, S*, 1901 *E, W*, 1902 *E, S, W*, 1903 *E, W*, 1904 *E, S, W*, 1906 *E, S, W*, 1907 *S, W*, 1908 *S, W*, 1909 *E, S, F*

Gardiner, J.B. (NIFC) 1923 *E, S, W, F*, 1924 *F, E, S, W, NZ*, 1925 *F, E, S, W*

Gardiner, S. (Belfast Albion) 1893 *E, S*

Gardiner, W. (NIFC) 1892 *E, S*, 1893 *E, S, W*, 1894 *E, S, W*, 1895 *E, S, W*, 1896 *E, S, W*, 1897 *E, S*, 1898 *W*

Garry, M.G. (Bective Rangers) 1909 *E, S, F*, 1911 *E, S, W*

Gaston, J.T. (Dublin U) 1954 *NZ, F, E, S, W,* 1955 *W,* 1956 *F, E*

Gavin, T.J. (Moseley, London Irish) 1949 *F, E*

Gibson, C.M.H. (Cambridge U, NIFC) 1964 *E, S, W, F,* 1965 *F, E, S, W, SA,* 1966 *F, E, S, W,* 1967 *A* 1, *E, S, W, F, A* 2, 1968 *E, S, W, A,* 1969 *E, S, W,* 1970 *SA, F, E, S, W,* 1971 *F, E, S, W,* 1972 *F* 1, *E, F* 2, 1973 *NZ, E, S, W, F,* 1974 *F, W, E, S, P,* 1975 *E, S, F, W,* 1976 *A, F, W, E, S, NZ,* 1977 *W, E, S, F,* 1978 *F, W, E, NZ,* 1979 *S, A* 1,2

Gibson, M.E. (Lansdowne) 1979 *F, W, E, S,* 1981 *W* (R)

Gifford, H.P. (Wanderers) 1890 *S*

Gillespie, J.C. (Dublin U) 1922 *W, F*

Gilpin, F.G. (Queen's U, Belfast) 1962 *E, S, F*

Glass, D.C. (Belfast Collegians) 1958 *F,* 1960, *W,* 1961 *W, SA*

Glennon, J.J. (Skerries) 1980 *E, S*

Godfrey, R.P. (UC Dublin) 1954 *S, W*

Goodall, K.G. (City of Derry and Newcastle U) 1967 *A* 1, *E, S, W, F, A* 2, 1968 *F, E, S, W, A,* 1969 *F, E, S,* 1970 *SA, F, E, S, W*

Gordon, A. (Dublin U) 1884 *S*

Gordon, T.G. (NIFC) 1877 *E, S,* 1878 *E*

Gotto, R.P.C. (NIFC) 1906 *SA*

Goulding, W.J. (Cork) 1879 *S*

Grace, T.P. (UC Dubln, St Mary's Coll) 1972 *F* 1, *E,* 1973 *NZ, E, S, W,* 1974 *E, S, P, NZ,* 1975 *E, S, F, W,* 1976 *A, F, W, E, S, NZ,* 1977 *W, E, S, F,* 1978 *S*

Graham, R.I. (Dublin U) 1911 *F*

Grant, E.L. (CIYMS) 1971 *F, E, S, W*

Grant, P.J. (Bective Rangers) 1894 *S, W*

Graves, C.R.A. (Wanderers) 1934 *E, S, W,* 1935 *E, S, W, NZ,* 1936 *E, S, W,* 1937 *E, S,* 1938 *E, S, W*

Gray, R.D. (Old Wesley) 1923 *E, S,* 1925 *F,* 1926 *F*

Gregg, R.J. (Queen's U, Belfast) 1953 *F, E, S, W,* 1954 *F, E, S*

Greene, E.H. (Dublin U, Kingstown) 1882 *W,* 1884 *W,* 1885 *E, S,* 1886 *E*

Greer, R. (Kingstown) 1876 *E*

Greeves, T.J. (NIFC) 1907 *E, S, W,* 1909 *W, F*

Griffin, C.S. (London Irish) 1951 *F, E*

Griffin, J.L. (Wanderers) 1949 *S, W*

Griffiths, W. (Limerick) 1878 *E*

Grimshaw, C. (Queen's U, Belfast) 1969 *E* (R)

Guerin, B.N. (Galwegians) 1956 *S*

Gwynn, A.P. (Dublin U) 1895 *W*

Gwynn, L.H. (Dublin U) 1893 *S,* 1894 *E, S, W,* 1897 *S,* 1898 *E, S*

Hakin, R.F. (CIYMS) 1976 *W, S, NZ,* 1977 *W, E, F*

Hall, R.O.N. (Dublin U) 1884 *W*

Hall, W.H. (Instonians) 1923 *E, S, W, F,* 1924 *F, S*

Hallaran, C.F.G.T. (Royal Navy) 1921 *E, S, W,* 1922 *E, S, W,* 1923 *E, F,* 1924 *F, E, S, W,* 1925 *F,* 1926 *F, E*

Halpin, T. (Garryowen) 1909 *S, W, F,* 1910 *E, S, W,* 1911 *E, S, W, F,* 1912 *F, E, S*

Hamilton, A.J. (Lansdowne) 1884 *W*

Hamilton, R.L. (NIFC) 1926 *F*

Hamilton, R.W. (Wanderers) 1893 *W*

Hamilton, W.J. (Dublin U) 1877 *E*

Hamlet, G.T. (Old Wesley) 1902 *E, S, W,* 1903 *E, S, W,* 1904 *S, W,* 1905 *E, S, W, NZ,* 1906 *SA,* 1907 *E, S, W,* 1908 *E, S, W,* 1909 *E, S, W, F,* 1910 *E, S, F,* 1911 *E, S, W, F*

Hanrahan, C.J. (Dolphin) 1926 *S, W,* 1927 *E, S, W, NSW,* 1928 *F, E, S,* 1929 *F, E, S, W,* 1930 *F, E, S, W,* 1931 *F,* 1932 *S, W*

Harbison, H.T. (Bective Rangers) 1984 *W* (R), *E, S*

Hardy, G.G. (Bective Rangers) 1962 *S*

Harman, G.R.A. (Dublin U) 1899 *E, W*

Harper, J. (Instonians) 1947 *F, E, S*

Harpur, T.G. (Dublin U) 1908 *E, S, W*

Harrison, T. (Cork) 1879 *S,* 1880 *S,* 1881 *E*

Harvey, F.M.W. (Wanderers) 1907 *W,* 1911 *F*

Harvey, G.A.D. (Wanderers) 1903 *E, S,* 1904 *W,* 1905 *E, S*

Harvey, T.A. (Dublin U) 1900 *W,* 1901 *S, W,* 1902 *E, S, W,* 1903 *E, W*

Headon, T.A. (UC Dublin) 1939 *S, W*

Healey, P. (Limerick) 1901 *E, S, W,* 1902 *E, S, W,* 1903 *E, S, W,* 1904 *S*

Heffernan, M.R. (Cork Institution) 1911 *E, S, W, F*

Hemphill, R. (Dublin U) 1912 *F, E, S, W*

Henderson, N.J. (Queen's U, Belfast, NIFC) 1949, *S, W*, 1950 *F*, 1951 *F, E, S, W, SA*, 1952 *F, S, W, E*, 1953 *F, E, S, W*, 1954 *NZ, F, E, S, W*, 1955 *F, E, S, W*, 1956 *S, W*, 1957 *F, E, S, W*, 1958 *A, E, S, W, F*, 1959 *E, S, W, F*

Henebrey, G.J. (Garryowen) 1906 *E, S, W, SA*, 1909 *W, F*

Heron, A.G. (Queen's Coll, Belfast) 1901 *E*

Heron, J. (NIFC) 1877 *S*, 1879 *E*

Heron, W.T. (NIFC) 1880 *E, S*

Herrick, R.W. (Dublin U) 1886 *S*

Heuston, F.S. (Kingstown) 1882 *W*, 1883 *E, S*

Hewitt, D. (Queen's U, Belfast, Instonians) 1958 *A, E, S, F*, 1959 *S, W, F*, 1960 *E, S, W, F*, 1961 *E, S, W, F*, 1962 *S, F*, 1965 *W*

Hewitt, F.S. (Instonians) 1924 *W, NZ*, 1925 *F, E, S*, 1926 *E*, 1927 *E, S, W*

Hewitt, J.A. (NIFC) 1981 *SA* 1 (R), 2 (R)

Hewitt, T.R. (Queen's U, Belfast) 1924 *W, NZ*, 1925 *F, E, S*, 1926 *F, E, S, W*

Hewitt, V.A. (Instonians) 1935 *S, W, NZ*, 1936 *E, S, W*

Hewitt, W.J. (Instonians) 1954 *E*, 1956 *S*, 1959 *W*, 1961 *SA*

Hewson, F.T. (Wanderers) 1876 *E*

Hickie, D.J. (St Mary's Coll) 1971 *F, E, S, W*, 1972 *F* 1, *E*

Higgins, J.A.D. (Civil Service) 1947 *S, W, A*, 1948 *F, S, W,*

Higgins, W.W. (NIFC) 1884 *E, S*

Hillary, M. (UC Dublin) 1952 *E*

Hingerty, D. (UC Dublin) 1947 *F, E, S, W*

Hinton, W.P. (Old Wesley) 1907 *W*, 1908 *E, S, W*, 1909 *E, S*, 1910 *E, S, W, F*, 1911 *E, S, W*, 1912 *F, E, W*

Hipwell, M.L. (Terenure Coll) 1962 *E, S*, 1968 *F, A*, 1969 *F* (R), *S* (R) *W*, 1971 *F, E, S, W*, 1972 *F* 2

Hobbs, T.H.M. (Dublin U) 1884 *S*, 1885 *E*

Hobson, E.W. (Dublin U) 1876 *E*

Hogg, W. (Dublin U) 1885 *S*

Holland, J.J. (Wanderers) 1981 *SA* 2, 1986 *W*

Holmes, G.W. (Dublin U) 1912 *SA*, 1913 *E, S*

Holmes, L.J. (Lisburn) 1889 *S, W*

Hooks, K.J. (Queen's U, Belfast) 1981 *S*

Horan, A.K. (Blackheath) 1920 *E, W*

Houston, K.J. (Oxford U, London Irish) 1961 *SA*, 1964 *S, W*, 1965 *F, E, SA*

Hughes, R.W. (NIFC) 1878 *E*, 1880 *E, S*, 1881 *S*, 1882 *E, S*, 1883 *E, S*, 1884 *E, S*, 1885 *E*, 1886 *E*

Hunt, E.W.F. de Vere (Army, Rosslyn Park) 1930 *F*, 1932 *E, S, W*, 1933 *E*

Hunter, D.V. (Dublin U) 1885 *S*

Hunter, L. (Civil Service) 1968 *W, A*

Hunter, W.R. (CIYMS) 1962 *E, S, W, F*, 1963 *F, E, S*, 1966 *F, E, S*

Hutton, S.A. (Malone) 1967 *S, W, F, A* 2

Ireland, J. (Windsor) 1876 *E*, 1877 *E*

Irvine, H.A.S. (Collegians) 1901 *S*

Irwin, D.G. (Queen's U, Belfast) 1980 *F, W*, 1981 *F, W, E, S, SA* 1,2, *A*, 1982 *W*, 1983 *S, F, W, E*, 1984 *F, W*

Irwin, J.W.S. (NIFC) 1938 *E, S*, 1939 *E, S, W*

Irwin, S.T. (Queen's Coll, Belfast) 1900 *E, S, W*, 1901 *E, W*, 1902 *E, S, W*, 1903 *S*

Jack, H.W. (UC Cork) 1914 *S, W*, 1921 *W*

Jackson, A.R.V. (Wanderers) 1911 *E, S, W, F*, 1913 *W, F*, 1914 *F, E, S, W*

Jackson, F. (NIFC) 1923 *E*

Jackson, H.W. (Dublin U) 1877 *E*

Jameson, J.S. (Lansdowne) 1888·*M*, 1889 *S, W*, 1891 *W*, 1892 *E, W*, 1893 *S*

Jeffares, E.W. (Wanderers) 1913 *E, S*

Johnston, J. (Belfast Acad) 1881 *S*, 1882 *S*, 1884 *S*, 1885 *S*, 1886 *E*, 1887 *E, S, W*

Johnston, M. (Dublin U) 1880 *E, S*, 1881 *E, S*, 1882 *E*, 1884 *E, S*, 1886 *E*

Johnston, R. (Wanderers) 1893 *E, W*

Johnston, R.W. (Dublin U) 1890 *S, W, E*

Johnston, T.J. (Queen's Coll, Belfast) 1892 *E, S, W*, 1893 *E, S*, 1895 *E*

Johnstone, W.E. (Dublin U) 1884 *W*

Johnstone-Smyth, T.R. (Lansdowne) 1882 *E*

Kavanagh, J.R. (UC Dublin, Wanderers) 1953 *F, E, S, W*, 1954 *NZ, S, W*, 1955 *F, E*, 1956 *E, S, W*, 1957 *F, E, S, W*, 1958 *A, E, S, W*, 1959 *E, S, W, F*, 1960

E, S, W, F, SA, 1961 *E, S, W, F, SA,*
1962 *F*
Kavanagh, P. (UC Dublin, Wanderers)
1952 *E,* 1955 *W*
Keane, M.I. (Lansdowne) 1974 *F, W, E,*
S, P, NZ, 1975 *E, S, F, W,* 1976 *A, F,*
W, E, S, NZ, 1977 *W, E, S, F,* 1978 *S,*
F, W, E, NZ, 1979 *F, W, E, S, A* 1,2,
1980 *E, S, F, W,* 1981 *F, W, E, S,* 1982
W, E, S, F, 1983 *S, F, W, E,* 1984 *F, W,*
E, S
Kearney, R.K. (Wanderers) 1982 *F,* 1984
A, 1986 *F, W*
Keeffe, E. (Sunday's Well) 1947 *F, E, S,*
W, A, 1948 *F*
Kelly, H.C. (NIFC) 1877 *E, S,* 1878 *E,*
1879 *S,* 1880 *E, S*
Kelly, J.C. (UC Dublin) 1962 *F, W,*
1963 *F, E, S, W, NZ,* 1964 *E, S, W, F*
Kelly, S. (Lansdowne) 1954 *S, W,* 1955
S, 1960 *W, F*
Kelly, W. (Wanderers) 1884 *S*
Kennedy, A.G. (Belfast Collegians) 1956
F
Kennedy, F. (Wanderers) 1880 *E,* 1881
E, 1882 *W*
Kennedy, F.A. (Wanderers) 1904 *E, W*
Kennedy, H. (Bradford) 1938 *S, W*
Kennedy, J.M. (Wanderers) 1882 *W,*
1884 *W*
Kennedy, K.W. (Queen's U, Belfast,
London Irish) 1965 *F, E, S, W, SA,*
1966 *F, E, W,* 1967 *A* 1, *E, S, W, F,*
A 2, 1968 *F, A,* 1969 *F, E, S, W,* 1970
SA, F, E, S, W, 1971 *F, E, S, W,* 1972
F 1, *E, F* 2, 1973 *NZ, E, S, W, F,* 1974
F, W, E, S, P, NZ, 1975 *F, W*
Kennedy, P. (London Irish) 1986, *W, E*
Kennedy, T. (St Mary's College) 1978
NZ, 1979 *F, W, E* (R), *A* 2, 1980 *E, S,*
F, W, 1981 *SA* 2, *A*
Keogh, F. (Bective Rangers) 1964 *W, F*
Keon, J.J. (Limerick) 1879, *E*
Keyes, R. (Constitution) 1986 *E*
Kidd, F.W. (Dublin U, Lansdowne)
1877 *E, S,* 1878 *E*
Kiely, M.D. (Lansdowne) 1962 *W,* 1963
F, E, S, W
Kiernan, M. (Dolphin, Lansdowne)
1982 *W* (R), *E, S, F,* 1983 *S, F, W, E,*
1984 *E, S, A,* 1985 *S, F, W, E,* 1986 *F,*
W, E, S

Kiernan, T.J. (UC Cork, Cork Const)
1960 *E, S, W, F, SA,* 1961 *E, S, W, F,*
SA, 1962 *E, W,* 1963 *F, S, W, NZ,*
1964 *E, S,* 1965 *F, E, S, W, SA,* 1966 *F,*
E, S, W, 1967 *A* 1, *E, S, W, F, A* 2,
1968 *F, E, S, W, A,* 1969 *F, E, S, W,*
1970 *SA, F, E, S, W,* 1971 *F,* 1972 *F* 1,
E, F 2, 1973 *NZ, E, S*
Killeen, G.V. (Garryowen) 1912 *E, S, W,*
1913 *E, S, W, F,* 1914 *E, S, W*
King, H. (Dublin U) 1883 *E, S*
Knox, J.H. (Dublin U, Lansdowne)
1904 *W,* 1905 *E, S, W, NZ,* 1906 *E, S,*
W, 1907 *W,* 1908 *S*
Kyle, J.W. (Queen's U, Belfast, NIFC)
1947 *F, E, S, W, A,* 1948 *F, E, S, W,*
1949 *F, E, S, W,* 1950 *F, E, S, W,* 1951
F, E, S, W, SA, 1952 *F, S, W, E,* 1953
F, E, S, W, 1954 *NZ, F,* 1955 *F, E, W,*
1956 *F, E, S, W,* 1957 *F, E, S, W,* 1958
A, E, S
Lambert, N.H. (Lansdowne) 1934 *S, W*
Lamont, R.A. (Instonians) 1965 *F, E,*
SA, 1966 *F, E, S, W,* 1970 *SA, F, E, S,*
W
Landers, M.F. (Cork Const) 1904 *W,*
1905 *E, S, W, NZ*
Lane, D. (UC Cork) 1934 *S, W,* 1935 *E,*
S
Lane, M.F. (UC Cork) 1947 *W,* 1949 *F,*
E, S, W, 1950 *F, E, S, W,* 1951 *F, S, W,*
SA, 1952 *F, S,* 1953 *F, E*
Lane, P. (Old Crescent) 1964 *W*
Langan, D.J. (Clontarf) 1934 *W*
Lavery, P. (London Irish) 1974 *W,* 1976
W
Lawler, P.J. (Clontarf) 1951 *S, SA,* 1952
F, S, W, E, 1953 *F,* 1954 *NZ, E, S,*
1956 *F, E*
Lawlor, P.J. (Bective Rangers) 1935 *E, S,*
W, 1937 *E, S, W*
Leahy, M.W. (UC Cork) 1964 *W*
Lee, S. (NIFC) 1891 *E, S, W,* 1892 *E,*
S, W, 1893 *E, S, W,* 1894 *E, S, W,*
1985 *E, W,* 1896 *E, S, W,* 1897 *E,*
1898 *E*
Le Fanu, V.C. (Cambridge U,
Lansdowne) 1886 *E, S,* 1887 *E, W,*
1888 *S,* 1889 *W,* 1890 *E,* 1891 *E,*
1892 *E, S, W*
Lenihan, D.G. (UC Cork, Cork Const)
1981 *A,* 1982 *W, E, S, F,* 1983 *S, F, W,*

E, 1984 F, W, E, S, A, 1985 S, F, W, E, 1986 F, W, E, S

L'Estrange, L.P.F. (Dublin U) 1962 E

Levis, F.H. (Wanderers) 1884 E

Lightfoot, E.J. (Lansdowne) 1931, F, E, S, W, SA, 1932 E, S, W, 1933 E, W, S

Lindsay, H. (Dublin U, Armagh) 1893 E, S, W, 1894 E, S, W, 1895 E, 1896 E, S, W, 1898 E, S, W

Little, T.J. (Bective Rangers) 1898 W, 1899 S, W, 1900 S, W, 1901 E, S

Lloyd, R.A. (Dublin U, Liverpool) 1910 E, S, 1911 E, S, W, F, 1912 F, E, S, W, SA, 1913 E, S, W, F, 1914 F, E, 1920, E, F

Lydon, C. (Galwegians) 1956 S

Lyle, R.K. (Dublin U) 1910 W, F

Lyle, T.R. (Dublin U) 1885 E, S, 1886 E, 1887 E, S

Lynch, J.F. (St Mary's Coll) 1971 F, E, S, W, 1972 F 1, E, F 2, 1973 NZ, E, S, W, 1974 F, W, E, S, P, NZ

Lynch, L. (Lansdowne) 1956 S

Lytle, J.H. (NIFC) 1894 E, S, W, 1895 W, 1896 E, S, W, 1897 E, S, 1898 E, S, 1899 S

Lytle, J.N. (NIFC) 1888 M, 1889 W, 1890 E, 1891 E, S, 1894 E, S, W

Lyttle, V.J. (Collegians, Bedford) 1938 E, 1939 E, S

McAllan, G.H. (Dungannon 1896 S, W

Macaulay, J. (Limerick) 1887 E, S

McBride, W.J. (Ballymena) 1962 E, S, F, W, 1963 F, E, S, W, NZ, 1964 E, S, F, 1965 F, E, S, W, SA, 1966 F, E, S, W, 1967 A 1, E, S, W, F, A 2, 1968 F, E, S, W, A, 1969 F, E, S, W, 1970 SA, F, E, S, W, 1971 F, E, S, W, 1972 F 1, E, F 2, 1973 NZ, E, S, W, F, 1974 F, W, E, S, P, NZ, 1975 E, S, F, W

McCall, B.W. (London Irish) 1985 F (R), 1986 E, S

McCallan, B. (Ballymena) 1960 E, S

McCarten, R.J. (London Irish) 1961 E, W, F

McCarthy, E.A. (Kingstown) 1882 W

McCarthy, J.S. (Dolphin) 1948 F, E, S, W, 1949 F, E, S, W, 1950 W, 1951 F, E, S, W, SA, 1952 F, S, W, E, 1953 F, E, S, 1954 NZ, F, E, S, W, 1955 F, E

MacCarthy, St G. (Dublin U) 1882 W

McCarthy, T. (Cork) 1898 W

McClelland, T.A. (Queen's U, Belfast) 1921, E, S, W, F, 1922 E, W, F, 1923 E, S, W, F, 1924 F, E, S, W, NZ

McClenahan, R.O. (Instonians) 1923 E, S, W

McClinton, A.N. (NIFC) 1910 W, F

McCombe, W.McM. (Dublin U, Bangor) 1968 F, 1975 E, S, F, W

McConnell, A.A. (Collegians) 1947 A, 1948 F, E, S, W, 1949 F, E

McConnell, G. (Derry, Edinburgh U) 1912 F, E, 1913 W, F

McConnell, J.W. (Lansdowne) 1913 S

McCormac, F.M. (Wanderers) 1909 W, 1910 W, F

McCormick, W.J. (Wanderers) 1930 E

McCoull, H.C. (Belfast Albion) 1895 E, S, W, 1899 E

McCourt, D. (Queen's U, Belfast) 1947 A

McCoy, J.J. (Dungannon) 1984 W, A, 1985 S, F, W, E

McCracken, H. (NIFC) 1954 W

McDermott, S.J. (London Irish) 1955 S, W

Macdonald, J.A. (Methodist Coll, Belfast) 1875 E, 1876 E, 1877 S, 1878 E, 1879 S, 1880 E, 1881 S, 1882 E, S, 1883 E, S, 1884 E, S

McDonnell, A.C. (Dublin U) 1889 W, 1890 S, W, 1891 E

McDowell, J.C. (Instonians) 1924 F, NZ

McFarland, B.A.T. (Derry) 1920 S, W, F, 1922 W

McGann, B.J. (Lansdowne) 1969 F, E, S, W, 1970 SA, F, E, S, W, 1971 F, E, S, W, 1972 F 1, E, F 2, 1973 NZ, E, S, W, 1976 F, W, E, S, NZ

McGown, T.M.W. (NIFC) 1899 E, S, 1901 S

McGrath, D.G. (UC Dublin) 1984 S

McGrath, N.F. (Oxford U, London Irish) 1934 W

McGrath, P.J. (UC Cork) 1965 E, S, W, SA, 1966 F, E, S, W, 1967 A 1, A, 2

McGrath, R.J.M. (Wanderers) 1977 W, E, F (R), 1981 SA, 1,2, A, 1982 W, E, S, F, 1983 S, F, W, E, 1984 F, W

McGrath, T. (Garryowen) 1956 W, 1958 F, 1960 E, S, W, F, 1961 SA

McGuire, E.P. (UC Galway) 1963 E, S, W, NZ, 1964 E, S, W, F

MacHale, S. (Lansdowne) 1965 *F, E, S, W, SA,* 1966 *F, E, S, W,* 1967 *S, W, F*

McIldowie, G. (Malone) 1906 *SA,* 1910 *E, S, W*

McIlrath, J.A. (Ballymena) 1976 *A, F, NZ,* 1977 *W, E*

McIlwaine, E.H. (NIFC) 1895 *S, W*

McIlwaine, E.N. (NIFC) 1875 *E,* 1876 *E*

McIlwaine, J.E. (NIFC) 1897 *E, S,* 1898 *E, S, W,* 1899 *E, W*

McIntosh, L.M. (Dublin U) 1884 *S*

MacIvor, C.V. (Dublin U) 1912 *F, E, S, W,* 1913 *E, S, F*

McKay, J.W. (Queen's U, Belfast) 1947 *F, E, S, W, A,* 1948 *F, E, S, W,* 1949 *F, E, S, W,* 1950 *F, E, S, W,* 1951 *F, E, S, W, SA,* 1952 *F*

McKee, W.D. (NIFC) 1947 *A,* 1948 *F, E, S, W,* 1949 *F, E, S, W,* 1950 *F, E,* 1951 *SA*

McKelvey, J.M. (Queen's U, Belfast) 1956 *F, E*

McKibbin, A.R. (Instonians, London Irish) 1977 *W, E, S,* 1978 *S, F, W, E, NZ,* 1979 *F, W, E, S,* 1980 *E, S*

McKibbin, C.H. (Instonians) 1976 *S* (R)

McKibbin, D. (Instonians) 1950 *F, E, S, W,* 1951 *F, E, S, W*

McKibbin, H.R. (Queen's U, Belfast) 1938 *W,* 1939 *E, S, W*

McKinney, S.A. (Dungannon) 1972 *F* 1, *E, F* 2, 1973 *W, F,* 1974 *F, E, S, P, NZ,* 1975 *E, S,* 1976 *A, F, W, E, S, NZ,* 1977 *W, E, S,* 1978 *S* (R), *F, W, E*

McLaughlin, J.H. (Derry) 1887 *E, S,* 1888 *W, S*

McLean, R.E. (Dublin U) 1881 *S,* 1882 *W, E, S,* 1883 *E, S,* 1884 *E, S,* 1885 *E*

Maclear, B. (Cork County, Monkstown) 1905 *E, S, W, NZ,* 1906 *E, S, W, SA,* 1907 *E, S, W*

McLennan, A.C. (Wanderers) 1977 *F,* 1978 *S, F, W, E, NZ,* 1979 *F, W, E, S,* 1980 *E, F,* 1981 *F, W, E, S, SA* 2

McLoughlin, F.M. (Northern) 1976 *A*

McLoughlin, G.A.J. (Shannon) 1979 *F, W, E, S, A* 2, 1980 *E,* 1981 *SA* 2, 1982 *W, E, S, F,* 1983 *S, F, W, E,* 1984 *F*

McLoughlin, R.J. (Blackrock Coll) 1962 *E, S, F,* 1963 *E, S, W, NZ,* 1964 *E, S,* 1965 *F, E, S, W, SA,* 1966 *F, E, S, W,*

1971 *F, E, S, W,* 1972 *F* 1, *E, F* 2, 1973 *NZ, E, S, W, F,* 1974 *F, W, E, S, P, NZ,* 1975 *E, S, F, W*

McMahon, L.B. (Blackrock Coll, UC Dublin) 1931 *E, SA,* 1933 *E,* 1934 *E,* 1936 *E, S, W,* 1937 *E, S, W,* 1938 *E, S*

McMaster, A.W. (Ballymena) 1972 *F* 1, *E, F* 2, 1973 *NZ, E, S, W, F,* 1974 *F, E, S, P,* 1975 *F, W,* 1976 *A, F, W, NZ*

McMordie, J. (Queen's Coll, Belfast) 1886 *S*

McMorrow, A. (Garryowen) 1951 *W*

McMullen, A.R. (Cork) 1881 *E, S*

McNamara, V. (UC Cork) 1914 *E, S, W*

McNaughton, P.P. (Greystones) 1978 *S, F, W, E,* 1979 *F, W, E, S, A* 2, 1980 *E, S, F, W,* 1981 *F*

MacNeill, H.P. (Dublin U, Oxford U, Blackrock Coll, London Irish) 1981 *F, W, E, S, A,* 1982 *W, E, S, F,* 1983 *S, F, W, E,* 1984 *F, W, E, A,* 1985 *S, F, W, E,* 1986 *F, W, E, S*

MacSweeney, D.A. (Blackrock Coll) 1955 *S*

McVicker, H. (Army, Richmond) 1927 *E, S, W, NSW,* 1928 *F*

McVicker, J. (Collegians) 1924 *F, E, S, W, NZ,* 1925 *F, E, S, W,* 1926 *F, E, S, W,* 1927 *F, E, S, W, NSW,* 1928 *W,* 1930 *F*

McVicker, S. (Queen's U, Belfast) 1922 *E, S, W, F*

Madden, M.N. (Sunday's Well) 1955, *E, S, W*

Magee, J.T. (Bective Rangers) 1895 *E, S*

Magee, A.M. (Louis) (Bective Rangers, London Irish) 1895 *E, S, W,* 1896 *E, S, W,* 1897 *E, S,* 1898 *E, S, W,* 1899 *E, S, W,* 1900 *E, S, W,* 1901, *E, S, W,* 1902, *E, S, W,* 1903 *E, S, W,* 1904 *W*

Maginiss, R.M. (Dublin U) 1875 *E,* 1876 *E*

Magrath, R.M. (Cork Constitution) 1909 *S*

Maguire, J.F. (Cork) 1884 *S*

Mahony, J. (Dolphin) 1923 *E*

Malcolmson, G.L. (RAF, NIFC) 1935 *NZ,* 1936 *E, S, W,* 1937 *E, S, W*

Maloney, J. (UC Dublin) 1950 *S*

Marshall, B.D.E. (Queen's U, Belfast) 1963 *E*

Massey-Westropp, R.H. (Limerick, Monkstown) 1866 *E*

Matier, R.N. (NIFC) 1878 *E*, 1879 *S*

Matthews, P.M. (Ards) 1984 *A*, 1985 *S*, *F*, *W*, *E*

Mattsson, J. (Wanderers) 1948 *E*

Mays, K.M.A. (UC Dublin) 1973 *NZ*, *E*, *S*, *W*

Mayne, R.B. (Queen's U, Belfast) 1937 *W*, 1938 *E*, *W*, 1939 *E*, *S*, *W*

Mayne, R.H. (Belfast Academy) 1888 *W*, *S*

Mayne, T. (NIFC) 1921 *E*, *S*, *F*

Meares, A.W.D. (Dublin U) 1899 *S*, *W*, 1900 *E*, *W*

Megaw, J. (Richmond, Instonians) 1934 *W*, 1938 *E*

Millar, A. (Kingstown) 1880 *E*, *S*, 1883 *E*

Millar, H.J. (Monkstown) 1904 *W*, 1905 *E*, *S*, *W*

Millar, S. (Ballymena) 1958 *F*, 1959 *E*, *S*, *W*, *F*, 1960 *E*, *S*, *W*, *F*, *SA*, 1961 *E*, *S*, *W*, *F*, *SA*, 1962 *E*, *S*, *F*, 1963 *F*, *E*, *S*, *W*, 1964 *F*, 1968 *F*, *E*, *S*, *W*, *A*, 1969 *F*, *E*, *S*, *W*, 1970 *SA*, *F*, *E*, *S*, *W*

Millar, W.H.J. (Queen's U, Belfast) 1951 *E*, *S*, *W*, 1952 *S*, *W*

Miller, F.H. (Wanderers) 1886 *S*

Milliken, R.A. (Bangor) 1973 *E*, *S*, *W*, *F*, 1974 *F*, *W*, *E*, *S*, *P*, *NZ*, 1975 *E*, *S*, *F*, *W*

Millin, T.J. (Dublin U) 1925 *W*

Minch, J.B. (Bective Rangers) 1912 *SA*, 1913 *E*, *S*, 1914 *E*, *S*

Moffat, J. (Belfast Academy) 1888 *W*, *S*, *M*, 1889 *S*, 1890 *S*, *W*, 1891 *S*

Moffat, J.E. (Old Wesley) 1904 *S*, 1905 *E*, *S*, *W*

Moffett, J.W. (Ballymena) 1961 *E*, *S*

Molloy, M.G. (UC Galway, London Irish) 1966 *F*, *E*, 1967 *A* 1, *E*, *S*, *W*, *F*, *A* 2, 1968 *F*, *E*, *S*, *W*, *A* 1969 *F*, *E*, *S*, *W*, 1970 *F*, *E*, *S*, *W*, 1971 *F*, *E*, *S*, *W*, 1973 *F*, 1976 *A*

Moloney, J.J. (St Mary's Coll) 1972 *F* 1, *E*, *F* 2, 1973 *NZ*, *E*, *S*, *W*, *F*, 1974 *F*, *W*, *E*, *S*, *P*, *NZ*, 1975 *E*, *S*, *F*, *W*, 1976 *S*, 1978 *S*, *F*, *W*, *E*, 1979 *A* 1,2, 1980 *S*, *W*

Moloney, L.A. (Garryowen) 1976 *W* (R), *S*, 1978 *S* (R), *NZ*

Monteith, J.D.E. (Queen's U, Belfast) 1947 *E*, *S*, *W*

Montgomery, A. (NIFC) 1895 *S*

Montgomery, F.P. (Queen's U, Belfast) 1914 *E* *S*, *W*

Montgomery, R. (Cambridge U) 1887 *E*, *S*, *W*, 1891 *E*, 1982 *W*

Moore, C.M. (Dublin U) 1887 *S*, 1888 *W*, *S*

Moore D.F. (Wanderers) 1883 *E*, *S*, 1884 *E*, *W*

Moore, F.W. (Wanderers) 1884 *W*, 1885 *E*, *S*, 1886 *S*

Moore, H. (Windsor) 1876 *E*, 1877 *S*

Moore, H. (Queen's U, Belfast) 1910 *S*, 1911 *W*, *F*, 1912 *F*, *E*, *S*, *W*, *SA*

Moore, T.A.P. (Highfield) 1967 *A* 2, 1973 *NZ*, *E*, *S*, *W*, *F*, 1974 *F*, *W*, *E*, *S*, *P*, *NZ*

Moore, W.D. (Queen's Coll, Belfast) 1878 *E*

Moran, F.G. (Clontarf) 1936 *E*, 1937 *E*, *S*, *W*, 1938 *S*, *W*, 1939 *E*, *S*, *W*

Morell, H.B. (Dublin U) 1881 *E*, *S*, 1882 *W*, *E*

Morgan, G.J. (Clontarf) 1934 *E*, *S*, *W*, 1935 *E*, *S*, *W*, *NZ*, 1936 *E*, *S*, *W*, 1937 *E*, *S*, *W*, 1938 *E*, *S*, *W*, 1939 *E*, *S*, *W*

Moriarty, C.C.H. (Monkstown) 1899 *W*

Moroney, J.C.M. (Garryowen) 1968 *W*, *A*, 1969 *F*, *E*, *S*, *W*

Moroney, R.J.M. (Lansdowne) 1984 *F*, *W*, 1985 *F*

Moroney, T.A. (UC Dublin) 1964 *W*, 1967 *A* 1, *E*

Morphy, E.McG. (Dublin U) 1908 *E*

Morris, D.P. (Bective Rangers) 1931 *W*, 1932 *E*, 1935 *E*, *S*, *W*, *NZ*

Morrow, D. (Bangor) 198 *F*, *E*, *S*

Morrow, J.W.R. (Queen's Coll, Belfast) 1882 *S*, 1883 *E*, *S*, 1884 *E*, *W*, 1885 *S*, 1886 *E*, *S*, 1888 *S*

Mortell, M. (Bective Rangers, Dolphin) 1953 *F*, *E*, *S*, *W*, 1954 *NZ*, *F*, *E*, *S*, *W*

Morton, W.A. (Dublin U) 1888 *S*

Moyers, L.W. (Dublin U) 1884 *W*

Mulcahy, W.A. (UC Dublin, Bective Rangers) 1958 *A*, *E*, *S*, *W*, *F*, 1959 *E*, *S*, *W*, *F*, 1960 *E*, *S*, *W*, *SA*, 1961 *E*, *S*, *W*, *SA*, 1962 *E*, *S*, *F*, *W*, 1963 *F*, *E*, *S*, *W*, *NZ*, 1964 *E*, *S*, *W*, *F*, 1965 *F*, *E*, *S*, *W*, *SA*

Mullan, B. (Clontarf) 1947 *F, E, S, W,*
1948 *F, E, S, W*
Mullane, J.P. (Limerick Bohemians)
1928 *W,* 1929 *F*
Mullen, K.D. (Old Belvedere) 1947 *F, E,*
S, W, A, 1948 *F, E, S, W,* 1949 *F, E, S,*
W, 1950 *F, E, S, W,* 1951 *F, E, S, W,*
SA, 1952 *F, S, W*
Mulligan, A.A. (Wanderers) 1956 *F, E,*
1957 *F, E, S, W,* 1958 *A, E, S, F,* 1959
E, S, W, F, 1960 *E, S, W, F, SA,* 1961
W, F, SA
Mullin, B.J. (Dublin U) 1984 *A,* 1985 *S,*
W, E, 1986 *F, W, E, S*
Murphy, C.J. (Lansdowne) 1939 *E, S,*
W, 1947 *F, E*
Murphy, J.G.M.W. (London Irish) 1951
SA, 1952 *S, W, E,* 1954 *NZ,* 1958 *W*
Murphy, J.J. (Greystones) *SA* 1, 1982 *W*
(R), 1984 *S*
Murphy, N.A.A. (Cork Constitution)
1958 *A, E, S, W, F,* 1959 *E, S, W, F,*
1960 *E, S, W, F, SA,* 1961 *E, S, W,*
1962 *E,* 1963 *NZ,* 1964 *E, S, W, F,*
1965 *F, E, S, W, SA,* 1966 *F, E, S, W,*
1967 *A* 1, *E, S, W, F,* 1969 *F, E, S, W*
Murphy, N.F. (Cork Constitution) 1930
E, W, 1931 *F, E, S, W, SA,* 1932 *E, S,*
W, 1933 *E*
Murphy-O'Connor, J. (Bective Rangers)
1954 *E*
Murray, H.W. (Dublin) 1877 *S,* 1878 *E,*
1879 *E*
Murray, J.B. (UC Dublin) 1963 *F*
Murray, P.F. (Wanderers) 1927 *F,* 1929
F, E, S, 1930 *F, E, S, W,* 1931 *F, E, S,*
W, SA, 1932 *E, S, W,* 1933 *E, W, S*
Murtagh, C.W. (Portadown) 1977 *S*
Myles, J. (Dublin U) 1875 *E*
Nash, L.C. (Queen's Coll, Cork) 1889 *S,*
1890 *W, E,* 1891 *E, S, W*
Neely, M.R. (Collegians) 1974 *F, E, S, W*
Neill, H.J. (NIFC) 1885 *E, S,* 1886 *S,*
1887 *E, S, W,* 1888 *W, S*
Neill, J.McF. (Instonians) 1926 *F*
Nelson, J.E. (Malone) 1947 *A,* 1948 *E, S,*
W, 1949 *F, E, S, W,* 1950 *F, E, S, W,*
1951 *F, E, W,* 1954 *F*
Nelson, R. (Queen's Coll, Belfast) 1882
E, S, 1883 *S,* 1886 *S*
Nesdale, T.J. (Garryowen) 1961 *F*
Neville, W.C. (Dublin U) 1879 *S, E*

Nicholson, P.C. (Dublin U) 1900 *E, S,*
W
Norton, G.W. (Bective Rangers) 1949 *F,*
E, S, W, 1950 *F, E, S, W,* 1951 *F, E, S*
Notley, J.R. (Wanderers) 1952 *F, S*
O'Brien, B. (Derry) 1893 *S, W*
O'Brien B.A.P. (Shannon) 1968 *F, E, S*
O'Brien, D.J. (London Irish, Cardiff,
Old Belvedere) 1948 *E, S, W,* 1949 *F,*
E, S, W, 1950 *F, E, S, W,* 1951 *F, E, S,*
W, SA, 1952 *F, S, W, E*
O'Brien, K.A. (Broughton Park) 1980 *E,*
1981 *SA* 1 (R), 2
O'Brien-Butler, P.E. (Monkstown) 1897
S, 1898 *E, S,* 1899 *S, W* 1900 *E*
O'Callaghan, C.T. (Carlow) 1910 *W, F,*
1911 *E, S, W, F,* 1912 *F*
O'Callaghan, M.P. (Sunday's Well)
1962 *W,* 1964 *E, F*
O'Callaghan, P. (Dolphin) 1967 *A* 1, *E,*
A 2, 1968 *F, E, S, W,* 1969 *F, E, S, W,*
1970 *SA, F, E, S, W,* 1976 *F, W, E, S,*
NZ
O'Connell, P. (Bective Rangers) 1913 *W,*
F, 1914 *F, E, S, W*
O'Connell, W.J. (Lansdowne) 1955 *F*
O'Connor, H.S. (Dublin U) 1957 *F, E, S,*
W
O'Connor, J. (Garryowen) 1895 *S*
O'Connor, J.H. (Bective Rangers) 1888
M, 1890 *S, W, E,* 1891 *E, S,* 1892 *E,*
W, 1893 *E, S,* 1894 *E, S, W* 1895 *E,*
1896 *E, S, W*
O'Connor, J.J. (Garryowen) 1909 *F*
O'Connor, J.J. (UC Cork) 1933 *S,* 1934
E, S, W, 1935 *E, S, W, NZ,* 1936 *S, W,*
1938 *S*
O'Connor, P.J. (Lansdowne) 1887 *W*
O'Donnell, R.C. (St Mary's Coll) 1979
A 1,2, 1980 *S, F, W*
O'Donoghue, P.J. (Bective Rangers)
1955 *F, E, S, W,* 1956 *W,* 1957 *F, E,*
1958 *A, E, S, W*
Odbert, R.V.M. (RAF) 1928 *F*
O'Driscoll, B.J. (Manchester) 1971 *F*
(R), *E, S, W*
O'Driscoll, J.B. (London Irish,
Manchester) 1978 *S,* 1979 *A* 1,2, 1980
E, S, F, W, 1981 *F, W, E, S, SA* 1,2, *A,*
1982 *W, E, S, F,* 1983 *S, F, W, E,* 1984
F, W, E, S
O'Flanagan, K.P. (London Irish) 1947 *A*

O'Flanagan, M. (Lansdowne) 1948 *S*

O'Hanlon, B. (Dolphin) 1947 *E, S, W,* 1948 *F, E, S, W,* 1949 *F, E, S, W,* 1950 *F*

O'Leary, A. (Cork Constitution) 1952 *S, W, E*

O'Loughlin, D.B. (UC Cork) 1938 *E, S, W,* 1939 *E, S, W*

O'Meara, J.A. (UC Cork, Dolphin) 1951 *F, E, S, W, SA,* 1952 *F, S, W, E,* 1953 *F, E, S, W,* 1954 *NZ, F, E, S,* 1955 *F, E,* 1956 *S, W,* 1958 *W*

O'Neill, H.O'H. (Queen's U, Belfast, UC Cork) 1930 *E, S, W,* 1933 *E, S, W*

O'Neill, J.B. (Queen's U, Belfast) 1920 *S*

O'Neill, W.A. (UC Dublin) 1952 *E,* 1953 *F, E, S, W,* 1954 *NZ*

O'Reilly, A.J.F. (Old Belvedere, Leicester, London Irish) 1955 *F, E, S, W,* 1956 *F, E, S, W,* 1957 *F, E, S, W,* 1958 *A, E, S, W, F,* 1959 *E, S, W, F,* 1960 *E,* 1961 *E, F, SA,* 1963 *F, S, W,* 1970 *E*

Orr, P.A. (Old Wesley) 1976 *F, W, E, S, NZ,* 1977 *W, E, S, F,* 1978 *S, F, W, E, NZ,* 1979 *F, W, E, S, A* 1,2, 1980 *E, S, F, W,* 1981 *F, W, E, S, SA* 1,2, *A,* 1982 *W, E, S, F,* 1983 *S, F, W, E,* 1984 *F, W, E, S, A,* 1985 *S, F, W, E,* 1986 *F, S*

O'Sullivan, A.C. (Dublin U) 1882 *S*

O'Sullivan, J.M. (Limerick) 1884, *S,* 1887 *S*

O'Sullivan, P.J.A. (Galwegians) 1957 *F, E, S, W,* 1959 *E, S, W, F,* 1960 *SA,* 1961 *E, S,* 1962 *F, W,* 1963 *F, NZ*

O'Sullivan, W. (Queen's Coll, Cork) 1895 *S*

Owens, R.H. (Dublin U) 1922 *E, S*

Parfrey, P. (UC Cork) 1974 *NZ*

Parke, J.C. (Monkstown) 1903 *W,* 1904 *E, S, W,* 1905 *W, NZ,* 1906 *E, S, W, SA,* 1907 *E, S, W,* 1908 *E, S, W,* 1909 *E, S, W, F*

Parr, J.S. (Wanderers) 1914 *F, E, S, W*

Patterson, C.S. (Instonians) 1978 *NZ,* 1979 *F, W, E, S, A* 1,2, 1980 *E, S, F, W*

Patterson, R.d'A. (Wanderers) 1912 *F, S, W, SA,* 1913 *E, S, W, F*

Payne, C.T. (NIFC) 1926 *E,* 1927 *F, E, S, NSW,* 1928 *F, E, S, W,* 1929 *F, E, W,* 1930 *F, E, S, W*

Pedlow, A.C. (CIYMS) 1953 *W,* 1954

NZ, F, E, 1955 *F, E, S, W,* 1956 *F, E, S, W,* 1957 *F, E, S, W,* 1958 *A, E, S, W, F,* 1959 *E,* 1960 *E, S, W, F, SA,* 1961 *S,* 1962 *W,* 1963 *F*

Pedlow, J. (Bessbrook) 1882 *S,* 1884 *W*

Pedlow, R. (Bessbrook) 1891 *W*

Pedlow, T.B. (Queen's Coll, Belfast) 1889 *S, W*

Peel, T. (Limerick 1892 *E, S, W*

Peirce, W. (Cork) 1881 *E*

Phipps, G.C. (Army) 1950 *E, W,* 1952 *F, W, E*

Pike, T.O. (Lansdowne) 1927 *E, S, W, NSW,* 1928 *F, E, S, W*

Pike, V.J. (Lansdowne) 1931 *E, S, W, SA,* 1932 *E, S, W,* 1933 *E, W, S,* 1934 *E, S, W*

Pike, W.W. (Kingstown) 1879 *E,* 1881 *E, S,* 1882 *E,* 1883 *S*

Pinion, G. (Belfast Collegians) 1909 *E, S, W, F*

Piper, O.J.S. (Cork Constitution) 1909 *E, S, W, F,* 1910 *E, S, W, F*

Polden, S.E. (Clontarf) 1913 *W, F,* 1914 *F,* 1920 *F*

Popham, I. (Cork Constitution) 1922 *S, W, F,* 1923 *F*

Potterton, H.N. (Wanderers) 1920 *W*

Pratt, R.H. (Dublin U) 1933 *E, W, S,* 1934 *E, S*

Price, A.H. (Dublin U) 1920 *S, F*

Pringle, J.C. (NIFC) 1902 *S, W*

Purcell, N.M. (Lansdowne) 1921 *E, S, W, F*

Purdon, H. (NIFC) 1879 *S, E,* 1880 *E,* 1881 *E, S*

Purdon, W.B. (Queen's Coll, Belfast) 1906 *E, S, W*

Purser, F.C. (Dublin U) 1898 *E, S, W*

Quinlan, S.V.J. (Blackrock Coll) 1956 *F, E, W,* 1968 *W*

Quinn, B.T. (Old Belvedere) 1947 *F*

Quinn, F.P. (Old Belvedere) 1947 *F, W, E*

Quinn, J.P. (Dublin U) 1910 *E, S,* 1911 *E, S, W, F,* 1912 *E, S, W,* 1913 *E, W, F,* 1914 *F, E, S*

Quinn, K. (Old Belvedere) 1947 *F, A,* 1953 *F, E, S*

Quinn, M.A.M. (Lansdowne) 1973 *F,* 1974 *F, W, E, S, P, NZ,* 1977 *S, F,* 1981 *SA* 2

Quirke, J.T.M. (Blackrock Coll) 1962 E, S, 1968 S

Rambaut, D.F. (Dublin U) 1887 E, S, W, 1888 W

Rea, H.H. (Edinburgh U) 1967 A 1, 1969 F

Read, H.M. (Dublin U) 1910 E, S, 1911 E, S, W, F, 1912 F, E, S, W, SA, 1913 E, S

Rearden, J.V. (Cork Constitution) 1934 E, S

Reid, C. (NIFC) 1899 S, W, 1900 E, 1903 W

Reid, J.L. (Richmond) 1934 S, W

Reid, P.J. (Garryowen) 1947 A, 1948 F, E, W

Reid, T.E. (Garryowen) 1953 E, S, W, 1954 F, NZ, 1955 E, S, 1956 F, E, 1957 F, E, S, W

Reidy, C.J. (London Irish) 1937 W

Reidy, G.F. (Dolphin, Lansdowne) 1953 W, 1954 F, E, S, W

Richey, H.A. (Dublin U) 1889 W, 1890 S

Ridgeway, E.C. (Wanderers) 1932 S, W, 1935 E, S, W

Ringland, T.M. (Queen's U, Belfast, Ballymena) 1981 A, 1982 W, E, F, 1983 S, F, W, E, 1984 F, W, E, S, A, 1985 S, F, W, E, 1986 F, W, E, S

Riordan, W.F. (Cork Constitution) 1910 E

Ritchie, J.S. (London Irish) 1956 F, E

Robb, C.G. (Queen's Coll, Belfast) 1904 E, S, W, 1905 NZ, 1906 S

Robbie, J.C. (Dublin U, Greystones) 1976 A, F, NZ, 1977 S, F, 1981 F, W, E, S

Robinson, T.T.H. (Wanderers) 1904 E, S, 1905 E, S, W, NZ, 1906 SA, 1907 E, S, W

Roche, J. (Wanderers) 1890 S, W, E, 1891 E, S, W, 1892 W

Roche, R.E. (UC Galway) 1955 E, S, 1957 S, W

Roche, W.J. (UC Cork) 1920 E, S, F

Roddy, P.J. (Bective Rangers) 1920 S, F

Roe, R. (Lansdowne) 1952 E, 1953 F, E, S, W, 1954 F, E, S, W, 1955 F, E, S, W, 1956 F, E, S, W, 1957 F, E, S, W

Rooke, C.B. (Dublin U) 1891 E, W, 1892 E, S, W, 1893 E, S, W, 1894 E, S,

W, 1895 E, S, W, 1896 E, S, W, 1897 E, S

Ross, D.J. (Belfast Academy) 1884 E, 1885 S, 1886 E, S

Ross, G.R.P. (CIYMS) 1955 W

Ross, J.F. (NIFC) 1886 S

Ross, J.P. (Lansdowne) 1885 E, S, 1886 E, S

Ross, N.G. (Malone) 1927 F, E

Ross, W.McC. (Queen's U, Belfast) 1932 E, S, W, 1933 E, W, S, 1934 E, S, 1935 NZ

Russell, J. (UC Cork) 1931 F, E, S, W, SA, 1933 E, W, S, 1934 E, S, W, 1935 E, S, W, 1936 E, S, W, 1937 E, S

Rutherford, W.G. (Tipperary) 1884 E, S, 1885 E, 1886 E, 1888 W

Ryan, E. (Dolphin) 1937 W, 1938 E, S

Ryan, J. (Rockwell Coll) 1897 E, 1898 E, S, W, 1899 E, S, W, 1900 S, W, 1901 E, S, W, 1902 E, 1904 E

Ryan, J.G. (UC Dublin) 1939 E, S, W

Ryan, M. (Rockwell Coll) 1897 E, S, 1898 E, S, W, 1899 E, S, W, 1900 E, S, W, 1901 E, S, W, 1903 E, 1904 E, S

Sayers, H.J.M. (Lansdowne) 1935 E, S, W, 1936 E, S, W, 1938 W, 1939 E, S, W

Schute, F. (Wanderers) 1878 E, 1879 E

Scute, F.G. (Dublin U) 1912 SA, 1913 E, S

Scott, D. (Malone) 1961 F, SA, 1962 S

Scott, R.D. (Queen's U, Belfast) 1967 E, F, 1968 F, E, S

Scovell, R.H. (Kingstown) 1883 E, 1884 E

Scriven, G. (Dublin U) 1879 S, E, 1880 E, S, 1881 E, 1882 S, 1883 E, S

Sealy, J. (Dublin U) 1896 E, S, W, 1897 S, 1899 E, S, W, 1900 E, S

Sexton, W.J. (Garryowen) 1894 A

Shanahan, T. (Lansdowne) 1885 E, S, 1886 E, 1888 S, W

Shaw, G.M. (Windsor) 1877 S

Sheehan, M.D. (London Irish) 1932 E

Sherry, B.F. (Terenure Coll) 1967 A 1, E, S, A 2, 1968 F, E

Sherry, M.J.A. (Lansdowne) 1975 F, W

Siggins, J.A.E. (Belfast Collegians) 1931 F, E, S, W, SA, 1932 E, S, W, 1933 E, W, S, 1934 E, S, W, 1935 E, S, W, NZ, 1936 E, S, W, 1937 E, S, W

Slattery, J.F. (UC Dublin, Blackrock Coll) 1970 *SA, F, E, S, W,* 1971 *F, E, S, W,* 1972 *F* 1, *E, F* 2, 1973 *NZ, E, S, W, F,* 1974 *F, W, E, S, P, NZ,* 1975 *E, S, F, W,* 1976 *A,* 1977 *S, F,* 1978 *S, F, W, E, NZ,* 1979 *F, W, E, S, A* 1,2, 1980 *E, S, F, W,* 1981 *F, W, E, S, SA* 1,2, *A,* 1982 *W, E, S, F,* 1983 *S, F, W, E,* 1984 *F*

Smartt, F.N.B. (Dublin U) 1908 *E, S,* 1909 *E*

Smith, J.H. (London Irish) 1951 *F, E, S, W, SA,* 1952 *F, S, W, E,* 1954 *NZ, W, F*

Smith, R.E. (Lansdowne) 1892 *E*

Smithwick, F.F.S. (Monkstown) 1898 *S, W*

Smyth, J.T. (Queen's U, Belfast) 1920 *F*

Smyth, P.J. (Belfast Collegians) 1911 *E, S, F*

Smyth, R.S. (Dublin U) 1903 *E, S,* 1904 *E*

Smyth, T. (Malone, Newport) 1908 *E, S, W,* 1909 *E, S, W,* 1910 *E, S, W, F,* 1911 *E, S, W,* 1912 *E*

Smyth, W.S. (Belfast Collegians) 1910 *W, F,* 1920 *E*

Solomons, B.A.H. (Dublin U) 1908 *E, S, W,* 1909 *E, S, W, F,* 1910 *E, S, W*

Spain, A.W. (UC Dublin) 1924 *NZ*

Sparrow, W. (Dublin U) 1893 *W,* 1894 *E*

Spillane, B.J. (Bohemians) 1985 *S, F, W, E,* 1986 *F, W, E*

Spring, D.E. (Dublin U) 1978 *S, NZ,* 1979 *S,* 1980 *S, F, W,* 1981 *W*

Spring, R.M. (Lansdowne) 1979 *F, W, E*

Spunner, H.F. (Wanderers) 1881 *E, S,* 1884 *W*

Stack, C.R.R. (Dublin U) 1889 *S*

Stack, G.H. (Dublin U) 1875 *E*

Steele, H.W. (Ballymena) 1976 *E,* 1977 *F,* 1978 *F, W, E,* 1979 *F, W, E, A* 1,2

Stephenson, G.V. (Queen's U, Belfast, London Hosp) 1920 *F,* 1921 *E, S, W, F,* 1922 *E, S, W, F,* 1923 *E, S, W, F,* 1924 *F, E, S, W, NZ,* 1925 *F, E, S, W,* 1926 *F, E, S, W,* 1927 *F, E, S, W, NSW,* 1928 *F, E, S, W,* 1929 *F, E, W,* 1930 *F, E, S, W*

Stephenson, H.W.V. (United Services) 1922 *S, W, F,* 1924 *F, E, S, W, NZ,*

1925 *F, E, S, W,* 1927 *NSW,* 1928 *E*

Stevenson, J. (Dungannon) 1888 *M,* 1889 *S*

Stevenson, J.B. (Instonians) 1958 *A, E, S, W, F*

Stevenson, R. (Dungannon) 1887 *E, S, W,* 1888 *M,* 1889 *S, W,* 1890 *S, W, E,* 1891 *W,* 1892 *W,* 1893 *E, S, W*

Stevenson, T.H. (Belfast Acad) 1895 *E, W,* 1896 *E, S, W,* 1897 *E, S*

Stewart, A.L. (NIFC) 1913 *W, F,* 1914 *F*

Stewart, W.J. (Queen's U, Belfast, NIFC) 1922 *F,* 1924 *S,* 1928 *F, E, S, W,* 1929 *F, E, S, W*

Stoker, E.W. (Wanderers) 1888 *W, S*

Stoker, F.O. (Wanderers) 1886 *S,* 1888 *W, M,* 1889 *S,* 1891 *W*

Stokes, O.S. (Cork Bankers) 1882 *E,* 1884 *E*

Stokes, P. (Garryowen) 1913 *E, S,* 1914 *F,* 1920 *E, S, W, F,* 1921 *E, S, F,* 1922 *W, F*

Stokes, R.D. (Queen's Coll, Cork) 1891 *S, W*

Strathdee, E. (Queen's U, Belfast) 1947 *E, S, W, A,* 1948 *W, F,* 1949 *E, S, W*

Stuart, C.P. (Clontarf) 1912 *SA*

Stuart, I.M.B. (Dublin U) 1924 *E, S*

Sugars, H.S. (Dublin U) 1905 *NZ,* 1906 *SA,* 1907 *S*

Sugden, M. (Wanderers) 1925 *F, E, S, W,* 1926 *F, E, S, W,* 1927 *E, S, W, NSW,* 1928 *F, E, S, W,* 1929 *F, E, S, W,* 1930 *F, E, S, W,* 1931 *F, E, S, W*

Sullivan, D.B. (UC Dublin) 1922 *E, S, W, F*

Sweeney, J.A. (Blackrock Coll) 1907 *E, S, W*

Symes, G.R. (Monkstown) 1895 *E*

Synge, J.S. (Lansdowne) 1929 *S*

Taggart, T. (Dublin U) 1887 *W*

Taylor, A.S. (Queen's Coll, Belfast) 1910 *E, S, W,* 1912 *F*

Taylor, D.R. (Queen's Coll, Belfast) 1903 *E*

Taylor, J. (Belfast Collegians) 1914 *E, S, W*

Taylor, J.W. (NIFC) 1879 *S,* 1880 *E, S,* 1881 *S,* 1882 *E, S,* 1883 *E, S*

Tector, W.R. (Wanderers) 1955 *F, E, S*

Tedford, A. (Malone) 1902 *E, S, W,* 1903 *E, S, W,* 1904 *E, S, W,* 1905 *E, S,*

W, NZ, 1906 E, S, W, SA, 1907 E, S,
W, 1908 E, S, W

Teehan, C. (UC Cork) 1939 E, S, W

Thompson, C. (Belfast Collegians) 1907
E, S, 1908 E, S, W, 1909 E, S, W, F,
1910 E, S, W, F

Thompson, J.A. (Queen's Coll, Belfast)
1885 S

Thompson, J.K.S. (Dublin U) 1921 W,
1922 E, S, F, 1923 E, S, W, F

Thompson, R.F. (Lansdowne) 1882 W

Thompson, R.H. (Instonians) 1951 SA,
1952 F, 1954 NZ, F, E, S, W, 1955 F,
S, W, 1956 W

Thornhill, T. (Wanderers) 1892 E, S, W,
1893 E

Thrift, H. (Dublin U) 1904 W, 1905
E, S, W, NZ, 1906 E, W, SA, 1907 E,
S, W, 1908 E, S, W, 1909 E, S, W,
F

Tierney, D. (UC Cork) 1938 S, W, 1939
E

Tillie, C.R. (Dublin U) 1887 E, S, 1888
W, S

Todd, A.W.P. (Dublin U) 1913 W, F,
1914 F

Torrens, J.D. (Bohemians) 1938 W,
1939 E, S, W

Tucker, C.C. (Shannon) 1979 F, W,
1980 F (R)

Tuke, B.B. (Bective Rangers) 1890 E,
1891 E, S, 1892 E, 1894 E, S, W, 1895
E, S

Turley, N. (Blackrock Coll) 1962 E

Tydings, J. (Young Munster) 1968 A

Tyrrell, W. (Queen's U, Belfast) 1910 F,
1913 E, S, W, F, 1914 F, E, S, W

Uprichard, R.J.H. (Harlequins, RAF)
1950 S, W

Waide, S.L. (Oxford U, NIFC) 1932 E,
S, W, 1933 E, W

Waites, J. (Bective Rangers) 1886 S,
1888 M, 1889 W, 1890 S, W, E, 1891
E

Waldron, O.C. (Oxford U, L. Irish)
1966 S, W, 1968 A

Walker, S. (Instonians) 1934 E, S, 1935
E, S, W, NZ, 1936 E, S, W, 1937 E, S,
W, 1938 E, S, W

Walkington, D.B. (NIFC) 1887 E, W,
1888 W, 1890 W, E, 1891 E, S, W

Walkington R.B. (NIFC) 1875 E, 1876

E, 1877 E, S, 1878 E, 1879 S, 1880 E,
S, 1882 E, S

Wall, H. (Dolphin) 1965 S, W

Wallace, Jas (Wanderers) 1904 E, S

Wallce, Jos (Wanderers) 1903 S, W,
1904 E, S, W, 1905 E, S, W, NZ, 1906
W

Wallace, T.H. (Cardiff) 1920 E, S, W

Wallis, A.K. (Wanderers) 1892 E, S, W,
1893 E, W

Wallis, C.O'N. (Old Granleighans,
Wanderers) 1935 NZ

Wallis, T.G. (Wanderers) 1921 F, 1922
E, S, W, F

Wallis, W.A. (Wanderers) 1880 S, 1881
E, S, 1882 W, 1883 S

Walmsley, G. (Bective Rangers) 1894 E

Walpole, A. (Dublin U) 1888 S, M

Walsh, E.J. (Lansdowne) 1887 E, S, W,
1892 E, S, W, 1893 E

Walsh, H.D. (Dublin U) 1875 E, 1876 E

Walsh, J.C. (UC Cork, Sunday's Well)
1960 S, SA, 1961 E, S, F, SA, 1963 E,
S, W, NZ, 1964 E, S, W, F, 1965 F, S,
W, SA, 1966 F, S, W, 1967 E, S, W, F,
A 2

Ward, A.J.P. (Garryowen, St Mary's
Coll, Greystones) 1978 S, F, W, E,
NZ, 1979 F, W, E, S, 1981 W, E, S, A,
1983 E (R), 1984 E, S, 1986 S

Warren, J.P. (Kingstown) 1883 E

Warren, R.G. (Lansdowne) 1884 W,
1885 E, S, 1886 E, 1887 E, S, W,
1888 W, S, M, 1889 S, W, 1890 S, W,
E

Watson, R. (Wanderers) 1912 SA

Wells, H.G. (Bective Rangers) 1891 S,
W, 1894 E, S

Westby, A.J. (Dublin U) 1876 E

Wheeler, G.H. (Queen's Coll, Belfast)
1884 S, 1885 E

Wheeler, J.R. (Queen's U, Belfast) 1922
E, S, W, F, 1924 E

Whelan, P.C. (Garryowen) 1975 E, S,
1976 NZ, 1977 W, E, S, F, 1978 S, F,
W, E, NZ, 1979 F, W, E, S, 1981 F, W,
E

White, M. (Queen's Coll, Cork) 1906 E,
S, W, SA, 1907 E, W

Whitestone, A.M. (Dublin U) 1877 E,
1879 S, E, 1880 E, 1883 S

Wilkinson, R.W. (Wanderers) 1947 A

Williamson, F.W. (Dolphin) 1930 *E, S, W*

Willis, W.J. (Lansdowne) 1879 *E*

Wilson, F. (CIYMS) 1977 *W, E, S*

Wilson, H.G. (Glasgow U, Malone) 1905 *E, S, W, NZ*, 1906 *E, S, W, SA*, 1907 *E, S, W*, 1908 *E, S, W*, 1909 *E, S, W*, 1910 *W*

Wilson, W.H. (Bray) 1877 *E, S*

Withers, H.H.C. (Army, Blackheath) 1931 *F, E, S, W, SA*

Wolfe, E.J. (Armagh) 1882 *E*

Wood, G.H. (Dublin U) 1913 *W*, 1914 *F*

Wood, B.G.M. (Garryowen) 1954 *E, S*, 1956 *F, E, S, W*, 1957 *F, E, S, W*, 1958 *A, E, S, W, F*, 1959 *E, S, W, F*, 1960 *E, S, W, F, SA*, 1961 *E, S, W, F, SA*

Woods, D.C. (Bessbrook) 1888 *M*, 1889 *S*

Wright, R.A. (Monkstown) 1912 *S*

Yeates, R.A. (Dublin U) 1889 *S, W*

Young, G. (UC Cork) 1913 *E*

Young, R.M. (Collegians) 1965 *F, E, S, W, SA*, 1966 *F, E, S, W*, 1967, *W, F*, 1968 *W, A*, 1969 *F, E, S, W*, 1970 *SA, F, E, S, W*, 1971 *F, E, S, W*

Ireland's leading cap winners (1875–1986 inclusive)

M. Gibson 69
W.J. McBride 63
F. Slattery 61
T. Kiernan 54
M. Keane 51
P. Orr 50
J. Kyle 46
K. Kennedy 45
G. Stephenson 42
W. Duggan 41
N. Henderson 40
R. McLoughlin 40
S. Millar 37
R. Kavanagh 35
W. Mulcahy 35
E. O'D Davy 34
C. Pedlow 30
G. Hamlet 30
E. Crawford 30
J. Clinch 30
J. Farrell 30
G. Wood 29
A. O'Reilly 29

M. Sugden 28
J. McCarthy 28
L. Magee 27
R. Dawson 27
M. Molloy 27
J. Moloney 27
J. Walsh 27
R. Young 26
J. O'Driscoll 26
G. Beamish 26
B. Bresnihan 25
A. Duggan 25
C. Fitzgerald 25
T. Grace 25
H. MacNeill 25
B. McGann 25
S. McKinney 25

Ireland's most capped player in each position

Full-back: T. Kiernan (UCC, Constitution) 54 (equals world record)

Wing: T. Grace (UCD St Mary's Coll) and A. Duggan (Lansdowne), 25

Centre: M. Gibson (Cambridge U and NIFC), 40

Outside-half: J. Kyle (Queen's U and NIFC), 46

Scrum-half: M. Sugden (Dublin U), 28

Prop: P. Orr (Old Wesley), 50 (equals world record)

Hooker: K. Kennedy (Queen's U, CIYMS, London Irish), 45 (world record)

Second-row: W.J. McBride (Ballymena), 63 (world record)

Flank-forward: F. Slattery (UCD, Blackrock Coll), 61 (world record)

Number eight: W. Duggan (Blackrock Coll), 39

Note: Gibson also won 25 caps at outside-half and four on the wing for a total of 69, to make him the world's most capped player.

W. Duggan also won two caps as a flank-forward.

W. J. McBride played in a record 17 tests for the Lions and made five Lions tours, as did Gibson, which is a record. McBride is also the world's most capped forward.

Leading appearances by Irish referees in full internationals

K.D. Kelleher 21 (equals world record)
R. Williams 20
M. Dowling 18
J. West 16
P. D'Arcy 14
D. Burnett 13
H. Lambert 11

CAPPED PLAYERS AT 'B' INTERNATIONAL LEVEL

The following players have represented Ireland at 'B' level

Legend: As for full international list

Aherne, D (Dolphin, St Mary's Coll) 1982 E, 1984 S
Barrett, G. (Constitution) 1979 S
Barry, J. (Bohemians, Constitution) 1982 E, 1983 S, 1984 S
Bowen, J. (Constitution) 1976 F
Bradley, M. (Constitution) 1983 S
Brady, R. (Queen's U Ballymena) 1984 S
Burns, I. (Wanderers) 1979 S
Byrne, E. (Blackrock Coll) 1975 F, 1976 F (R)
Canniffe, D. (Lansdowne) 1975 F
Cantillon, C. (Constitution) 1982 E
Cantrell, J. (UCD, Blackrock Coll) 1975 F
Carr, N. (Queen's U, Ards) 1979 S, 1980 E, 1982 E, 1984 S
Casserley, M. (Galwegians) 1975 F, 1976 F (R)
Clancy, T. (Lansdowne) 1984 S
Coleman, J. (Highfield) 1975 F
Condon H. (London Irish) 1975 F, 1983 S
Cosgrave, V. (Wanderers) 1976 F
Dalton, D. (Malone) 1975 F, 1976 F
D'Arcy, M. (Terenure Coll) 1984 S
Dean, P. (St Mary's Coll) 1980 E
Derham, P. (UCC, Constitution) 1982 E
Ennis, F. (Clontarf, Wanderers) 1977 S
Fanning, D. (St Mary's Coll) 1983 S, 1984 S
Feely, M. (Old Belvedere) 1984 S
Feighery, T. (St Mary's Coll) 1975 F, 1976 F
Finn, M. (UCC, Constitution) 1977 S

Fitzgerald, C. (St Mary's Coll) 1976 F, 1977 S
Fitzgerald, D. (Lansdowne) 1983 S
Fitzpatrick, M. (Wanderers) 1977 S
Fortune, J. (UCD) 1975 F
Glennon, J. (Skerries) 1979 S
Goodrich, A. (Ballymena) 1982 E
Harbison, H. (UCD, Bective Rangers) 1980 E, 1983 S
Haycock, P. (Terenure Coll) 1982 E
Henry, A. (Sale) 1975 F (R)
Hewitt, J. (NIFC) 1980 E
Hitchcock C (UCG) 1982 E
Holland, J. (Wanderers) 1980 E
Hooks, K. (Queen's U) 1979 S, 1980 E
Irwin, A. (Queen's U) 1977 S, 1980 E
Irwin, D. (Queen's U) 1979 S
Jackman, M. (Old Wesley) 1979 S
Kavanagh, T. (Bective Rangers) 1980 E
Kearney, R. (Wanderers) 1979 S, 1980 E
Keyes, R. (Constitution) 1984 S
Kidd, I. (Instonians) 1979 S
Langbroek, J. (Blackrock Coll) 1983 S
Lenihan, D. (UCC, Constitution) 1980 E
Miles, J. (Malone) 1976 F
Molloy, E.J. (Garryowen) 1975 F
Moloney, L. (Garryowen) 1975 F
Moroney, R. (Lansdowne) 1983 S
Morrow, D. (Bangor) 1984 S
Moylett, M. (Manchester, Shannon) 1982 E, 1983 S
Mullin, B. (Dublin U) 1983 S
Murtagh, C (Portadown) 1976 F
MacNeill, H. (Dublin U), Blackrock Coll, London Irish) 1980 E
McCall, B. (London Irish) 1983 S, 1984 S
McCann, D. (Dungannon) 1976 F
McCarthy, C. (Coventry) 1977 S
McComish, G. (NIFC) 1979 S
McCoy, J. (Dungannon, Bangor) 1979 S, 1982 E
McCracken, D. (London Irish) 1979 S
McDonald, J. (Malone) 1984 S
McGeady, J. (Lansdowne) 1983 S
McGrath, D. (UCD) 1983 S
McGrath, R. (Wanderers) 1976 F
McGuire, H. (St Mary's Coll) 1980 E
McKibbin, A. (Instonians) 1976 F
McLean, S. (Ballymena) 1975, F, 1977 S
McLoughlin, G. (Shannon) 1977 S

McMaster, T. (Bangor) 1984 *S*
McNaughton, P. (Greystones) 1977 *S*
O'Brien, K. (Broughton Park) 1979 *S*
O'Carroll, C. (Bective Rangers) 1976 *F*
O'Connor B. (Palmerston) 1980 *E*
O'Driscoll, J. (London Irish, Manchester) 1976 *F*
O'Leary, A. (Constitution, Wanderers, London Irish) 1979 *S*, 1980 *E*, 1982 *E*
O'Neill, J. (Waterpark) 1984 *S*
O'Regan, A. (St Mary's Coll) 1982 *E*
O'Rafferty, E. (Wanderers) 1977 *S*
Palmer, R. (Collegians) 1982 *E*, 1983 *S*
Patterson, C. (Instonians) 1977 *S*
Quinn, F. (Old Belvedere) 1980 *E*
Ryan, M. (Shannon) 1982 *E*
Sexton, W. (Garryowen) 1983 *S*
Smith, B. (Constitution) 1975 *F*
Spring, D. (Dublin U, Lansdowne) 1976 *F*, 1977 *S*
Steele, H. (Ballymena) 1975 *F*
Stewart, R. (Queen's U) 1979 *S*
Tarpey, M. (Galwegians) 1984 *S*
Tucker, C. (Shannon) 1977 *S*
Wallace, G. (Old Wesley) 1982 *E*
Ward, A.J. (Garryowen, St Mary's Coll, Greystones) 1976 *F*, 1977 *S*
Wilson, F. (CIYMS) 1976 *F*

Capped players at schools international level

The following have represented Ireland at schools level.

Legend: As for full international list with *J* – Japan.

Ahern, J. (St Munchin's) 1982 *A*(R), *W*, *S*
Anderson, R. (Coleraine AL) 1981 *S*, *E*, 1982 *A*
Archer, A.P. (RS Dungannon) 1984 *S*, *E*, 1985 *NZ*
Armstrong, C. (RS Dungannon) 1976 *S*, *W*
Barry, N. (Crescent Comprehensive) 1986 *A*, *E*, *J*, *W*
Bauress, P. (Blackrock Coll) 1977 *A*, 1978 *S*, *E*
Bell, P. (Castleknock) 1981 *S*, *E*
Beverland, C. (MCB) 1980 *A*
Blair, A. (The High School) 1977 *A*, 1978 *E*, *S*

Blair, R. (MCB) 1977 *A*, 1978 *S*, *E*
Booth, S. (Ballymena Academy) 1986 *A*, *J*
Bowen, J. (PBC Cork) 1975 *E*
Bradley, M. (PBC Cork) 1980 *E*, *A*, 1981 *S*, *E*
Brady, M. (PBC Cork) 1985 *W*
Brown, L. (BRA) 1876 *S*, *W*
Browne, T. (Armagh RS) 1977 *E*(R)
Bryce, D. (The King's Hospital) 1982 *W*, *S*
Burns, W. (Clongowes Wood and PBC Birr) 1979 *W*, *S*, 1980 *W*, *E*, *A*
Campbell, C. (Rainey Endowed) 1983 *E*, *W*
Carroll, J. (PBC Cork) 1986 *A*
Chambers, P. (Coleraine AI) 1985 *S*, *W*, *A*
Clarke, A. (RYS Dungannon) 1986 *A*, *J*
Clarke, J. (Rockwell) 1986 *A*, *E*, *J*, *W*
Clarke, R. (PBC Cork) 1981 *S*, *E*
Clifford, B. (PBC Cork) 1975 *E*
Coleman, P. (CBC Cork) 1984 *S*, *E*, 1985 *NZ*
Collins, P. (CBC Cork) 1977 *A*, 1978 *E*, *S*
Connolly, M. (Gonzaga) 1981 *E*
Costello, M. (Terenure) 1984, *S*, *E*
Coughlan, G. (CBC Cork) 1986 *E*, *W*
Coulter, E. (Bangor GS) 1981 *S*, *E*
Crawford, D. (RBAI) 1981 *S*, *E*
Cremin, C. (CBC Cork) 1979 *S*, 1980 *W*, *A*
Cross, G. (St Mary's Dublin) 1983 *E*(R), *W*
Crotty, O. (CBC Cork) 1979 *W*, *S*
Crotty, T. (CBC Cork) 1978 *S*
Cullen, R. (RBAI) 1984 *S*, *E*
Cunningham, V. (St Mary's Dublin) 1985 *W*
Curran, P. (Rockwell) 1976 *S*, *W*
Danaher, P. (St Munchin's) 1983 *E*, *W*
Davidson, M. (RS Dungannon) 1981 *S*, *E*
Dean, P. (St Mary's Dublin) 1977 *W*, *E*, *A* 1978 *E*, *S*
Derham, P. (Castleknock) 1976 *S*, *W*
Dineen, L. (Crescent Comprehensive) 1984 *S*, *E*, 1985 *NZ*, *S*, *W*
Donnelly, H. (RS Dungannon) 1975 *E*
Douglas, T. (MCB) 1977 *A*, 1978 *E*, *S*
Dowling, D. (De La Salle Churchtown) 1981 *S*, *E*, 1982 *A*, *W*, *S*

Duggan, J. (Rockwell) 1977 *W, E*
Ennis M. (CBC Monkstown) 1982
 A, W, S
Farren, N. (CBC Monkstown) 1980
 W, E, A
Feely, M. (De La Salle Churchtown)
 1983 *E, W*
Ferguson, S. (RBAI) 1985 *NZ*
Finn, M. (PBC Cork) 1975 *E*
Fitzgibbon, M. (Rockwell and St Enda's)
 1982 *A, W* 1983 *E, W (R)*
Flanagan, C. (Belfast Model) 1982
 W, S
Foley, C. (St Mary's Dublin) 1985 *S, W*
Foley, M. (The King's Hospital) 1986
 E, W
Forkin, K. (St Michael's) 1977 *A*
Francis, N. (Blackrock Coll) 1981 *S, E*
 1982 *A, W, S*
Fraser, S. (Regent House) 1983 *E*
Gardiner, J. (Blackrock Coll) 1981
 S, E
Garvey, J. (Blackrock Coll) 1980 *W, E, A*
Gaston, D. (Dalriada) 1980 *W, E, A*
Glennon, B. (De La Salle Churchtown)
 1984 *S, E* 1985 *NZ, S, W*
Graham, G.K. (RBAI) 1979 *W, S*
Grier, S. (Bangor GS) 1983 *E, W*
Greally, P. (Blackrock Coll) 1986
 E, J, W
Griffin, F. (Blackrock Coll) 1985 *W*
 1986 *A, J*
Hall, S. (Portadown) 1982 *W,*
 S
Halpin, G. (Rockwell Coll) 1983
 E, W 1984 *S, E*
Haly, C. (PBC Cork) 1986 *A, E, W*
Harbison, H. (Blackrock Coll.) 1975 *E*
Hartnett, J. (Blackrock Coll) 1977
 W, E
Harvey, M. (Portora) 1980 *W, E, A*
Hastings, N. (Rainey Endowed) 1981 *S*
Hewitt, J. (Carrickfergus GS) 1979
 W, S
Hoey, A. (St Mary's Dublin) 1986 *A*
Hoey, B. (De La Salle Churchtown)
 1980 *A*
Hooks, D. (Bangor GS) 1979 *W, S*
Hooks, K. (Bangor GS) 1977 *E, A,*
 1978 *E, S*
Hopkins, R. (Terenure) 1977 *A*, 1978
 E, S

Horner, P. (Campbell) 1980 *W, E*
Howard, W. (Wallace HS) 1975 *E*
Hutton, S. (Belfast HS) 1980 *W, E, A*
 1981 *S, E*
Hyland B (PBC Cork) 1985 *NZ*
Hyland, D. (PBC Cork) 1982 *W(R)*
Iveson, W. (Regent House) 1977 *A*
 1978 *E, S*
Jenkinson, C. (Newbridge) 1979 *W, S*
Jennings, C. (St Gerard's) 1977 *A,*
 1978 *E*
Johns, P. (RS Dungannon) 1986
 A, E, J, W
Johnston, I. W. (MCB) 1977 *W, E*
Johnston, N. (Campbell) 1983 *E, W*
Kearney, N. (De La Salle Churchtown)
 1980 *A*
Kearney, R. (Newbridge) 1975 *E (R)*
Kennelly, B. (De La Salle Churchtown)
 1980 *W, E, A*
Keogh, B. (CBC Monkstown) 1977 *A,*
 1978 *S, E*
Keogh, M. (CBC Monkstown) 1977 *W*
Kiernan, M. (PBC Cork) 1979 *W, S*
Kingston, T. (CBC Cork) 1982 *A, W, S*
Kinsella, A. (Belvedere) 1982 *S*
Langbroek, J. (Blackrock Coll) 1975 *E*
Larkin, D. (St Munchin's) 1984 S, E
 1985 NZ, S, W
Larmour, D. (Bangor GS) 1980 *W, E, A*
Leahy, K. (Crescent Comprehensive)
 1984 *S, E*
Lenihan, D. (CBC Cork) 1977 *W, E*
Livesey, J. (PBC Cork) 1982 *A*
Loughran, P. (Castleknock) 1976 *S, W*
Lowry, T. (Rainey Endowed) 1982 *A*
Lynch, D. (St Mary's Dublin) 1985 *S, W*
Madden, P. (CBC Cork) 1980 *W(R)*
Madden, P.D. (CBC Cork) 1984 *S, E,*
 1985 *NZ*
Madigan, D. (Gonzaga) 1984 *S, E*
Mahon, M. (CBC Monkstown) 1983
 E, W
Malcolmson, N. (MCB) 1979 *W, S*
Malone, J. (CBC Monkstown) 1979
 W, S
Matthews, N. (Portadown) 1982 *W*
Matthews, P. (Regent House) 1977
 W, E, A 1978 *E, S*
Maxwell, G. (Bangor GS) 1979 *W*
Meharg, (Campbell) 1981 *S, E*
Melville, P. (Wallace HS) 1977 *W*

Millar, R. (Regent House) 1977 W, E
Molloy, G. (Blackrock Coll) 1975 E
Molloy, J. (Castleknock) 1975 E
Moloney, J. (Crescent Comprehensive) 1982 A, W
Monahan, L. (Blackrock Coll) 1976 S, W
Montford, R. (PBC Bray) 1984 S, E 1985 NZ, S
Morris, D. (BRA) 1982 S
Morris, G. (MCB) 1976 S, W
Moylett, M. (Castleknock) 1977 A 1978 E, S
Muldowney, N. (De La Salle Churchtown) 1983 E (R), W
Mullin, B. (Blackrock Coll) 1981 S, E 1982 A, W, S
Murphy, B. (De La Salle Churchtown) 1976 S, W
Murphy, E. (Newbridge) 1982 A
Murphy, J. (PBC Bray) 1975 E
Murphy, K. (CBC Cork) 1985 NZ
Murray, P. (St Munchin's) 1982 W, S
MacGoey, B. (Rockwell) 1986 A, E, J, W
MacNeill, H. (Blackrock Coll) 1976 S, W 1977 W, E
MacWhite, M. (Castleknock) 1977 W, E
McBride, D. (Belfast HS) 1983 E, W
McCall, B. (Armagh RS) 1977 W, E
McCall, M. (Bangor GS) 1985 NZ S 1986 A, E, J, W
McCormack, P. (Clongowes Wood) 1976 S, W
McCoy, J. (Portora) 1975 E, 1976 S, W
McDonnell, P. (St Mary's Coll) 1977 E, A 1978 E, S
McElroy, P. (BRA) 1980 E (R)
McFarland, B. (BRA) 1984 S, E 1985 NZ
McGuire, J. (Blackrock Coll) 1980 W, E, A
McKibbin, A. (RBAI) 1975 E 1976 S, W
McKibbin, B. (RBAI) 1979 W, S
McLaughlin, N. (Carrickfergus GS) 1979 S
McLoughlin, C. (Blackrock Coll) 1983 E, W
McMahon, G. (Blackrock Coll) 1979 W, S 1980 W, E, A
Neill, G. (Grosvenor HS) 1980 W
Nowlan, P. (Wesley) 1977 A, 1978 E, S
O'Callaghan, C. (CBC Cork) 1980 E, A

O'Connell, B. (St Michael's) 1981 S
O'Connell, K. (PBC Cork) 1986 A, E, J, W
O'Connor, M. (Rockwell) 1980 W
O'Connor, P. (Blackrock Coll) 1977 W, E
O'Connor, T. (St Munchin's) 1983 W
O'Donoghue, M. (Crescent Comprehensive) 1986 E, J, W
O'Farrell, K.(Clongowes Wood) 1983 E, W
O'Flaherty (Blackrock Coll) 1985 S, W
O'Kelly, G. (PBC Cork) 1982 A
O'Loane, K. (Rainey Endowed) 1976 S, W 1977 W, E
O'Shaughnessy, B. (PBC Cork) 1982 S
Pollock, P. (RBAI) 1986 E, J, W
Poole, C. (Clongowes Wood) 1983 E
Porter, S. (The King's Hospital) 1985 S, W
Potts, K. (Templeogue) 1985 NZ, S, W
Prendergast, J. (Crescent Comprehensive) 1986 E (R)
Quaid, M. (Rockwell) 1975 E
Quaid, M. (St Munchin's) 1981 E
Reid, S. (Campbell) 1982 A
Reynolds, M. (BRA) 1982 W, S 1983 E, W
Rhodes, B. (Ballymena Academy) 1984 S, E
Ridgeway, N. (Wesley) 1979 W, S
Riordan, J. (Rockwell) 1984 S, E
Russell, P. (RBAI) 1980 W, E
Semple, M. (Grosvenor HS) 1982 A
Semple, R. (RBAI) 1986 A (R), E, W
Sexton, W. (Castleknock) 1976 S, W
Sheehan, D. (Clongowes Wood) 1981 S, E
Shields, P. (RBAI) 1983 E
Simpson, H. (VRA) 1976 S, W
Spring, D. (Roscrea) 1975 E
Stewart, C. (Wallace HS) 1985 W
Stewart, S. (RBAI) 1983 W
Sweeney, N. (Wesley) 1986 A, E, J, W
Todd, D. (RBAI) 1986 A
Waldron, B. (St Michael's) 1980 E
Walsh, B. (Crescent Comprehensive) 1985 S, 1986 A, E, J, W
Webb, D. (Terenure) 1979 W, S
Webb, M. (Bangor GS) 1985 W
Wylie, C. (BRA) 1985 S

Capped players at under-23 international level

Ireland has played only one match at under-23 level, against Holland at Hilversum on 13 October 1979. The score was Ireland 31 Holland 3. The following team represented Ireland:

R. O'Donnell (St Mary's Coll), J. Bowen (Constitution), D. Irwin (Queen's U), C. Hitchcock (UCG), J. Crotty (UCC), M. Finn (UCC), R. Stewart (Queen's U), B. O'Connor (Young Munster), H. Harbison (UCD), J. McCoy (Dungannon), D. Lenihan (UCC), B. McCall (Queen's U), D. Hanrahan (Blackrock Coll), D. Spring (Dublin U) capt., N. Carr (Queen's U).

Full and 'B' caps

The following players have represented Ireland at full international and 'B' levels. The years of first cap at 'B' and full levels are given.

Bowen, J. (Constitution) 1976 (B) 1977
Bradley, M. (Constitution) 1983 (B) 1984
Burns, I. (Wanderers) 1979 (B) 1980
Byrne, E. (Blackrock Coll) 1975 (B) 1977
Canniffe, D. (Lansdowne) 1975 (B) 1976
Cantrell, J. (UCD, Blackrock Coll), 1975 (B) 1976
Carr, N. (Queen's U, Ards) 1979 (B) 1985
Condon, H. (London Irish) 1975 (B) 1984
Dean, P. (St Mary's Coll) 1980 (B) 1981
Ennis, F. (Clontarf, Wanderers) 1977 (B) 1979
Feighery, T. (St Mary's Coll) 1975 (B) 1977
Finn, M. (UCC Constitution) 1977 (B) 1979
Fitzgerald, C. (St Mary's Coll) 1976 (B) 1979
Fitzgerald, D. (Lansdowne) 1983 (B) 1984
Fitzpatrick, M. (Wanderers) 1977 (B) 1978
Glennon, J. (Skerries) 1979 (B) 1980

Harbison, H. (UCD, Bective Rangers) 1980 (B) 1984
Hewitt, J. (NIFC) 1980 (B) 1981
Holland, J. (Wanderers) 1980 (B) 1981
Hooks, K. (Queen's U) 1979 (B) 1981
Irwin, D. (Queen's U, Instonians) 1979 (B) 1980
Kearney, R. (Wanderers) 1979 (B) 1982
Keyes, R. (Constitution) 1984 (B) 1986
Lenihan, D. (UCC, Constitution) 1980 (B) 1981
Moloney, L. (Garryowen) 1975 (B) 1976
Moroney, R. (Lansdowne) 1983 (B) 1984
Morrow, D. (Bangor) 1984 (B) 1986
Mullin, B. (Dublin U) 1983 (B) 1984
Murtagh, C. (Portadown) 1976 (B) 1977
MacNeill, H. (Dublin U, Blackrock Coll, Oxford U, London Irish) 1980 (B) 1981
McCall, B. (London Irish) 1983 (B) 1985
McCoy, J. (Dungannon, Bangor) 1979 (B), 1984
McGrath, D. (UCD) 1983 (B), 1984
McGrath (Wanderers) 1976 (B), 1977
McKibbin, A. (Instonians, London Irish) 1976 (B) 1977
McLoughlin, G. (Shannon) 1977 (B) 1979
McNaughton, P. (Greystones) 1977 (B) 1978
O'Brien, K. (Broughton Park) 1979 (B) 1980
O'Driscoll, J. (London Irish, Manchester) 1976 (B) 1978
Patterson, C. (Instonians) 1977 (B) 1978
Quinn, F. (Old Belvedere) 1980 (B) 1981
Sexton, W. (Garryowen) 1983 (B) 1984
Spring, D. (Dublin U, Lansdowne) 1976 (B) 1978
Steele, H. (Ballymena) 1975 (B) 1976
Tucker, C. (Shannon) 1977 (B) 1979
Ward, A.J. (Garryowen, St Mary's Coll, Greystones) 1976 (B) 1978
Wilson, F. (CIYMS) 1976 (B) 1977

Full and schools Caps

The following players have represented Ireland at full and schools international levels. The year of the first cap in each grade is given.

Legend: S – Schools, F – Full.

Bowen, J. (PBC Cork, Constitution) 1975 *S*, 1977 *F*

Bradley, M. (PBC Cork, Constitution) 1980 *S* 1984 *F*

Dean, P. (St Mary's Dublin, St Mary's Coll) 1977 *S*, 1981 *F*

Finn, M. (PBC Cork, UCC, Constitution) 1975 *S*, 1979 *F*

Harbison, H. (Blackrock Coll, UCD, Bective Rangers) 1975 *S*, 1984 *F*

Hewitt, J. (Carrickfergus GS, NIFC) 1979 *S*, 1981 *F*

Hooks, K. (Bangor GS) 1977 *S*, 1981 *F*

Kearney, R. (Newbridge, Wanderers) 1975 *S*, 1982 *F*

Kiernan, M. (PBC Cork, Dolphin, Lansdowne) 1979 *S*, 1982 *F*

Lenihan, D. (CBC Cork, UCC, Constitution) 1977 *S*, 1980 B, 1981 *F*

Matthews, P. (Regent House, Queen's U, Ards) 1977 *S*, 1984 *F*

Mullin, B. (Blackrock, Dublin U) 1981 *S*, 1984 *F*

Murphy, J. (PBC Bray, Greystones) 1975 *S*, 1981 *F*

MacNeill, H. (Blackrock Coll, Dublin U, Oxford U, London Irish) 1977 *S*, 1981 *F*

McCall, B. (Armagh RS, Queen's U, London Irish) 1977 *S*, 1985 *F*

McCoy, J. (Portora, Dungannon, Bangor) 1975 *S*, 1984 *F*

McKibbin, A. (RBAI, Instonians, London Irish) 1975 *S*, 1977 *F*

Sexton, W. Castleknock, Garryowen) 1976 *S*, 1984 *F*

Spring, D. (Roscrea, Dublin U) 1975 *S*, 1978 *F*

O'Donnell, R. (St Mary's Coll) represented Ireland at full level (1980) and under 23 level (1979)

Hitchcock, C. (UCG) represented Ireland at 'B' level (1982) and under 23 (1979)

Derham, P. (Castleknock, Constitution) represented Ireland at Schools (1976) and 'B' (1982)

Stewart, R. (Queen's U) represented Ireland at under 23 (1979) and 'B' (1979)

Langbroek, J. (Blackrock Coll)

represented Ireland at schools (1975) and 'B' levels (1983)

Moylett, M. (Castleknock, Manchester, Shannon) represented Ireland at schools (1977) and 'B' (1982)

Full 'B' and schools caps

The following players have represented Ireland at Full, 'B' and schools levels. The year of first cap at each level is given.

Legend: F – Full, 'B' – B, S – Schools.

Bowen, J. (PBC Cork, Constitution) 1975 *S*, 1976 *B*, 1977 *F*

Bradley, M. (PBC Cork, Constitution) 1980 *S*, 1983 *B*, 1984 *F*

Dean, P. (St Mary's Dublin, St Mary's Coll) 1977 *S*, 1980 *B*, 1981 *F*

Finn, M. (PBC Cork, UCC, Constitution) 1975 *S*, 1977 *B*, 1979 *F*

Harbison, H. (Blackrock Coll, UCD Bective Rangers) 1975 *S*, 1980 *B*, 1984 *F*

Hewitt, J. (Carrickfergus GS, NIFC) 1979 *S*, 1980 *B*, 1981 *F*

Hooks, K. (Bangor GS, Queen's U) 1977 *S*, 1979 *B*, 1981

Kearney, R. (Newbridge, Wanderers) 1975 *S*, 1979 *B*, 1982 *F*

Lenihan, D. (CBC Cork, UCC, Constitution) 1977 *S*, 1980 *B*, 1981 *F*

MacNeill, H. (Blackrock, Dublin U, Oxford U, London Irish) 1976 *S*, 1980 *B*, 1981 *F*

McCall, B. (Armagh, RS, Queen's U, London Irish) 1977 *S*, 1983 *B*, 1985 *F*

McCoy, J. (Portora, Dungannon, Bangor) 1975 *S*, 1979 *B*, 1984 *F*

McKibbin, A. (RBAI, Instonians, London Irish) 1975 *S*, 1976 *B*, 1977 *F*

Mullin, B. (Blackrock, Dublin U) 1982 *S*, 1983 *B*, 1984 *F*

Sexton, W. (Castleknock) 1976 *S*, 1983 *B*, 1984 *F*

Spring, D. (Roscrea, Dublin U) 1975 *S*, 1976 *B*, 1978 *F*

Full, 'B' and under-23 caps

The following players represented Ireland at full, 'B', and under-23 levels. In each instance the date of first cap at each level is given.

Legend: 'B' – B, Under 23 – U23, F – Full

Bowen, J. (Constitution) 1976 *B,* 1979 *U23,* 1977 *F*

Carr, N. (Queen's U, Ards) 1979 *U23,* 1979 *B,* 1985 *F*

Finn, M. (UCC, Constitution) 1977 *B,* 1979 *U23,* 1979 *F*

Harbison, H. (UCD, Bective Rangers) 1979 *U23,* 1980 *B,* 1984 *F*

Irwin, D. (Queen's U, Instonians) 1979 *U23,* 1979 *B,* 1980 *F*

Lenihan, D. (UCC, Constitution) 1979 *U23,* 1980 *B,* 1981 *F*

McCall, B. (Queen's U, London Irish) 1979 *U23,* 1983 *B,* 1985 *F*

McCoy, J. (Dungannon Bangor) 1979 *U23,* 1979 *B,* 1984 *F*

Spring, D. (Dublin U) 1976 *B,* 1979 *U23,* 1977 *F*

Full 'B' under-23 and schools caps

The following are the only seven players to have represented Ireland at all four levels in which the country has participated. In each instance the date of first cap at each level is given.

Legend F – Full cap, B – 'B' cap, U23 – Under 23, S – Schools

Bowen, J. (PBC Cork, Constitution) 1975 *S,* 1976 *B,* 1977 *F,* 1979 *U23*

Finn, M. (PBC Cork, UCC, Constitution) 1975 *S,* 1977 *B,* 1979 *U23,* 1979 *F*

Harbison, H. (Blackrock Coll, UCD, Bective Rangers) 1975 *S,* 1979 *U23,* 1980 *B,* 1984 *F*

Leniham, D. (CBC Cork, UCC, Constitution), 1977 *S,* 1979 *U23,* 1980 *B,* 1981 *F*

McCall, B. (Armagh RS, Queen's U, London Irish) 1977 *S,* 1979 *U23,* 1983 *B,* 1984 *F*

McCoy, J. (Portora, Dungannon, Bangor) 1975 *S,* 1979 *U23,* 1979 *B,* 1984 *F*

Spring, D. (Roscrea, Dublin U) 1975 *S,* 1976 *B,* 1977 *F,* 1979 *U23*

APPENDIX 4

Captains of Ireland

1874–75 G.H. Stack (Dublin U)

1875–76 R. Bell (NIFC)

1876–77 R. Galbraith (Dublin U) (*v* E); W.H. Wilson (Dublin U, Bray) (*v* S)

1877–78 R.B. Walkington (NIFC)

1878–79 C.W. Neville (Dublin U)

1879–80 H.C. Kelly (NIFC)

1880–81 A.J. Forrest (Wanderers)

1881–82 J.W. Taylor (NIFC) (*v* S, E); A.J. Forrest (Wanderers) (*v* W)

1882–83 G. Scriven (Dublin U)

1883–84 J.A. MacDonald (Methodist Coll) (*v* E, S); D.F. Moore (Wanderers) (*v* W)

1884–85 W. Rutherford (Lansdowne, Clanwilliam)

1885–86 M. Johnston (Wanderers) (*v* E); J.P. Ross (Wanderers) (*v* S)

1886–87 R.G. Warren (Lansdowne)

1887–88 H.J. Neill (NIFC)

1889–89 R.G. Warren (Lansdowne)

1889–90 R.G. Warren (Lansdowne)

1890–91 R. Stevenson (NIFC, Dungannon) (*v* W); D.B. Walkington (NIFC, Dublin U) (*v* SE)

1891–92 V.C. Le Fanu (Lansdowne)

1892–93 S. Lee (NIFC)

1893–94 E.G. Forrest (Wanderers) (Triple Crown)

1894–95 J.H. O'Conor (Bective Rangers) (*v* E); E.G. Forrest (Wanderers) (*v* W); C.V. Rooke (Dublin U) (*v* S)

1895–96 S. Lee (NIFC)

1896–97 E.G. Forrest (Wanderers)

1897–98 S. Lee (NIFC) (*v* E); G. Allen (Derry) (*v* S); W. Gardiner (NIFC) (*v* W)

1898–99 L.M. Magee (Bective Rangers, London Irish) (Triple Crown)

1899–1900 L.M. Magee (Bective Rangers, London Irish)

1900–01 L.M. Magee (Bective Rangers, London Irish)

1901–02 J. Fulton (NIFC)

1902–03 H.H. Corley (Dublin U)

1903–04 H.H. Corley (Dublin U) (*v* S); C.E.Allen (Derry) (*v* E, W)

1904–05 C.E. Allen (Derry)
1905–06 C.E. Allen (Derry)
1906–07 C.E. Allen (Derry) (*v* S, W);
A. Tedford (Malone) (*v* E); J.C. Parke
(Monkstown) (*v* S, A)
1907–08 H. Thrift (Dublin U) (*v* E),
J.C. Parke (Monkstown) (*v* W)
1908–09 F. Gardiner (NIFC) (*v* E, S, F),
G. Hamlet (Old Wesley) (*v* W)
1909–10 G. Hamlet (Old Wesley)
(*v* E, S, F), T. Smyth (Malone and
Newport) (*v* W)
1910–11 G.T. Hamlet (Old Wesley)
1911–12 R.A. Lloyd (Dublin U)
(*v* S, W), A.R. Foster (Queen's U)
(*v* E, F)
1912–13 R.A. Lloyd (Dublin U)
1913–14 R.A. Lloyd (Dublin U) (*v* F, E);
A.R. Foster (Derry) (*v* W), J.P. Quinn
(Dublin U) (*v* S)
1919–20 R.A. Lloyd (Dublin U) (*v* E,F),
T. Wallace (Queen's U) (*v* W),
W.D. Doherty (Guy's Hospital) (*v* S)
1920–21 W.D. Doherty (Guy's
Hospital, Cambridge U)
1921–22 W.P. Collopy (Bective
Rangers)
1922–23 J.K.S. Thompson (Dublin U)
1923–24 W.E. Crawford (Lansdowne)
(*v* E, W), W.P. Collopy (Bective
Rangers) (*v* S)
1924–25 W.E. Crawford (Lansdowne)
1925–26 W.E. Crawford (Lansdowne)
1926–27 W.E. Crawford (Lansdowne)
1927–28 G.V. Stephenson (NIFC,
London Hospital)
1928–29 G.V. Stephenson (London
Hospital) (*v* E, W, F), E.O'D. Davy
(Lansdowne) (*v* S)
1929–30 G.V. Stephenson (London
Hospital
1930–31 M. Sugden (Wanderers)
1931–32 G.R. Beamish (RAF, London
Irish)
1932–33 E.O'D. Davy (Lansdowne)
1933–34 J.A. Siggins (Collegians)
1934–35 J.A. Siggins (Collegians)
1935–36 J.A. Siggins (Collegians)
1936–37 G.J. Morgan (Clontarf)
1937–38 G.J. Morgan (Old Belvedere)
(*v* E, S), S. Walker (Instonians) (*v* W)
1938–39 G.J. Morgan (Old Belvedere)

1946–47 C.J. Murphy (Lansdowne)
(*v* F, E), J.D. Monteith (Queen's U)
(*v* S, W)
1947–48 E. Strathdee (Queen's U)
(*v* F, A), K.D. Mullen (Old Belvedere)
(*v* E, S, W), (Triple Crown)
1948–49 K.D. Mullen (Old Belvedere)
(Triple Crown)
1949–50 K.D. Mullen (Old Belvedere)
1950–51 K.D. Mullen (Old Belvedere)
1951–52 D. O'Brien (Cardiff)
1952–53 J.W. Kyle (NIFC)
1953–54 J.W. Kyle (NIFC) (*v* NZ, F),
J.S. McCarthy (Dolphin) (*v* E, S, W)
1954–55 R.H. Thompson (Instonians)
(*v* F, S, W) J.S. McCarthy (Dolphin)
(*v* E)
1955–56 J.S. Ritchie (London Irish)
(*v* F, E), N.J. Henderson (NIFC)
(*v* S, W)
1956–57 N.J. Henderson (NIFC)
1957–58 N.J. Henderson (NIFC)
1958–59 A.R. Dawson (Wanderers)
1959–60 A.R. Dawson (*v* F),
A.A. Mulligan (Cambridge U)
(*v* E, S, W)
1960–61 A.R. Dawson (Wanderers)
1961–62 W.A. Mulcahy (Bohemians)
1962–63 W.A. Mulcahy (Bective
Rangers) (*v* W in match postponed
from previous season, *v* E, S, W),
T.J. Kiernan (UCC) (*v* F)
1963–64 J. Kelly (UCD) (*v* NZ),
W.A. Mulcahy (Bective Rangers)
(*v* E, S, W, F)
1964–65 R.J. McLoughlin (Gosforth)
1965–66 R.J. McLoughlin (Gosforth)
(*v* F, E, S), T.J. Kiernan Cork
Constitution) (*v* W)
1966–67 N.A. Murphy (Cork
Constitution) (*v* A in Dublin, *v*
E, S, W), T.J. Kiernan (Cork
Constitution) (*v* A in Sydney)
1967–68 T.J. Kiernan (Cork
Constitution)
1968–69 T.J. Kiernan (Cork
Constitution)
1969–70 T.J. Kiernan (Cork
Constitution)
1970–71 T.J. Kiernan (Cork
Constitution) (*v* F), C.M.H. Gibson
(NIFC) (*v* E, S, W)

1971–72 T.J. Kiernan (Cork
Constitution)
1972–73 T.J. Kiernan (Cork
Constitution) (*v* NZ, E, S),
W.J. McBride (Ballymena) (*v* W, F)
1973–74 W.J. McBride (Ballymena)
1974–75 W.J. McBride (Ballymena)
1975–76 M. Gibson (NIFC) (*v* A,F),
T. Grace (St Mary's Coll) (*v* E, S, W,
NZ)
1976–77 T. Grace (St Mary's Coll)
1977–78 J. Moloney (St Mary's Coll)
1978–79 S. Deering (St Mary's Coll)
(*v* NZ), E. Slattery (Blackrock Coll)
(*v* E, S, W, F, A)
1979–80 F. Slattery (Blackrock Coll)
1980–81 F. Slattery (Blackrock Coll)
1981–82 F. Slattery (Blackrock Coll)
(*v* A), C. Fitzgerald (St Mary's Coll)
(*v* E, S, W, F)
1982–83 C. Fitzgerald (St Mary's Coll)
1983–84 C. Fitzgerald (St Mary's Coll)
(*v* F, W), W. Duggan (Blackrock
Coll) (*v* E, S)
1984–85 C. Fitzgerald (St Mary's Coll)
1985–86 C. Fitzgerald (St Mary's Coll)

In the seasons where a player captained
Ireland in all matches played, the
countries are not listed.

T.J. Kiernan (UCC and Constitution)
holds the record for having captained
Ireland on most occasions (24)

The following players have captained
Ireland at 'B' level.

D. Canniffe (Lansdowne) *v* France 1975
D. Fanning (St Mary's Coll) *v* Scotland
1983 and 1984
C. Fitzgerald (St Mary's Coll) *v* Scotland
1977
I. Kidd (Instonians) *v* Scotland 1979
R. McGrath (Wanderers) *v* France 1976
A. O'Leary (Wanderers, Constitution) *v*
England 1980 and 1982

The most capped player for Ireland at
'B' level is Nigel Carr (Queen's U, Ards)
with 4 caps.

The following players have captained
Ireland at schools international level.

L. Dineen (Crescent Comprehensive)
1985 *v*·NZ, S

B. Glennon (De La Salle Churchtown)
1985, *v* W
G.K. Graham (RBAI) 1979 *v* W, S
M. McCall (Bangor GS) 1986 *v*
A, E, J, W
G. McMahon (Blackrock Coll) 1980 *v*
W, E, A
H. MacNeill (Blackrock Coll) 1976
v S, W, 1977 *v* W, S
P. Matthews (Regent House) 1977 *v*
A, E, S
B. Mullin (Blackrock Coll) 1982 *v*
A, W, S
M. Bradkey (PBC Cork) 1981 *v* S, E
T. O'Connor (St Munchin's) 1983 *v* W
M. Reynolds (BRA) 1983 *v* E
B. Rhodes (Ballymena Academy) 1984
v S, E
D. Spring (Dublin U) 1975 *v* E

APPENDIX 5
RELATED PLAYERS
WHO HAVE
REPRESENTED IRELAND

The following fathers and sons have
played for Ireland. *In each instance the
years of first and last caps are given.*

A.D. Clinch (Dublin U, Wanderers)
1885–97
J.D. Clinch (Dublin U, Wanderers)
1924–32

W. Collis (Wanderers) 1884
W.R. Collis (Harlequins, K.C.H.)
1924–26

M.P. Crowe (Blackrock C, Lansdowne)
1929–34
J. Crowe (U.C.D.) 1974

G. Collopy (Bective Rangers) 1891–92
W.P. Collopy (Bective Rangers)
1914–24
R. Collopy (Bective Rangers) 1923–25

S.J. Deering (Bective Rangers) 1935–37
S.M. Deering (Garryowen, St. Mary's
College) 1974–78

T.R. Hewitt (Queen's U) 1924–26
D. Hewitt (Queen's U, Instonians)
1958–65

S.T. Irwin (Queen's U) 1900–03

J.W.S. Irwin (Queen's U and N.I.F.C.) 1938–39

N.F. Murphy (Constitution) 1930–33
N.A. Murphy (Constitution) 1958–69

P.F. Murray (Wanderers) 1927–33
J. Murray (U.C.D.) 1963

H.R. McKibbin (Queen's U, Instonians) 1938–39
C.H. McKibbin (Instonians) 1976
A.R. McKibbin (Instonians, London Irish) 1977–80

F. Schute (Wanderers) 1878–79
F.G. Schute (Dublin U) 1913

The following is a list of brothers who have played for Ireland.

E. Doran (Lansdowne) 1890
G. P. Doran (Lansdowne) 1899–1904
B.R. Doran (Lansdowne) 1900–02

A.J. Forrest (Wanderers) 1880–83
E.G. Forrest (Wanderers) 1889–97
H. Forrest (Wanderers) 1893

T.A. Harvey (Dublin U) 1900–03
A.D. Harvey (Wanderers) 1903–05
F.M.W. Harvey (Wanderers) 1907–11

F.S. Hewitt (Instonians) 1926–27
T.R. Hewitt (Queen's U) 1924–26
V.A. Hewitt (Instonians) 1935–36

W.E. Johnstone (Dublin U) 1884
R.W. Johnstone (Dublin U) 1890
R. Johnstone (Wanderers) 1893

S. McVicker (Queen's U) 1922
J. McVicker (Collegians) 1924–30
H. McVicker (Army) 1927–28

D.F. Moore (Wanderers) 1883–84
F.W. Moore (Wanderers) 1884–86
C.M. Moore (Dublin U) 1887–88

J. Pedlow (Bessbrook) 1882–84
T.B. Pedlow (Queen's U) 1889
R. Pedlow (Bessbrook) 1891

D.J. Ross (Belfast Albion) 1884–86
J.P. Ross (Lansdowne) 1885–86
J.F. Ross (NIFC) 1886

T. Smyth (Malone) 1908–12
W.S. Smyth (Collegians) 1910–20
P.J. Smyth (Collegians) 1911

C. Glynn Allen (Derry, Liverpool) 1896–99
C. Elliott Allen (Derry, Liverpool) 1900–07

George R. Beamish (Coleraine, RAF) 1925–33
Charles E. Beamish (Coleraine, RAF) 1935–36

H. Brown (Windsor) 1877
T. Brown (Windsor) 1877

M.J. Bulger (Dublin U, Lansdowne) 1899
L. Q. Bulger (Dublin U, Lansdowne) 1896–98

F. Byrne (UCD) 1962
S.J. Byrne (Lansdowne, UCD) 1953–55

W.P. Collopy (Bective Rangers) 1914–24
R. Collopy (Bective Rangers) 1923–25

M.P. Crowe (Lansdowne) 1929–34
P. Crowe (Blackrock Coll) 1935

M. Deering (Bective Rangers) 1929
S.J. Deering (Bective Rangers) 1935–37

C.J. Dick (Ballymena) 1961–63
J.S. Dick (Queen's U) 1962

M. Doyle (Cambridge U, Blackrock Coll) 1965–68
T. Doyle (Wanderers) 1968

C. Feighery (Lansdowne) 1972
T. Feighery (St. Mary's Coll) 1977

E. Galbraith (Dublin U) 1875
R. Galbraith (Dublin U) 1875–77

W. Gardiner (NIFC) 1892–98
F.T. Gardiner (NIFC) 1900–09

L.H. Gwynn (Dublin U) 1894–98
A.P. Gwynn (Dublin U) 1895

J. Heron (NIFC) 1877–79
W.T. Heron (NIFC) 1880

L. Hunter (Civil Service) 1968
W.R. Hunter (CIYMS) 1962–66

P. Kavanagh (UCD) 1952
R. Kavanagh (UCD, Wanderers) 1953–61

F. Kennedy (Wanderers) 1880–82
J.M. Kennedy (Wanderers) 1882–84

J. Lyttle (NIFC) 1889–94
J.H. Lyttle (NIFC) 1894–99

L.M. Magee (Bective Rangers, London Irish) 1895–1904

J.T. Magee (Bective Rangers) 1895

E.H. McIlwaine (NIFC) 1895

J. E. McIlwaine (NIFC) 1897–99

H.R. McKibbin (Queen's U, Instonians) 1938–39

D.E. McKibbin (Instonians) 1950–51

C.H. McKibbin (Instonians) 1976

A.R. McKibbin (Instonians, London Irish) 1977–80

R.J. McLoughlin (Gosforth, Blackrock Coll) 1962–75

F. McLoughlin (Northern) 1976

R.B. Montgomery (Queen's U, Cambridge U) 1887–92

A. Montgomery (NIFC) 1895

H. Moore (Windsor) 1876–77

W. Moore (Queen's U) 1878

Jack O'Connor (Garryowen) 1895

Joe O'Connor (Garryowen) 1910

B. O'Driscoll (Manchester) 1971

J. O'Driscoll (London Irish) 1978–82

K.P. O'Flanagan (London Irish) 1947

M. O'Flanagan (Lansdowne) 1949

T.O. Pike (Lansdowne) 1927–28

V.J. Pike (Lansdowne) 1931–34

M. Ryan (Rockwell Coll) 1897–1904

J. Ryan (Rockwell Coll) 1897–1904

D. Scott (Malone) 1961–62

R.D. Scott (Queen's U) 1967–68

Donal Spring (Dublin U, Lansdowne) 1978–81

Dick Spring (Lansdowne) 1979

G.V. Stephenson (Queen's U, United Services) 1920–30

H.W. Stephenson (United Services) 1922–28

Stevenson (Lisburn, NIFC Dungannon) 1889

R. Stevenson (Lisburn, NIFC Dungannon) 1887–1893

F.O. Stoker (Wanderers) 1886–89

E.W. Stoker (Wanderers) 1888

R.B. Walkington (NIFC) 1875–82

D.B. Walkington (Dublin U) 1887–91

Joseph Wallace (Wanderers) 1902–06

James Wallace (Wanderers) 1904

W.A. Wallis (Wanderers) 1881–83

A.K. Wallis (Wanderers) 1892–93

APPENDIX 6

IRISH PARTICIPATION IN UNOFFICIAL MATCHES: 1942–46

Irish XV v British Army

7 Feb. 1942 (Ravenhill): lost: 1 try, 1 penalty goal (6) to 2 tries, 1 penalty goal (9).

30 Jan. 1943 (Ravenhill): lost: 1 goal, 2 tries (11) to 1 goal, 1 try, 1 dropped goal (12).

12 Feb. 1944 (Ravenhill): lost: 0 to 3 tries, 2 penalty goals (15).

10 Feb. 1945 (Ravenhill): lost: 1 goal (5) to 1 try, 2 penalty goals (9).

15 Dec. 1945 (Ravenhill): won: 2 goals, 2 tries, 1 penalty goal (19) to 1 penalty goal (3).

The following were the Irish XVs that played against the British Army.

7 Feb. 1942

M.R. Williams (Clontarf)

K.P. O'Flanagan (UCD)

S.D. Walsh (Dublin U)

J.D. Torrens (Bohemians)

T. Chamberlain (Blackrock Coll)

H. Greer (NIFC)

H. de Lacy (Dublin U)

D. Riordan (UCC)

M.R. Neely (Queen's U)

D. Ryan (UCD)

T. Headon (UCD)

E. Keeffe (Sunday's Well)

R. Alexander (NIFC)

J.J. Guiney (Clontarf)

K. O'Brien (Bective Rangers)

30 Jan. 1943

C. Murphy (Lansdowne)

W.J. Higson (Queen's U)

S.D. Walsh (Dublin U)

H. Greer (NIFC)

T. Chamberlain (Blackrock Coll)

E.A. Carry (Old Wesley)

S.J. McComb (Malone)

F. Cromey (Collegians)
E.G. Ryan (Blackrock Coll)
J. Griffin (Corinthians)
J. Joyce (Galwegians)
E. Keeffe (Sunday's Well)
K. O'Brien (Bective Rangers)
D.B. O'Loughlin (Dolphin)
J.J. Guiney (Clontarf)

12 Feb. 1944
C. Murphy (Lansdowne)
F.G. Moran (Clontarf)
G.J. Quinn (Old Belvedere)
L. O'Brien (UCC)
N. Burke (Lansdowne)
H. Greer (NIFC)
J.W. Adrain (NIFC)
W.J. Moynan (Dublin U)
F. Cromey (Collegians)
J. Corcoran (UCC)
E. Keeffe (Sunday's Well)
J.E. Nelson (Malone)
K. O'Brien (Bective Rangers)
D.B. O'Loughlin (Dolphin)
T. Halpenny (UCD)

10 Feb. 1945
C. Murphy (Lansdowne)
F.G. Moran (Clontarf)
G. Quinn (Old Belvedere)
K. Quinn (Old Belvedere)
W.H. Miller (Queen's U)
E.A. Carry (Old Wesley)
E. O'Mullane (UCC)
J. Belton (Old Belvedere)
H. Dudgeon (Collegians)
C. Callan (Lansdowne)
J.E. Nelson (Malone)
J. Guiney (Bective Rangers)
D.B. O'Loughlin (Dolphin)
D. Hingerty (Lansdowne)

15 Dec. 1945
C. Murphy (Lansdowne)
F. G. Moran (Clontarf)
H. Greer (NIFC)
K. Quinn (Old Belvedere)
B. Quinn (Old Belvedere)
J. Kyle (Queen's U)
D. Thorpe (Old Belvedere)
J. Belton (Old Belvedere)
K.D. Mullen (Old Belvedere)
J. Corcoran (UCC)

C. Callan (Lansdowne)
R. D. Agar (Malone)
J. Guiney (Bective Rangers)
H. Dudgeon (Collegians)
D. McCourt (Instonians)

Unofficial Internationals 1946
Irish XV French XV
26 Jan. 1946 (Lansdowne Road): lost:
1 penalty goal (3) to 1 dropped goal
(4).

Irish XV English XV
6 Feb. 1946 (Lansdowne Road): lost:
2 tries (6) to 1 goal, 1 try, 2 penalty
goals (14)

Irish XV Welsh XV
9 Mar. 1946 (Cardiff): lost: 1 dropped
goal (4) to 2 tries (6).

Irish XV Scottish XV
23 Mar. 1946 (Murrayfield): lost: 0 to 1
goal, 1 dropped goal (9).

The following players represented
Ireland in the unofficial internationals
of 1946.

J. Belton (Old Belvedere) (F, E)
C. Callan (Lansdowne) (F, E, S, W)
E.A. Carry (Old Wesley) (S, W)
J. Corcoran (UCC) (S, W)
R. E. Coolican (Dublin U) (W)
T. Coveney (St Mary's Coll) (S)
H. Dolan (UCD) (F)
H.G. Dudgeon (Collegians) (S, W)
H. Greer (NIFC) (F)
J.J. Guiney (Bective Rangers) (F, E)
D. Hingerty (Lansdowne) (E, S, W)
E. Keeffe (Sunday's Well) (E, S, W)
J.W. Kyle (Queen's U) (F, E)
D. McCourt (Instonians) (F, E)
F.G. Moran (Clontarf) (F, E, S)
K.D. Mullen (Old Belvedere)
(F, E, S, W)
C. Murphy (Lansdowne) (F, E, S, W)
M.R. Neely (Royal Navy and Queen's
U) (F, E, S, W)
K.P. O'Flanagan (London Irish) (F)
D.B. O'Loughlin (Dolphin) (F, E)
B.T. Quinn (Old Belvedere) (E, S, W)
G.T. Quinn (Old Belvedere) (E, W)
K. Quinn (Old Belvedere) (E, S, W)
P. Reid (Garryowen) (F, W)

E. Strathdee (Queen's U) (S, W)
D. Thorpe (Old Belvedere) (F, E)

APPENDIX 7

IRELAND'S OVERSEAS TOURS

Canada 1899

Players
J.G. Franks (Dublin U), Capt.
C.A. Boyd (Dublin U)
R.R. Boyd (Lansdowne)
J. Byers (NIFC)
I.G. Davidson (NIFC)
F. Dinsmore (NIFC)
B.W. Doran (Lansdowne)
I. Grove-White (Dublin U)
T.A. Harvey (Dublin U)
J.C. Lepper (NIFC)
H.A. Macready (Dublin U)
J.S. Myles (Derry)
P.C. Nicholson (Dublin U)
B.W. Rowan (Lansdowne)
A.C. Rowan (Lansdowne)
H. Stevenson (Dungannon)
J. Stokes (Lansdowne)

Tour Record: P. 11. W. 10. D. 0. L. 1.

Team played in Halifax, Montreal, Ottawa, Brockville, Peterborough, Quebec, Toronto, Hamilton.

Argentina and Chile 1952

Players
Backs:
R. Gregg (Queen's U)
M.F. Lane (UCC)
R.R. Chambers (Instonians)
J. Notley (Wanderers)
M. Hillary (UCD)
J.T. Horgan (UCC)
W.J. Hewitt (Instonians)
J.A. O'Meara (UCC)
M. Birthistle (Old Belvedere)

Forwards:
D.J. O'Brien (Cardiff), Capt.
W.J. O'Neill (UCD)
D. Crowley (Cork Constitution)
J.H. Smith (Collegians)
P.J. Lawler (Clontarf)
A.F. O'Leary (Cork Constitution)

P.J. Kavanagh (UCD)
J.S. McCarthy (Dolphin)
M.J. Dargan (Old Belvedere)
F.E. Anderson (Queen's U)
P.P. Traynor (Clontarf)
J.R. Kavanagh (UCD)

Manager: G.P.S. Hogan
Secretary: R.W. Jeffares, jr
Referee: O.B. Glasgow

Tour record:
(All matches played at Buenos Aires except where indicated)
Beat Chilean All-Stars 30–0 (Santiago)
Beat Capital 12–6
Lost to Pucara 6–11
Drew with Buenos Aires Provincial XV 6–6
Beat Argentine 'A' Selection 19–3
Drew with Argentina 3–3
Beat Argentine 'B' Selection 25–3
Beat Argentina 6–0
Beat Buenos Aires University Past and Present 19–11
P. 9. W. 6. D. 2. L. 1. F. 126 A. 43

South Africa 1961

Players
Backs:
T.J. Kiernan (UCC)
A.J.F. O'Reilly (Leicester and Old Belvedere)
N.H. Brophy (UCD)
J.C. Walsh (UCC)
K.J. Houston (London Irish and Oxford U)
W.J. Hewitt (Instonians)
J.F. Dooley (Galwegians)
W.G. Tormey (UCD)
D.C. Glass (Collegians)
A.A. Mulligan (Cambridge U)
T.J. Cleary (Bohemians)

Forwards
A.R. Dawson (Wanderers), Capt.
S. Millar (Balymena)
B.G. M. Wood (Garryowen)
J.N. Thomas (Blackrock Coll)
J.S. Dick (Queen's U)
W.A. Mulcahy (UCD)
M.G. Culliton (Wanderers)
C.J. Dick (Ballymena)
N.A. Murphy (Cork Constitution)

D. Scott (Malone)
J.R. Kavanagh (UCD)
T. McGrath (Garryowen)

Manager: N.F. Murphy
Hon. assistant manager: T. O'Reilly

Tour record:
Lost to South Africa (International)
 8–24 (Cape Town)
Beat South Western Districts XV 11–6
 (Mossel Bay)
Beat Western Transvaal 16–6
 (Potschefstroom)
Beat Rhodesia 24–0 (Salisbury)
P. 4. W. 3. D. 0. L. 1. F. 59. A. 36.

Team in international: Kiernan,
O'Reilly, Walsh, Houston, Hewitt,
Glass, Mulligan, Wood, Dawson,
Millar, Mulcahy, G. J. Dick, McGrath,
Kavanagh, Scott.

Australia 1967

Players
Backs:
T.J. Kiernan (Cork Constitution), Capt.
A.T.A. Duggan (Lansdowne)
F.P.K. Bresnihan (UCD)
J.C. Walsh (Sunday's Well)
N.H. Brophy (Blackrock Coll)
P.J. McGrath (UCC)
J.B. Murray (UCD)
C.M.H. Gibson (NIFC)
B.F. Sherry (Terenure Coll)
L. Hall (UCC)

Forwards:
S.A. Hutton (Malone)
K.W. Kennedy (CIYMS)
S. MacHale (Lansdowne)
P. O'Callaghan (Dolphin)
W.J. McBride (Ballymena)
M.G. Molloy (UCG)
K.G. Goodall (City of Derry)
T.A. Moore (Highfield)
M.G. Doyle (Edinburgh Wanderers)
L.G. Butler (Blackrock Coll)
J. Flynn (Wanderers)
D.J. Hickie (St Mary's Coll)

Manager: E. O'D. Davy
Assistant manager: D. McKibbin

Tour record:
Beat Queensland 41–8 (Brisbane)

Lost to New South Wales 9–21 (Sydney)
Beat New South Wales County Districts
 XV 31–11 (Wollogong)
Beat Australia (International) 11–5
 (Sydney)
Lost to Sydney 8–30 (Sydney)
Beat Victoria 19–5 (Melbourne)
P. 6. W. 4. D. 0. L. 2. F. 119. A. 80.

Team in international: Kiernan, Duggan,
Walsh, McGrath, Brophy, Gibson,
Sherry, Hutton, Kennedy, O'Callaghan,
McBride, Molloy, Goodall, Moore,
Doyle.

Argentina 1970

Players
Backs:
T.J. Kiernan (Cork Constitution), Capt.
B. O'Driscoll (Manchester)
A.T. A. Duggan (Lansdowne)
W. Brown (Malone)
T.O. Grace (UCD)
F.P. K. Bresnihan (London Irish)
F. O'Driscoll (UCD)
H. Murphy (UCD)
B.J. McGann (Cork Constitution)
J. Moloney (St Mary's Coll)
L. Hall (Garryowen)

Forwards:
J.F. Lynch (St Mary's Coll)
S. Millar (Ballymena)
P. O'Callaghan (Dolphin)
P. Madigan (Old Belvedere)
J. Birch (Ballymena)
W.J. McBride (Ballymena)
M. Molloy (London Irish)
P. Cassidy (Corinthians)
T. Moore (Highfield)
M. Hipwell (Terenure Coll)
R. Lamont (Instonians)
J. Buckley (Sunday's Well)

Manager: E. Patterson
Assistant manager and coach:
A.R. Dawson

Tour record:
(All matches played at Buenos Aires
except where indicated)
Beat Interior Selection 33–11
Beat Rosario 11–6 (Rosario)
Beat Argentine 'B' Selection (Junior
 Pumas) 9–6

Beat Argentine 'D' Selection 14–3
Lost to Argentina 3–8
Lost to Argentine 'C' Selection 0–17
Lost to Argentina 3–6
P. 7. W. 4. L. 3. F. 73. A. 57.

New Zealand and Fiji 1976

Players
Backs:
A. Ensor (Wanderers)
L. Moloney (Garryowen)
T. Grace (St Mary's Coll) Capt.
W. McMaster (Ballymena)
J. Brady (Wanderers)
M. Gibson (NIFC)
I. McIrath (Ballymena)
B. McGann (Constitution)
M. Quinn (Lansdowne)
D. Canniffe (Lansdowne)
J. Robbie (Dublin U)
R. McGrath (Wanderers) Joined tour as replacement

Forwards:
P. Orr (Old Wesley)
R. Clegg (Bangor)
P. O'Callgahan (Dolphin)
T. Feighery (St Mary's Coll)
E. O'Rafferty (Wanderers)
J. Cantrell (UCD)
P. Whelan (Garryowen)
E. O'Rafferty (Wanderers)
B. Foley (Shannon)
M. Keane (Lansdowne)
R. Hakin (CIYMS)
H. Steele (Ballymena)
J. Davidson (Dungannon) Joined tour as replacement
S. McKinney (Dungannon)
S. Deering (Garryowen)
W. Duggan (Blackrock Coll)

Manager: K. Quilligan
Assistant Manager (Coach) R. Meates
Medical Officer: T.C.J. O'Connell

Tour Record:
Played 8. W. 5. D. 0. L. 3. F. 96. A. 68.
Beat South Canterbury 19–4 (Timaru)
Beat North Auckland 12–3 (Whangarei)
Lost to Auckland 10–13 (Auckland)
Beat Manawatu 22–16
Lost to Canterbury 18–4 (Christchurch)
Beat Southland 18–3 (Invercargill)

Lost to New Zealand (Test) 3–11 (Wellington)
Beat Fiji 8–0 (Suva)

Team in Test Match (*v* New Zealand):
Ensor, Grace, Gibson, McIlrath, McMaster, McGann, Robbie, Orr, Whelan, O'Callaghan, Keane, Hakin, Davidson, Duggan, McKinney.

Australia 1979

Players
Backs:
F. Ennis (Wanderers)
R. O'Donnell (St Mary's Coll)
M. Gibson (NIFC)
T. Kennedy (St Mary's Coll)
A. McLennan (Wanderers)
P. Andreucetti (St Mary's Coll)
D. Irwin (Queen's U)
P. McNaughton (Greystones)
O. Campbell (Old Belvedere)
A. Ward (Garryowen)
J. Moloney (St Mary's Coll)
C. Patterson (Instonians)

Forwards:
P. Orr (Old Wesley)
G. McLoughlin (Shannon)
E. Byrne (Blackrock Coll)
M. Fitzpatrick (Wanderers) Joined Tour as replecment
C. Fitzgerald (St Mary's Coll)
P. Whelan (Garryowen)
B. Foley (Shannon)
M. Keane (Lansdowne)
H. Steele (Ballymena)
W. Duggan (Blackrock Coll)
C. Cantillon (Constitution)
A. McLean (Ballymena)
J. O'Driscoll (London Irish)
F. Slattery (Blackrock Coll) Capt.

Manager: J. Coffey
Assistant Manager (Coach): N. Murphy
Medical Officer: T.C.J. O'Connell

Tour Record:
P. 8. W. 7. D. 0. L. 1. F. 184. A. 75
Beat Western Australia 39–3 (Perth)
Beat ACT 35–7 (Canberra)
Beat New South Wales 16–12 (Sydney)
Beat Queensland 18–15 (Brisbane)
Beat Australia (First Test) 27–12 (Brisbane)

Beat New South Wales Country 28–7 (Orange)

Lost to Sydney 12–16 (Sydney)

Beat Australia (Second Test) 9–3 (Sydney)

Teams in Test Matches:

First Test: O'Donnell, Moloney, Gibson, McNaughton, Kennedy, Campbell, Patterson, Orr, Fitzgerald, McLoughlin, Keane, Steele, O'Driscoll, Duggan, Slattery. Replacement: Ennis for O'Donnell (45 minutes).

Second Test: O'Donnell, Moloney, McNaughton, Gibson, Kennedy, Campbell, Patterson, Orr, Fitzgerald, McLoughlin, Keane, Steele, O'Driscoll, Duggan, Slattery

South Africa 1981

Players

Backs:

J. Murphy (Greystones)

K. O'Brien (Broughton Park)

K. Crossan (Instonians)

T. Kennedy (St Mary's Coll)

M. Kiernan (Dolphin)

A. McLennan (Wanderers)

J. Hewitt (NIFC)

A. Irwin (Queen's U)

D. Irwin (Queen's U)

O. Campbell (Old Belvedere)

P. Dean (St Mary's Coll)

J. Robbie (Greystones)

R. McGrath (Wanderers)

M. Quinn (Lansdowne) Joined tour as replacement

B. O'Connor (Palmerston) Joined tour as replacement

Forwards:

P. Orr (Old Wesley)

G. McLoughlin (Shannon)

D. Fitzgerald (Dublin U)

J. Cantrell (Blackrock Coll)

H. Harbison (UCD)

J. Holland (Wanderers)

G. Wallace (Old Wesley)

B. Foley (Shannon)

A. O'Leary (Constitution and Wanderers)

J. O'Driscoll (London Irish)

R. Kearney (Wanderers)

W. Duggan (Blackrock Coll)

F. Slattery (Blackrock Coll) Capt.

Manager: P. Madigan

Assistant Manager (Coach): T. Kiernan

Medical Officer: M. Little

Tour record:

P. 7. W. 3. D. 0. L. 4. F. 207. A. 90

Lost to SA Gazelles (15–18 (Pretoria)

beat SA Mining XV 46–7 (Potchefstroom)

beat President's Trophy XV 54–3 (East London)

Lost to SA Country District's XV 16–17 (Wellington)

Lost to South Africa (First Test) 15–23 (Cape Town)

Beat Gold Cip XV 51–10 (Dudtshoorn)

Lost to South Africa (Second Test) 10–12 (Durban)

Teams in Test Matches:

First Test: Murphy, Kennedy, D. Irwin, Campbell, McLennan, Dean, McGrath, Orr, Cantrell, McLoughlin, Foley, Holland, O'Driscoll, Duggan, Slattery. Replacements: Hewitt for Campbell (56 minutes), O'Brien for Murphy (62 minutes).

Second Test: O'Brien, Kennedy, D. Irwin, Dean, McLennan, Quinn, McGrath, Orr, Cantrell, McLoughlin, Holland, Foley. O'Driscoll, Duggan, Slattery. Replacement: Hewitt for Dean 75 minutes.

Japan 1985

Players:

Backs:

P. Rainey (Ballymena)

H. MacNeill (Oxford U and London Irish)

T. Ringland (Ballymena)

K. Crossan (Instonians)

M. Kiernan (Lansdowne and Dolphin)

B. Mullin (Dublin U)

M. Finn (Constitution)

T. McMaster (Bangor)

J. Hewitt (NIFC) Joined tour as replacement

P. Dean (St Mary's Coll)

R. Keyes (Constitution)

M. Bradley (Constitution)

R. Brady (Ballymena)

Forwards:
P. Kennedy (London Irish)
M. Fitzpatrick (Wanderers)
J. McCoy (Dungannon)
P. Orr (Old Wesley)
C. Fitzgerald (St Mary's Coll) Capt.
H. Harbison (Bective Rangers)
B. McCall (London Irish)
W. Anderson (Dungannon)
D. Lenihan (Constitution)
N. Carr (Ards)
P. Matthews (Ards)
B. Spillane (Bohemians)
P. Kenny (Wanderers)
P. Collins (Highfield)

Manager: D. McKibbin
Assistant Manager (Coach) M. Doyle
Medical Officer: J. Gallagher

Tour Record:
P. 5. W. 5. D. 0. L. 0. F. 201. A. 66
Beat Kansai 44-13 (Morioka)
Beat Japan 'B' 34-10 (Sendai)
Beat Japan (First Test) 48-13 (Osaka)
Beat Kanto 42-15 (Nagoya)
Beat Japan (Second Test) 33-15 (Tokyo)

Teams in test matches:
First test: Macneill, Ringland, Kiernan, Mullin, Crossan, Dean, Bradley, Orr, Fitzgerald, McCoy, Anderson, Lenihan, Kenny, Spillane, Matthews.

Second test: MacNeill, Ringland, Kiernan, Mullin, Crossan, Dean, Bradley, Orr, Fitzgerald, McCoy, Anderson, Lenihan, Matthews, Spillane, Kenny

Replacements: Keyes for Dean (Second Half), Brady for Bradley (Second Half)

APPENDIX 8
IRELAND PLAYERS ON COMBINED BRITISH AND IRISH TOURS

Ireland has been represented on all British and Irish sides that have toured Australia, New Zealand and South Africa since 1896. The number of each players test match appearances are given in brackets after each tour entry.

Legend: A – Australia; NZ – New Zealand, SA – South Africa

Where a player joined the tour as a replacement it is indicated by an asterisk (*) and where a player came on as a replacement for a test match it is indicated by 'S' with the number of substitutions in brackets.

R. Alexander (North of Ireland) SA 1938 (3)
W. Ashby (UCC) SA 1910 (0)
G. Beamish (Leicester) A, NZ 1930 (5: 1 *v* A, 4 *v* NZ)
C.A. Boyd (Dublin U) SA 1896 (1)
C.V. Boyle (Dublin U) SA 1938 (3)
M.J. Bradley (Dolphin) SA 1924 (0)
T.N. Brand (North of Ireland) SA 1924 (2)
F.P.K. Bresnihan (UCD and Blackrock Coll) A, NZ 1966, SA 1968 (3 *v* SA)
N.H. Brophy (UCD) A, NZ 1959, SA 1962 (2: 2 *v* SA)
L.Q. Bulger (Dublin U, Lansdowne) SA 1896 (4)
T. Clifford (Young Munster) A, NZ 1950 (5: 2 *v* A; 3 *v* NZ)
S.O. Campbell (Old Belvedere) SA 1980 (3) (1S); NZ 1983 (4)
A.D. Clinch (Dublin U) SA 1896 (4)
J.D. Clinch (Dublin U) SA 1924 (0)
T. J. Crean (Wanderers) SA 1896 (4)
G.E. Cromey (Queen's U) SA 1938 (1)
W.A. Cunningham (Lansdowne) SA 1924 (1)
I.G. Davidson (North of Ireland) SA 1903 (1)
A.R. Dawson (Wanderers) A, NZ 1959 (6: 2 *v* A, 4 *v* NZ)
G.P. Doran (Lansdowne) A 1899 (2)
M.G. Doyle (Blackrock Coll) SA 1968 (1)
W.P. Duggan (Blackrock Coll) NZ 1977 (4)
M.J. Dunne (Lansdowne) A, NZ 1930 (0)
R.W. Edwards (Malone) A, NZ 1904 (3: 2 *v* A, 1 *v* NZ)
M.F. English (Bohemians) A, NZ 1959 (0)
J.L. Farrell (Bective Rangers) A, NZ 1930 (5: 1 *v* A, 4 *v* NZ)

C. Fitzgerald (St Mary's Coll) NZ 1983 (4)

A.R. Foster (Derry) SA 1910 (2)

C.M.H. Gibson (Cambridge U, NIFC) NZ 1966, SA 1968, A, NZ 1971 (12: 4 *v* NZ 1966, 4 *v* SA 1968, 4 *v* NZ 1971), SA 1974 (0) NZ 1977 (0)

K. Goodall (City of Derry) SA 1968 (0)

T.O. Grace (St Mary's Coll) SA 1974 (0)

C.R.A. Graves (Wanderers) SA 1938 (2)

N.J. Henderson (Queen's U) A, NZ 1950 (2: 2 *v* NZ)

D. Hewitt (Queen's U) A, NZ 1959, SA 1962 (6: 3 *v* NZ, 2 *v* A; 1 *v* SA)

M.L. Hipwell (Terenure Coll) A, NZ 1971 (0)

W.R. Hunter (CIYMS) SA 1962 (0)

D. Irwin (Queen's U, Instonians) NZ 1983 (3)

R. Johnston (Wanderers) SA 1896 (3)

M.I. Keane (Lansdowne) NZ 1977 (1)

K.W. Kennedy (CIYMS and London Irish) A, NZ 1966 (4 2 *v* A, 2 *v* NZ), SA 1974 (0)

M. Kiernan (Dolphin and Lansdowne) NZ 1983 (3)

T.J. Kiernan (UCC Constitution) SA 1962 (1), SA 1968 (4)

J.W. Kyle (Queen's U) A, NZ 1950 (2 *v* A, 4 *v* NZ)

R.A. Lamont (Instonians) A, NZ 1966 (4 *v* NZ)

M.F. Lane (UCC) A, NZ 1950 (1 *v* A)

D. Lenihan (UCC and Constitution) NZ 1983 (0)

J.F. Lynch (St Mary's Coll) A, NZ 1971 (4 *v* NZ)

W.J. McBride (Ballymena) SA 1962 (2) A, NZ 1966 (3 *v* NZ), SA 1968 (4), A, NZ 1971 (4) *v* NZ), SA 1974 (4)

H. MacNeill (Dublin U, Oxford U, London Irish) NZ 1983 (3, 1S)

J.S. McCarthy (Dolphin) A, NZ 1950 (0)

A.N. McClinton (NIFC) SA 1910 (0)

T.M.W. MCGown (NIFC) A 1899 (4)

J.W. McKay (Queen's U) A, NZ 1950 (6: 2 *v* A; 4 *v* NZ)

H.R. McKibbin (Queen's U) SA 1938 (3)

S. McKinney (Dungannon) SA 1974 (0)

G. McLoughlin (Shannon) NZ 1983 (0)

R.J. McLoughlin (Gosforth and Blackrock Coll) A, NZ 1966; A, NZ 1971 (3: 2 *v* A 1966; 1 *v* NZ 1966)

J. McVicker (Collegians) SA 1924 (3)

J.T. Magee (Bective Rangers) SA 1896 (2)

L.M. Magee (Bective Rangers) SA 1896 (4)

B.S. Massey (Hull, ER, Ulster) A, NZ 1904 (1: *v* A)

E. Martinelli (Dublin U) A 1899 (1)

R.B. Mayne (Queen's U) SA 1938 (3)

A.D. Meares (Dublin U) SA 1896 (2)

S. Millar (Ballymena) A, NZ 1959, SA 1962, SA 1968 (9: 2 *v* A 1959, 1 *v* NZ 1959, 4 *v* SA 1962, 2 *v* SA 1968)

R. Milliken (Bangor) SA 1974 (4)

J.J. Moloney (St Mary's Coll) SA 1974 (0)

G.J. Morgan (Clontarf) SA 1938 (1)

W.A. Mulcahy (UCD, Bohemians) A, NZ 1959, SA 1962, (7: 1 *v* A 1959, 2 *v* NZ 1959, 4 *v* SA 1962)

K.D. Mullen (Old Belvedere) A, NZ 1950 (Capt.) (3: 1 *v* A; 2 *v* NZ)

A.A. Mulligan (Cambridge U) A, NZ 1959 (1 *v* NZ)

N.A.A. Murphy (Cork Constitution): A, NZ 1959, A, NZ 1966, (8: 1 *v* A 1959, 3 *v* NZ 1959, 2 *v* A 1966, 2 *v* NZ 1966)

P.F. Murray (Wanderers) A, NZ 1930 (4: 1 *v* A; 3 *v* NZ)

J.E. Nelson (Malone) A, NZ *1950* (4: 2 *v* A; 2 *v* NZ)

G.W. Norton (Bective Rangers) A, NZ 1950 (0)

R. O'Donnell (St Mary's Coll) SA 1980 (1)

J. O'Driscoll (London Irish, Manchester) SA 1980 (4), NZ 1983 (2)

H. O'Neill (Queen's U) A, NZ 1930 (1 *v* A; 4 *v* NZ)

A.J.F. O'Reilly (Old Belvedere, Leicester) SA 1955 (4) A, NZ 1959 (2 *v* A, 4 *v* NZ)

P. Orr (Old Wesley) NZ 1977 (1) SA 1980 (0)

C. Patterson (Instonians) SA 1980 (3)

C.D. Patterson (Malone) A, NZ 1904 (0)
A.C. Pedlow (Queen's U) SA 1955 (2)
O.S. Piper (Constitution) SA 1910 (1)
T. Reid (Garryowen) SA 1955 (2)
J.C. Robbie (Dublin U, Cambridge U, Greystones) SA 1980 (1)
W. J. Roche (UCC, Newport) SA 1924 (0)
T. Ringland (Ballymena) NZ 1983 (1)
R. Roe (Lansdowne) SA 1955 (0)
J. Sealy (Dublin U) SA 1896 (4)
F. Slattery (UCD) A, NZ 1971 (0) SA 1974 (4)
R.S. Smyth (Dublin U) SA 1903 (3)
T. Smyth (Malone) SA 1910 (2)
A. Tedford (Malone) SA 1903 (3)
R.H. Thompson (Instonians, London Irish) SA 1955 (3)
C.C. Tucker (Shannon) SA 1980 (2)
W. Tyrrell (Queen's U) SA 1910 (0)
James Wallace (Wanderers) SA 1903 (0)
Joseph Wallace (Wanderers) SA 1903 (3)
S. Walker (Instonians) SA 1938 (3)
J.C. Walsh (Sunday's Well) A 1966 (0)
A.J. Ward (Garryowen) SA 1980 (1)
B.G.M. Wood (Garryowen); A, NZ 1959 (2: *v* NZ)
R.M. Young (Queen's U); A, NZ 1966; SA 1968 (4: 1 *v* NZ; 2 *v* A, 1 *v* SA)

In April 1986, a special match to mark the centenary of the International Board was played in Cardiff between the Lions and the Rest of the World. Full Lions honours were awarded to the 21 players chosen. The six Irishmen so honoured were:
T. Ringland (Ballymena), B. Mullin (Dublin University), M. Kiernan (Dolphin), D. Fitzgerald (Lansdowne), D. Lenihan (Constitution), N. Carr (Ards)

The following Irishmen have captained Lions' teams:
T. Smythe (Malone) to South Africa in 1910
S. Walker (Instonians) to South Africa in 1938
K. Mullen (Old Belvedere) to Australia and New Zealand in 1950

R.H. Thompson (Instonians and London Irish) to South Africa 1955
A.R. Dawson (Wanderers) to Australia and New Zealand 1959
T.J. Kiernan (Constitution) to South Africa in 1968
W.J. McBride (Ballymena) to South Africa in 1974
C. Fitzgerald (St Mary's Coll) to New Zealand in 1983

APPENDIX 9
IRELAND'S INTERNATIONAL MATCHES AT ALL LEVELS

Uniform scoring values were adopted in 1890. In 1893–94 the try was valued at three points; it was revalued to four points in 1971–72.

The dropped goal was valued at four points from 1891 until 1948 when it was devalued to three points. A goal from a mark was devalued from four to three points in 1905–06.

FULL INTERNATIONAL MATCHES

Ireland v Scotland
P.96 W.44 D.4 L.48

1877 *Belfast*
  Scotland 4G 2DG 2T to 0
1878 No match
1879 *Belfast*
  Scotland 1G 1DG 1T to 0
1880 *Glasgow*
  Scotland 1G 2DG 2T to 0
1881 *Belfast*
  Ireland 1DG to 1T
1882 *Glasgow*
  Scotland 2T to 0
1883 *Belfast*
  Scotland 1G 1T to 0
1884 *Raeburn Place* (Edinburgh)
  Scotland 2G 2T to 1T
1885 *Raeburn Place*
  Scotland 1G 2T to 0
1886 *Raeburn Place*
  Scotland 3G 1DG 2T to 0
1887 *Belfast*
  Scotland 1G 1GM 2T to 0

1888 *Raeburn Place*
Scotland 1G to 0
1889 *Belfast*
Scotland 1DG to 0
1890 *Raeburn Place*
Scotland 1DG 1T to 0
1891 *Belfast*
Scotland 3G 1DG 2T (14) to 0
1892 *Raeburn Place*
Scotland 1T (2) to 0
1893 *Belfast*
Drawn no score
1894 *Dublin*
Ireland 1G (5) to 0
1895 *Raeburn Place*
Scotland 2T (6) to 0
1896 *Dublin*
Drawn no score
1897 *Powderhall* (Edinburgh)
Scotland 1G 1PG (8) to 1T (3)
1898 *Belfast*
Scotland 1G 1T (8) to 0
1899 *Inverleith* (Edinburgh)
Ireland 3T (9) to 1PG (3)
1900 *Dublin*
Drawn no score
1901 *Inverleith* (Edinburgh)
Scotland 3T (9) to 1G (5)
1902 *Belfast*
Ireland 1G (5) to 0
1903 *Inverlieth*
Scotland 1T (3) to 0
1904 *Dublin*
Scotland 2G 3T (19) to 1T (3)
1905 *Inverleith*
Ireland 1G 2T (11) to 1G (5)
1906 *Dublin*
Scotland 2G 1GM (13) to 2T (6)
1907 *Inverleith*
Scotland 3G (15) to 1PG (3)
1908 *Dublin*
Ireland 2G 2T (16) to 1G 1PG 1T (11)
1909 *Inverleith*
Scotland 3T (9) to 1PG (3)
1910 *Belfast*
Scotland 1G 3T (14) to 0
1911 *Inverleith*
Ireland 2G 2T (16) to 1DG 2T (10)
1912 *Dublin*
Ireland 1DG 1PG 1T (10) to 1G 1T (8)

1913 *Inverleith*
Scotland 4G 3T (29) to 2G 1DG (14)
1914 *Dublin*
Ireland 2T (6) to 0
1920 *Inverleith*
Scotland 2G 1PG 2T (19) to 0
1921 *Dublin*
Ireland 3T (9) to 1G 1T (8)
1922 *Inverleith*
Scotland 2T (6) to 1T (3)
1923 *Dublin*
Scotland 2G 1T (13) to 1T (3)
1924 *Inverleith*
Scotland 2G 1T (13) to 1G 1T (8)
1925 *Dublin*
Scotland 2G 1DG (14) to 1G 1PG (8)
1926 *Murrayfield*
Ireland 1T (3) to 0
1927 *Dublin*
Ireland 2T (6) to 0
1928 *Murrayfield*
Ireland 2G 1T (13) to 1G (5)
1929 *Dublin*
Scotland 2G 2T (16) to 1DG 1T (7)
1930 *Murrayfield*
Ireland 1G 3T (14) to 1G 2T (11)
1931 *Dublin*
Ireland 1G 1T (8) to 1G (5)
1932 *Murrayfield*
Ireland 4G (20) to 1G 1T (8)
1933 *Dublin*
Scotland 2DG (8) to 2T (6)
1934 *Murrayfield*
Scotland 2G 1PG 1T (16) to 3T (9)
1935 *Dublin*
Ireland 4T (12) to 1G (5)
1936 *Murrayfield*
Ireland 1DG 2T (10) to 1DG (4)
1937 *Dublin*
Ireland 1G 2T (11) to 1DG (4)
1938 *Murrayfield*
Scotland 2G 1DG 1PG 2T (23) to 1G 3T (14)
1939 *Dublin*
Ireland 1PG 1GM 2T (12) to 1T (3)
1947 *Murrayfield*
Ireland 1T (3) to 0
1948 *Dublin*
Ireland 2T (6) to 0
1949 *Murrayfield*
Ireland 2G 1PG (13) to 1PG (3)

1950 *Dublin*
 Ireland 3G 2PG (21) to 0
1951 *Murrayfield*
 Ireland 1DG 1T (6) to 1G (5)
1952 *Dublin*
 Ireland 1PG 3T (12) to 1G 1PG (8)
1953 *Murrayfield*
 Ireland 4G 2T (26) to 1G 1PG (8)
1954 *Belfast*
 Ireland 2T (6) to 0
1955 *Murrayfield*
 Scotland 2PG 1DG 1T (12) to 1PG
 (3)
1956 *Dublin*
 Ireland 1G 3T (14) to 2G (10)
1957 *Murrayfield*
 Ireland 1G (5) to 1PG (3)
1958 *Dublin*
 Ireland 2PG 2T (12) to 2T (6)
1959 *Murrayfield*
 Ireland 1G 1PG (8) to 1PG (3)
1960 *Dublin*
 Scotland 1DG 1T (6) to 1G (5)
1961 *Murrayfield*
 Scotland 2G 1PG 1T (16) to 1G 1T
 (8)
1962 *Dublin*
 Scotland 1G 1DG 2 PG 2T (20)
 to 1PG 1T (6)
1963 *Murrayfield*
 Scotland 1PG (3) to 0
1964 *Dublin*
 Scotland 2PG (6) to 1PG (3)
1965 *Murrayfield*
 Ireland 2G 1DG 1T (16) to 1DG
 1PG (6)
1966 *Dublin*
 Scotland 1G 2T (11) to 1PG (3)
1967 *Murrayfield*
 Ireland 1G (5) to 1PG (3)
1968 *Dublin*
 Ireland 1G 1PG 2T (14) to 2PG (6)
1969 *Murrayfield*
 Ireland 2G 2T (16) to 0
1970 *Dublin*
 Ireland 2G 2T (16) to 1G 1DG 1T
 (11)
1971 *Murrayfield*
 Ireland 1G 2PG 2T (17) to 1G (5)
1972 No Match
1973 *Murrayfield*
 Scotland 2PG 3DG 1T (19)
 to 2PG 2T (14)

Ireland v England
P. 98 W. 35 D. 8 L. 55

1875 *The Oval*
 England 1G 1DG 1T to 0
1876 *Dublin*
 England 1G 1T to 0
1877 *The Oval*
 England 2G 2T to 0
1878 *Dublin*
 England 2G 1T to 0
1879 *The Oval*
 England 2G 1DG 2T to 0
1880 *Dublin*
 England 1G 1T to 1T
1974 *Dublin*
 Ireland 1G 1PG (9) to 2PG (6)
1975 *Murrayfield*
 Scotland 2PG 2DG 2T (20)
 to 1G 1PG 1T (13)
1976 *Dublin*
 Scotland 4PG 1DG (15) to 2PG (6)
1977 *Murrayfield*
 Scotland 2PG 1DG 3T (21)
 to 1G 3PG 1DG (18)
1978 *Dublin*
 Ireland 1G 2PG (12) to 3PG (9)
1979 Murrayfield
 Drawn 1PG 2T (11) each
1980 *Dublin*
 Ireland 1G 3PG 1DG 1T (22) to
 2G 1PG (15)
1981 *Murrayfield*
 Scotland 1PG 1DG 1T (10) to
 1G 1PG (9)
1982 *Dublin*
 Ireland 6PG 1DG (21) to 1G 2PG (12)
1983 *Murrayfield*
 Ireland 1G 3PG (15) to 2PG 1DG
 1T (13)
1984 *Dublin*
 Scotland 3G 1T 1PT 2PG (32)
 1G 1PG (9)
1985 *Murrayfield*
 Ireland 2G 1DG 1PG (18)
 to 4PG 1DG (15)
1985 *Dublin*
 Scotland 1T 2PG (10)
1986 *Dublin*
 Scotland 1T 2PG (10) to 1 G1 1PG
 (9)
1986 *Murrayfield*
 Ireland 1T 2PG (6)

1881 *Manchester*
England 2G 2T to 0
1882 *Dublin*
Drawn 2T each
1883 *Manchester*
England 1G 3T to 1T
1884 *Dublin*
England 1G to 0
1885 *Manchester*
England 2T to 1T
1886 *Dublin*
England 1T to 0
1887 *Dublin*
Ireland 2G to 0
1888 No Match
1889 No Match
1890 *Blackheath* (London)
England 3T to 0
1891 *Dublin*
England 2G 3T (9) to 0
1892 *Manchester*
England 1G 1T (7) to 0
1893 *Dublin*
England 2T (4) to 0
1894 *Blackheath*
Ireland 1DG 1T (7) to 1G (5)
1895 *Dublin*
England 2T (6) to 1T (3)
1896 *Leeds*
Ireland 2G (10) to 1DG (4)
1897 *Dublin*
Ireland 1GM 3T (13) to 2PG 1T (9)
1898 *Richmond* (London)
Ireland 1PG 2T (9) to 1PG 1T (6)
1899 *Dublin*
Ireland 1PG 1T (6) to 0
1900 *Richmond*
England 1G 1DG 2T (15) to 1DG (4)
1901 *Dublin*
Ireland 2G (10) to 1PG 1T (6)
1902 *Leicester*
England 2T (6) to 1T (3)
1903 *Dublin*
Ireland 1PG 1T (6) to 0
1904 *Blackheath*
England 2G 3T (19) to 0
1905 *Cork*
Ireland 1G 4T (17) to 1T (3)
1906 *Leicester*
Ireland 2G 2T (16) to 2T (6)
1907 *Dublin*
Ireland 1G 1GM 3T (17) to 1PG 2T
(9)

1908 *Richmond*
England 2G 1T (13) to 1PG (3)
1909 *Dublin*
England 1G 2T (11) to 1G (5)
1910 *Twickenham*
Drawn no score
1911 *Dublin*
Ireland 1T (3) to 0
1912 *Twickenham*
England 5T (15) to 0
1913 *Dublin*
England 1PG 4T (15) to 1DG (4)
1914 *Twickenham*
England 1G 4T (17) to 1G 1DG 1T
(12)
1920 *Dublin*
England 1G 3T (14) to 1G 1PG 1T
(11)
1921 *Twickenham*
England 1G 1DG 2T (15) to 0
1922 *Dublin*
England 4T (12) to 1T (3)
1923 *Leicester*
England 2G 1DG 3T (23) to 1G (5)
1924 *Belfast*
England 1G 3T (14) to 1T (3)
1925 *Twickenham*
Drawn 2T (6) each
1926 *Dublin*
Ireland 2G 1PG 2T (19) to 3G (15)
1927 *Twickenham*
England 1G 1T (8) to 1PG 1T (6)
1928 *Dublin*
England 1DG 1T (7) to 2T (6)
1929 *Twickenham*
Ireland 2T (6) to 1G (5)
1930 *Dublin*
Ireland 1DG (4) to 1T (3)
1931 *Twickenham*
Ireland 1PG 1T (6) to 1G (5)
1932 *Dublin*
England 1G 2PG (11) to 1G 1PG
(8)
1933 *Twickenham*
England 1G 4T (17) to 1PG 1T (6)
1934 *Dublin*
England 2G 1T (13) to 1T (3)
1935 *Twickenham*
England 1G 3PG (14) to 1T (3)
1936 *Dublin*
Ireland 2T (6) to 1T (3)
1937 *Twickenham*
England 1PG 2T (9) to 1G 1T (8)

1938 *Dublin*
England 6G 1PG 1T (36) to 1G 3T (14)
1939 *Twickenham*
Ireland 1G (5) to 0
1947 *Dublin*
Ireland 2G 1PG 3T (22) to 0
1948 *Twickenham*
Ireland 1G 2T (11) to 2G (10)
1949 *Dublin*
Ireland 1G 2PG 1T (14) to 1G (5)
1950 *Twickenham*
England 1T (3) to 0
1951 *Dublin*
Ireland 1PG (3) to 0
1952 *Twickenham*
England 1T (3) to 0
1953 *Dublin*
Drawn 2PG 1T (9) each
1954 *Twickenham*
England 1G 1PG 2T (14) to 1PG (3)
1955 *Dublin*
Drawn Ireland 1PG 1T (6)
England 2T (6)
1956 *Twickenham*
England 1G 3PG 2T (20) to 0
1957 *Dublin*
England 1PG 1T (6) to 0
1958 *Twickenham*
England 1PG 1T (6) to 0
1959 *Dublin*
England 1PG (3) to 0
1960 *Twickenham*
England 1G 1DG (8) to 1G (5)
1961 *Dublin*
Ireland 1G 2PG (11) to 1G 1T (8)
1962 *Twickenham*
England 2G 1PG 1T (16) to 0
1963 *Dublin*
Drawn no score
1964 *Twickenham*
Ireland 3G 1T (18) to 1G (5)
1965 *Dublin*
Ireland 1G (5) to 0
1966 *Twickenham*
Drawn 1PG 1T (6) each
1967 *Dublin*
England 1G 1PG (8) to 1PG (3)
1968 *Twickenham*
Drawn England 2PG 1DG (9)
Ireland 3PG (9)

1969 *Dublin*
Ireland 1G 2PG 1DG 1T (17) to 4PG 1T (15)
1970 *Twickenham*
England 2DG 1T (9) to 1PG (3)
1971 *Dublin*
England 3PG (9) to 2T (6)
1972 *Twickenham*
Ireland 1G 1DG 1PG 1T (16) to 1G 2PG (12)
1973 *Dublin*
Ireland 2G 1PG 1DG (18) to 1G 1PG (9)
1974 *Twickenham*
Ireland 2G 1PG 1DG 2T (26) to 1G 5PG (21)
1975 *Dublin*
Ireland 2G (12) to 1G 1DG (9)
1976 *Twickenham*
Ireland 2PG 1DG 1T (13) to 4PG (12)
1977 *Dublin*
England 1T (4) to 0
1978 *Twickenham*
England 2G 1PG (15) to 2PG 1DG (9)
1979 *Dublin*
Ireland 1G 1PG 1DG (12) to 1PG 1T (7)
1980 *Twickenham*
England 3G 2PG (24) to 3PG (9)
1981 *Dublin*
England 1G 1T (10) to 2DG (6)
1982 *Twickenham*
Ireland 1G 2PG 1T (16) to 1G 3PG (15)
1983 *Dublin*
Ireland 1G 5PG 1T (25) to 5PG (15)
1984 *Twickenham*
England 1DG 3PG (12) to 3PG (9)
1985 *Dublin*
Ireland 1DG 2PG 1T (13) to 2PG 1T (10)
1986 *Twickenham*
England 3G 1PT 1PG (25) to 1G 2T 2PG (20)

Ireland v Wales
P. 88 W. 29 D. 5 L. 54
1882 *Dublin*
Wales 2G 2T to 0
1883 No Match
1884 *Cardiff*
Wales 1DG 2T to 0

1885 No Match
1886 No Match
1887 *Birkenhead*
 Wales 1DG 1T to 3T
1888 *Dublin*
 Ireland 1G 1DG 1T to 0
1889 *Swansea*
 Ireland 2T to 0
1890 *Dublin*
Drawn 1G each
1891 *Llanelli*
 Wales 1G 1DG (6) to 1DG 1T (4)
1892 *Dublin*
 Ireland 1G 2T (8) to 0
1893 *Llanelli*
 Wales 1T (2) to 0
1894 *Belfast*
 Ireland 1PG (3) to 0
1895 *Cardiff*
 Wales 1G (5) to 1T (3)
1896 *Dublin*
 Ireland 1G 1T (8) to 1DG (4)
1897 No Match
1898 *Limerick*
 Wales 1G 1PG 1T (11) to 1PG (3)
1899 *Cardiff*
 Ireland 1T (3) to 0
1900 *Belfast*
 Wales 1T (3) to 0
1901 *Swansea*
 Wales 2G (10) to 3T (9)
1902 *Dublin*
 Wales 1G 1DG 2T·(15) to 0
1903 *Cardiff*
 Wales 6T (18) to 0
1904 *Belfast*
 Ireland 1G 3T (14) to 4T (12)
1905 *Swansea*
 Wales 2G (10) to 1T (3) ·
1906 *Belfast*
 Ireland 1G 2T (11) to 2T (6)
1907 *Cardiff*
 Wales 2G 1DG 1PG 4T (29) to
 0
1908 *Belfast*
 Wales 1G 2T (11) to 1G (5)
1909 *Swansea*
 Wales 3G 1T (18) to 1G (5)
1910 *Dublin*
 Wales 1DG 5T (19) to 1T (3)
1911 *Cardiff*
 Wales 2G 1PG 1T (16) to 0

1912 *Belfast*
 Ireland 1G 1DG 1T (12) to 1G (5)
1913 *Swansea*
 Wales 2G 1PG 1T (16) to 2G 1PG
 (13)
1914 Belfast
 Wales 1G 2T (11) to 1T (3)
1920 *Cardiff*
 Wales 3G 1DG 3T (28) to 1DG (4)
1921 *Belfast*
 Wales 1PG 1T (6) to 0
1922 *Swansea*
 Wales 1G 2T (11) to 1G (5)
1923 *Dublin*
 Ireland 1G (5) to 1DG (4)
1924 *Cardiff*
 Ireland 2G 1T (13) to 1DG 2T (10)
1925 *Belfast*
 Ireland 2G 1PG 2T (19) to 1T (3)
1926 *Swansea*
 Wales 1G 2T (11) to 1G 1PG (8)
1927 Dublin
 Ireland 2G 1PG 2T (19)
 to 1G 1DG (9)
1928 *Cardiff*
 Ireland 2G 1T (13) to 2G (10)
1929 *Belfast*
 Drawn 1G (5) each
1930 *Swansea*
 Wales 1PG 3T (12) to 1DG 1PG (7)
1931 Belfast
 Wales 1G 1DG 2T (15) to 1T (3)
1932 *Cardiff*
 Ireland 4T (12) to 1DG 2T (10)
1933 *Belfast*
 Ireland 1DG 1PG 1T (10) to 1G (5)
1934 *Swansea*
 Wales 2G 1T (13) to 0
1935 *Belfast*
 Ireland 2PG 1T (9) to 1PG (3)
1936 *Cardiff*
 Wales 1PG (3) to 0
1937 *Belfast*
 Ireland 1G (5) to 1PG (3)
1938 *Swansea*
 Wales 1G 1PG 1T (11) to 1G (5)
1939 *Belfast*
 Wales 1DG 1T (7) to 0
1947 Swansea
 Wales 1PG 1T (6) to 0
1948 *Belfast*
 Ireland 2T (6) to 1T (3)

1949 Swansea
Ireland 1G (5) to 0
1950 *Belfast*
Wales 2T (6) to 1PG (3)
1951 *Cardiff*
Drawn Wales 1PG (3)
to Ireland 1T (3)
1952 *Dublin*
Wales 1G 1PG 2T (14) to 1PG (3)
1953 *Swansea*
Wales 1G (5) to 1T (3)
1954 *Dublin*
Wales 1DG 3PG (12) to 2PG 1T (9)
1955 *Cardiff*
Wales 3G 1PG 1T (21) to 1PG (3)
1956 *Dublin*
Wales 1G 1DG 1PG (11) to 1PG (3)
1957 *Cardiff*
Wales 2PG (6) to 1G (5)
1958 *Dublin*
Wales 3T (9) to 1PG 1T (6)
1959 *Cardiff*
Wales 1G 1T (8) to 1PG 1T (6)
1960 *Dublin*
Wales 2G (10) to 2PG 1T (9)
1961 *Cardiff*
Wales 2PG 1T (9) to 0
1962 *Dublin*
Drawn Ireland 1 DG (3) Wales 1PG
(3)
1963 *Cardiff*
Ireland 1G 1DG 2PG (14)
to 1DG 1T (6)
1964 *Dublin*
Wales 3G (15) to 2PG (6)
1965 *Cardiff*
Wales 1G 1DG 1PG 1T (4)
to 1G 1PG (8)
1966 *Dublin*
Ireland 1DG 1PG 1T (9)
to 1PG 1T (6)
1967 *Cardiff*
Ireland 1T (3) to 0
1968 *Dublin*
Ireland 1PG 1DG 1T (9)
to 1PG 1DG (6)
1969 *Cardiff*
Wales 3G 1DG 1PG 1T (24)
to 1G 2PG (11)
1970 *Dublin*
Ireland 1G 1DG 1PG 1T (14) to 0

Ireland v France
P. 59 W. 25 D. 5 L. 29
1909 *Dublin*
Ireland 2G 1PG 2T (19) to 1G 1T (8)
1910 *Paris*
Ireland 1G 1T (8) to 1T (3)
1911 *Cork*
Ireland 3G 1DG 2T (25) to 1G (5)
1912 *Paris*
Ireland 1G 2T (11) to 2T (6)
1913 *Cork*
Ireland 3G 3T (24) to 0
1971 *Cardiff*
Wales 1G 2PG 1DG 3T (23)
to 3PG (9)
1972 No Match
1973 *Cardiff*
Wales 1G 2PG 1T (16)
to 1G 2PG (12)
1974 *Dublin*
Drawn Ireland 3PG (9)
Wales 1G 1PG (9)
1975 *Cardiff*
Wales 3G 2PG 2T (32) to 1T (4)
1976 *Dublin*
Wales 3G 4PG 1T (34) to 3PG (9)
1977 *Cardiff*
Wales 2G 2PG 1DG 1T (25)
to 3PG (9)
1978 *Dublin*
Wales 4PG 2T (20)
to 3PG 1DG 1T (16)
1979 *Cardiff*
Wales 2G 4PG (24) to 2G 3PG (21)
1980 *Dublin*
Ireland 3G 1PG (21) to 1PG 1T (7)
1981 *Cardiff*
Wales 2PG 1DG (9) to 2T (8)
1982 *Dublin*
Ireland 1G 2PG 2T (20)
to 1G 1PG 1DG (12)
1983 *Cardiff*
Wales 1G 3PG 2T (23) to 3PG (9)
1984 *Dublin*
Wales 1G 4PG (18) to 3PG (9)
1985 *Cardiff*
Ireland 2G 3PG (21) to 1G 1DG (9)
1986 *Dublin*
Wales 1G 1T 3PG (19)
to 1G 2PG (12)

1914 *Paris*
Ireland 1G 1T (8) to 2T (6)
1920 *Dublin*
France 5T (15) to 1DG 1T (7)
1921 *Paris*
France 4G (20) to 2G (10)
1922 *Dublin*
Ireland 1G 1PG (8) to 1T (3)
1923 *Paris*
France 1G 3T (14) to 1G 1T (8)
1924 *Dublin*
Ireland 2T (6) to 0
1925 *Paris*
Ireland 1PG 2T (9) to 1T (3)
1926 *Belfast*
Ireland 1G 1PG 1T (11) to 0
1927 *Paris*
Ireland 1G 1PG (8) to 1T (3)
1928 *Belfast*
Ireland 4T (12) to 1G 1T (8)
1929 *Paris*
Ireland 2T (6) to 0
1930 *Belfast*
France 1G (5) to 0
1931 *Paris*
France 1T (3) to 0
1947 *Dublin*
France 4T (12) to 1G 1PG (8)
1948 Paris
Ireland 2G 1T (13) to 2T (6)
1949 *Dublin*
France 2G 2PG (16) to 3PG (9)
1950 Paris
Drawn France 1DG (3) Ireland 1PG (3)
1951 *Dublin*
Ireland 1PG 2T (9) to 1G 1T (8)
1952 *Paris*
Ireland 1G 1PG 1T (11) to 1G 1PG (8)
1953 *Belfast*
Ireland2G 2T (16) to 1DG (3)
1954 *Paris*
France 1G 1T (8) to 0
1955 *Dublin*
France 1G (5) to 1PG (3)
1956 *Paris*
France 1G 2DG 1T (14) to 1G 1PG (8)
1957 *Dublin*
Ireland 1G 1PG 1T (11) to 2PG (6)

1958 *Paris*
France 1G 1DG 1PG (11) to 2PG (6)
1959 *Dublin*
Ireland 1DG 1PG 1T (9) to 1G (5)
1960 *Paris*
France 1G 3DG 3T (23) to 2T (6)
1961 *Dublin*
France 2DG 2PG 1T (15) to 1PG (3)
1962 *Paris*
France 1G 2T (11) to 0
1963 *Dublin*
France 3G 2DG 1T (24) to 1G (5)
1964 *Paris*
France 3G 1DG 3T (27) to 1DG 1T (6)
1965 *Dublin*
Drawn 1T (3) each
1966 *Paris*
France 1G 1PG 1T (11) to 1DG 1PG (6)
1967 *Dublin*
France 1G 2DG (11) to 1PG 1T (6)
1968 *Paris*
France 2G 1PG 1DG (16) to 2PG (6)
1969 *Dublin*
Ireland 1G 1DG 3PG (17) to 2PG 1T (9)
1970 *Paris*
France 1G 1DG (8) to 0
1971 *Dublin*
Drawn Ireland 2PG 1T (9) France 2PG 1DG (9)
1972 *Paris*
Ireland 2PG 2T (14) to 1G 1PG (9)
*1972 *Dublin*
Ireland 3G 2PG (24) to 1G 2T (14)
1973 *Dublin*
Ireland 2PG (6) to 1T (4)
1974 *Paris*
France 1G 1PG (9) to 2PG (6)
1975 *Dublin*
Ireland 2G 1PG 2DG 1T (25) to 1PG 1DG (6)
1976 *Paris*
France 2G 2PG 2T (26) to 1PG (3)
1977 *Dublin*
France 1G 3PG (15) to 2PG (6)
1978 *Paris*
France 2PG 1T (10) to 3PG (9)

APPENDIX 10
FOUR COUNTRIES MATCHES
SCOTLAND IRELAND
v
ENGLAND WALES

1 Nov. 1923 (Centenary Match, Rugby School Close)
England-Wales 2 goals, 1 try, 2 dropped goals (21)
Scotland-Ireland 2 goals, 2 tries (16)
Scotland-Ireland W.E. Crawford *I*, H.W. Stephenson *I*, G.V. Stephenson *I*, A.L. Gracie *S*, D.J. Cussen *I*, J.C. Dykes *S*, W.E. Bryce *S*, Capt., J. MacD. Bannerman *S*, J.C.R. Buchanan *S*, L.M. Stuart *S*, J.R. Lawrie *S*, D.S. Davies *S*, W.P. Collopy *I*, T.A. McClelland *I*, R.Y. Crichton *I*

5 Oct. 1929 (Rowland Hill Memorial Match, Twickenham)
Scotland-Ireland 2 goals, 1 dropped goal, 2 tries (20);
England-Wales 2 goals, 1 try (13)
Scotland-Ireland T.G. Aitchison *S*, I.S. Smith *S*, G.P.S. MacPherson *S*, capt., P. Murray *I*, W.M. Simmers *S*, E.O'D. Davy *I*, M. Sugden *I*, J.W. Allen *S*, G.R. Beamish *I*, W.B. Welsh *S*, H.S. Mackintosh *S*, M.J. Dunne *I*, J.L. Farrell *I*, C.T. Payne *I*, R.T. Smith *S*

31 Dec. 1955 (opening of new West Stand, Lansdowne Road)
England-Wales 3 goals, 1 penalty goal (18);
Scotland-Ireland 4 tries, 1 penalty goal (15)
Scotland-Ireland R.W. Chisholm *S*, A.R. Smith *S*, A.C. Pedlow *I*, A.J. O'Reilly *I*, J.S. Swan *S*, J.W. Kyle *I*, Capt., A.F. Dorward *S*, H.F. McLeod *S*, R. Roe *I*, P.J. O'Donoghue *I*, J.R. Brady *I*, P.J. Lawlor *I*, J. Greenwood *S*, T.E. Reid *I*, A. Robson *S*.

17 Oct. 1959 (Twickenham Jubilee Match)
England-Wales 4 goals, 2 tries (26);

Scotland-Ireland 1 goal, 3 tries, 1 penalty goal (17)
Scotland-Ireland K.J.F. Scotland *S*, A.R. Smith *S*, M.K. Flynn *I*, D. Hewitt *I*, A.J.F. O'Reilly *I*, G. Sharpe *S*, A.A. Mulligan *I*, H.F. McLeod *S*, A.R. Dawson *I*, Capt., S. Millar *I*, J.W.Y. Kemp *S*, W.A. Mulcahy *I*, N.A. Murphy *I*, J.T. Greenwood *S*, G.K. Smith *S*.

3 Oct. 1970 (Rugby Union Centenary Match, Twickenham)
Scotland-Ireland 1 goal, 2 tries, 1 penalty goal (14);
England-Wales 1 goal, 3 tries (14)
Scotland-Ireland T.J. Kiernan *I*, Capt., A.T.A. Duggan *I*, C.M.H. Gibson *I*, J.N.M. Frame *S*, A.G. Biggar *S*, B.J. McGann *I*, D.S. Paterson *S*, P.J. O'Callaghan *I*, F.A. Laidlaw *S*, N. Suddon *S*, W.J. McBride *I*, P.C. Brown *S*, R.J. Arneil *S*, T.A.P. Moore *I*, T.G. Elliot *S*.
Substitutes: M.G. Molloy *I* for Moore; J. Moloney *I* for Biggar.

14 Oct 1972 (Scottish RU Centenary Match, Murrayfield)
Scotland-Ireland 2 goals, 3 tries, 2 penalty goals (30);
England-Wales 1 goal, 3 tries, 1 penalty goal (21)
Scotland-Ireland A.R. Brown *S*, T.O. Grace *I*, J. Frame *S*, J. Renwick *S*, W.C. Steele *S*, C.M.H. Gibson *I*, J. Moloney *I*, A.B. Carmichael *S*, K.W. Kennedy *I*, N. Suddon *S*, W.J. McBride *I*, G. Brown *S*, F. Slattery *I*, P. Brown *S*, N. McEwan *S*.

19th April 1975 (IRFU Centenary Match, Lansdowne Road)
Scotland-Ireland 2 tries, 3 penalty goals (17)
England-Wales 1 goal, 1 try (10)
Scotland-Ireland A. Ensor *I*, T. Grace *I*, I. McGeechan *S*, R. Milliken *I*, A. Irvine *S*, M. Gibson *I*, J. Moloney *I*, I. McLaughlan *S*, K. Kennedy *I*, A. Carmichael *S*, W. J. McBride *I* Capt., G. Brown *S*, W. Lauder *S*, D. Leslie *S*, F. Slattery *I*.

Replacement – W. Duggan *I* for Leslie second half.

29th November 1980 (Welsh RU Centenary Match, National Stadium Cardiff)

England-Wales 3 goals, 4 tries, 3 dropped goals (37)

Scotland-Ireland 5 goals, 1 penalty goal (33)

Scotland-Ireland A. Irvine *S*, Capt., D. Johnston *S*, J. Renwick *S*, D. Irwin *I*, B. Hay *S*, A. Ward *I*, J. Robbie *I*, P. Orr *I*, C. Deans *S*, M. Fitzpatrick *I*, A. Tomes *S*, D. Spring *I*, J. O'Driscoll *I*, J. Beattie *S*, F. Slattery *I*.

Replacement – K. Robertson *S* for Irwin 75 minutes.

IRELAND'S INTERNATIONAL RECORD AGAINST ALL COUNTRIES

(X) denotes matches for which caps were not awarded. Caps were awarded for the match in 1974 against the President's XV.

opponents	P	W	D	L
England	98	35	8	55
Scotland	96	44	4	48
Wales	88	29	5	54
France	59	25	5	29
New Zealand	9	0	1	8
S.Africa	10	1	1	8
Australia	10	6	0	4
The Maoris	1	0	0	1
The Warathas (NSW)	1	0	0	1
Romania (X)	1	0	1	0
Argentina (X)	5	2	1	2
Japan (X)	2	2	0	0
Fiji (X)	2	2	0	0
President's XV	1	0	1	0

The scoring records are against international board countries only and tours by and to international board countries, except where stated.

Highest Score by Ireland in international: 27 *v* Australia (Brisbane 1979)

Highest winning points margin by Ireland: 24 *v* France (Cork 1913)

Highest score conceded by Ireland in International: 38 *v* South Africa (Dublin 1912)

Biggest losing points margin in International: 38 *v* South Africa (38–0) (Dublin 1912)

Highest number of points by Ireland in International Championship in one season: 71 (season 1982–83)

Most tries by Ireland in International: 6 *v* France (Cork 1913) *v* Scotland (Murrayfield 1953)

Highest number of tries scored against Ireland in international: 10 (South Africa 1912)

Record points scorer in internationals; O. Campbell (Old Belvedere) (1976–84): 217

Highest total by individual in international: O. Campbell: 21 (*v* Scotland 1982) 21 (*v* England 1983)

Most tries by individual in internationals: 11 A. Duggan (Lansdowne) 1963–1972

Note: Some contemporary reports credit G. Stephenson (Queen's U London Hospital) (1920–1930) with 13 tries.

Most tries by individual in an international: 3 R. Montgomery (Queen's U, Cambridge U) *v* Wales 1887, J.P. Quinn (Dublin U) *v* France 1913, E.O.D. Davy (Lansdowne) *v* Scotland 1930, S. Byrne (Lansdowne) *v* Scotland 1950

Most points by an individual in international Championship in a season: O. Campbell: 52 (1982–83)

Most tries by an individual in International Championship in a season: 5 J. Arigho (Lansdowne) 1927–28

Most points for Ireland on overseas tour: O. Campbell: 60 (In Australia 1979)

Most points in a match on tour: 19 A. Ward (Garryowen, St Mary's College, Greystones) (*v* ACT Cangerra 1979); O. Campbell (*v* Australia, 1st Test Brisbane 1979)

Note: M.J. Kiernan (Dolphin, Lansdowne) scored 25 points for Ireland against Japan in Tokyo

1979 *Dublin*
  Drawn Ireland 3PG (9)
  France 1G 1PG (9)
1980 *Paris*
  France 1G 2PG 1DG 1T (19)
  to 1G 3PG 1DG (18)
1981 *Dublin*
  France 3PG 2DG 1T (19)
  to 3PG 1T (13)
1982 Paris
  France 1G 4PG 1T (22) to 3PG (9)
1983 *Dublin*
  Ireland 1G 4PG 1T (22)
  to 1G 2PG 1T (16)
1984 *Paris*
  France 1G 4PG 1DG 1T (25)
  to 4PG (12)
1985 *Dublin*
  Drawn Ireland 5PG (15)
  France 2G 1PG (15)
1986 *Paris*
  France 1G 2T 1DG 5PG (29)
  to 3PG (9) (X) Extra match not in
  championship

Ireland v New Zealand
P. 9 W. 0 D. 1 L. 8

1905 *Dublin*
  New Zealand 3G (15) to 0
1924 *Dublin*
  New Zealand 1 T 1 PG (6) to 0
1935 *Dublin*
  New Zealand 1 G 2T 2PG (17)
  to 1T 2PG (9)
1954 *Dublin*
  New Zealand 1G 1T 1DG 1PG (14)
  to 1PG (3)
1963 *Dublin*
  New Zealand 1T 1PG (6) to 1G (5)
1973 *Dublin*
  Drawn Ireland 1T 2PG (10)
  to 1G 1T (10)
1974 *Dublin*
  New Zealand 1G 3PG (15) to 2PG (6)
1976 *Wellington*
  New Zealand 2T 1PG (11) to 1PG (3)
1978 *Dublin*
  New Zealand 1T 2DG (10) to 2PG (6)

Ireland v South Africa
P. 10 W. 1 D. 1 L. 8

1906 *Belfast*
  South Africa 4T 1PG (15)
  to 3T 1PG (12)
1912 *Dublin*
  South Africa 6T 4G (38) to 0
1931 *Dublin*
  South Africa 1G 1T (8) to 1PG (3)
1951 *Dublin*
  South Africa 1G 3T 1DG (17)
  to 1G (5)
1960 *Dublin*
  South Africa 1G 1T (8) to 1PG (3)
1961 *Cape Town*
  South Africa 3G 2T 1PG (24)
  to 1G 1PG (8)
1965 *Dublin*
  Ireland 1T 2PG (9) to 1T 1PG (6)
1970 *Dublin*
  Drawn Ireland 1G 1PG (8)
  to 1G 1PG (8)
1981 *Cape Town*
  South Africa 1G 2T 3PG (23)
  to 2G 1PG (15)
1981 *Durban*
  South Africa 1PG 3DG (12)
  to 1T 2PG (10)

Ireland v Australia
P. 10 W. 6 D. 0 L. 4

1947 *Dublin*
  Australia 2G 2T (16) to 1PG (3)
1958 *Dublin*
  Ireland 2T 1PG (9) to 2T (6)
1967 *Dublin*
  Ireland 2T 2DG 1PG (15)
  to 1G 1DG (8)
1967 *Sydney*
  Ireland 1G 1T 1DG (11) to 1G (5)
1968 *Dublin*
  Ireland 2G (10) to 1T (3)
1976 *Dublin*
  Australia 1G 2T 2PG (20)
  to 1T 2PG (10)
1979 *Brisbane*
  Ireland 2G 4PG 1DG (27)
  to 1G 2PG (12)
1979 *Sydney*
  Ireland 1PG 2DG (9) to 1PG (3)
1981 *Dublin*
  Australia 1T 3PG 1DG (16)
  to 4PG (12)
1984 *Dublin*

Australia 1T 3DG 1PG (16)
to 3PG (9)

Ireland v President's XV

1974 *Dublin*
Drawn Ireland 2G 2PG (18)
to 2G 2PG (18)
NB Caps awarded for this special match
arranged to mark IRFU centenary

IRELAND v THE MAORIS

1888 *Dublin*
Maoris 4G 1T (13) to 1G, 1T (4)

Ireland v 'The Warathas' (New South
Wales)

1927 *Dublin*
Warathas 1G (5) to 1PG (3)

'B' INTERNATIONAL MATCHES

Ireland v France

1975 Ireland 9 France 6
(Lansdowne Road)
1976 Ireland 3 France 16 (Dijon)

Ireland v Scotland

1977 Ireland 7 Scotland 3 (Murrayfield)
1979 Ireland 13 Scotland 20
(Lansdowne Road)
1983 Ireland 13 Scotland 22 (Melrose)
1984 Ireland 23 Scotland 20 (Galway)

Ireland v England

1980 Ireland 15 England 18
(Twickenham)
1982 Ireland 6 England 10 (Ravenhill)

Ireland has played only once at under-23
level

1979 Ireland 31 Holland 3 (Hilversum)

SCHOOLS INTERNATIONAL MATCHES

Ireland v England

1975 Ireland 3 England 6
(Lansdowne Road)
1977 Ireland 7 England 37 (Gloucester)
1978 Ireland 22 England 16
(Lansdowne Road)
1980 Ireland 7 England 12
(Twickenham)

1981 Ireland 11 England 16
(Lansdowne Road)
1983 Ireland 0 England 16 (Moseley)
1984 Ireland 15 England 7 (Ravenhill)
1986 Ireland 6 England 13 (Nottingham)

Ireland v Scotland

1976 Ireland 16 Scotland 4
(Lansdowne Road)
1978 Ireland 21 Scotland 7 (Inverleith)
1979 Ireland 19 Scotland 0
(Lansdowne Road)
1981 Ireland 14 Scotland 12
(Braidholm Glasgow)
1982 Ireland 42 Scotland 0
(Musgrave Park)
1984 Ireland 26 Scotland 13
(Braidholm Glasgow)
1985 Ireland 3 Scotland 9
(Lansdowne Road)

Ireland v Wales

1976 Ireland 10 Wales 26 (Aberavon)
1977 Ireland 4 Wales 10
(Lansdowne Road)
1979 Ireland 15 Wales 20
(Arms Park, Cardiff)
1980 Ireland 7 Wales 13
(Thomond Park)
1982 Ireland 9 Wales 17 (Neath)
1983 Ireland 10 Wales 24
(Musgrave Park)
1985 Ireland 10 Wales 7 (St David's)
1986 Ireland 17 Wales 3 (Galway)

Ireland v Australia

1977 Ireland 10 Australia 12
(Thomond Park)
1980 Ireland 7 Australia 10 (Sydney)
1982 Ireland 0 Australia 24
(Donnybrook)
1986 Ireland 9 Australia 13 (Ravenhill)

Ireland v New Zealand

1985 Ireland 3 New Zealand 17
(Donnybrook)

Ireland v Japan
1986 Ireland 16 Japan 6
(Lansdowne Road)

on 1st June 1986 in second test. Caps were not awarded for this which was not an official international. Kiernan also scored a total of 65 points in four appearances on that tour to Japan in 1986.

Captained Ireland most occasions in internationals T.J. Kiernan (UCC, Constitution) (1960–1973): 24

APPENDIX 11
INTERPROVINCIAL CHAMPIONSHIP RESULTS

While the first interprovincial took place between Leinster and Ulster in 1875–76, the four province interprovincial championship did not start until 1946–47 season. The results in the series from that date are:

LEINSTER *v* ULSTER

1946–47 Ulster 16–8
1947–48 draw 0–0
1948–49 Leinster 8–0
1949–50 Leinster 6–3
1950–51 Ulster 10–3
1951–52 Ulster 17–14
1952–53 Leinster 5–3
1953–54 Ulster 3–0
1954–55 Leinster 5–3
1955–56 Ulster 21–6
1956–57 Ulster 17–8
1957–58 Ulster 24–13
1958–59 Leinster 16–12
1959–60 Leinster 16–6
1960–61 draw 9–9
1961–62 Leinster 8–3
1962–63 Ulster 11–8
1963–64 Leinster 12–8
1964–65 draw 8–8
1965–66 Leinster 8–6
1966–67 Ulster 8–6
1967–68 Ulster 9–5
1968–69 Ulster 14–8
1969–70 Ulster 8–3
1970–71 Ulster 6–3
1971–72 Leinster 12–10
1972–73 Leinster 11–6
1973–74 Leinster 20–13
1974–75 Ulster 22–9
1975–76 Leinster 16–9
1976–77 Ulster 36–21
1977–78 Leinster 29–18
1978–79 Leinster 9–3
1979–80 Leinster 18–12
1980–81 Leinster 39–9
1981–82 Leinster 19–6
1982–83 Leinster 15–9
1983–84 Leinster 20–16
1984–85 Ulster 16–3
1985–86 Ulster 19–13

LEINSTER *v* MUNSTER

1946–47 Leinster 15–11
1947–48 Munster 14–11
1948–49 Leinster 6–0
1949–50 draw 3–3
1950–51 Leinster 8–6
1951–52 Leinster 12–9
1952–53 Munster 3–0
1953–54 draw 0–0
1954–55 Munster 9–8
1955–56 Leinster 12–9
1956–57 Leinster 19–9
1957–58 Munster 19–12
1958–59 Leinster 32–0
1959–60 Munster 18–14
1960–61 Leinster 14–9
1961–62 Leinster 6–3
1962–63 Munster 14–6
1963–64 Leinster 10–6
1964–65 Leinster 14–3
1965–66 Munster 6–3
1966–67 Munster 9–5
1967–68 Leinster 8–5
1968–69 Munster 12–8
1969–70 Leinster 12–6
1970–71 Leinster 10–0
1971–72 Leinster 9–0
1972–73 Munster 17–3
1973–74 Munster 13–3
1974–75 Leinster 9–6
1975–76 Munster 9–0
1976–77 Leinster 12–6
1977–78 Munster 15–10
1978–79 Munster 12–3
1979–80 Leinster 4–3
1980–81 Leinster 18–9
1981–82 draw 15–15
1982–83 Munster 9–6

1983–84 Leinster 22–13
1984–85 Leinster 15–9
1985–86 Leinster 15–6

LEINSTER *v* CONNACHT

1946–47 draw 5–5
1947–48 Leinster 15–0
1948–49 Leinster 3–0
1949–50 Leinster 31–3
1950–51 Connacht 10–6
1951–52 Leinster 39–3
1952–53 Leinster 35–0
1953–54 Leinster 34–14
1954–55 Leinster 6–3
1955–56 Connacht 8–6
1956–57 Leinster 19–3
1957–58 Leinster 9–3
1958–59 Leinster 9–3
1959–60 draw 3–3
1960–61 draw 0–0
1961–62 Leinster 13–9
1962–63 Leinster 18–17
1963–64 Leinster 11–6
1964–65 draw 6–6
1965–66 Leinster 13–6
1966–67 Leinster 26–3
1967–68 Leinster 24–11
1968–69 Leinster 15–6
1969–70 Leinster 26–6
1970–71 Leinster 11–3
1971–72 Leinster 12–6
1972–73 Leinster 13–0
1973–74 Leinster 20–13
1974–75 Leinster 12–3
1975–76 Leinster 7–0
1976–77 Leinster 21–7
1977–78 Leinster 30–9
1978–79 Leinster 13–6
1979–80 Leinster 25–10
1980–81 Leinster 18–9
1981–82 Leinster 20–10
1982–83 Leinster 13–7
1983–84 Leinster 29–6
1984–85 Leinster 14–3
1985–86 Copnnacht 9–6

ULSTER *v* MUNSTER

1946–47 Ulster 6–3
1947–48 draw 6–6
1948–49 Ulster 13–6
1949–50 Ulster 11–0

1950–51 Ulster 6–3
1951–52 Ulster 16–3
1952–53 draw 0–0
1953–54 Munster 11–6
1954–55 Ulster 3–0
1955–56 Ulster 6–3
1956–57 Ulster 5–3
1957–58 Munster 11–6
1958–59 Ulster 8–6
1959–60 Munster 18–0
1960–61 Ulster 13–3
1961–62 Ulster 26–3
1962–63 Munster 11–0
1963–64 draw 0–0
1964–65 Munster 9–8
1965–66 Munster 13–6
1966–67 draw 3–3
1967–68 Ulster 13–6
1968–69 Munster 17–9
1969–70 draw 3–3
1970–71 Ulster 8–3
1971–72 Ulster 13–6
1972–73 Ulster 4–3
1973–74 draw 6–6
1974–75 draw 6–0
1975–76 Ulster 9–7
1976–77 Ulster 27–24
1977–78 Ulster 9–6
1978–79 Munster 11–6
1979–80 Munster 15–11
1980–81 Munster 21–10
1981–82 Ulster 18–16
1982–83 Ulster 19–10
1983–84 Ulster 13–12
1984–85 Ulster 14–6
1985–86 Ulster 23–3

ULSTER *v* CONNACHT

1946–47 Ulster 26–3
1947–48 Ulster 19–0
1948–49 Ulster 30–6
1949–50 Ulster 12–3
1950–51 Ulster 26–3
1951–52 Ulster 13–0
1952–53 Ulster 28–3
1953–54 Ulster 11–3
1954–55 Connacht 14–6
1955–56 Connacht 12–9
1956–57 Connacht 6–3
1957–58 Ulster 23–12
1958–59 Connacht 14–5

1959–60 Ulster 9–3
1960–61 Connacht 6–3
1961–62 Ulster 11–0
1962–63 Ulster 19–6
1963–64 Connacht 13–3
1964–65 Ulster 5–0
1965–66 draw 3–3
1966–67 Ulster 9–8
1967–68 Ulster 14–12
1968–69 Ulster 11–9
1969–70 Ulster 20–0
1970–71 Ulster 42–0
1971–72 Ulster 13–0
1972–73 Ulster 37–6
1973–74 Ulster 17–14
1974–75 Ulster 29–6
1975–76 Ulster 6–3
1976–77 Ulster 13–3
1977–78 Ulster 18–3
1978–79 Ulster 11–4
1979–80 draw 6–6
1980–81 Ulster 13–12
1981–82 Ulster 6–3
1982–83 Ulster 22–21
1983–84 Connacht 9–4
1984–85 Ulster 28–6
1985–86 Ulster 12–6

MUNSTER *v* CONNACHT

1946–47 Munster 13–10
1947–48 Munster 24–3
1948–49 Munster 20–6
1949–50 Munster 6–5
1950–51 Munster 12–8
1951–52 Munster 28–3
1952–53 Munster 8–0
1953–54 Connacht 3–0
1954–55 Munster 8–3
1955–56 Munster 8–3
1956–57 Connacht 10–3
1957–58 Munster 3–0
1958–59 Munster 9–0
1959–60 Munster 6–0
1960–61 Munster 5–0
1961–62 Munster 11–3
1962–63 Munster 6–0
1963–64 Munster 12–8
1964–65 draw 5–5
1965–66 Munster 9–3
1966–67 Munster 12–6
1967–68 Munster 11–9
1968–69 Munster 12–3

1969–70 Munster 22–0
1970–71 Munster 9–0
1971–72 Munster 10–0
1972–73 Munster 12–3
1973–74 Munster 29–7
1974–75 draw 6–6
1975–76 Munster 16–6
1976–77 Munster 13–6
1977–78 Munster 10–6
1978–79 Munster 19–3
1979–80 Connacht 20–16
1980–81 Munster 16–0
1981–82 Munder 21–8
1982–83 Munster 9–7
1983–84 Munster 29–7
1984–85 Munster 15–9
1985–86 Munster 16–9

APPENDIX 12

SENIOR CUP AND LEAGUE WINNERS IN FOUR PROVINCES

Leinster Senior Cup winners

1882 Dublin U
1883 Dublin U
1884 Dublin U
1885 Wanderers
1886 Dublin U
1887 Dublin U
1888 Wanderers
1889 Bective Rangers
1890 Dublin U
1891 Lansdowne
1892 Bective Rangers
1893 Dublin U
1894 Wanderers
1895 Dublin U
1896 Dublin U
1897 Dublin U
1898 Dublin U
1899 Monkstown
1900 Dublin U
1901 Lansdowne
1902 Monkstown
1903 Lansdowne
1904 Lansdowne
1905 Dublin U
1906 Wanderers
1907 Dublin U
1908 Dublin U

1909 Old Wesley
1910 Bective Rangers
1911 Wanderers
1912 Dublin U
1913 Dublin U
1914 Bective Rangers
1915–1919 No Competition
1920 Dublin U
1921 Dublin U
1922 Lansdowne
1923 Bective Rangers
1924 UCD
1925 Bective Rangers
1926 Dublin U
1927 Lansdowne
1928 Lansdowne
1929 Lansdowne
1930 Lansdowne
1931 Lansdowne
1932 Bective Rangers
1933 Lansdowne
1934 Bective Rangers
1935 Bective Rangers
1936 Clontarf
1937 Blackrock Coll
1938 UCD
1939 Blackrock Coll
1940 Old Belvedere
1941 Old Belvedere
1942 Old Belvedere
1943 Old Belvedere
1944 Old Belvedere
1945 Old Belvedere
1946 Old Belvedere
1947 Wanderers
1948 UCD
1949 Lansdowne
1950 Lansdowne
1951 Old Belvedere
1952 Old Belvedere
1953 Lansdowne
1954 Wanderers
1955 Bective Rangers
1956 Bective Rangers
1957 Blackrock Coll
1958 St Mary's Coll
1959 Wanderers
1960 Dublin U
1961 Blackrock Coll
1962 Bective Rangers
1963 UCD
1964 UCD

1965 Lansdowne
1966 Terenure
1967 Terenure
1968 Old Belvedere
1969 St Mary's Coll
1970 UCD
1971 St Mary's Coll
1972 Lansdowne
1973 Wanderers
1974 St Mary's Coll
1975 St Mary's Coll
1976 Dublin U
1977 UCD
1978 Wanderers
1979 Lansdowne
1980 Lansdowne
1981 Lansdowne
1982 Wanderers
1983 Blackrock Coll
1984 Wanderers
1985 Old Wesley
1986 Lansdowne

Leinster Senior League winners

1971–72 St Mary's Coll
1972–73 Wanderers
1973–74 Lansdowne
1974–75 Blackrock Coll
1975–76 Wanderers
1976–77 Lansdowne
1977–78 St Mary's Coll
1978–79 Wanderers
1979–80 St Mary's Coll
1980–81 Lansdowne
1981–82 Blackrock Coll
1982–83 Blackrock Coll
1983–84 Terenure
1984–85 Wanderers
1985–86 Lansdowne

Munster Senior Cup winners

1886 Bandon
1887 Queen's Coll
1888 Queen's Coll
1889 Garryowen
1890 Garryowen
1891 Garryowen
1892 Garryowen
1893 Garryowen
1894 Garryowen
1895 Garryowen
1896 Garryowen

1897 Queen's Coll
1898 Garryowen
1899 Garryowen
1900 Queen's Coll
1901 Queen's Coll
1902 Garryowen
1903 Garryowen
1904 Garryowen
1905 Constitution
1906 Constitution
1907 Constitution
1908 Garryowen
1909 Garryowen
1910 Constitution
1911 Garryowen
1912 UCC
1913 UCC
1914 Garryowen
1915–1919 No competition
1920 Garryowen
1921 Dolphin
1922 Constitution
1923 Constitution
1924 Garryowen
1925 Garryowen
1926 Garryowen
1927 Bohemians
1928 Young Munster
1929 Constitution
1930 Young Munster
1931 Dolphin
1932 Garryowen
1933 Constitution
1934 Constitution
1935 UCC
1936 UCC
1937 UCC
1938 Young Munster
1939 UCC
1940 Garryowen
1941 UCC
1942 Constitution
1943 Constitution
1944 Dolphin
1945 Dolphin
1946 Constitution
1947 Garryowen
1948 Dolphin
1949 Sunday's Well
1950 UCC
1951 UCC
1952 Garryowen

1953 Sunday's Well
1954 Garryowen
1955 UCC
1956 Dolphin
1957 Constitution
1958 Bohemians
1959 Bohemians
1960 Shannon
1961 Constitution
1962 Bohemians
1963 UCC
1964 Constitution
1965 Constitution
1966 Highfield
1967 Constitution
1968 Highfield
1969 Garryowen
1970 Constitution
1971 Garryowen
1972 Constitution
1973 Constitution
1974 Garryowen
1975 Garryowen
1976 UCC
1977 Shannon
1978 Shannon
1979 Garryowen
1980 Young Munster
1981 UCC
1982 Shannon
1983 Constitution
1984 Young Munster
1985 Constitution
1986 Shannon

Munster Senior League winners

1902–03 Garryowen
1903–04 Garryowen
1904–05 Garryowen
1905–06 Garryowen
1906–07 Garryowen
1907–08 Garryowen
1908–09 Garryowen
1909–10 Garryowen
1910–11 Garryowen/Constitution
  (shared)
1911–12 Garryowen/Constitution
  (shared)
1912–13 UCC
1913–14 UCC/Constitution (shared)
1914–15 to 1920–21 No Competition
1921–22 Constitution

1922–23 Constitution
1923–24 Dolphin
1924–25 Garryowen
1925–26 Dolphin
1926–27 Constitution
1927–28 Sunday's Well
1928–29 Dolphin
1929–30 Young Munster
1930–31 Bohemians/UCC (shared)
1932–33 UCC
1933–34 UCC
1934–35 Sunday's Well
1935–36 Garryowen/UCC (shared)
1936–37 Unfinished
1937–38 Unfinished
1938–39 Constitution
1939–40 Unfinished
1940–41 Unfinished
1941–42 UCC
1942–43 UCC
1943–44 Young Munster
1944–45 Unfinished
1945–46 Garryowen
1946–47 Unfinished
1947–48 Sunday's Well
1948–49 Dolphin
1949–50 UCC
1950–51 Sunday's Well
1951–52 Young Munster
1952–53 Constitution
1953–54 Garryowen
1954–55 Dolphin
1955–56 Dolphin
1956–57 Constitution
1957–58 UCC
1958–59 Bohemians
1959–60 Sunday's Well
1960–61 UCC
1961–62 UCC
1962–63 UCC
1963–64 Constitution
1964–65 Constitution
1965–66 Constitution
1966–67 Constitution
1967–68 Constitution
1968–69 Constitution
1969–70 Constitution
1970–71 Constitution
1971–72 Constitution
1972–73 Dolphin
1973–74 UCC
1974–75 Constitution

1975–76 Constitution
1976–77 Constitution
1977–78 UCC
1978–79 Constitution
1979–80 UCC
1980–81 Shannon
1981–82 Garryowen
1982–83 Garryowen
1983–84 Constitution
1984–85 UCC
1985–86 Shannon

Ulster Senior Cup winners

1885 NIFC
1886 Queen's U
1887 Queen's U
1888 Lisburn
1889 Albion
1890 Queen's U
1891 Queen's U
1892 Queen's U
1893 NIFC
1894 NIFC
1895 NIFC
1896 NIFC
1897 NIFC
1898 NIFC
1899 NIFC
1900 Queen's U
1901 NIFC
1902 NIFC
1903 Queen's U
1904 Malone
1905 Malone
1906 Collegians
1907 Malone
1908 NIFC
1909 Queen's U
1910 Collegians
1911 Knock
1912 Queen's U
1913 Collegians
1914–1919 No Competition
1920 NIFC
1921 Queen's U
1922 Instonians
1923 Instonians
1924 Queen's U
1925 Queen's U
1926 Collegians
1927 Instonians
1928 Instonians

1929 Instonians
1930 NIFC
1931 Instonians
1932 Queen's U
1933 Queen's U
1934 Instonians
1935 NIFC
1936 Queen's U
1937 Queen's U
1938 Instonians
1939 NIFC
1940–1945 No Competition
1946 Instonians
1947 Queen's U
1948 Instonians
1949 Instonians
1950 Instonians
1951 Queen's U
1952 Collegians
1953 CIYMS
1954 Instonians
1955 NIFC
1956 Instonians
1957 Instonians
1958 Instonians
1959 Queen's U
1960 Queen's U
1961 Collegians
1962 Collegians
1963 Ballymena
1964 Dungannon
1965 Instonians
1966 CIYMS
1967 CIYMS
1968 Dungannon
1969 NIFC
1970 Ballymena
1971 Malone
1972 CIYMS
1973 NIFC
1974 CIYMS
1975 Ballymena
1976 Dungannon
1977 Ballymena
1978 CIYMS
1979 Instonians
1980 Bangor
1981 Queen's U
1982 Bangor
1983 Collegians
1984 Malone
1985 Ards
1986 Bangor

Ulster Senior League winners

1890–91 Queen's U
1891–92 NIFC
1892–93 NIFC
1893–94 NIFC
1894–95 NIFC
1895–96 NIFC
1896–97 NIFC
1897–98 NIFC
1898–99 NIFC
1899–1900 Queen's U
1900–01 NIFC
1901–02 NIFC
1902–03 Collegians
1903–04 Malone
1904–05 Malone
1905–06 Malone
1906–07 Malone
1907–08 Collegians
1908–09 NIFC
1909–10 No Competition
1910–11 Collegians
1911–12 Queen's U
1912–13 Collegians
1913–19 No competition
1919–20 Queen's U
1920–21 NIFC
1921–22 Queen's U
1922–23 Queen's U
1923–24 Queen's U
1924–25 Instonians
1925–26 Instonians
1926–27 NIFC/Instonians (shared)
1927–28 Instonians
1928–29 Civil Service
1929–30 Bangor
1930–45 No League Competition
1945–46 NIFC
1946–47 Queen's U
1947–48 Queen's U
1948–49 Queen's U
1949–50 Queen's U
1950–51 Collegians/Instonians (shared)
1951–52 Collegians
1952–53 Instonians/Queen's U (shared)
1953–54 Collegians/Queen's U (shared)
1954–55 NIFC
1955–56 Collegians
1956–57 Instonians/Queen's U (shared)
1957–58 Instonians
1958–59 NIFC
1959–60 Instonians
1960–61 Dungannon

1961–62 Collegians
1962–63 CIYMS
1963–64 Queen's U
1964–65 Dungannon
1965–66 NIFC
1966–67 Queen's U
1967–68 Dungannon
1968–69 Malone
1969–70 Civil Service
1970–71 CIYMS
1971–72 CIYMS
1972–73 Ballymena/CIYMS (shared)
1973–74 CIYMS
1974–75 Bangor
1975–76 Ballymena
1976–77 Bangor
1977–78 Ballymena
1978–79 Ballymena
1979–80 Queen's U
1980–81 Bangor
1981–82 Bangor
1982–83 Bangor
1983–84 Ards
1984–85 Instonians
1985–86 Ballymena

Connacht Senior Cup winners

1896 Galway Town
1897 Queen's Coll
1898 Galway GS
1899 Queen's Coll
1900 No Competition
1901 No Competition
1902 No Competition
1903 Queen's Coll
1904 Queen's Coll
1905 Queen's Coll
1906 Galway Town
1907 Queen's Coll
1908 Queen's Coll
1909 UCG (X)
1910 UCG
1911 Galway Town
1912 UCG
1913 Galway Town
1914 Sligo Town
1915–1921 no competition

(X) Queen's Coll
Galway renamed University Coll
Galway (UCG)

1922 Galway Town

1923 UCG
1924 UCG
1925 UCG
1926 Galwegians
1927 Galwegians
1928 Galwegians
1929 Galwegians
1930 UCG
1931 Loughrea
1932 UCG
1933 Corinthians
1934 Corinthians
1935 UCG
1936 UCG
1937 UCG
1938 Galwegians
1939 UCG
1940 UCG
1941 Corinthians
1942 UCG
1943 Galwegians
1944 UCG
1945 UCG
1946 UCG
1947 Corinthians
1948 Ballinasloe
1949 Corinthians
1950 Ballinasloe
1951 Ballina
1952 Galwegians
1953 UCG
1954 Corinthians
1955 Athlone
1956 Galwegians
1957 Galwegians
1958 Galwegians
1959 Galwegians
1960 Galwegians
1961 UCG
1962 UCG
1963 Galwegians
1964 UCG
1965 Galwegians
1966 UCG
1967 UCG
1968 Galwegians
1969 Galwegians
1970 UCG
1971 Galwegians
1972 Corinthians
1973 Galwegians
1974 UCG
1975 Galwegians

1976 Athlone
1977 Athlone
1978 Corinthians
1979 Ballina
1980 Galwegians
1981 Galwegians
1982 Corinthians
1983 Galwegians
1984 Corinthians
1985 Corinthians
1986 Galwegians

Connacht Senior League winners

1925–26 Galwegians
1926–27 Loughrea
1927–28 Ballinasloe
1928–29 Ballina
1929–30 Ballina
1930–31 UCG
1931–32 UCG
1932–33 UCG
1933–34 Corinthians
1934–35 UCG
1935–36 Corinthians
1936–37 UCG
1937–38 UCG
1938–39 Corinthians
1939–40 Corinthians
1940–41 Corinthians
1941–42 UCG
1942–43 Corinthians
1943–44 Corinthians
1944–45 Ballinasloe
1945–46 Ballinasloe
1946–47 Galwegians
1947–48 UCG
1948–49 Ballinasloe
1949–50 Corinthians
1950–51 Corinthians/Ballina (shared)
1951–52 Corinthians
1952–53 Ballina
1953–54 Corinthians
1954–55 UCG
1955–56 Athlone
1956–57 Galwegians
1957–58 Galwegians
1958–59 Galwegians
1959–60 Galwegians
1960–61 Galwegians
1961–62 UCG
1962–63 UCG
1963–64 Galwegians

1964–65 Corinthians
1965–66 UCG/Galwegians (shared)
1966–67 UCG
1967–68 UCG
1968–69 UCG
1969–70 Galwegians
1970–71 Galwegians
1971–72 Galwegians
1972–73 UCG
1973–74 UCG
1974–75 UCG
1975–76 Corinthians
1976–77 Athlone
1977–78 Corinthians
1978–79 Corinthians
1979–80 Corinthians
1980–81 Corinthians
1981–82 Corinthians
1982–83 Corinthians
1983–84 Galwegians
1984–85 Galwegians
1985–86 Corinthians

Ulster Schools Senior Cup winners

1876 Armagh RS
1877 Armagh RS
1878 Methodist Coll
1879 Armagh RS
1880 Armagh RS
1881 Armagh RS
1882 Methodist Coll
1883 Armagh RS
1884 Coleraine AI
1885 Armagh RS
1886 Coleraine AI
1887 Coleraine AI
1888 RBAI
1889 Methodist Coll
1890 RBAI
1891 Methodist Coll
1892 Methodist Coll
1893 Methodist Coll
1894 Coleraine AI
1895 RBAI
1896 Methodist Coll
1897 Coleraine AI
1898 Campbell Coll
1899 Methodist Coll
1900 Foyle Coll
1901 Methodist Coll
1902 Methodist Coll
1903 RBAI

1904 Methodist Coll
1905 Portora RS
1906 Portora RS
1907 Dungannon RS
1908 Portora RS
1909 Portora RS
1910 Campbell Coll
1911 Competition not completed
1912 RBAI
1913 Campbell Coll
1914 Methodist Coll
1915 Foyle Coll
1916 RBAI
1917 Campbell Coll
1918 RBAI
1919 RBAI
1920 Coleraine AI
1921 Campbell Coll
1922 Campbell Coll
1923 Campbell Coll
1924 Campbell Coll
1925 Coleraine AI
1926 Campbell Coll
1927 Methodist Coll
1928 Methodist Coll
1929 Methodist Coll
1930 RBAI
1931 Campbell Coll
1932 Campbell Coll
1933 RBAI
1934 RBAI
1935 RBAI
1936 Methodist Coll
1937 Methodist Coll
1938 RBAI
1939 Coleraine AI
1940 Portora RS
1941 Portora RS
1942 Portora RS/RBAI (shared)
1943 RBAI
1944 RBAI
1945 RBAI
1946 RBAI
1947 RBAI
1948 RBAI
1949 Methodist Coll
1950 Campbell Coll
1951 RBAI
1952 Methodist Coll
1953 Methodist Coll/Campbell Coll
   (shared)
1954 Campbell Coll/RBAI (shared)

1955 Campbell Coll
1956 Campbell Coll
1957 RBAI
1958 Annadale GS
1959 RBAI
1960 Campbell Coll/RBAI (shared)
1961 Campbell Coll
1962 BRA/RBAI (shared)
1963 BRA/Rainey Endowed (shared)
1964 BRA/Campbell Coll (shared)
1965 Campbell Coll
1966 Campbell Coll
1967 Rainey Endowed
1968 Campbell Coll
1969 Bangor GS
1970 RBAI
1971 Belfast Model
1972 Ballymena Academy
1973 Ballyclare HS
1974 Methodist Coll
1975 Methodist Coll
1976 Methodist Coll
1977 Armagh RS
1978 Bangor GS
1979 Methodist Coll
1980 Campbell Coll
1981 Ballymena Academy
1982 Rainey Endowed
1983 Grosvenor HS
1984 Methodist Coll
1985 Bangor GS
1986 Bangor GS

Ulster Schools Medallion winners

1910 Methodist Coll
1911 RBAI
1912 RBAI
1913 RBAI
1914 Methodist Coll
1915 RBAI
1916 RBAI
1917 RBAI
1918 Dungannon RS
1919 Dungannon RS
1920 RBAI
1921 RBAI
1922 RBAI
1923 RBAI
1924 Methodist Coll
1925 RBAI
1926 RBAI
1927 Methodist Coll

1928 Methodist Coll
1929 Methodist Coll
1930 RBAI
1931 RBAI
1932 Methodist Coll
1933 RBAI
1934 Methodist Coll
1935 Coleraine AI
1936 Bangor GS
1937 Coleraine AI
1938 Coleraine AI
1939 RBAI
1940 Methodist Coll
1941 Methodist Coll
1942 RBAI
1943 RBAI
1944 Coleraine AI
1945 Methodist Coll
1946 Methodist Coll
1947 Methodist Coll
1948 Methodist Coll
1949 Methodist Coll
1950 Coleraine AI
1951 Ballymena Academy/RBAI
   (shared)
1952 RBAI
1953 RBAI
1954 Annadale GS/Methodist Coll
   (shared)
1955 RBAI
1956 RBAI
1957 Methodist Coll
1958 RBAI
1959 RBAI
1960 Annadale GS/RBAI (shared)
1961 RBAI
1962 Methodist Coll
1963 Coleraine AI
1964 Methodist Coll
1965 BRA
1966 Bangor GS
1967 Annadale GS/BRA (shared)
1968 BRA
1969 Ballymena Academy/BRA (shared)
1970 Ballymena Academy
1971 Methodist Coll
1972 Methodist Coll/RBAI (shared)
1973 Methodist Coll
1974 Methodist Coll
1975 Coleraine AI
1976 Regent House
1977 Rainey Endowed

1978 BRA
1979 BRA
1980 RBAI
1981 RBAI
1982 RBAI
1983 Methodist Coll
1984 Campbell Coll
1985 Bangor GS
1986 Methodist Coll

Leinster Schools Senior Cup winners

1887 Blackrock Coll
1888 Blackrock Coll
1889 Corrig
1890 Blackrock Coll
1891 Rathmines
1892 Corrig
1893 Blackrock Coll
1894 Blackrock Coll
1895 Blackrock Coll
1896 Blackrock Coll
1897 Blackrock Coll
1898 Wesley
1899 St Columba's
1900 Blackrock Coll
1901 Blackrock Coll
1902 Blackrock Coll
1903 Blackrock Coll
1904 Blackrock Coll
1905 Blackrock Coll
1906 St Andrew's
1907 Blackrock Coll
1908 Blackrock Coll
1909 Blackrock Coll
1910 Blackrock Coll
1911 St Andrew's
1912 Blackrock Coll
1913 Castleknock
1914 Mountjoy
1915 Blackrock Coll
1916 Blackrock Coll
1917 Blackrock Coll
1919 Blackrock Coll
1920 Castleknock
1921 St Andrew's
1922 St Andrew's
1923 Belvedere
1924 Belvedere
1925 Blackrock Coll
1926 Clongowes
1927 Blackrock Coll
1928 Blackrock Coll

1929 Blackrock Coll
1930 Blackrock Coll
1931 Castleknock
1932 PBC Bray
1933 Blackrock Coll
1934 Blackrock Coll
1935 Blackrock Coll
1936 Blackrock Coll
1937 Castleknock
1938 Belvedere
1939 Blackrock Coll
1940 Blackrock Coll
1941 Newbridge
1942 Blackrock Coll
1943 Blackrock Coll
1944 Castleknock
1945 Blackrock Coll
1946 Belvedere
1947 Castleknock
1948 Blackrock Coll
1949 Blackrock Coll
1950 Blackrock Coll
1951 Belvedere
1952 Terenure
1953 Blackrock Coll
1954 Blackrock Coll
1955 Blackrock Coll
1956 Blackrock Coll
1957 Blackrock Coll
1958 Terenure
1959 Castleknock
1960 Blackrock Coll
1961 St Mary's
1962 Blackrock Coll
1963 Blackrock Coll
1964 Blackrock Coll
1965 Castleknock
1966 St Mary's
1967 Blackrock Coll
1968 Belvedere
1969 St Mary's
1970 Newbridge
1971 Belvedere
1972 Belvedere
1973 High School
1974 Blackrock Coll
1975 Blackrock Coll
1976 CBC Monkstown
1977 Blackrock Coll
1978 Clongowes
1979 Terenure
1980 Terenure

1981 Blackrock Coll
1982 Blackrock Coll
1983 De La Salle Churchtown
1984 Terenure
1985 De La Salle Churchtown
1986 Blackrock Coll

Leinster Schools Junior Cup winners

1909 St Andrew's
1910 Blackrock Coll
1911 Blackrock Coll
1912 Blackrock Coll
1913 Belvedere
1914 Belvedere
1915 Castleknock
1916 Belvedere
1917 Belvedere
1918 Belvedere
1919 Belvedere
1920 Castleknock
1921 Castleknock
1922 Castleknock
1923 Blackrock Coll
1924 Castleknock
1925 Belvedere
1926 Castleknock
1927 Blackrock
1928 Castleknock
1929 Belvedere
1930 PBC Bray
1931 Belvedere
1932 Blackrock Coll
1933 Blackrock Coll
1934 St Mary's
1935 Blackrock Coll
1936 Blackrock Coll
1937 Belvedere
1938 High School
1939 Roscrea
1940 Belvedere
1941 Blackrock Coll
1942 Blackrock Coll
1943 Blackrock Coll
1944 Clongowes
1945 Blackrock Coll
1946 Blackrock Coll
1947 Clongowes
1948 Blackrock Coll
1949 Clongowes
1950 Newbridge
1951 Blackrock Coll
1952 Clongowes

1953 Blackrock Coll
1954 Blackrock Coll
1955 Terenure
1956 Blackrock Coll
1957 Blackrock Coll
1958 Terenure
1959 Blackrock Coll
1960 Belvedere
1961 Belvedere
1962 Blackrock Coll
1963 St Mary's
1964 Blackrock Coll
1965 Blackrock Coll
1966 Castleknock
1967 Terenure
1968 Blackrock Coll
1969 Blackrock Coll
1970 Blackrock Coll
1971 St Mary's
1972 Blackrock Coll
1973 Blackrock Coll
1974 St Mary's
1975 PBC Bray
1976 Terenure
1977 Terenure
1978 Terenure
1979 Blackrock Coll
1980 Blackrock Coll
1981 Blackrock Coll
1982 Blackrock Coll
1983 Terenure
1984 Blackrock Coll
1985 PBC Bray
1986 Blackrock Coll

Munster Schools Senior Cup winners

1909 CBC Cork
1910 Rockwell
1911 Rockwell
1912 Rockwell
1913 CBC Cork
1914 Rockwell
1915 Rockwell
1916 CBC Cork
1917 Rockwell
1918 PBC Cork
1919 CBC Cork
1920 PBC Cork
1921 The Abbey, Tipperary
1922 CBC Cork
1923 No Competition
1924 CBC Cork

1925 CBC Cork
1926 CBS Limerick
1927 PBC Cork
1928 Rockwell
1929 Rockwell
1930 Rockwell
1931 CBS Limerick
1932 PBC Cork
1933 CBS Limerick
1934 CBS Limerick
1935 PBC Cork
1936 CBC Cork
1937 Rockwell
1938 PBC Cork
1939 PBC Cork
1940 Rockwell
1941 Mungret
1942 Rockwell
1943 CBC Cork
1944 CBC Cork
1945 PBC Cork
1946 PBC Cork
1947 Crescent
1948 PBC Cork
1949 Crescent
1950 Rockwell
1951 Crescent
1952 PBC Cork
1953 Rockwell
1954 PBC Cork
1955 Rockwell
1956 CBC Cork
1957 PBC Cork
1958 PBC Cork
1959 Rockwell
1960 Rockwell
1961 Rockwell
1962 CBC Cork
1963 Crescent
1964 Rockwell
1965 PBC Cork
1966 PBC Cork
1967 Rockwell
1968 St Munchin's
1969 PBC Cork
1970 Rockwell
1971 CBC Cork
1972 CBC Cork
1973 CBC Cork
1974 CBC Cork
1975 PBC Cork
1976 CBC Cork

1977 CBC Cork
1978 PBC Cork
1979 CBC Cork
1980 CBC Cork
1981 PBC Cork
1982 St Munchin's
1983 Crescent Comprehensive
1984 CBC Cork
1985 Rockwell
1986 Crescent Comprehensive

Munster Schools Junior Cup winners

1932 CBS Limerick
1933 PBC Cork
1934 Rockwell
1935 Rockwell
1936 Rockwell
1937 Rockwell
1938 CBC Cork
1939 Mungret
1940 Mungret
1941 Mungret
1942 Rockwell
1943 Rockwell
1944 PBC Cork
1945 PBC Cork
1946 PBC Cork
1947 Rockwell
1948 Rockwell
1949 Rockwell
1950 Crescent
1951 PBC Cork
1952 Crescent
1953 CBC Cork
1954 PBC Cork
1955 Rockwell
1956 Rockwell
1957 PBC Cork
1958 Rockwell
1959 Rockwell
1960 PBC Cork
1961 Crescent
1962 CBC Cork
1963 PBC Cork
1964 PBC Cork
1965 PBC Cork
1966 PBC Cork
1967 Rockwell
1968 Rockwell
1969 CBC Cork
1970 St Munchin's
1971 CBC Cork

1972 Rockwell
1973 PBC Cork
1974 Rockwell
1975 CBC Cork
1976 PBC Cork
1977 PBC Cork
1978 CBC Cork
1979 PBC Cork
1980 PBC Cork
1981 CBC Cork
1982 Rockwell
1983 PBC Cork
1984 PBC Cork
1985 PBC Cork
1986 PBC Cork

Connacht Schools Senior Cup winners

1913 St Joseph's Garbally
1914 St Joseph's Garbally
1915 St Joseph's Garbally
1916 St Joseph's Garbally
1917 No Competition
1918 St Joseph's Galway
1919 Ranelagh Athlone
1920 No Competition
1921 No Competition
1922 St Joseph's Galway
1923 Ranelagh Athlone
1924 Colaiste Iognaid
1925 Colaiste Iognaid
1926 St Joseph's Garbally
1927 Colaiste Iognaid
1928 Colaiste Iognaid
1929 St Joseph's Garbally
1930 St Joseph's Galway
1931 St Joseph's Garbally
1932 Collegians/St Joseph's Galway
   (shared)
1933 No Competition
1934 No Competition
1935 St Joseph's Garbally
1936 St Joseph's Garbally
1937 No Competition
1938 No Competition
1939 No Competition
1940 No Competition
1941 Galway GS
1942 No Competition
1943 No Competition
1944 No Competition
1945 No Competition
1946 No Competition

1947 No Competition
1948 No Competition
1949 St Joseph's Garbally
1950 St Joseph's Garbally
1951 Collegians
1952 St Joseph's Garbally
1953 St Joseph's Garbally
1954 St Joseph's Galway
1955 St Joseph's Garbally
1956 St Joseph's Garbally
1957 St Joseph's Garbally
1958 St Joseph's Garbally
1959 St Joseph's Galway
1960 St Joseph's Galway
1961 Sligo GS
1962 Sligo GS
1963 Sligo GS
1964 St Joseph's Galway
1965 St Joseph's Galway
1966 Wilson's Hospital
1967 No Competition
1968 No Competition
1969 Sligo GS
1970 St Joseph's Galway
1971 St Joseph's Garbally
1972 St Joseph's Garbally
1973 St Joseph's Garbally
1974 St Joseph's Garbally
1975 Clifden Community School
1976 St Joseph's Garbally
1977 Marist Athlone
1978 St Joseph's Garbally
1979 Colaiste Iognaid
1980 Sligo GS
1981 St Joseph's Galway
1982 St Joseph's Garbally
1983 St Joseph's Garbally
1984 St Joseph's Garbally
1985 Colaiste Iognaid
1986 St Joseph's Garbally

Connacht Schools Junion Cup winners

1915 Galway GS
1916 St Joseph's Garbally
1917 Ranelagh Athlone
1918 Colaiste Iognaid

1919 Ranelagh Athlone
1920 No Competition
1921 No Competition
1922 No Competition
1923 Ranelagh Athlone
1924 St Joseph's Galway
1925 St Joseph's Garbally
1926 Ranelagh Athlone
1927 St Joseph's Garbally
1928 Ranelagh Athlone
1929 St Joseph's Galway
1930 St Joseph's Galway
1931–1948 No Competition
1949 St Joseph's Garbally
1950 St Joseph's Garbally
1951 St Joseph's Garbally
1952 St Joseph's Garbally
1953 No Competition
1954 St Joseph's Garbally
1955 No Competition
1956 No Competition
1957 No Competition
1958 Galway GS
1959 Sligo GS
1960 St Joseph's Galway
1961 No Competition
1962 No Competition
1963 St Joseph's Galway
1964–1969 No Competition
1970 St Joseph's Garbally
1971 St Joseph's Garbally
1972 No Competition
1973 No Competition
1974 St Joseph's Garbally
1975 Colaiste Iognaid
1976 St Joseph's Galway
1977 Clifden Community School
1978 Colaiste Iognaid
1979 St Joseph's Garbally
1980 St Joseph's Garbally
1981 Colaiste Iognaid
1982 St Joseph's Garbally
1983 St Joseph's Garbally
1984 St Joseph's Garbally
1985 St Joseph's Garbally
1986 St Joseph's Galway

INDEX